Primary-Level Government

Jing Zhang

Primary-Level Government

Issues in Rural Governance in China

Translated by Xiaoyan Li

palgrave
macmillan

Jing Zhang
Peking University
Beijing, China

Translated by
Xiaoyan Li
Beijing Forestry University
Beijing, China

Sponsored by the Chinese Fund for the Humanities and Social Sciences.

ISBN 978-981-96-6208-1 ISBN 978-981-96-6209-8 (eBook)
https://doi.org/10.1007/978-981-96-6209-8

This Palgrave Macmillan imprint is published by the registered company Springer Nature Singapore Pte Ltd.
The registered company address is: 152 Beach Road, #21-01/04 Gateway East, Singapore 189721, Singapore

Foreword to the First Edition

The Issues

Since 1996 I have taken part in a research project studying politics and power at the primary level in rural China. The project appealed to me because of the opportunities it would offer me to work with materials and on issues that I had not studied before, which represented a fresh challenge. In the existing literature on political sociology that I have seen, studies of historical documents account for the majority of those that focus on rural China. However, those studying contemporary China have tended to turn their attention to cities or the urban society. This may be attributable to a combination of how rapidly changes happen in and to cities, their importance in political, economic, and cultural transformation, and the ready availability of well-preserved documents and materials that researchers in political sociology can work with. By contrast, anyone trying to undertake a political sociological study of the countryside in contemporary China is immediately confronted with a cardinal difficulty, namely, the dearth of firsthand material. In fact, this kind of "shortage" reflects what exactly a particular investigator is interested in. It is common for researchers interested in questions related to "conflict" and "order", which are among the most basic of concepts in political sociology, to want to study lives in cities, where institutions and organizational structures are relatively well established and which are more culturally influential. By contrast, when the countryside is the subject, research questions, e.g., how township enterprises, organizational mode of production, and its relationship with agricultural output changed over time, tend to be about either "economic development" or how organizations related to economic development have evolved. This pattern in research focus is more or less revelatory of the prevailing tendency to treat rural issues primarily as issues of economics, amenable only to economic investigation.

It must not be gainsaid, of course, that this approach to studying the countryside has afforded us an expansive field of vision, which is especially useful for analyzing the evolution of social and economic relations in rural China. Some of their findings have been impressive. Still, the issue with which those who frame these questions in economic terms are primarily concerned is agricultural productivity. Starting with the assumption that the People's Commune was a failed economic experiment, these studies are in search of more efficient development models of economic organizations or relations. To that end, these researchers try to answer, primarily by applying the principle of efficiency, such questions as how to maximize the utility of factors of production, increase land productivity, raise funds for public-interest causes, strengthen institutional incentives by proper configuration of property rights, among others. All these questions are motivated by the desire to find a path toward prosperity for rural China, or, in the words of the person in the street, to rid it of "poverty". From this point of view, rural political power is first and foremost seen as playing an active economic role, whose basic function consists in mobilizing resources for agricultural production and assembling efficient organizations.[1] While our knowledge about life in rural China has grown considerably as a result of these analyses, the economic approach is of limited value for studying the tension and conflicts that have become increasingly common in rural communities. In fact, reducing everything to economics makes it too tempting to attribute the lack of "order and stability" in rural China to economic underdevelopment, or poverty, and to conclude that economic growth and income increase hold the key to solving these problems of social order at the primary level.

Indeed, we may as a result end up overlooking other causes that might be more important. There has been a growing body of evidence generated by recent investigations for the conflict between political power at the primary level and rural society. For example, a 1997 study done in Suichang in Zhejiang province concluded that "primary-level government has very little credibility among the villagers", a study done in the outskirt of Jiaxing, also in Zhejiang province, in 1997 revealed that a total of 46.6 percent of respondents rated the job performance of CPC village committee either "barely acceptable" or "quite unsatisfactory"; a 1997 study done in the Huali village, Lanxi City, Zhejiang province showed "worsening relationship between cadres and the public, and [the existence of] a large volume of letters of complaint from the public"; a 1997 study done in Xihu District in the city of Hangzhou showed that "It's an enormous challenge to get administrative work done at the primary level, some tension has almost reached a tipping point".[2] Still other investigations revealed that in some places 63.1 percent of all villages disapprove, either "somewhat" or "strongly", of the job the cadres were doing, and as high as 74.3 percent of villagers thought the relationship between the public and the cadres was either

[1] Xiwen Chen, "Share-holding Cooperative: A New Model of Operation and Organization in the Countryside", in *On Rural China: Scholarly Voices from China and Beyond*, ed. Jianping Mou (Huaxia Press, 1994), 270; *In-depth Field Investigation of Rural Zhejiang in the New Era: A Study of Primary-level CPC Party Building under Different Economic Models*, ed. Office of Research and Investigation, Organizational Division, Zhejiang Provincial CPC Committee, unpublished, 1997; Jean C. Oi, "The Role of the Local State in China's Transitional Economy," *The China Quarterly* 144 (1995): 1132–1149.

[2] In-depth Field Investigation of Rural Zhejiang in the New Era, 1997.

"not good " or "very bad".[3] Obviously, all these studies have uncovered one basic fact, namely, that the widespread disconnect between primary-level government and rural society, on which that power depends, has become a source of constant conflict between the two. It is small wonder, therefore, that civil affairs departments should have admitted that "in some places it is almost impossible for village meetings to take place"[4] or that "many villages do not feel that appointed cadres represent them at all".[5] These phenomena are undoubtedly symptomatic of the structural predicament, on both the social and political dimensions, facing primary-level government, namely, the erosion of the strong bond and unity it once had with the society subject to its authority.

From a strictly economic point of view, reality has turned out to be exactly the opposite of what most would predict. Even though, thanks to economic development, people have become materially better off than they had ever been, the level of dissatisfaction with local authorities among and the number of complaints filed by the public has gone up, not down as one might imagine. How could this be? What it suggests is that despite the foundational and sustained importance of economic growth, the fissure described above cannot be attributable entirely to "poverty". In other words, from the point of view of political sociology, prosperity alone provides no guarantee for order in rural communities. Understanding conflicts and order at that level of society requires us to treat primary-level government as a key factor in political analyses. However, while some works have been published in Chinese in recent years that look at the social and political dimensions of political authority in rural communities,[6] including some that have put forward "plans" for its transformation,[7] on the whole academic interests in its economic functions

[3] Houan Zhang & Yong Xu, *Political Stability and Development in Rural China* (Wuhan: Wuhan Press, 1995), 158.

[4] Xueju Li, Zhenyao Wang and Pusu Tang, eds. *Rural and Township Polity in China: Current State and Reform* (Beijing: China Society Press, 1994); Chinese Society for the Study of Primary-level Polity, Villager Self-Governance System in Rural China Project Team, ed. *Village Council Electoral System in Rural China* (Beijing: China Society Press, 1993); Chinese Society for the Study of Primary-level Polity, Villager Self-Governance System in Rural China Project Team, ed. *Villager Delegation System in Rural China* (Beijing: China Society Press, 1994).

[5] Xueju Li, Zhenyao Wang and Pusu Tang, eds. *Rural and Township Polity in China: Current State and Reform* (Beijing: China Society Press, 1994); Chinese Society for the Study of Primary-level Polity, Villager Self-Governance System in Rural China Project Team, ed. *Village Council Electoral System in Rural China* (Beijing: China Society Press, 1993); Chinese Society for the Study of Primary-level Polity, Villager Self-Governance System in Rural China Project Team, ed. *Villager Delegation System in Rural China* (Beijing: China Society Press, 1994).

[6] Mou, *On Rural China: Scholarly Voices from China and Beyond*, 273); Jing Zhang, "Several Issues in the Study of Primary-level Polity in Rural China", in *China Book Review*, No. 10 (1996): 165; Zhenyao Wang, "A Decade of Building Primary-level Polity", Conference Proceedings (Nov. 1997).

[7] Yong Xu, *Villager Self-Governance in Rural China* (Shanghai: Huazhong Normal University Press, 1997); Houan Zhang, Yong Xu, *Political Stability and Development*, 1995; Zhongtian Wang, *Villager Delegation System: Structure, Functions and the Foundation of Authority*, Conference Proceedings (Nov. 1997).

have far outweighed those in its political functions. What is the source of its mandate? How do public interests factor in it? How does it function as a leverage to balance the institutional objectives at the primary level and the national levels against each other? What kind of institutional support do social organizations provide to political conduct at that level? And what does rural politics say about who the stakeholders are in rural communities and how their interests are interconnected? These are just some of the many questions that have so far received very little attention from researchers.

This neglect can have worrying consequences. For example, until and unless we have an adequate understanding of what rural primary-level government is and does, how do we determine the right strategy for building and strengthening it? What is it about it that might be "strengthened"? And why should we be confident that what is being "built" is what is really needed? In fact, if anything, some of the conflicts and perhaps even contradiction that can exist among "building" activities currently under way at different levels have already been exposed. For the state, the goal is to restore oversight of primary-level politics in order to help local political authorities improve governance and ease the tension between these authorities and the rural population.[8] The state has come to the realization that rather than functioning as a nexus linking state institutions and society, primary-level organizations in rural China have instead pit the two against each other, thereby posing a threat to social stability in rural communities. The state is hoping that strengthening rural primary-level political apparatus would help boost its level of self-restraint and openness to public oversight. But so far as the rural cadres are concerned, "strengthening rural primary-level political apparatus" engendered a feeling of insecurity because it signified restoration of some of the rights of which operators of such apparatus had been stripped. For example, one rural cadre said: "Now people can run things on their own, they would turn to the market instead of the cadres when they need something done, so control and manage are a lot harder than before" (1997 study in Zhejiang). A cadre from a city government said: "For primary-level political apparatus to be competent and effective, make sure to heed the principle that things are as well done as they are well-funded by public funds; so it is necessary to facilitate the development of collectivized economy if primary-level political apparatus is have access to the resources it needs" (1997 study in Zhejiang). It is true that changes in the relative values of the means of agricultural production, including, for example, the diminishing returns farmlands are able to generate, have reduced villagers' dependency on and obedience toward primary-level political authorities by upending the resource monopoly on which such relationships are predicated. This undermined the standing of primary-level political authorities, which found themselves urgently in need of new sources of mandate and scrambling to reestablish both their prominence and their dominance in the rural communities. Unfortunately,

[8] Daniel Kelliher, "The Chinese Debate over Village Self-Government", *The China Journal*, No. 37 (Jan., 1997): 63–86.

what they failed to realize is that "commandeering resources", the traditional means for expanding one's power, has demonstrably proven to have just the opposite effect to what is intended. Insofar as it was completely immaterial to the issue of how primary-level political authorities secure the mandate of the rural population, "commandeering resources" not only does not allow one to consolidate power the way one could through a system of representation, more often than not, it erodes instead of strengthening the power base.

One would fairly easily notice after reviewing discussions over these issues in modern times that the kind of political predicament rural primary-level political authorities now face has appeared many times throughout Chinese history. Within the last century, there had been many incidents of "popular revolt in the countryside" across China. Their political and economic legacy has long been a topic of great interest to Chinese history scholars for whom English is the *lingua franca*. We have learned from these studies that unlike in European societies, in China, the incidence of popular revolt is far high in the countryside than in urban areas, and they tend to be directed at governments at the sub-national level, instead of the national institutions.[9] Evidently, the precarious nature of "stability" at the rural primary level is nothing new (even though the way it manifests itself evolves as society changes), and it is really just another episode of a recurring crisis of the model and principle of rural governance. Such recurrence has provided us with ample reason to investigate the possibility of tension between social structure and institutional configuration in rural China. Could it be that this tension has been both sustained and strengthened by a series of institutional transformations (e.g. the People's Commune system) and is for a variety of reasons rearing its ugly head again today? Could it be that, despite continuous search by several political regimes under different political systems for over more than a century, answers have yet to be found to the question of how rural primary-level political authorities can govern effectively while at the same time accomplishing those things with which they have been tasked by the central government? And why has massive economic transformation in rural communities in recent times done nothing to mitigate social tension and conflict? We are left with no other choice but to resort to political analysis, and perhaps even more broadly, analysis from the point of view of social institutions.

This shift in perspective may well make is easier to see the role other factors might play in social order in rural communities. We might, for example, adopt the analytical method of political sociology and try to understand how rural primary-level political authorities function as agents of social cohesion in rural communities. The key question in such analysis is not the administrative and economic efficiency of rural primary-level political authorities, i.e., their performance in completing tasks assigned to them by higher levels of government and in coordinating agricultural production. While I do touch upon these

[9] Guobin Wang, *China Under Transformation: Historical Evolution and Limits to the European Experience* (Nanjing: Jiangsu People's Publishing House, 1998).

issues of efficiency, they are not my primary concerns. What I am most interested in is the structure and dynamics of primary-level political apparatus, i.e., how power is distributed, exercised and its ramifications. I want to understand the genesis of political power in rural communities, the structural determination of its obtainment, operation, expansion or decline, and how it shapes both social order and social conflict within rural communities.

Basic Argument

In Chap. 1 I trace changes in modern Chinese history in the source of power for primary-level political authorities, and look at the kinds of impact these changes have had on social structure in rural communities. My hope is to offer an account (albeit a rough one) of this evolutionary process that may serve as the basis of discussions later in the book. Chapter 2 examines the ways in which primary-level political apparatus in rural communities are multi-lateral, complex, and at odds with itself, especially the inherent tension between its economic role and its political role, which, in my view, constitutes a source of conflict within these communities. Both of these chapters address the relationship between the gradual detachment of the primary-level political apparatus from rural communities' public interest on the one hand and the structural instability caused by such detachment on the other. This detachment is, in my view, the structural reason for social instability in these communities.

But if this is true, why is it that in many places primary-level political power holders not only still have but are able to continue to exercise their power, and even maintain dominance? Starting with Chap. 3, my focus shifts to those aspects of and elements in the rural social institutions that are favorable to, or "facilitate", the coalescence of political power. For example, centralized accounting, deficit-neutral tax codes, and other extra-legal instruments allowed the tax and fiscal systems to strengthen the taxation power of primary-level political authorities. Key figures engaged in power play, which was a crucial part of rural politics. The cadres recruitment mechanism spurred the emergence of factions (political support system), which sought to advance their own long-term interests and security through strategic nomination of candidates. There were also a myriad of norms and conventions that had been passed down, both written and un-written, from generations before that lent themselves to being capitalized on by primary-level political figures to strengthen their hold on power.

What I intend to demonstrate is that despite the fact that the cleavage between primary-level political power holders and the interests of the rural communities in which they inhabit had become a source of tension and instability, it nonetheless continued to deepen under existing rural social institutions. This only led to the expansion of power for the local political figures, and further cemented their dominance within those rural communities. In a sense, this meant that not only was the severance of the tie between the two allowed to persist, the power relation between the two was becoming increasingly lopsided. Against the backdrop of waning institutional oversight, and being pulled as it was in these two opposite directions, primary-level political authorities managed to "produce" instability while at the same time maintaining absolute economic, political, and social dominance. This is the defining feature of social conflict and order in rural communities.

This state of affairs had social and political ramifications. On the one hand it detracted from the moral and jurisdictional legitimacy of primary-level political power holders and threatened social cohesion among their constituency; on the other hand, it exacerbated the disconnect between rural communities and the national bureaucratic institutions and apparatus (as evidenced by petitioners' preference to file their grievances with agencies higher on the government hierarchy), since primary-level political authorities provided, at least in this system, the only formal conduit between the two. This meant that the long-held image of these figures as agents acting on behalf of the state was becoming increasingly difficult to maintain. Even today, primary-level political authorities in rural China do not simply take orders from the central government. Instead, they have managed to carve out for themselves some space in which to act "autonomously" (though not in the legal sense of the term). In terms of both their position in society and the constitution of their interests, they stand in a competitive relationship with the developing power of the state on one hand and the society on the other. These political power holders tend to play both sides against each other by using them as leverage, while avoiding taking side.

The book, therefore, contains extensive discussions of the "nature" or "essence" of primary-level government, especially how far it still falls short of what government power in a modern nation-state ought to be insofar as its operating principles are fundamentally incommensurate with constitutional principles. This is closely related to the idea of the "state-building" that has become a basic premise in many studies, one that presupposes a definitive stance on the logically prior question of whether the "building" of a state-centered mobilization system, a system of rights and organizations, of legal accountability and sources of solidarity and integration are in fact complete. For a very long time, academics have focused primarily on the organizational development of a nation state's political system and how capable and effective it is in collecting taxes. However, there is growing realization that such "building" has yet to lead to the emergence of the kind of polity consistent with constitutional rule, i.e., the kind that is to be exercised on behalf of the public's interests. Nevertheless, it is a given within the analytical framework predicated on "state-building" that primary-level political authorities are an integral part of the state's political system, and that the two are in perfect unity with each other. This explains why some of the conduct of rural primary-level officials, most notably those related to levying taxes and collecting fees, have often been seen as state actions, and why conflicts involving these primary-level political authorities have been thought of as conflicts involving the state itself. The fact is that whatever that passes for "state-building" has done little if anything to extend the jurisdictional reach of the state's mandate to rule and to govern, and still less to foster the development of a set of institutions by means of which the symbolic significance of the power of the state translates into actionable mandates. Better understanding of these basic facts about rural politics at the primary level can enhance our ability to identify the structural impediments to the expansion of the scope of the mandate to rule and to govern. I discuss these in the chapters on the compartmentalization of the mandate to rule and on issues of rural institutions.

Sources

Several types of sources were used for writing this book. The first consists of materials professor Yuejin Jing of China Renmin University and myself collected during fieldwork we did in 1997–1998 at a number of rural sites in northern and southern parts of the country. These materials call into three sub-categories. First, there are documents related to the day-to-day operations of public administration in townships and villages, name lists for various purposes, statistics, meeting minutes and memoranda, arbitration notices, rules, regulations, and ordinances. Second, there are archival materials, including documents obtained from local archives. Thirdly, there are records of interviews we did of a range of individuals, including officials in sub-county-level cities, townships and villages, workers, and ordinary villages.

The second type of materials is a treasure trove of textual and written documents that we were able to obtain through the generous assistance from others. These would be things such as supporting documents in a petition filing, letters of complaint, replies to complaints and petitions, certificate letters. Included in the third category were materials that had already appeared in other publications or works or places in the public domain, such as publications in recent years by research teams from the Ministry of Internal Affairs, some master's theses, published investigative reporting, the internet, newspapers, radio shows, and the television. All of these sources are documented in the footnotes. A very small proportion of these sources received multiple mentions across different chapters, but for different purposes. I am grateful to the many people whose hard work, understanding, and assistance made it possible for me to not only gain access to but also make use of these materials.

Questions may be raised about the appropriateness of using certain historical documents for a study about the contemporary period. At a conference on "rural laws" where I presented a paper about "village conventions and ordinances" I was asked why I would make an "abruptly" turn towards historical documents while discussing contemporary issues. Those who were concerned noted that they "could not quite see" the reasons for this apparent temporal discontinuity in my choice of research material. For me, it's important to try to uncover whatever connections there may be between institutions in place today and historical legacies. I am animated by the desire to find out if the commonly held hypothesis that "state-building" has been going on for over half a century is true, and if it has gotten to the crux of the issue. If we are able to trace many features of current institutions at the rural primary level to traditional materials, doubt has to be cast on this hypothesis. I am not using historical documents in order to establish some historical facts, or to establish the historical lineage of current institutions. Instead, my goal is to find out what has or has not changed over time, and I feel strongly that historical documents would be very helpful in that regard. Another concern that was raised had to do with my use of materials from different locations. I was asked why I had not chosen to focus on one village, one township, or one rural community. Perhaps, I did not intend to write about any one place but wanted to extrapolate from the experiences of different places with rural primary-level political activities something that hold true generally. I do not mean to suggest that primary-level politics behave the same way in different places. In fact, there can be substantial dissimilarities. However, what I am most interested in is whether there may nonetheless be some underlying commonalities in terms of fundamental principles and basic structure.

One question that could not be gotten around when I was going over these materials was deciding which one was a more reliable source of information, the textual documents or transcripts of oral history (interviews). I was especially concerned with how much we could trust the portrayal of life in the countryside provided by textual documents that had been processed and that reflected the government's reigning ideology. In my view, there is little if anything that researchers can do about this. The most we can do is to avoid being "deceived" by the materials we have to work with. Since primary-level authority figures were involved in the production of a good amount of the textual documents sourced from rural localities, these documents were in some measure a reflection of these people's governing philosophy and style. But there is also a significant portion of the documents that was churned out as a matter of expedience, i.e., simply for the sake of fulfilling a bureaucratic requirement and as such lacked substantive import. The researcher must therefore stay alert, and do what is necessary to find out where the documents belie the facts, especially if the "discrepancy" is the result of deviation from certain fundamental principles or basic rules. Defects of interview records are caused by such contingent factors as the mood of those involved, recollection, interests and stakes, and relationships, all of which can make proper assessment of the credibility of these record difficult. On top of that, the objectives of the researcher also affect the responses, and the ends towards which these responses are used. These problems should keep us constantly reminded of the importance of exercising caution when working with these materials, and of not putting more faith in them than they merit. Abundance of research material does not obviate the need for perspicacity and insights. This is why Max Weber's insightful analysis of the Chinese society, his inability to read Chinese notwithstanding, has continued to be hugely influential after so many years.

It has long been my belief that the significance of materials for any research lies in its explanatory value. The dispute between those who hold the view that "[one ought to] try to uncover problems and issues by examining the material" and those who believe that a researcher "[ought to] find the materials that would be useful for studying a particular issue" is largely immaterial. There is this notion with which many academics are sympathetic that the first of these two views is more "down to earth" insofar as it goes from facts and empirical evidence to theory, while the second one starts from a framework, and is therefore hollowed of substance. As far as I am concerned, regardless of where one starts, any researcher must take evidence seriously, because that is what they will rely on to show that a problem actually does exist. Meanwhile, the researcher must genuinely care about theoretical questions if the value of the research materials can be realized to the maximum. How useful a theory is depends on whether it can guide researchers in their quest to make sense of the materials and to understand a problem. Indeed, even the very ability to "uncover" problems and issues through examining the research material presupposes a kind of problematization sensitivity that training in theoretical analysis can instill in one. What a researcher wants their research material to provide them with—whether it is empirical evidence or a collection of materials, a cognitive framework or theoretical elucidation, advocacy for some "ism" or criticism of some institutions—will shape the way they treat both the research material and theories. There seems no reason why we should not allow each researcher the space to make that decision for themselves based on their own personality. A one-size-fits-all requirement or prohibition is not necessary. What is important is what they are able to produce with their work. In the marketplace of knowledge, trade-offs are inevitable.

Methodology

Finally, a few words about the "method" used in this study. Method is necessarily related to methodology, so the following is likely to be fairly drab and abstract.

As I was nearing the completion of the first draft of the manuscript, my colleague Professor Liping Sun sent me by email a recent article on rural studies. In the piece the author makes the case for an analytical method that focuses on "process-event", a method, according to Professor Sun, quite different from the one that revolves around "structure-institutions". And he wanted to hear what others had to say about it. His suggestion, it turned out, gave me an opportunity to reflect on the analytical method on which I myself had been relying, and on my own characteristics and limitations. I had had discussion about this issue with graduate students enrolled in the elective seminar on "Research on select topics in political sociology", and their opinions, which they wrote about in their reports, covered a wide range. Here, I would like to offer an elucidation of the method that has been defined in terms of "structure-institution", and I shall do so by connecting the "process-event" method with some of the issues raised by these graduate students. My main aim is not to comment on the "process-event" method, but rather to register my reaction and response to some of the criticisms that have been leveled against it. They matter because they have bearing on the analytical approach I used for this book.

This clarification is important also because of its implications for a debate about methodology that has raged on for nearly half a century, albeit in slightly different forms and couched in somewhat different terminologies across different disciplines. The central animating question in this debate is whether it is structure (or institutions [that embody it]) or actions (or individual agents [who do them]) that is explanatorily more fundamental for social phenomena. In other words, which perspective produces a deeper understanding of the basic order that makes co-existence in groups even possible for human beings. Discussions about this issue have taken place in fields such as sociology, anthropology, history, political sciences, among others. And it is not uncommon to find references to it in the recent debate about "rational choice" vs. "neo-institutionalism".

To make sure such a debate about a foundational question stays relevant, there is no getting around, in my view at least, some philosophical questions. These debates took place at a time when they could not have been couched in vocabulary now associated with post-modernism, nor did they, for that reason, have anything at all to say about some of the basic premises on which post-modern discourse had been built. These include questions such as whether normative statements can be derived from descriptive ones, and whether the reader can have certain control over the text that transcends the original intent of the narrator because they occupy a vantage point higher than that of the latter. These issues have direct implications for the kind of relationship a subject stands to and can have with the object (the socio-cultural environment), and what one's presumptions are with regard to these questions obviously has significant impact on what one understands the objectives of their research project to be. On the approach to this question that is characteristic to modernist thinking, two questions are distinguished and addressed separately. One question is epistemological, having to do with the subject seeking to understand the world, while the other is empirical, having to do with the objective entities that populate the world and that the subject is trying to understand. This creates something of a dichotomy, with determination by what (structure-institutions) has objective existence on one hand and subjective (chosen) actions on the other. While this dichotomy may not be among the premises sanctioned by postmodernism, it is widely accepted by many followers of modernist thinking. I am keenly aware of my own intellectual limitations when it comes to these issues. There is obviously great need for what insights studies in other fields beside sociology can offer.[10]

Now let us return to the traditional intellectual paradigm. The structure-institution analysis emphasizes the ways in which actions conform to social rules. However, rules are not the same thing as laws. Rules are always

[10] I gave a brief introduction to post-modernist philosophy and constructivism, and continued the discussion in my *Notes from Harvard* (Beijing: Higher Education Press, 2005).

changing, responsive to and reflective of changes in society and how people live as a matter of course. By contrast, laws are believed to be essentially absolute "truth", to which the world must conform, by bending itself if necessary (hence its evocativeness of "fatalism"). In my view, the most salient form in which progress humanity is able to make in controlling our own orderliness manifests itself in the way we try (formally or informally) to establish justification for whatever new thing we are exploring. This amounts to the establishment of new social norms. Leading thinkers do this, that is done through theoretical proofs and arguments, and it is also what ordinary people do in their daily lives. Creating justification (normativity) for our actions is a need that is a natural part of our lives. To human beings, norms are not something external, and while they are imposed on us, we do often need them for the sense of security and a basis for expectations they can provide.

Proponents of the "process-event" analytical framework contend that those who adopt the "structure-institution" framework lay too much emphasis on rules. But I think this reflects differences in what animates researchers. And these differences can in turn be attributable to differences in intellectual background, academic training, personal experiences and even basic philosophy and systems of values. These differences determine how important different "problems" are to different people. And such assessment has consequences for what they are trying to accomplish in either deciding on (or constructing) a theoretical and analytical framework. For they are committed to ascertaining the essence of the thing to which they have attached great importance. Application of the "structure-institution" analytical framework entails putting a premium on what specific "events" or "processes" can reveal about social (structural) relationships. This is because proponents of this framework start with the assumption that the actions of human beings reflect how the institutions (both formal and informal) in which we are existentially embedded stimulate, encourage, guide, and also limit us. They argue, therefore, that "events" are the products of the complex interrelations among institutions and social relations. It is implied in this assumption that institutions are, relative to actions, more consequential, insofar as different institutions can engender different actions (and events). The causal link between the abolition of (the system) of fully subsidized medical care and the (act of) binge purchase and hording of medicines is a case in point. Obviously, the occurrence of "events" has much to do with institutional reconfiguration, which is essentially shifts in the balance of power (structure) among different groups.

The term "institution" as it is used here is not quite what is ordinarily meant by "rules", because "rules" that lack practical import do not constitute "institutions" as the embodiment of *social norms*. Even if institutions lie underneath the surface, they still must be capable of effecting conformity to norms. Generally speaking, I interpret the notion of "institution" broadly, and use it to refer to the overarching system that provides the justificatory basis for our actions. Since "justification" also means the delimitation of people's rights, responsibilities, and duties, and that all of our political, economic, and social relationship are fundamentally subject to these constraints (with some measure elasticity of course), "institutions" play a decisive role in shaping the "structural" relationship among people. Institutions may be written or unwritten, and many of them exist in unwritten form, e.g., conventions, traditions, or culture. Still, regardless of their mode of existence, they must be normatively efficacious over people's actions and constitutive of basic principles that people are already familiar, try to comply and even identify with. When an action [involving two parties] runs afoul of such a basic principle, both parties would regard it as unjustified. A recurrence, under a certain set of conditions, of conducts exemplifying such a principle would constitute sufficient evidence that such an institution (norm) is in effect in this area.

Differences in the degrees to which institutions are honored is not one of the premises of the "structure-institutions" analytical framework, in which deviation from an institution is not even considered comprehensible. One reason for this might be that "institutions", when understood as social norms, have their origin in contracts, which came into existence at all because of general agreement among a group of individuals (and for that reason include stipulations about penalty for those who do not comply). But there are other institutions that are made up of "rules" that reflect only one party's wishes. They have no built-in punishment mechanism, or otherwise only mete out punishments haphazardly, or do not enforce punishments that exist "on paper" because of the prohibitively high costs associated with enforcement. Institutions like these have no normative effects on a society. For proponents of institutionalists, "institutions" must have built into them a system of enforcement and oversight, whose goal is to identify and eliminate those who disobey the rules, and whose existence makes widespread non-compliance almost impossible. All of this is presuppositional to the idea of "institutions". Therefore, "institutions" that are not broadly honored are indeed not genuine institutions, and proponents of the institution-based analytical framework would unlikely be swayed by criticisms of that framework that cite the failures of these pseudo-institutions. To them, such criticism is predicated on a misapplication of the notion of "institution", and that what these critics should do instead is to find out what the rules are that do explain the way people actually behave.

We can, of course, purse this line of questioning further still, and ask whether the fact that different operational strategies appear to be at work behind different events indicates changes in rules. My answer to that would be that strategies are chosen insofar as they are demonstrably *effective* within a certain set of institutions (including both formal and informal structural relationships). The outcome of the inner workings of these institutions allows the agents involved to anticipate the effects of adopting any particular strategy, effects that would not obtain under a different set of institutions or relationships. This means which operational system is in place can have consequences for both the choice and the efficaciousness of the "strategy", i.e., directional shifts in strategies and their magnitude do to some extent obey some kind of institutional logic. Therefore, "events" analyses would not, contrary to what their proponents might have liked to see, do much at all to detract from the functions of institutions. In fact, just the opposite may be true: such analysis may provide evidence for the strong connection between "institutions" and "action strategies". It should be noted, however, that the focus in "event" are strategies and related processes, and not the underlying mechanisms behind the choice. In other words, "event" analysis does not seek to deepen our understanding about institutions.

Now when we step back, it is easy to see that in China, a large proportion of institutions and rules are not in fact operational (and for that reason ought not be regarded as *bona fide* "institutions", i.e., as embodiments of social norms). Still, that does not make them utterly useless to researchers undertaking "institutional analysis", and this may be particularly true for those working in China studies. In his recent works, Professor Philip Huang sees the "discrepancy" between "representation" and "practice" as what constitutes the very *institutional essence* of the legal codes of the Qing Dynasty. For example, while the political class's hifalutin rhetoric and their actions can often seem to stand in stark contrast to each other, much like the apparent tension between the timidity and compliance some defendants in legal cases display and the shamelessness and cunningness that led them to their alleged crimes, these seemingly jarring contradictions are not incomprehensible once we looked at them from a perspective from which both expression and practice—which often run counter to each other—are taken into consideration.[11] It can also sometimes happen that apparently contradictory institutional factors act upon one another, such as when rural officials exercise their authority to buy grains from the farmers to stock the public supply. In so doing, they are responding to changes in multilateral institutions. On the one hand, the market price (and the pricing mechanism) of grains presents farmers with other opportunities for disposing of their harvest, which increased the opportunity costs of selling to the government, which had been the traditional practice. However, the reason why a "binding" contract for the buying and selling of grains between the farmers and the government is nonetheless possible is the underlying ("collective" or "public") ownership of the land. Under this ownership structure, the failure to sign such a contract would constitute justification for stripping, or the policy to that effect, the land from the farmer. Both [the market price of grains and land ownership] play an important role in shaping the expectations of both farmers and rural officials. The emergence of market rules weakens rural officials' mandatory claim upon farmer's grain harvest, while collective land ownership does the exact opposite. The conclusion we can draw, therefore, is both the degree to which rural officials succeed in convincing farmers to sell them their grains and what course of action farmers choose to follow will change according to how the range of institutional relationships these actors find themselves operating under shape their behavior. And these institutions represent different

[11] Philip C. C. Huang, *Civil Justice in China: Representation and Practice in the Qing* (Beijing: China Social Sciences Press, 1998), 3.

systems of power distribution, with some tending to boost the political mandate of rural officials, while others to augment farmers' right to choose.

It is of course not true that structure-institution-based analysis does not take processes (history) seriously. For example, T. Skocpol has been trying to identify factors in the historical development of the Russian, French, and Chinese societies that may have contributed to macroscopic structural changes. For V. Shue, China's traditional social structure offers foundational historical resources for understanding contemporary transformation in the country's rural areas. V. Nee, who took it upon himself to explore areas in sociology for application of the institutional analysis, sees transformation as indicative of changes in rules (institutions), changes that in turn alter the structure of the action space for those who produce and those who redistribute. More notably still, much of the work by the economist D. North, a prominent institutionalist, has been in trying to understand economic history through the lens of the evolution of structure and institutions. In Philip A. Kuhn's *Soulstealers*, a historical study whose Chinese translation was recently published, the author probes the tense relationship and inter-dependency between monarch and bureaucrat by analyzing a community "event". What these remarkable works illustrate is that the structure-institution framework and the process-event framework are not opposed to each other, nor are they mutually exclusive. They simply differ in where they place their emphasis. And this difference, in my view, has directly to do with the motive and objectives of the researcher.

Another criticism of the structure-institution analysis is that it is overly "simplistic". It is true that those who apply such analysis have often tried to bring into sharp relief the key features of certain relationships by capturing their simplest and purest form with generalizations couched in technical terms. However, simplicity and superficiality are not the same thing. Many simple formulas capture abstract relationships that most probably would not have been identified had it not been for close examination of a rich body of materials, including those on processes and events. The structure institution analysis does not trivialize rich and complex narratives of facts, or at least is not opposed to them. But generating descriptive accounts is not the ultimate goal of such analysis, nor is the collection of research materials. In applying the structure-institution perspective, one is trying to assess and evaluate concepts and frameworks that are used as cognitive apparatus. This is, in my understanding, one particular kind of academic work. Other kinds include interviewing, documenting, collecting material, describing, commenting or appraising, criticizing or defending, all of which are motivated by different ideas, animated by different concerns and are trying to accomplish different objectives. What is achieved by the use of analytical tools, insofar as such exercise tends to "simplifies" and "formalizes", is obviating the need for vast amounts of materials through abstraction: descriptions of specific phenomena are generalized into evaluations of and deductions based on conceptual frameworks, the richness of historical facts is condense into compact and concise abstract concepts. Such transcendence from particularity does not result in the loss of the richness [of concrete facts]. Instead, such richness has been woven into the fabrics of what the apparently simple formal expressions are intended to capture.

It seems, therefore, that the issue is not so much whether frameworks should be constructed as it is why frameworks are invariably simple. In my view, this has a great deal to do with the level on which the act of "abstracting" is done on a scale. In the words of A. J. Nathan, who sees this as a philosophical issue, "uniqueness is thus a function of location on what Giovanni Sartori has called the 'ladder of abstraction'".[12] In other words, how unique something is depends on where the abstraction is done. Moving up on this ladder is to move towards greater simplicity and abstractness, moving down is to move towards greater complexity and richness. Therefore, depending on which direction in which our analysis proceeds, we may end up with either a complex, specific, and unique account of events or simple, abstract, and general account of the same events. For researchers, such a ladder of abstractness is an analytical instrument that allows them to identify, sort, and characterize their subject matters. On which specific rung on this ladder abstraction is to be carried out is to be dictated by the inherent needs of the research project.

It is important, however, for the researcher to be cognizant of certain side effects of the adoption of any particular framework. While it can and does guide one's thinking on a subject, a framework may also increase the likelihood of an event being treated as an empirical "given", and make it harder for the researcher to discover new things. Unfortunately, in this sense, unless the subject matter concerns things that have thus far fallen outside the purview of scholarly attention, a lot of what researchers do amounts to producing interpretations of empirical facts constructed on the basis of facts that are "given" by stipulation. In other words, once something enters a researcher's field of vision, the "pre-conception" (framework and assumptions) about it would inevitably impact the researcher's perception of its reality. The obvious consequence of this is that, to a considerable degree, "reality" becomes a production of conceptual stipulation. Faced with this restrictive effect of cognitive frameworks, a conscientious researcher must remain at once open-minded and vigilant about all kind of possible frameworks.

I encourage researchers to be receptive to those elements of different frameworks that may be beneficial, instead of rejecting them outright. I believe that different methods can help researchers discover different things, so the right attitude is open-mindedness, and willingness to try. Insofar as we can all agree that the world is inherently uncertain, no one knows the real answers to the questions we face.[13] That means, naturally, that no one can be sure what the best methods are for understanding this problem, or whether there exists any such thing as the single correct method.

[12] Andrew J. Nathan, "Is Chinese Culture Distinctive?—A Review Article" *The Journal of Asian Studies* 52 (1993): 927.

[13] Joseph Stiglitz, *Why the Government Interferes in the Economy?* (Beijing: China Resource Press, 1998), 163.

It is also possible that it is not the simplicity of the frameworks *per se* that is a source of danger, but rather the simplistic way in which frameworks are put to work, which is commonplace. The Coase Theorem, for example, has been subject to derision: Why do monkeys climb up trees? Because the transaction costs are right. Other examples of simplistic answers abound in political sociology. Why do rural conflicts occur? Because of the tension between the state and society; Why establish primary-level organizations? It's part of the "state-building"; What caused social movements? The existence of civil society; Why elections? Because that is what is needed to establish democracy. Surely, the reader can already tell that the reason these diagnoses lack credibility is due not so much to any inherent problem with any particular framework, but more to the problematic ways the frameworks have been applied. The researcher alone is in a position to decide, on the basis of what they are interested in and what materials they have available to them, whether to resort to causal, or process, or structural or event analysis. I see little evidence for any mutual exclusivity among these analytical perspectives, and still less reason to be able to know ahead of time if the different analyses would yield similar results. Even if the process-event analysis aims to and succeeds in providing an account that is rich, specific, and raw (i.e., with minimal treatment of the research materials), it does not therefore preclude the possibility of such an account being supplemented by further analysis that is abstract and formulaic. There is no fundamental opposition between the two approaches.

It is quite possible that I will be open in future studies to using alternative analytical methods, if that is what is appropriate given the subject matter and the materials available to me. But empirical materials, theoretical questions, historical legacy, the roles and institutions and organizations will always be important to me, so will absorbing as much that is useful for advancing understanding as possible from other methods. This is the essence of my basic research "method".

Peking University
Beijing, China

Jing Zhang

Preface to the 2018 Revised Edition

When Social Sciences Academic Press decided to release a new edition of *Primary-level Government: Issues in Rural Governance in China*, 12 years had passed since the publication of the second edition in 2006. Harking back to the year 2000, when the first edition was published by Zhejiang People's Publishing House, this book has become a historical study.

Among the issues primary-level government has faced over the past 12 years, some are old, others are new. As urbanization continues apace, the value of land, a factor in agricultural economy, is changing, so are rural institutions. Primary-level polity's role has declined in some tasks, such as tax collection and distribution, but grown in others, such as project management and digital information collection. While primary-level government must constantly respond to social change, there has been no systematic change to the principle of governance and norm of conduct (insofar as primary-level government is distinct not only from social act in the ordinary sense but also from how things had been in the past) that define its essence. In my view, this is precisely why we are discussing the topic of promoting the modernization of the system of governance today.

I would rather not see the book getting thicker and thicker. Therefore, for this edition, except for a few revisions (to improve precision), I have left most of the contents intact, to make sure the book reflects history. With regard to some new issues, I plan to address them in an upcoming edited volume *Social Governance: Theory, Organization and Methods* (Commercial Press, 2018). That book will focus on the cities, while the old book mainly draws on materials about the countryside. The hope is that the new book and new editions of the old book will supplement each other and form a continuity.

I would like to thank Xiaofei Zhang, the in-house editor, for her excellent work on the manuscript, without which there would have been many more errors in the published book.

Beijing, UK — Jing Zhang

Contents

About the Author

Jing Zhang is Professor of Sociology at Peking University. Zhang received her BA from Sichuan University, MA from Nankai University, and Ph.D. from the Chinese University of Hong Kong. Zhang specializes in political sociology, and her representative publications include: *The State and the Society* (chief editor), *The Institutionalization of Interests and Its Organizational Embodiment: Case Studies of Corporate Employee Delegation*, *Corporatism*, *Identification: Beliefs, Attitudes and Justifications* (chief editor), *China in Transition: Ideas of Social Justice* (chief editor), *Structural Origins of Social Conflicts*, *Social Organizing: Case Studies* (chief editor).

List of Tables

CHAPTER 1

Background: The Source(s) of Rural Political Power and Authority

1.1 Local Governance in China: A Parallel Regime to Imperial Rule

Historical studies have shown that China's governance structure has traditionally consisted of two distinct components. On top was the central government, which sat at the top of a massive bureaucratic hierarchy; and in the lower level were local governing bodies controlled by lineage leaders, rural gentry, and local authority figures.[1] A basic feature of a political power configuration like this is the co-existence of cultural and ideological unity on one hand and the "compartmentalization" of the *de facto* mandate to govern across different jurisdictions on the other. At the primary level, community leaders exercised full control over local affairs, i.e., affairs internal to the locality. This power did not derive from delegation by the central government, those who commanded it held no office within the state's bureaucratic hierarchy and rarely came into contact with the authority represented by that structure. All of this made it difficult for the central government to extend its reach and authority to the primary-level community level and become a significant player in local governance. On the surface, orders and directives issued by the central government would be orderly transmitted to lower rungs on the subnational structure of authority, thereby maintaining the integrity of that very structure. But in practice, the involvement of intermediaries at each step in the process, who invariably exercised a certain measure of discretion, prevented the central authority from having much meaningful influence over local governance. Where the demarcation line is between local governance and central government rule is a delicate matter, and one of tacit (strategic?) consent for both sides, and only

[1] Xianming Wang, *Surviving Feudalism: The Modern Transformation of China's Gentry* (Tianjin: Tianjin People's Publishing House, 1997), 21.

J. Zhang, *Primary-Level Government*,
https://doi.org/10.1007/978-981-96-6209-8_1

those cases that community leaders were genuinely incapable of handling were reported to higher authorities. The "autonomy" or "self-rule" of the local communities, therefore, faced little threat. The central government and community leaders at the primary level managed to mind their own businesses. While such *de facto* compartmentalization of governing power and authority in the country was never openly acknowledged by the state, evidence of it was ubiquitous.[2]

If we follow Vivienne Shue in applying the concept of "locality" to refer to the geographical area covered by the jurisdiction under any local authority such as described by Xiaotong Fei (Hsiao-tung Fei), we would then see the co-existence throughout Chinese history of two separate and mutually independent centers of social order. One consisted of the official system of state bureaucracy that revolved around the central government. For those at the primary level of society, however, the unifying power this bureaucratic system had consisted in its symbolic value as something culturally significant. The *in situ* political authority at each specific locality was the other center [of social order], which had more substance to it, insofar as it is where the real power to govern lied. After centuries of co-existence, both systems of order have developed into centers of power and authority unto themselves within their respective domains. Those operating in either one understood that beyond following the protocol of formality necessary for maintaining amicable relations between the two systems, they were to refrain from trespassing into the others' turf. This long-standing practice of mutual non-interference effectively created a gap between them. It stands to reason, therefore, that a political system based on a compartmentalized structure of authority can only provide the foundation of national unity on the cultural level. Political cohesiveness on the structural level, however, was forged within each locality, since it fell upon the local authority to manage the day-to-day operation of local affairs. This explains why, so long as its authority over the country as a whole is symbolically accepted by local communities and their leaders, the state never sought to take control of local governance, which would have been seen as an act of provocation.[3] Indeed, for a very long time the state was not even able to adopt a uniform set of principles for governance applicable across the country, so different places followed their own customs and traditions. The validity and legitimacy of the maxim "do what makes the most sense locally", predicated on the premise that in the state lies the symbolic unifying entity, have never been in dispute. The state long relied on community leaders to govern as its proxy at the local level, and showed little if any interest in usurping that power. Within each locality,

[2] Hsiaotong Fei, *China's Gentry: Essays in Rural - Urban Relations* (University of Chicago Press, 1953).

[3] Vivienne Shue, *The Reach of the State: Sketches of the Chinese Body Politic*, (Stanford: Stanford University Press, 1988).

especially at the most primary level of rural society, community leaders built solidarity and cohesion within the local population, something the state was unable to do.

That solidarity and cohesion could be forged at the local level is indicative of the close connection between the source of local leader's power and authority and the locality within which that power and authority are exercised. Not everyone can become a community leader, and the power and standing attendant to such a position were only obtainable to those who satisfied three conditions: sufficient wealth, academic credentials, and the status as a public figure within the locality. Possessing all of these three forms of capital is a necessary, though not necessarily a sufficient, condition for becoming part of the rural authority. Of these three, academic credential was what a person earned after passing imperial examinations. It can redound to the esteem of the holders of these titles. The other two, by contrast, were strictly related to social conditions inside each locality. Wealth is by its very nature a form of family or private property, and is thus constitutive of the economic foundations of primary-level power and authority. However, while wealth did boost the social standing of those who had it, it did not automatically endow them with the power and authority to lead. Some scholars have argued that academic credentials actually carried greater weight. For example, it has been pointed out that "during much of the Ming and Qing dynasties, wealth played a relatively minor role in determining if someone would become a government official, and by comparison, academic credentials (earned by passing imperial examinations) were more strongly correlated with a person's political career prospects".[4] But if this described the average member of the gentry, it may not be as true of people who occupied leadership positions in rural society, who would have been the elites among the gentry, that is, belonging to the upper echelons within that class. They acquired that status by getting actively involved in community affairs. In other words, people who became leaders at the primary level were not only well educated but also deeply involved in local governance, they were held in high regard by the local population on account of that hands-on involvement. The reason why, despite having both "academic degrees" and sufficient wealth, a good many members of the gentry did not become community leaders was that they led mostly private lives and did little that would help establish them as public figures among the local population. On this particular phenomenon, some anthropological studies done in southern China have produced interesting findings based on close observations.

> The Pearl River delta region has historically been known for its highly developed lineage-based customs and practices. There were many single-lineage villages, whose leaders were usually chosen by lineage members, and their selection would typically be accepted by the government. These community leaders were mostly

[4] Bingdi He, cited in Xianming Wang, *Surviving Feudalism: The Modern Transformation of China's Gentry* (Tianjin: Tianjin People's Publishing House, 1997), 47.

> in charge of religious affairs, ancestor worship, education, water supply, and commerce. A myriad of matters fell within the scope of their official duties, which encompassed legislative power (to draft lineage ordinances), judicial power (in some cases the power to order execution) and enforcement power. These are in addition to officiating at ancestral worship ceremonies, organizing economic production, overseeing educational institutions and activities, administering conflict resolution, coordinating emergency management and disaster relief, and dealing with government bureaucracy. This is why the bar for becoming a leader at the primary level had to be as high as it was. First and foremost, one had to be intelligent.[5] Secondly, one had to have commonsense and be rational, and familiar with local norms and customs; and thirdly, one had to want to serve the community, to further the public interest... Not only did he have to make known to those in the community that he was willing to work for them, but he also had to demonstrate his competency. In addition, this person had to have what it takes to represent the village, such that when people from outside needed to speak to somebody in charge in the village, he could be that person, as the head of the village. This position was not filled by appointment, but when someone became the go-to person for all other villagers, especially when they needed an opinion on something, and when this person was asked to officiate at ceremonies and rituals, he became the *de facto* leader, or at least one of them... Alternatively, one could also, if they had the financial means, build shrines, or otherwise do something to win the hearts and minds of lineage members, and become as a matter of course a leader of the lineage or a particular branch thereof.[6]

Hands-on engagement with local public affairs was necessary for becoming a public figure. This can be clearly seen in the kinds of social responsibilities placed on them. Historians have identified three areas in which these individuals were expected to serve their community: education, common assets, and public works. With respect to education, their responsibilities included but were not limited to drafting development plans, building schools, recruiting and training teachers, maintaining education facilities, and compiling gazetteer. As for common assets, i.e., facilities and establishments collectively owned by and served the community, such as nurseries, nursing homes, food banks, and township and village granary reserves, the local leaders were responsible for their operation, staffing, financial and accounting management, and donation solicitation. Given the paramount importance of township granary reserves to the economic security of the community, their management fell squarely on these local leaders. Public works, the third area of their duties, were related to infrastructure, such as water supply and conservation facilities, bridges, ferry services, and other construction projects.[7] For those things that required close interaction with members of the community, such as civic education, public

[5] The requirement for academic titles most likely reflected this.

[6] Xiuguo Li, Shilian Shan, "Leadership Selection Mechanism in pre-modern Southern China," Unpublished project proposal (1999), 3.

[7] Wang, *Surviving Feudalism*, 52–55.

security (militia drills), litigation, arbitration, ancestor worship, religious ceremonies, document transcription, bookkeeping, and public assistance, nobody was better suited than members of the gentry. This was how they earned the status as public figures, and the esteem that came with that status.

What is important to understand here is that these individuals' status as "public figures" was indicative of a kind of alignment or unity in terms of basic interests and objectives between themselves and the community. That is to say they had to be able somehow to either merge their personal interests (i.e., household property and economic gains) and the interests of the local community (its development, security, and order) by obliterating the line between them. One could not build a reputation as or earn esteem for being a person of authority in a rural community unless they were able to fuse these two spheres together. Success at running a private business, while useful for acquiring wealth, apparently did not necessarily confer on one of the kind of social standing that comes only with a track record for serving the local population. One needed to show they could get things done for the community if they were to be recognized as a public figure, a person of authority. These lettered men also played a number of other roles, including facilitating communications between the local population and those from the outside, organizing ancestor worship ceremonies, arbitrating disputes, and serving as intermediaries or guardians, among others. Their status as public figures within the local community was predicated upon their regular performance of these tasks, and that status in turn also afforded them protection from what might hurt their own wealth and property. What peace and stability a locality enjoyed, we might say, was a result of what these community leaders did to forge the identification between their own political economic interests and those of the community, so that whatever that benefited one also benefited the other.

As a type of political resource, "public figure status" comes with social responsibility. It put leadership power and authority in the hands of members of the gentry, whose role in the management of local public affairs made them the bedrock of primary-level governance. The geographical reach of their responsibilities was, however, clearly delimited, and did not extend beyond the locality. While the power of rural gentry was recognized and approved by the central government, the latter was never the source of the former's mandate to govern. In fact, every effort was made by the gentry to avoid entanglement between their power and those of government officials, and the latter were likewise opposed to the gentry "overreaching and meddling in affairs (outside their own locality) that fell within the government's jurisdiction". Moreover,

> Local community leaders must not seek out government officials or try to associate with people with power and prestige in order to advance themselves.... Enter ministry buildings at one's own peril.[8]

[8] Wang, *Surviving Feudalism*, 51, quoting from *Da Qing Hui Dian*.

Granary reserves are to set up in townships and villages, and local authority is to be in charge of their management, with which government official must not interfere.[9]

1.2 Becoming a Public Figure: The Institutional Framework

The power and the authority to govern at the local level, as was just shown, were not conferred onto rural leaders by the state. Nor were these automatically inherited, still less a bequest the way a piece of property might be. One attained them by actually partaking in running local affairs.

It was not enough for village landlords to exercise great power over their tenants and debtors; to gain legitimacy they also had to be responsible kinsmen and social leaders. Watson argues that the ideal of brotherhood within the lineage justified elite domination. But she makes it equally clear that lineages did not automatically confer authority to these elites; they needed to build up their symbolic capital within the lineage by engaging in philanthropy and other community tasks.[10]

Any individual could attain status as an elite only within the parameters of a set of rules and institutions, as well as cultural tradition. For example, the social responsibility shouldered by those in positions of power and authority ultimately manifested itself inside each and every rural household, in the form of a dominating, paternalistic, and moralizing force. So these leaders had to tend to every aspect, big or small, of the lives of those living in their community, whether it was related to production or personal welfare. Unlike other landlords, in years of poor harvest they either reduced or waived rent, or met with tenants to express their concerns and sympathy. All of this goes to show that it was incumbent upon local leaders to serve as both "caretaker" and "guardian" of the community. While the account below may arguably have made rural leaders look nicer than they in fact were, it does add credence to the view that public figures, i.e., people in positions of authority, were not held to the same moral standards as were average members of the rural gentry.

On the day rent was due, expressions of concern were offered [to the tenants]... and whenever something bad happened [to them], such as injuries or disasters, legal disputes, sickness, death, bereavement and economic hardship, efforts were made to provide them with what they lacked, be it things to know or things to have. The caring attention [the tenants] received was not unlike what would be given to [the landlord's] own family... On the opening day of the rent period, a visit was paid to [the tenant's] residence, aimed at learning about where he lived, if he was diligent and industrious, the number of dependents in the household,

[9] Wang, *Surviving Feudalism*, 54, quoting from *Qingchao Xu Wenxian Tongkao*.

[10] Prasenjit Duara, "Elites and the Structures of Authority in the Villages of North China," in Joseph W. Esherick, Mary Backus Rankin, eds., *Chinese Local Elites and Patterns of Dominance* (University of California Press, 1990), 265.

and identifying the hardworking and upright, and offer special support for those who had many to support and showed determination.[11]

What is especially noteworthy is that, while it might seem as though whether somebody did these things depend mostly on their personality and character, throughout history, at least in parts of the country, such activities had long been codified into the social norm, and become something that was required. These rules also stipulated that land mostly belonged to the lineage, instead of any individual, so that funds needed to pay for public expenditure would not be subject to the kinds of restrictions that often applied to private property. Studies have shown that in some southern Chinese provinces, single-family landlords were far less powerful and influential both economically and politically than "landlord groups", essentially associations comprising multiple land-owning families in a village. In addition to taking on tenants, these groups were required to allocate a portion of the earnings from the use of the land towards public expenditure, either directly or indirectly. The means of production controlled by such groups would be apportioned among different community causes and proceeds from each apportionment would be earmarked for investment toward that cause, and cannot be claimed by any one person or family. For example, there would be so-called "school land", "temple land", and "association land" owned by trade groups or professional associations, and "lineage land", a designation given to whatever land that is yet unclaimed by individual households in the lineage.[12] Pertinent ordinance would typically stipulate that proceeds from these lands must be set aside for very specific public interest purposes. Such a system no doubt played a key role in adjudicating the distribution of benefits between what was the "public's interest" and what was "private interests" within rural communities.

> Rent earnings from leasing out the common land are used to pay for community religious ceremonies, financial assistance for students from poor households, public education, stipend for defraying living expenses, travel allowance for those taking exams in the city, subsidy for scholars, old-age and disability assistance, disaster relief, sometimes even the costs of weddings and funerals within the lineage.[13]

Other measures were introduced over time to ensure the reliability and sustainability of this revenue stream. For example, selling or claiming as one's own land or other common property belonging to the lineage was strictly

[11] Lüxiang Zhang, ed., *An Annotated Supplement to Agricultural Book* (*Bunongshu Jiaoshi*), (Beijing: Agriculture Press, 1983), quoted in Huilin Lu, "The Transformation of the Gentry and Social Erosion (thesis)", in *Graduate Student Forum* (published by Peking University Department of Sociology), No. 1.

[12] Han-Sheng Chen, *Landlord and Peasant in China* (New York, International Publishers, 1936), quoting from Mei County Gazetteer.

[13] Chen, *Landlord and Peasant in China*.

prohibited,[14] and land sales that had not been reviewed for approval by lineage members would be declared null.[15] Moreover, a principle was adopted that required "communal living and common ownership of property" within the lineage, meant to ensure that all lineage assets were collectively owned.[16] More people may know about the requirement that close relations be given priority in the transfer of household assets, the so-called "close relations first" principle. According to it, "should a seller fail to consider close relations as potential buyers first, and instead go directly to people belonging to another lineage, his own relations could come forward and contest the sale".[17] The *raison d'être* for this and similar rules was obviously to ensure that the lineage as a whole benefited from the value generated by its collectively owned property, and to protect the community against resource losses that might threaten its survival that could result from private land trades. These prohibitions may seem unreasonable from a modern economic point of view, but they make a good deal of sense from the perspective of rural governance and solidarity- and cohesion-building.

Xiaoli Zhao has surmised, for example, that the principle of "close relations first" was an expression of the long-standing norm in the rural "moral" economy that was meant to encourage "mutually beneficial" behaviors. Some scholars in North America and Europe have tried to explain these practices and customs among the gentry by reference to Confucian teachings about culture and civility. My own view, however, is that these conventions were adhered to because of their political significance. They were put in place in order to guarantee adequate funding for public causes within the rural community, to sustain and protect the community, and to maintain cohesion and internal order. Of course, these rules were also instrumental for safeguarding the economic underpinnings of the power and authority of community leaders. They helped to realize structural balance among the different interest groups and stakeholders, to protect the community's assets, and to maintain social and political stability. On this point, I concur with Philip Kuhn, who has argued that (within the Chinese context), protection of public assets is best understood as being motivated by a community's concern for its own *shared interests*. In other words, wealth is not needed to protect welfare *per se*, but to protect the community. Any individual with means became *recognized* and *approved of* by the community only if he had contributed toward its collective wellbeing.[18]

[14] Chen, *Landlord and Peasant in China*.

[15] Prasenjit Duara, *Culture, Power, and the State: Rural North China, 1900-1942* (Stanford University Press, 1991), quoting from the *Manchurian Railroad Survey*, 1988.

[16] Zhiping Liang, *Common Law in Qing Dynasty: Society and the State* (China University of Political Science and Law Press, 1996), 75, quoting unknown sources.

[17] Xiaoli Zhao, "Contracts and Customs in Land Transactions in the Rural China in the Modern Times," *Journal of the Student Union of Peking University*,1996 (8), 8, quoting unknown sources.

[18] Philip A. Kuhn, *Rebellion and Its Enemies in Late Imperial China* (Harvard University Press, 1980).

1.3 The Basis of Power: Forging a Body of Shared Interest

The analysis above suggests that it was not the state that gave primary-level authority figures the mandate to rule. Nor was it control over private wealth, or still less the aura of prestige surrounding "academic credentials". More than just power, mandate is recognition and endorsement by the community and it is something that one earns by demonstrating their ability to build a *body of shared interests.* In other words, one must be capable of coalescing disparate interest groups into an entity whose members are willing to identify themselves with a set of shared, but also structured political and economic interests. Moreover, there must also be mechanisms in place to ensure cohesion within that entity. This is also why establishing local authority and cultivating a body of shared economic and political interests must go hand-in-hand. Contribution toward the construction of this cohesive entity is a prerequisite for the establishment of one's elite status as a leader, and wealth and education attainment, either by itself or together, is insufficient.

From the point of view of rural polity, these constraints amounted to a system of checks and balances between politics and economics. Rules about "collective" ownership of property restrict what people could do in selling and buying, thereby obliterating the distinction between private affairs and the public interest. This was an effective measure against resource effluence, insofar as it made it difficult for anybody to take proceeds from commonly owned land with them when they relocated, and the revenue apportionment funding system sustained the community's shared interests. The social status and power possessed by elites derived from their proven ability to forge and maintain such a body of shared interest, which is essentially a form of political capital. There was, moreover, no tension between the need to protect these shared interests and the need to protect the elites' own economic interest, since power, claims, and accountability were always intricately connected with one another, such that should the political power structure be perturbed, so would the control of wealth, including the assignment of responsibility and the distribution of benefits and related privileges.[19] Over the course of Chinese history, a system of governance emerged that was based on a synergism among economic management, political cohesiveness building, wealth distribution, and the administration of public responsibility. This system is the fulcrum of solidarity and cohesion at the rural primary level.

Certain rules about property were designed specifically for the political purpose of coordinating the relationship between the public and the private spheres, and safeguarding both primary-level government and public property. These rules provided clear definitions of and as such helped to reinforce the

[19] William H Riker and Itai Sened, "A Political Theory of the Origin of Property Rights: The Case of Airport Slots," in Lee J Alston, Thráinn Eggertsson and Douglass C North, eds. *Empirical Studies in Institutional Change* (Cambridge University Press, 1996), 286.

trust, obligations, and duties community members have in and towards one another. They formed an integral part of the institutional apparatus instrumental for maintaining order in the community. While in modern society it is the government that is expected to formulate and enforce such rules, in premodern societies this responsibility may fall on any [competent] body or organization. Villages and lineages always tried, especially when they were more or less settled and engaged in limited trade, to build a regime of shared, public interest, to which their members would be required to subordinate their personal interests. So long as individual members were reliant upon this constructed regime of shared interests for their long-term security, they had no choice but to comply with its terms, and in doing so they also helped to shield the local community from the damages that could result from internal conflicts.

In sum, in pre-modern China, the status of authority at the primary level was something one earned by taking part in community affairs, and contributing towards the construction and maintenance of an internally cohesive regime of shared interests. The state had no role to play in granting that authority, nor could it strip it from those who had it. While holding a position in the state's bureaucratic system could enhance a primary-level leader's prestige, this was no more than a protective veneer. So as far as the rural society was concerned, at the primary level, the construction of a regime of shared interest played an irreplaceable role in guaranteeing the internal cohesion of naturally occurring collective entities such as those based on lineage, bloodlines, or geography. This goes some way towards explaining why, in the rural reform in the 1920s–1930s, occupants of positions such as village chief, neighborhood chief, and their staff had mostly been nominated by lineage leaders. Indeed, more than a few of those who became state-approved village chiefs and neighborhood chiefs were people who already held key positions within their lineage.[20]

To reiterate, an important fact about authority and legitimacy at the primary level was that they were not existentially dependent on the state (and conferral by the state would anyway not have been of much help for the construction of the regime of shared interests in rural society). People who had authority and claimed legitimacy were *de facto* figureheads within the community, and they earned that political capital by working to bring the community together around a shared set of interests. The structure of power at the primary level would not have been altered if local leaders had been appointment by the state, since that structure is fundamentally built upon and sustained by the community members' recognition of and support for their leaders. In other words, the only thing that might pose a genuine threat to the power possessed by primary-level authority is a crisis of cohesion and solidarity within the locality. While state approval may either provide a buffer against potential threats or add to the aura of honor and prestige surrounding them, under ordinary circumstances, community leaders had no particular reason to turn to the state for assistance. With the exception of their academic credentials, which they would

[20] Chen, *Landlord and Peasant in China*.

have to obtain by passing imperial exams, all the other resources and support they would need to draw upon, whether it is wealth or political power, to discharge their responsibilities were endogenous to the community.

1.4 Incorporation of Rural Authority into State Bureaucracy

The cohesion of interests within each locality was predicated upon, in premodern China, the separation between two distinct administrative regimes. One was made up of rural authority (i.e., rural gentry, who had jurisdiction over villages, and lower levels of administrative units), and the other of state bureaucracy (i.e., government ministries, in whose jurisdictional scope fell all counties and higher-level administrative units).[21] Ordinarily, the two would, while by no means sealed off from each other, mostly keep to themselves when it came to governance and administration. There was little power entanglement between them. While state approval of their authority may have been worth flaunting for rural gentry who wanted to show they had brought pride to their lineage, it was a glossy coating at best and had little substantive to it. Neither did state approval expand the power of these primary-level leaders, nor did it confer on them the authority to act officially on behalf of the state. For governments at and above the county level, whose coffers were filled with payment from rural communities, what mattered more than anything was securing sources of revenue that would reliably support their standard of living. As long as rural communities provided them with this, these officials had little interest in how the communities were actually run. While rural gentry and landlords were for the most part deferential toward the government, they never ceded control of their communities to it. Indeed, both sides did their best to prevent the other from encroaching upon their turf. The existence of the two concepts of "imperial power" and "gentry power" attests to this bifurcation.

Things changed, rather drastically too, in modern times. The two hitherto separate administrative regimes began to inch closer toward each other, and gradually merged to form a mixed system. Against the backdrop of commercialization, urbanization, imperial exam reform, and wars, there were fewer opportunities for climbing the political or social ladder simply by earning academic titles. Farming became less profitable and more risky all the time, while more opportunities for a growing variety of commercial activities became available in the cities. Many members of the rural gentry sent their children to the cities, where some of them moved, and settled down themselves, with the hope of finding new opportunities for personal advancement. In the meantime, a string of violent outbreaks in different parts of the country forced the

[21] Kathryn Bernhardt, *Rents, Taxes, and Peasant Resistance in The Lower Yangzi Region, 1840-1950* (Stanford: Stanford University Press, 1992).

government to raise agricultural taxes, and to take mobilization at the primary level more seriously than it had ever done before. As a result of these developments, the government began to pay more attention to local governance. In modern times, the state has tried to transform rural authority and incorporate it into the official bureaucratic structure through a series of institutional reconfiguration, including setting up offices and departments and power delegation procedures. These moves were meant not only to turn primary-level government into bodies that could be appropriated to serve the national interests in key areas such as military draft, taxation and tribute payment but also to put them under the direct control of the state.

In fact, it was against this larger historical background that the series of local political system reform in the first half of the twentieth century unfolded. This is even true of what has oxymoronically been called the "local self-rule" movement, whose real objective was not to split up the power to govern, but rather to demarcate a space within the state's official bureaucratic structure for the existence and exercise of local authority. At the time of the movement, people pushed, in the name of "local self-rule", for the classification and differential handling of administrative tasks, and called for setting up a *xiangguanzhi*, or "rural officialdom" where members of the local gentry would become officials in charge of local affairs. Suggestions abounded for conferring official bureaucratic titles on community leaders, which would put them on a par with all other government officials with clearly defined job duties, only that they were to carry out these responsibilities within rural communities.

> On cases involving political crimes that might merit imprisonment, local officials should work with their superior to find the most appropriate punishment or remedy. Over matters related to material and economic welfare of the local population, each community was allowed to make its own decisions. (Hundred Day's Reform)[22]

Proposals were made for instituting a recruitment system for village and community leaders that is similar to the one in place for positions within the officialdom of the state government, with a four-year term, and similar performance evaluation mechanisms.

> Community leaders would be evaluated for their ethical cleanliness, political acumen and professional competency.... to make sure they abide by the law of the land.[23]

The philosophy driving these reform measures was not so much a commitment to the cause of "advancing modern local self-rule"[24] but more a belief in the need to fold the governing responsibilities of local authority into the state

[22] Xuguang Ding, *Studies on Self-rule in Modern China* (Guangzhou Publishing House, 1993), 12, quoting from *Resources for the Reform Movement of 1898 (Volume I).*

[23] Ding, *Studies on Self-rule,* 12, Quoting Chen Zhi.

[24] Ding, *Studies on Self-rule,* 12.

government's official duties by instituting a delegation system. Rural officialdom was incorporated into the bureaucratic structure, located below the county level governments. And people who held positions in it would be provided "handsome remuneration, official residence and real power" to ensure transparency within the structure.[25] As can be seen in the statements below, what was nominally considered "self-rule" was, as an ideal, animated by the desire to bring primary-level government and the state government in line with each other in terms of job duties and official responsibilities.

> The function of self-rule: To provide remedy where the government fell short, so the two are supplemental to each other.
>
> Local self-rule is able to: "help lessen the weight of the burden borne by the government, expedite reform, increase the public's political awareness and build their governance capacity so they become prepared for a constitutional republic."
>
> Identity and nature of the body administering self-rule: "To the community it is a community administrative authority, to the state, it is an integral part of the state administrative system."
>
> What is self-rule: "direct rule [by the state] is government-rule, indirect rule [by the state] is self-rule," and self-rule "has been practiced in China since ancient times"; "Conditions conducive for self-rule had always existed in rural China, that there were no more cases of success than there in fact was due to the lack of a proper organizational setup," which means that in China, self-rule was the *de facto* practice in even though nobody called it by that name."
>
> The practice of self-rule: "Within rural communities, an assembly comprised of members of the local gentry would make up the leadership, which has two branches: the legislative and the executive, and their heads are elected by the local gentry."[26]

It follows from statements as these that local "self-rule" was not meant to replace government rule or be an alternative system of governance but instead a supplement to government rule. Therefore, those reform-minded who advocated for strengthening self-rule were not calling for the replacement of the government system with something new and different. They were really trying to help the government in those areas where its oversight over local governance was ineffectual. As one scholar noted, almost all of those who have offered suggestions regarding self-rule, including Yanwu Gu from the Ming dynasty and Guifen Feng from the Qing dynasty, have argued for strict control of local interest groups, which are seen as essentially representing private interests, and for converting them into organizations that serve the public interest.[27] So on the assumption that what is needed is a monolithic government bureaucracy, "compartmentalized governance" can only apply to the definition and assignment of specific duties and tasks, and not to ideology, basic governance

[25] Ding, *Studies on Self-rule,* 12.

[26] Ding, *Studies on Self-rule,* 36, quoting Fazi Gong, "To My Compatriot."

[27] Philip A. Kuhn, "Local Self-Government under the Republic: Problems of Control, Autonomy and Mobilization," in *The Conflict and Control in Late Imperial China*, eds. Frederic Wakeman and Carolyn Grant (University of California Press, 1975), 257.

principle or philosophy, or power structure. And the real question facing those seeking to improve primary-level "self-rule" is how to strengthen community leadership by having it incorporated into the state's bureaucratic apparatus, so that it can, as the government's proxy, achieve what the latter cannot by itself, i.e., through direct rule.

> In the 18th year of the Republic of China, *County Organization Law* was promulgated. In the 20th year of the Republic, *Tentative Regulation for Supervision of Local Self-Rule by Government-Appointed Monitors*, the first ever basic law on local self-rule, was promulgated. However, there was not a single provision in the *County Organization Law*, researchers have found, on fiscal policy at the county level, in effect leaving the old system standing under which land tax (or advance payment thereof) formed the sole source of county revenue. In *New Ordinance for County Governance* that was promulgated in the 29th year of the Republic the legitimacy of self-rule was formally recognized, and the document contained clear provisions covering a range of related matters. It required the establishment of a uniform system of governance by county governments; it defined the dual identity of counties, villages and townships as both legal persons and bodies charged with administering local self-rule; it prohibited members of the public to either join or exist such an organization at will, and that every change must be carried out according to laws and regulations; those who failed to pay their dues would be subject to collection efforts; the relationship between local authority and those in their jurisdiction is the same as the relationship between the state and its nationals; organizations administering local self-rule and the geographic area of the jurisdiction stand in the same relationship to each other as what exists between a country and its territory, and that local self-rule consists in the exercise of power and authority granted by the state exclusive of any other kinds of power; administrative power is equivalent to the power belonging to a legal person, which encompasses the right to make decisions about one's property; personnel turnover does not entail discontinuity in the legal personhood of the organization, which cannot be disbanded except in ways that comply with the law. *New Ordinance for County Governance* allots a much larger support staff to county leadership than it does to leadership at the village and township levels. Moreover, no longer would villages and townships be allowed to make fiscal decisions for themselves. Instead, their expenditures would be included in the county budget, and their revenues would also be subject to review by the county government. There were other provisions. The lowest rungs in the government's bureaucratic hierarchy and those organizations that had been administering community self-rule at the primary level of society would now be consolidated. Government rule and self-rule thus became irredeemably entangled and a clear line separating fiscal matters of the government and fiscal matters of self-governing communities from each other no longer existed. In the 31st year of the Republic, provinces were stripped of their fiscal independence, their revenue and expenditure would be aggregated into the national, i.e., central budget. The fiscal independence of counties as self-ruling administrative units was formally approved. The framework of rural governance was thus complete.[28]

[28] Yicheng Ruan, *Local Self-rule and New County Regulation* (Linking Publishing Co., Ltd, 1978), 10–13.

1.5 Disintegration of Local Self-rule: Severance of Rural Authority from the Rural Society

The subsumption of local authority under the regime of state bureaucracy, or its "bureaucratization", had notable impact on the "basic structure" of rural society. First and foremost, the source of the power and authority to govern at the primary level changed. While for a long time primary-level leaders' status as "public figures" formed endogenously, now it was conferred by the state government. This reflected the diminishing importance of the connections these leaders had with local political and economic interests. The development was tantamount to ripping rural polity away from its constituency, and shoehorn it into government officialdom. This dissolved the set of "shared and common interests" that once served as the bonding agent between those who governed and those who were governed in primary-level society. As this alignment in basic interests deteriorated, so did the structural cohesiveness of the community, and the linkage between local leaders' legitimacy and their social, political, and economic ties within the community was broken. Xiaotong Fei used the phrase "erosion of primary-level community" to describe the deleterious effects of this political reform on rural communities. Measures that were intended to expand the scope of the government's control inevitably clashed with the *status quo* at the local level, and undermined community governance. What was gained was more efficient downward transmission of orders of the central government, but what was lost was an efficient conduit for conveying values created locally to higher levels of government. The result is what has sometimes been called "monorail politics" at the primary level.[29]

Another significant effect of this "bureaucratization" of primary-level governance[30] related to changes in the distribution of benefits and burdens within the local power structure. Those changes in turn perturbed the governance order that had been built on the power configuration. Monorail politics meant that, instead of having to demonstrate their adeptness at handling community affairs and readiness to put their personal wealth to use for advancing the public's interest in order to earn the community's trust and establish their credibility, local leaders now needed to show they had government connections. As local elites grew closer to state bureaucracy, they became less and less dependent on the local community. This gradual shift in the source of their mandate to rule meant that it became less and less important for local politicians to cultivate organic ties with the community for purpose of securing power. In many cases, it was people who already *de facto* held power and had authority who was *ex post facto* granted the mandate to rule by the government.[31] But still, this was

[29] Xiaotong Fei, *From the Soil: The Foundations of Chinese Society* (Tianjin: Tianjin People's Publishing House, 1994).

[30] Zhongli Zhang, *Role of Gentry in the 19th Century Chinese Society* (Shanghai: Shanghai Academy of Social Sciences Press, 1991).

[31] Philip A. Kuhn, *Rebellion and Its Enemies in Late Imperial China*, Trans. Xie Liangsheng (Beijing: China Social Sciences Press, 1990), 231.

further evidence that while the mandate to rule once rose from nothing else besides a person's standing in the community, now it had dual sources: the community and the state. The role of the primary-level politician as an intermediary who communicated about and protect a community's shared interests weakened considerably as a result. The buffer that was once provided by the local community that protected the local politicians from assault from outside became unnecessary, because now, in their new capacity as office holders in the state's bureaucratic regime, they could enjoy backing from a different source, namely, their "superiors", whose support that was much stronger than what the community could offer. More important, this change in the genetic makeup of power at the local level triggered fission within the rank of primary-level leadership, and contributed to the decline in the sense of duty and responsibility to the community in individuals who hold leadership positions. After all, they no longer needed the community's endorsement to sustain their authority status. Over time, they became more interested in state-organized functions and activities and lost interest in those that had directly to do with the affairs of the community.

From the point of view of political sociology, reform measures designed to subsume primary-level government under the state's massive government bureaucracy did not achieve the intended outcome, which was to "open up a conduit through which information and resources can flow freely up and down the hierarchy, and between the government and the people". All it did was to create positions in the bureaucratic machine that could be filled by, because only suitable for, elites. This reconfiguration did not manufacture new dynamics of social integration centered around a new political body (the state), on the contrary, the dissipation of rural authority led to a decline in social cohesion and increased fragmentation. At the primary level, the entanglement between power of the state and power of the local community left the goal of solidarity- and unity-building without any means for achieving it. This shows that political modernization is but a superficial exercise if it involved no more than decentralization and consolidation; organizational restructuring and instituting a system of appointment and delegation are no substitute for concrete changes in *ruling* and *governance*. At the primary level, having been folded into the state's bureaucratic structure neither automatically rendered existing norms null nor put an end to how things had been done. With the exception of taxes, rents and land tax, for which new targets set by the state were now imposed on local authorities, on just about everything else there were no changes in either how much local politicians could do and how they could to do it. In other words, the state neither helped to overhaul local governance nor put something else in its place that embodied the principle of state governance. Rural society, as a result, was still largely outside its purview for all practical purposes. And much like before, so long as continuation of local practices did not get in the way of their making timely payment of dues in taxes to the central government, the state more or less turned a blind eye towards how things were run at the local level. On the surface it might seem as though the new system of state control with tax collection at its core is more powerful and effective, the fact is that under the new system the state became more and not less dependent for tax collection on collection agencies in rural communities. Indeed, the state was indifferent to how much power local authorities had, all it wanted is that they helped meet state targets. Therefore, we may say that despite the bureaucratization at the superficial level on which official titles were granted, no new relationship formed between the state and society, nor did new principles for power sharing.

Still, in rural society, an official title was no small matter to either those who held it or others. It elevated the title-holder's standing in the community, expanded their power, and gave them access to more resources, even as the community's role as the source of their authority and legitimacy diminished. Without a doubt, this had deleterious effects on the community, especially in terms of its internal cohesion. Changes to both whom primary-level leaders *depended on for benefits and resources* and who they believed they were supposed to serve led to changes in their incentives and value orientation. The absence of a new set of power relations also meant they now operated under different constraints from before, which certainly did not help them adapt to the separation between their public persona and their private identity. They were not given the opportunity to learn how "to be" a government official, even if a low-ranking one, and were therefore ill prepared for performing tasks such as those associated with fiscal planning and management. The co-existence in the old days of private ownership of land and common ownership by lineage to some extent made the fuzzy distinction between what was public and what was private more or less acceptable, especially since community undertakings often needed to be paid for by proceeds from privately or lineage-owned land.

Obviously, the critical issue is the total absence of a new set of rules and norms centered around the state to replace the old one that featured a hybrid model of governance, which mixed the public with the private. The establishment of a new kind of relationship between rural authority and state government in which the former serves the ends of and using power granted by the latter was not enough to effect the severance between private affairs and public affairs. What it did do was to blur the line between the private objectives of primary-level leaders and those of others' or the community's. In fact, it became just as difficult to distinguish between codes of conduct governing public activities and those governing private ones, public finance and private/personal finance, the imperative to advance the public's good and that to advance one's own goals, public and private rules about procedure, and so on. In this process primary-level authority saw the growth of both their opportunities and their space of action, which would later become the societal foundation of a new kind of governance regime. Not only did local leaders not try to rectify the increasing ambiguity of the public-private distinction, they took advantage of this development and used their official titles to justify the new rules with dubious value commitment underpinnings. In fact, the normalization of this condition would become a prominent feature of local governance in the decades to come. When the principle of maximizing one's own material wealth became embedded in the ideological scaffold of officialdom, it also marked the institutionalization of a fusion of official matters and private matters.

We are able to conclude, therefore, that "state-building" in the modern period posed no existential threat to the authority of those community leaders that wielded power at the primary level. What the series of reform measures achieved were changes to the status and identity of local elites. They were now part of a state-approved primary-level organization that at once served and was controlled by state bureaucracy. Of course, these seemingly superficial changes did have significant consequences, most important of which being the enlarged space in which local leaders could carry out their activities. And their official titles made it easier for them to justify adhering to their *modus operandi*, and treating public and private affairs as if they were the same thing. This was a far cry from the old political ecology in which local leaders drew their power from the support of the primary-level community. In the new one where support and legitimization came from above, ties to local political and economic interests became less and less relevant or useful. The gap that once existed between state bureaucracy and primary-level government did not go away. It shifted downward and was now located between local authority and local community. Little improvement was made in the relationship between the state and the society, in the reconstitution of a set of shared interests, or in the construction of modern institutions through which the people and the government can meaningfully engage with each other.

1.6 Persistence of the Cleavage

In mid-twentieth century, a new political regime, a people's republic, was established in China, setting off a new round of primary-level governance reform. As a result of the decades-long push for centralization and consolidation in the first half of the century, the organizational structure previously in place in rural society had been eroded, peasants had nothing around which they could rally and whatever that passed as local governance was ineffectual.[32] The construction of the new political regime, therefore, had to begin with finding ways to reunite the peasants around a common cause into which their energy can be channeled, and to connect them with the new regime. This was historic, as it helped to project an image of the new regime as one that genuinely cared about serving the interests of the society, and of peasants in particular. In theory, this was an opportunity for uncovering that thing around which people could rally, and for realizing a "fundamental transformation" of the Chinese society by "mobilizing the masses" to the maximum. For example, in

[32] Xiaotong Fei, *China's Gentry: Essays in Rural – Urban Relations* (University of Chicago Press, 1953); Joseph W. Esherick and Amary Backus Rankin, *Chinese Local Elites and Patterns of Dominance* (University of California Press, 1990); Kathryn Bernhardt, *Rents, Taxes, and Peasant Resistance—The Lower Yangzi Region, 1840 - 1950* (Stanford University Press, 1992).

the 1940s, a number of reform measures were introduced in parts of Shaanxi, Gausu, and Ningxia, three contiguous regions, aimed at promoting equality between the sexes, consensual marriage, the use of written contracts and certificates, and so forth. People were encouraged to overcome outdated ideas, and to adjudicate conflicts among them by themselves through arbitration.[33] Another example was the land reform movement in the liberated areas in the 1940s 1950s. In 1957 there was an intense push for so-called "democratic management of the communes"[34] and in 1961 clear definitions and clarifications were released regarding leadership selection for the people's communes (according to which final decisions rest with either the full congress made up of all commune members or the delegate committee, it was up to these two bodies to choose commune leaders through elections and to remove them from their posts)[35]. The common goal of these movements and others like them, which took place mostly at the primary level, was to redistribute powers among peasants, so as to increase the level of control these people as a group had over their lives, their land, public matters that impacted them and to help them become more informed, more prepared and willing to become more involved in the community, even to help monitor and regulate it.

It is worth noting, however, that all of these movements presupposed that primary-level government and the peasants belonged to the same class and had shared interests, such that the former was capable of representing and did fully represent the will of the latter. This presumption may have been informed by the idea, or indeed the ideal, that there should be fit between people's socio-economic background and their class identity. Subscription to this notion among many at the time led them to believe that people can only be effectively represented by those who share their social, political, and economic interests. It follows from this belief that so long as strict eligibility requirements were put in place for primary-level leadership positions, these leaders would become advocates for the peasants. Many at the time were convinced that the only way to unite people around a set of common interests is by building classes and constructing class identity, so they tried to make sure only the right kinds of people became local leaders. The hope was that if these positions were filled with peasants, they would then go on to act as advocates for the interests of those with similar social, political, and economic backgrounds.

[33] Shigong Qiang, "Organizational Nexus of Power and Governmentality of Law: Formation of New Legal Tradition in 1940s Communist China," *Peking University Law Review*, 2000 (2).

[34] "Notice of the CPC Central Committee on Several Issues Relating to the Establishment of the People's Commune" (March 5, 1957); Zhenlin Tan, "Report on Implementing the Establishment of the People's Commune Democratically and the Launch of the Rectification Campaign in Youxian County, Hunan Province" (June 24, 1957).

[35] "Jiaying Tian's Speech at the '60 Articles' Pilot Work Conference of Weitang Commune" (March 31, 1961), in *Investigation of Jiaying Tian in Jiashan and the Formulation of the "60 Articles" of the People's Commune*, ed. Party History Research Office of Jiashan County (Dongfang Press, 1997), 118.

> All cooperatives must make sure their leadership positions are occupied by either poor peasants or borderline-poor peasants.[36]

> A majority of seats on the Chinese Communist Party committees at the primary level must be reserved for poor peasants, and every effort must be made to increase the representation of other poor and disenfranchised peasants among senior leadership.[37]

What many failed to realize, however, is that people who have similar socio-economic background and nominally belong to the same class may nonetheless have other identities or roles that can shape their outlooks. This may explain why little was done to engineer changes to the *de facto* distribution of benefits between the "leaders" and the "peasants". On the contrary, it was believed that the kind of change to the membership composition of the primary-level government brought about by a political revolution such as the one that took place in China would be enough to coalesce the social, political, and economic interests of the leaders and those they lead. But facts have proven otherwise. As the organizational structure of rural society became more complex, with more people being made to join production teams, associations, and communes, powers they once had were also being transferred to those who allegedly "represented" them. At the time the people in rural China were primarily intent on taking control over resources out of the hands of those old elites, consigning these people to the dustbin of history, as it were, and setting up representative organizations that they could claim to be their own. So the political and economic standing of these new organizations rose quickly. And people's commune, the very embodiment of a new model of primary-level government, took center stage in China's rural society.

> In the current phase, communes are primary-level political organs… in the future they will be the primary-level entities within a communist social structure.[38]

People's communes became the center around which reconfiguration of the power structure at the primary level was carried out. Almost all decisions about production, trade, housing, and relocation were made by these primary-level power organs, which also had control over key agricultural resources and how they were to be allocated. But all of this was but an exercise in organizing production, mobilizing resources, and mechanizing management, and it was

[36] "The Central Committee Forwards the Report of and Commentaries by the Fujian Provincial Committee on the Issues of the Cooperatives" (September 7, 1955), in *Manuscripts of Zedong Mao since the Founding of the People's Republic of China, Vol. V*, ed. Editorial Department of Party History Documents of the CPC Central Committee (Central Party Literature Press, 1987), 351.

[37] "Report by the Fujian Provincial Party Committee," in *Manuscripts of Zedong Mao*, 353.

[38] "Revisions to and Letters regarding the 'Resolution of the Zhengzhou Conference on Several Issues Concerning the People's Commune'" (November 1958), in *Manuscripts of Zedong Mao*, 515.

not a process for fusing together the interests of all stakeholders. That these initiatives met little resistance was likely due to the fact that many people accepted the theoretical justification marshaled to support them that made reference to the notion of "economic exploitation" and also approved of "dividing up the wealth". But if these helped to mitigate the economic tensions between classes, they also covered up or divert attention away from tensions between people with different social status. As these new forms of local authority, i.e., primary-level organizations, were being built and grew, the system of political and economic power these organs were meant to supplant atrophied. Peasants were quick to gravitate towards these new entities, which, thanks to what they did to alleviate peasants' economic hardship and to give them a political voice, soon took on a central role in engineering social solidarity and cohesion.

> It is the responsibility of all cooperatives to look after those whose spouse is deceased, those who live alone and those who are unmarried, and also those who cannot work (all of whom should be admitted into cooperatives). And for those cooperative members who are able to work but who suffer extraordinary hardship, assistance should be provided. Socialism that does not show benevolence towards those experiencing hardship is categorically wrong. Rural poverty alleviation funds should be set up quickly, and we should tell those who have yet to join a cooperative that, whenever they do, they would immediately become eligible for aid paid for with money from this fund.[39]

At this time, efforts to reform governing authority at the primary level had two components. One was aimed at its political dimension, and involved changes to the membership composition of the leadership, and the other at its economic aspects, which involved giving the leadership the power to make equitable allocation and equal distribution decisions about property. The latter in particular involved confiscating property from the "haves" and giving it to the "have nots",[40] which helped to turn the latter group into a most potent source of support for the new primary-level authority.

> Peasants who were living in poverty saw that, now they had a voice, and the state provided loans to help them out… when production under the collectivist model adopted by the communes did not seem to be doing well, those impoverish peasants became terribly worried, and were concerned about the viability of the communes. Even though they thought many things could be done better, they had no resentment towards either the Chinese Communist Party or the people's government. The Party's policy of providing economic assistance to impoverished peasants, in place since liberation, had greatly benefited these peasants, so they had nothing but gratitude towards the Party and the government. They

[39] "Zedong Mao's Commentaries," in *Manuscripts of Zedong Mao*, 531, 506.

[40] See Letian Zhang, *A Farewell to the Ideal: Institutional Studies on the People's Commune* (Orient Publishing Center, 1998), 53-56, on the distributions log for confiscated property.

> never tire of talking about how much the government's assistance and loans had meant to them, and have confidence in the prospect of a bright future for socialism.[41]

At one point, primary-level government became so unprecedentedly closely identified with the community in their basic interests that whenever it put out a mobilization call it would immediately be answered with enthusiasm by hundreds if not thousands. But because structural issues centered around the vertical distribution of benefits were never really solved, this kind of massive appeal of the primary-level government was quickly in danger of fizzling out under structural constraints related to these very issues. Effective mobilization depended more and more on cadres' ability to pitch ideas to the people, and to plead with them to "rally with enthusiasm" and less and less on the peasants' seeing it as genuinely in their own interest to do whatever they were asked. The presumption that those who nominally or otherwise belonged to the same class were therefore homogeneous in what they wanted simply lacked structural support. It was not difficult to find evidence, especially in how the cadre and ordinary members of the community related to each other, and in the dynamic relationship between what is public and what is private, for tension and conflicts that pit the local authority and the peasants against each other.

> At the moment what agricultural commune members are most concerned about, which is also a key source of conflict between members and commune leaders, is the way finances are managed. In many communes the books were kept from the members, who became suspicious about what the leaders may be up to. Leaders have been accused of greed, exploitation, and free-riding.[42]

What the state wanted and what the peasants wanted were also quite different.

> It is imperative to raise awareness about the importance of love of country among the rural population, so that peasants produced what the country needed, and it would be wrong to only encourage people to get rich.[43]

Primary-level authority had to choose between two mutually exclusive sides, and surely the side from which it had received the power it was exercising would be chosen. Little surprise, therefore, that in the years following the

[41] See the Appendix to the "Investigation Report of the Central Investigation Team on Weitang People's Commune and Production Team" (1961), in *Investigation of Jiaying Tian*, 75–76.

[42] "Notice of the CPC Central Committee on Several Issues Related to the Operations of the People's Commune," (March 5, 1957); Zhenlin Tan, "Report on Implementing the Establishment of the People's Commune Democratically and the Launch of the Rectification Campaign in Youxian County, Hunan Province" (June 24, 1957).

[43] "Draft Resolution on Mutual Assistance and Cooperation in Agricultural Production" (December 19, 1951), in *Manuscripts of Zedong Mao*, 579.

commencement of collectivization peasants did not see the kind of drastic improvements to their conditions they had hoped for.

> Income rose fairly slowly for impoverished peasants, and 36.9 percent of them had a material standard of living that was about the same as before land reform. For those peasants who had been borderline poor and a small percentage of the well-to-do peasants, in part because each such household had fewer people who were able-bodied workers, they often received less from the wealth redistribution, and add to that lost income due to the ban on exploitation, their standards of living declined notably.[44]

Not unlike earlier "self-governance" initiatives, the disunity within the structure of interests means that primary-level authority tended to side with their superior, those who had granted them the mandate to rule. But the more they saw themselves as answerable to the needs and wants of those above them, the less they felt compelled to serve those under them. Empowerment of the community would threaten to weaken, not reinforce, such a structure, so the bond between local authority and their societal base eroded even further. By the end of 1950s, Zedong Mao, sensing the looming danger in this situation, became alarmed,[45] but the solutions that were put forward were all based on the idea that further delegation was needed within the existing power structure. And no attempt was made to address the issue of the coalescence, or rather the absence thereof, of interests of different groups using political instruments. Even though Mao realized that "only one thing turned cadres on, which is to go out and collect whatever is due, whether it is grain or pigs, they are tone deaf to anything else, whichever side it may come from".[46] While it did not escape Mao's notice that some commune members were complaining that they "had no idea how much commune leaders were spending", and he even tried to draw attention to the fact that "as the amount of cash and things – including grains, grain coupons, work points tickets, produce, domestic animals and farming instruments – that needs to be handled by cadres grows, everybody through whom the process goes has to take a cut", still:

> [f]rom what we can see in the recent crackdown on embezzlement, wastefulness and bureaucratic formalism, over-spending and taking more than one's fair share is rather common among cadres, 23 percent of them have committed embezzlement, and 63 percent have engaged in petty theft.[47]

Yet for the most part these cases were seen as individual cadres having "put themselves above the masses", and failed to sound the alarm about the severe political consequences of the identity and ideological disunity within the power

[44] Cited in *Investigation of Jiaying Tian*, 74.
[45] "Party Communication" (March 15, 1959), *Manuscripts of Zedong Mao*, 111.
[46] Zedong Mao, source unknown.
[47] Cited in *Investigation of Jiaying Tian*, 53.

structure, which include the growing chasm between the authority and the people within rural communities, the increasing irrelevance of the latter to the former as a source of support, the diminishing role primary-level leaders played in effecting social cohesion, and ultimately the total alienation of these local leaders from their subjects. Such infraction was either labeled work style problems (long on rigid adherence to bureaucratic protocol and short on trying to get things done) or chalked up to partisanship left over from an earlier era.

> Under bureaucracy, people answer to their superiors and not to those who are in their charge, and treat the masses as an afterthought... People first, this is our mantra, which is the exact opposite of what the Kuomintang stood for. To them, the masses were dirt, which the authority could mistreat in any way it wished, humiliating them, brutalizing them, exploiting them, anything but what it should do, which is to serve their interests... The Kuomintang believed that cadre should enjoy special privileges denied everybody else. Some of the dissenting opinions we have received from some comrades regarding the size of the communes show they care little about what the masses want, and more about whether something worked in their favor, which is patent indifference towards the masses.[48]

Precisely because these infractions were seen as moral failing of the individuals involved and not a problem of public rules, few if anybody thought to look for structural causes or to try to address them by improving the institutional configuration. Why might the cadre, who themselves had come from humble backgrounds not unlike those of any other member of the masses, show a "lack of concern for what the masses wanted"? Why was it that, even though they belonged to the same "class" as the masses, the cadres did not feel it was their duty to serve them, but instead only wanted to "please their superior"? This goes to show that having similar "socioeconomic background" and belonging to the same "class" may do little to ensure alignment between the interests of the leaders and of those they lead. Instead, the only way such alignment can be achieved and sustained is if primary-level leaders receive the mandate to rule (and can be rejected by) and earn their standing in the community from its members. The fact that these problems occurred in these early years of the new republic suggests that, despite changes in the kinds of people who became primary-level leaders, the power structure by virtue of which the basic social order was maintained remained largely intact. The disunity between local authority and the communities persisted, the establishment of a new political regime in the country notwithstanding. In fact, such cleavage continued to play a role in pitting the leader against the led, and it manifested itself in a myriad of ways.

First, instead of trying to do what furthered the interests of the peasants, local authorities were trying to meet targets imposed from above or otherwise to benefit themselves. So when [production] came up short, they would inflate

[48] "Jiaying Tian's Speech at the '60 Articles' Pilot Work Conference of Weitang Commune" (March 31, 1961), in *Investigation of Jiaying Tian*, 124–125.

the numbers, sometimes solely for the purpose of advancing their own political career. This institutionalized the incentive to "lie", and lying became commonplace.

> Just when Baojing Wang was flamboyantly boasting to people in Shaanxi province about the scientific experiments that had allegedly been carried out in Fenghuo Village, new cotton, corn and wheat varieties these experiments produced that could be harvested twice a year, improved farming methods, and the promise of high yields year after year, Shaanxi was in fact the midst of a spring food shortage, and half of the population in Fenghuo Village did not have enough to eat.[49]

Secondly, neither the local authority nor the peasants trusted each other.

> Within the five communes included in the first group to undergo disciplinary review and overhaul, 56 cadres were suspected by commune members of embezzlement, with the largest sum embezzled by any one person reaching a whopping 500 yuan. But according to reports by the cadres, whatever charges that had been made about embezzlement, blah blah, it was all just suspicion, without concrete evidence. At the beginning I was reluctant to do anything, worried that any misstep would either draw the ire of commune members, or hurt the village cadre.[50]

Thirdly, local authority had become brazen, trying to justify anything they have done that may have been harmful to the community's interest by claiming they were acting on work assignment in their "official" capacities. According to the central task force reports:[51]

> Since the people's communes were set up, the portion of the commune budget that was retained (to cover various expenditure) grew each year, while the amount that was used towards paying commune members decreased. Most people said that, since 1958, the number of points they earned for work done went up year after year, but the amount of cash they received went down year after year (see Table 1.1).

A large proportion of the money that was retained was used by the cadre to cover their own expenses. For example, in a report from Anhui province on the results of "adjustments", the breakdown among national taxes, endowment, and production costs was 7 percent, 18 percent, and 20 percent, respectively.[52]

[49] Yuegang Lu, *Great Country, Weak People* (Beijing: China Film Press, 1998), 239.

[50] "Notice of the CPC Central Committee on Several Issues Relating to the Establishment of the People's Commune," (March 5 1957); Zhenlin Tan, "Report on Running the People's Commune Democratically and the Rectification Campaign in Youxian County, Hunan Province" (June 24, 1957).

[51] "Jiashan Investigation Report of the Central Working Group: Living Conditions and Thoughts of the Commune Members," in *Investigation of Jiaying Tian*, 65–66.

[52] "On the Ten Rules of Anhui" (March 26 1959), in *Manuscripts of Zedong Mao*, 160.

Table 1.1 Relative proportions of public fund and member pay in commune budget in one commune in Jiashan, 1956–1960

	1956	*1957*	*1958*	*1959*	*1960*
Revenue(1000 yuan)	137.3	123.6	142.7	168.9	102.2
Increase (%)	–	−9. 8	+15	+18.1	−39. 65
Public fund (%)	49.0	61.5	57.8	65.8	78.2
Taxes (%)	20.2	26.4	24.2	21.3	23.1
Production costs (%)	25.4	29.1	32.3	33.2	51.1
Management fees (%)	0.9	1.8	1.3	2.1	2.6
Commune endowment (%)	2.5	4.0	–	9.2	1.4
Member pay (%)	51.0	38.5	42.2	34.2	21.8
Per capita (yuan)	57.5	39.25	46.95	45.3	17.96

These numbers were 6 percent, 17.5 percent, and 20–30 percent in Sichuan province, where there was also a management surcharge that took up 0.3 percent; the endowment was allocated among management zone, which receives 30–35 percent, the commune, which receives 60–65 percent, and the county federation of social organizations, which receives 5 percent.[53] The main aim of re-allocation policies at this time was to put more money in the hands of the smallest organizational units, so if the communes were still claiming a lion's share of the amount that was "retained" after the disciplinary review and overhaul, the portion that was under the control of local authority must have been even larger before the overhaul. In other words, most of what was retained at the time was allocated to local authority at the village and township levels and below. Authorities at these levels heedlessly squandered the funds they had at their disposal on wasteful things. According to one report about one commune: "way too many people on the payroll, one department in a commune has more than 3000 people getting paid for doing nothing, of those as many as 180 are full-time members of the performance troupe".[54]

With their close social and economic ties with rural communities broken and their dependency on community members for status recognition and popular support greatly reduced, local authority was now subject to few if any social constraints on what it could do. It could with impunity make any arbitrary decision about public property, and to justify excluding others from access to confiscated assets by claiming that it is set aside for "public use", or otherwise needed for "official purposes". For example, clear stipulation in *Commune Resolution* that houses and objects for daily use were private property did not stop authorities from commandeering them at will as though they were marshaling resources to support a war effort. Whether it was houses, grains, produce, equipment, or furniture, the authorities took whatever they wanted whenever they wanted and effectively declared them to be public property.

[53] "Comments on the Sichuan Experience" (March 1959), in *Manuscripts of Zedong Mao*, 134, 151.

[54] "The Outline of the Speech at the Zhengzhou Meeting" (February 1959), in *Manuscripts of Zedong Mao*, 62.

Statistics show that, since 1959, all of the land, fertilizer, seeds, and labor needed for the "agricultural products and processed foods production bases" set up by 312 government departments in Hebei province had been provided by the local communities. The entire harvest [on these bases] was hauled away. Dongjie work team, part of Guangong Commune in Lintao County, had 426 *mu* of irrigated fields, and 310 *mu* of those was requisitioned by the authority.[55] Whether it wanted to or not, given their position, local authority had no choice but be the body to implement these acts of repurposing private property. In one especially egregious case, the local authority in Zhejiang province, intent on not just using somebody's house as the place to set up their office but also doing so in a way that appears legal, went so far as to classify the target household as landlord, so they could legitimately seize their property and hand it over to the village leaders.

> We wanted to take over his house, so we classified the household as landlord. During the land reform follow-up check, we changed their designated status to business owner/landlord, since it was discovered that the size of the land they owned fell a bit short [of the threshold for landlord status]. Once this was done, all of the family's land and most of the things they had owned were seized. The multi-story building where the family had lived became the office for the village council ... The three multi-story buildings used by village officials were at the time the best in the entire Taiping village, the village chief's desk is the one that was once used by the landlord to do his bookkeeping, and the landlord's favorite chair featuring intricate carving was now also his.[56]

Fourthly, information flow between the cadre and the peasants became obstructed, such that most of the rules and regulations peasants had to comply with were created by the local authority, behind closed doors, i.e., without any input from or consultation with the community. Tax collection is one example. Whatever "power" to collect taxes the local authority claimed to have as part of its mandate for "self-rule" often went beyond what they were allowed to do by either higher levels of government or their own constituents. More often than not, since how much they needed to collect was contingent on their fiscal needs, which were always changing, they did not feel bound by existing guidelines on such matters. In order to make room for a larger budget for themselves they would cite the alleged need to increase the value of the collective assets, and they never bothered to put in place a consultation mechanism for soliciting input from all stakeholders. The "approval" that was given after alleged review and examination was nothing more than a decision made internally, and one that had no participation by members of the community. According to one "tax collection work report":

[55] Yibo Bo, *Review of Certain Major Decisions and Events* (Beijing: The Central Committee of CPC Party School Press, 1993), 763–764.

[56] Cited in Zhang, *A Farewell to Ideals*, 51, 54.

> If we are serious about changing the way financial and taxation matters are managed, the first order of business is to change the way cadre on different levels of local government think about these things, and then they should try to educate and mobilize the masses. We convened a meeting attended by county and lower level cadres, and county officials explained in detail the close connection between the importance of fiscal decentralization and revenue and expenditure at the county level, and called on cadres up and down to correct whatever misunderstanding they had. Since counties took control of their own fiscal matters, sources of income have diversified, and their powers have expanded, and all must work together, each taking due diligence, and formally incorporate this into cadres' official responsibilities so it becomes a regular part of their job.[57]

Scholars who study "state-building" in China tend to assume that giving local authorities greater power over taxation is a necessary step towards increasing the government's tax collection efficacy. But there is a large body of evidence suggesting that the amount of payment made by local governments to the central government has remained unchanged, even though the amount they kept for themselves had changed. Moreover, the central government has never either been involved in collection and allocation decisions at the local level or played a supervisory role. In Henan province, for example, in 1959, just 7 percent of the earnings form agricultural production ended up in the central government's coffer, "communes and management zones" took in 26 percent, and 20 percent went toward "production costs", adding up to a subtotal of 53 percent. On top of those there were various "charitable funds" and "management fees" for which exact figures are not available, and commune members received less than 47 percent.[58] In Qinggang county in Heilongjiang province, since 1957, when the county (commune) took control of its own fiscal management, it had been ranking in more in tax revenue than the amount it was required to collect. Local tax payment itself accounted for 242 percent of the target (overshooting was considered an achievement and not disallowed under the law); at the sub-county levels local authorities created more kinds of taxes (no doubt under the aegis of references to "the public" or even "the country"), which communes were then required to collect, and these targets became a powerful driver for primary-level cadre, who spared no efforts pursuing them. One of the tax collectors in the above-mentioned village was met with resistance from the villagers on one of his collection trips. They asked him to go away. The village council then "studied the matter" and decided to furnish him with a piece of document, i.e., a certification saying in effect that he

[57] Taxation Bureau of Department of Finance of Heilongjiang Province, "From Three Contracts to Three Nonexistence," in *Compilation of the Experience of Taxation Work in the "Great Leap Forward" Movement*, ed. "Leap Forward" Office of the Department of Finance (Beijing: China Financial and Economic Publishing House, 1958), 227–228.

[58] "The Outline of the Speech at the Zhengzhou Meeting" (February 1959), in *Manuscripts of Zedong Mao*, 62.

had been officially authorized to engage in tax collection activities. Certificate in hand, this tax collector was greatly "emboldened", and became "more dedicated" to his work.[59]

As local leaders amassed more power over more things, including the power to collect taxes and to allocate revenue, administrative power and the power to make decisions about public property, and as they became more dependent on the state for their legitimacy, they had less and less need for the primary-level community as a form of political capital. For them, adeptness at wielding power, that is, not just knowing how to use it but also not being afraid to use it (in the words of Baojing Wang, the cadre from Shaanxi province), holds the key to securing the population's compliance. Under such a binary, leaders felt less and less beholden to or dependent on the led. They became increasingly preoccupied with doing things that would please their superiors, and indifferent to the needs and wants of those in their charge. In the meantime, however, they also became invigorated, more convinced than ever of the role local authority could play in mobilizing and educating the ordinary people, and in reforming the society. All of this has much to do with their growing dependency on the government, and diminishing dependency on their local constituents. As these primary-level leaders continued to peel away from the community and its concerns and interests, they gradually became a powerful group in its own rights. The group did not worry about whether their own power and authority were in or out of sync with the interests of the community, since it did not get its power from the community to begin with. And it certainly did not think it necessary to set up a supervisory system that allows ordinary people to provide oversight where state oversight falls short, precisely because it never doubted for a moment that it represented the community's interests.

1.7 The Source(s) of Power and State-Building

The national government's inability to perform effective oversight of officials at the primary level is a stubborn problem that has long eluded solutions. While "office holders should stay in touch with the masses" has always been the official tagline, there has otherwise rarely been any serious effort to understand how the source of primary-level officials' mandate to rule may be related to this problem. Nor, for that matter, has the question of what kinds of institutional reforms are needed to limit the structural unlinking of the interests of officials from those of the community they are meant to serve. While the "Production team-based three-level ownership system"[60] introduced at the end of the 1950s

[59] *Compilation of the Experience of Taxation Work in the "Great Leap Forward" Movement*, 228–229.

[60] Under the "Three-level ownership system", means of production belonged to the people's commune, the production brigade and the production team, the three levels of administrative units, in descending order, in rural China during the first decades of the People's Republic of China. And since the production team was the organizational level at which budgetary planning and fiscal accounting were done, it was "the most basic unit" for accounting and performance evaluation purposes.

represented something of an improvement, it essentially involved adjusting the allocation of resources among the different strata within the primary-level structure, namely, the county (*xiang*), village by administrative designation (*xingzheng cun*) and hamlets or historical settlements (*ziran cun*). As a result, those occupying positions at the lower strata were given more opportunities than they had ever had before, thereby easing, albeit only temporarily and superficially, some of the tension that had been building among the three organizational levels. Still, the failure to address adequately the question about the social source of mandate for those who held political power at the primary level made it all but impossible to achieve a more rational and equitable distribution of power among the villagers, or for a political oversight mechanism based on the separation of powers to form. As such, the structural misalignment of basic interests between officials and those they rule persisted. Under the commune system, more than ever, those occupying each rung on the political pecking order received their power through conferral from those above them, a mechanism that has functioned as something of a "protective shield" for rural primary-level leaders. Thanks to the firm grip of administrative control essential to this system, the growing distance between the interests represented by primary-level political operatives and those of the community they serve managed to elude any serious attention.

Still, it does not follow from the systematic conferral of administrative power by the central upon sub-national governments that the state's political power such as represented by the central government has been firmly established in the countryside. I beg to differ, therefore, from views such as this:

> Thanks to land reform and tax increases, the long arm of national political apparatus has reached more deeply than ever before into hamlets across the rural areas. The trilateral relationship that had long prevailed throughout Chinese history among national political authority, gentry or landlords, and the peasants has been gradually replaced by the bilateral relationship between a newly established national political authority and the peasants. For peasants such as those from Xue Jiadi village, their relationship with the central government was no longer necessarily mediated by landowners in the cities or the gentry ... Similarly, land reform and new tax policies marked the beginning of strong presence of the national government in the lives of villagers.[61]

Just because the gentry and landlords, who had long wielded the real power in rural communities, saw their social standing decline rapidly, it did not mean the central government could immediately take their place. It still had no direct control of rural communities, could not get around local authorities and form close connections with them, and certainly was in no position to enlist the help of the rural population to monitor these authorities. During the people's

[61] Philip C. C. Huang, *The Peasant Family and Rural Development in the Yangzi Delta, 1350–1988*, see https://www.sup.org/books/title/?id=2761 (Beijing: Zhonghua Book Publishing, 1992), 173.

commune era, primary-level bureaucratic organizations were officially given the mandate to rule by the state. However, while that did facilitate the development of these low-ranking officials' ability to advance their own collective and individual interests, it did little to help the rural communities themselves become better organized. These officials, who could now act in the name of the state, pursued the central government's policy objectives only selectively, and were far more concerned with capitalizing on this recognition to maximize political and economic gains for themselves. In theory at least, as the national political regime matures over time, the seat of political power moves upward along the bureaucratic chain of command. But in practice, rural officials continued to enjoy considerable autonomy, and were able to rule rural communities with minimal interference from or oversight by higher governments. Indeed, it is one of the defining features of politics in the modern era that the national government has more symbolic significance than practical relevance for rural governance. The state apparatus relied on the rural primary-level officials to execute administrative tasks on the ground. These officials operated with certain "autonomy" in their management of local affairs and certain "independence" from state and public oversight (albeit in the legal sense of neither term), and were able to exercise their powers in a way that suited the cultural, historical, developmental, and social conditions of the community. While rural primary-level political authority is not legally required to be functionally independent of more massive administrative bodies, it is, in practice, capable of using their own methods and procedures and staff in discharging their responsibilities. It did not depend on more broadly applicable laws to determine the scope of its mandate, as the central government's authorization provided solid base for its legitimacy. Even though political reforms led to changes in the kinds of ruling entities that existed, they did not change fundamentally the basic structural relationship between rural primary-level political authority and the communities, such that whichever group that ended up in the position to rule at the primary level would do so under the same set of constraints as have always existed.

Once we realize this, we would no longer be surprised by what is described in the passage below. Contrary to the commonly held perception about the land revolution, it suggests that even land reform failed in many places to alter the distribution of the right to the use of the land.

> The relative proportions of land owned by members of the different social classes were largely the same after land reform as what they had been before. Take the Yanguan area as an example. After land reform, per capita land ownership for landlords, rich peasants, middle peasants, poor peasants and farm laborers were 1.33 mu, 3.274 mu, 2.571 mu, 1.833 mu and 1.849 mu, respectively, roughly the same as prior to land reform.[62]

[62] Zhang, A Farewell to the Ideal, 52.

Political revolutions saw the constant replacement of the occupants of primary-level political positions and, with that, changes in the fortunes of individuals. But what remained unchanged despite shifting rhetoric and discourse was the way politics actually worked at the primary level. Wielders of political powers at this level had total control over both what information was to be released to higher authorities and how resources would be allocated within the community. The only way the state, i.e., the central government, could find out about conditions at the rural primary level was through reports and fact-finding teams. Whether it was announcement of government policies, release of subsidies, providing information feedback, and even fact-finding teams trying to carry out their missions, none of these could be done without first overcoming the layers upon layers of structural barriers and information firewalls that had been erected by the primary-level authorities. But since doing so would run afoul of administrative protocols, most of the time, the state would simply turn to the rural authority, on whose arrangement and cooperation it depended to get even the smallest of things done. Ordinarily, the state could not by itself, i.e., without the cooperation of primary-level cadres or some sort of shared understanding or agreement between the two, establish direct contact with members of the community, whose lives and work were shaped by and under the control of these local leaders. On the surface, even though a different group of people were now in charge of resource allocation in rural communities, and, moreover, they were acting as agents of the government, a status that the gentry of the old days did not enjoy, there was little change to how they carried out governance. They did not adopt any uniform and universal governing principles, nor did they try to protect people's rights by increasing their reliance on state rules and regulations, and still less did they do anything that might have strengthened the substantive connections between rural communities and state apparatus.

This kind of structure gave rise to a governance dilemma that was impossible to overcome. On one hand, to adjudicate conflicts at the primary level and to maintain political stability, the state must do all it could to prevent reckless behavior among primary-level cadres, including through, e.g., certain tax (dis) incentives. But on the other hand, the central government's *de facto* reliance on local officials for carrying out such tasks as disbursing subsidies, implementing tax exemptions, charitable giving and providing welfare in effect helped bolster the latter's legal standing and strengthened their hold on power. This means that the central government often found itself having to strike a difficult balance between the need to back the authority and reputation of primary-level officials, which could exacerbate their existing conflicts with the community in their charge, and the need to safeguard the rights and interests of the villagers, which would invariably "hurt" the interests of the primary-level officials. The state had to oscillate between these competing demands, and to do whatever that was expedient for purpose of keeping tension between the local officials and the communities under control. This suggests that the default strategy of strengthening the primary-level political authority within the existing framework of state bureaucracy could no longer improve either the latter's efficiency or its underlying operational principles. Nor could effective control of the primary-level political authority be achieved in this way, insofar as there was no mechanism for establishing linkages of share interests between those who had power and those who were ruled.

If we are going to build a structurally balanced system, we must confront the issue of the normative basis of primary-level political authority's power. Obviously, if and when that power is granted directly by the community itself, the primary-level authority and the community are properly aligned with each other in terms of basic interests. And this offers some immunity against the kind of political conflicts and governing difficulties that can arise when the two become disengaged with each other. Therefore, the key to realizing sustained stability at the primary level are institutional guarantees that local political authority receives its mandate from the community. For this to happen, political change must, at the appropriate time, graduate into social change. A mechanism must be established by which any wielder of power purportedly acting on behalf of the public receives their mandate from and is recognized by the society, individuals, and organizations. Such a mechanism ensures close links between the two parties in terms of basic interests, and compels the wielder of power to act in the best interest of those who gave them that power. This kind of political power that serves the public can only emerge from a relationship of equality between the society and authority, yet the commune system never did produce such a relationship. In fact, under it primary-level authority continued to operate as it always had since the beginning of the modern era. If anything, that model became ever more deeply entrenched.

Such a basic understanding of the place primary-level authority occupied in relation to the society serves as the starting point of the discussions to follow.

CHAPTER 2

Role Conflict: Public Service Provision and Operational Monopoly

As was shown in Chap. 1, the external impetus of the various changes in rural politics in modern times had been the desire to strengthen control by the central government. Not only was the reach of the national bureaucratic regime extended to cover the primary level, but primary-level bureaucrats were also granted the power and authority they needed to rule. While this might leave the impression that rural areas had kept apace with "state-building", that appearance is misleading. Even though the central government succeeded in setting up bureaucratic infrastructures in rural communities, its ruling power never managed to penetrate deep into the tissues of these communities, nor was it ever able to establish standing among these populations that was independent of the primary-level political authority. The structural changes were, therefore, merely superficial, and did not translate into substantive expansion of the scope of the central government's political mandate in the country. All that the central government managed to accomplish was replacing one source of political mandate with another: while political power at the rural primary level had traditionally been given to those who exercised it by members of the community, now it was granted by the central government. This was by no means a reconfiguration of the balance of political powers across different bureaucratic levels, but rather an attempt to augment cities' ability to extract resources needed for their own development and growth from the rural areas by altering the nominal identity of primary-level authorities while preserving the original power relations within the bureaucratic ecosystem.

> In the 1950s, the government levied agricultural taxes not in order to contribute towards the distribution of rents on land or to help cover budgetary expenditure by boosting fiscal income but rather to guarantee the central government's access to adequate supply of agricultural output.[1]

[1] Tiejun Wen & Shouyin Zhu, "Research Report on the Rural Tax and Fee Reform". China Economic Information Network (https://www.cei.cn), 1999.

J. Zhang, *Primary-Level Government*,
https://doi.org/10.1007/978-981-96-6209-8_2

The model of state governance that had been in place for a long time remained largely intact. On this model, rural communities accepted the symbolic significance of the state bureaucracy with the central government at the summit and its role in sustaining cultural cohesion of the country. So long as primary-level political authority complied, in spirit, with its directives and orders, the central government was more than happy to task them with the day-to-day management of local affairs. Therefore, despite superficial similarities between the bureaucratic structure at the local and the national levels, the primary-level authority [running the local structures] continued to think of these communities as turf they could rule "on their own terms". While the ruling principles adopted by these primary-level authorities changed little, the fact that now they were no longer given the mandate to rule by their subjects but by the central government effectively severed the organic bonds—built on shared interests—that had long existed between them and the rural communities. This is what I mean by "structural separation". It was thanks to the powerful administrative oversight under the people's commune system that the adverse political ramifications of such separation were temporarily rendered invisible.

For example, under such tight oversight, primary-level political authority was allowed very limited space to pursue commercial interests. Despite having absolute control over the means of production, primary-level cadres could only exercise this control in their capacity as administrators, and not in their capacity as operators. And most of them could claim no greater share of the total profit than was permitted under the terms of their administrative privileges, which typically amounted to no more than a puny amount. This made it all but impossible for these positions as a whole to become increasingly specialized in commercial operations. For this reason, it would be reasonable to conclude that for people occupying those positions their incentives were not so much whatever control they may have had over surpluses,[2] but rather the ability to work and live in a way that distinguished them from the peasants, and the sense of prestige and respectability that ability engenders. The cadres' duties included such tasks as agricultural administration, coordinating and allocating resources for agricultural labor and production, managing financial matters and physical properties. And performing these duties afforded them the opportunity to be promoted, to visit cities, to receive training and education, to go on sightseeing trips, to attend meetings and banquets, among others. For the cadres, these "perks", which came with a particular kind of work, were a badge of honor that could be worn conspicuously, something only people who occupy their position are entitled to. By contrast, using public property as a way of aggregating or concentrating the collective wealth of this group would have been both harder and less effective. This means that even though under the

[2] For the economic perspective, see Qiren Zhou, "China's rural and ownership reform: a review of the history of the economic system transition", in *Chinese and Foreign Scholars on the Countryside*, ed. Jianping Miu (Beijing: Huaxia Publishing House, 1994), 326.

commune system the primary-level cadres had become increasingly alienated from the community with respect to their interests and goals, for the most part the role they played in their positions was still relatively simple, and the kind of competition for gains that deep involvement in economic operations typically leads to was at the time not a prominent issue.

However, things began to change when the source of the power primary-level authority was exercising shifted upward from the community to the central government. This shift effectively created the precondition for the primary-level authority to become an economic interest group in its own right. Such precondition included certain kinds of "standing" the government bureaucracy bestowed on these local cadres. For example, standing with respect to resources entails access to state-supplied resources, state-sanctioned taxation right, and the right to manage financial affairs of rural communities, and standing with respect to status, i.e., one's identity as a representative of an administrative unit such as a village or town. Nobody who is not a member of the primary-level cadre could ever, by any other means, gain access to such status. At the most they might be given something of a simulacrum of such status that has little more than symbolic value. They would certainly not have standing with respect to either organization or decision-making. In other words, they would lack the official titles and proper authorization needed for organizing meetings, formulating and submitting policy proposals, instituting procedures and protocols, collecting information or engaging in outreach. During the marketization process these types of status turn into valuable symbolic capital, and translate easily into economic gains: monopoly power and control power. Obviously one can obtain these powers without relying on the local community, and one's status and experience as a cadre would suffice for that purpose. Their nominal titles within established "organs", and their status as the representatives of certain "collectives"—both of which making these individuals "public" figures—became the logical antecedent to their right to exercise operational control over publicly owned assets. This is absolutely beyond what is possible for any other kind of organizations that require operations or economic actor.

2.1 A New Role: A Group with Monopolistic Operational Control over Collectively Owned Assets

Since the means of agricultural production is collectively owned, and primary-level political authority represents the collective (i.e., the commons), putting the local government in charge of affairs of the public in rural collectives is considered a matter of course. Under the people's commune system, having the standing to act on behalf of a collective was nothing remarkable, because such a system afforded few opportunities to these individuals to engage in lucrative economic activities. So while the bond forged with shared interests that had always held between them and the community was already beginning to fray, no serious tension or conflict existed yet. In a market economy, however, occupants of these primary-level leadership positions took on a prominent new role, namely, as operators, i.e., as economic players or business people. On one hand, this new role allowed those playing it to contribute to the local economy (e.g., by creating employment opportunities and generating income for the local government); but on the other hand, it also gave rise to conflicts and tension between these people and other economic players (e.g. competition for control over resources, capital, opportunities, and market share). The changes brought about by the emergence of this new role are best illustrated by the following changes in the organizational structure of township government.

In each village, three nominally separate bodies were set up: CPC committee, village council, and economic cooperative. Yet there was no clear division of tasks among them, nor did each have its own staff. In several places in Zhejiang province, for example, the head of the CPC committee was also the head of the economic cooperative, so this person could "sign contracts on behalf of the village as its legal representative" in economic matters. At the township level, senior cadres also served as the chair of the board of directors, manager and deputy manager of the township flagship agricultural, industrial and commercial corporations, making them the most prominent figures among corporate managers and boards of directors. As an increasing number of government departments and agencies in charge of industry, agriculture, commerce, and foreign trade became corporatized, it also became commonplace for these emerging corporations to make appointment decisions for operational positions at subordinate levels, or even to get involved in business operations directly. In addition to finding out about pertinent policies, it was necessary for people to come in frequent contact with primary-level political authority for a variety of matters, such as business negotiations, securing collateral for a loan, making pitches to investor and applying for land use licenses. We found that not only was the economic role (i.e., related to for-profit activities) that these individuals took on widely regarded favorably, it was seen as indicative of the development of public-interest undertakings, and for that reason raised no suspicion or concern as to its potential for generating "illicit gains". Primary-level political leadership was even more deeply involved in business operations in places where the market infrastructure was relatively well-established.

Because of their status, these business operators operate in an environment defined by different rights, obligations, and duties from those faced by ordinary business people. When bureaucrats engaged in business activities, they were not on the same playing field as everyone else, and the advantages they enjoyed generated envy, and also resentment. They were able to make use of public resources such as real estate, land, and capital either for free or for but a nominal fee that was more symbolic than anything else. To attain them they needed to show neither credit nor other proof of their ability to repay [loans], and their status as persons occupying position of "authority" sufficed. This amounted to a kind of monopoly over what was "public", lent legitimacy to utilizing public resources for purpose of commercial operations, provided rationalization for raising public fund, and justification for commandeering "public" assets and wealth. But when these business initiatives ended in failure, the costs of the losses were usually borne by the "public", instead of those involved in the ventures. These people, in other words, faced no economic risks, and stood only to gain.

> In the mid 1980s, our village got into the frozen vegetable business. The village lacked capital, so people were asked to help raise fund by buying stock, and were told that the company would belong to all of us, and everybody would stand to profit. The villagers figured that a company had to be more profitable than the land, and since the cadres had already bought stocks, surely they were not going to end up losing money? So most households bought stocks. Things were very different then, when a few hundred yuan was a considerable sum for people in the countryside. I also bought 300-yuan worth of stock, but not without having to borrow from a number of people. More than a decade later, nobody has yet seen any dividend payment, and the company performance was only going downhill. Some cadres said the company was not profitable, and sold it to some cadres at a dirty cheap price, turning it into a private firm. What the village received from the sales was less than what was needed to recoup the cost for villagers who had bought stocks. Not only did we see no interests, we could not even get back the principal. That several hundred yuan would most probably have yielded a handsome amount in interest had we deposited it in a bank, no? In the end, we had no idea if the company made money. But it is a plain fact that for more than a decade family members of cadres have been making more money working in companies than one would farming. Obviously we have been taken unfair advantage of, and they stood to gain from taking unfair advantage of others.[3]

It was not because of their business skills or sound credit that the cadres were legally allowed to run businesses using public assets. Rather, it was because they had the power to control and make decisions regarding these assets. For people charged to providing public services, this kind of power was probably something necessary, but there were obvious drawbacks to allowing people who had to make investment decisions and run businesses to have such power. The case below shows how the exercise of such power could lead to waste of public assets.

> In 1985 the CPC secretary decided to start a cardboard box factory, and the village raised 40,000 yuan to purchase equipment, built the manufacturing plants, and invested another 100,000 yuan as liquid. The factory went bust shortly after, the intermediate products in the inventory, equipment and machines were worth maybe 200,000–300,000 yuan, all of which was sold at a discount to pay off debts. In the end it fell short by more than 100,000 yuan. A plastic factory was built in the same year, where the capital needed for building the plants, fixed assets and liquid had also come from the village. Two years later another 150,000-yuan loan was taken out on collateral. But the factory ended up going belly-up.

[3] Transcript of the March 1999 interviews with rural residents in Anhui province.

> The head was never held to account, and just took off and left the village as if nothing had happened. Later the accountant checked the account book, and the village couldn't come up with any strategy to deal with the situation, so the whole thing just ended like that, leaving all these questions unanswered.[4]

Under the people's commune system, positions of authority at the primary level did provide their occupants with the facility and opportunity to rake in economic gains. But the size of the gains they were able to secure was nothing compared to what we see today, in terms of either quantity or substance. What primary-level political leaders can gain today from what they do in their capacity as commercial operators of collective assets is a far cry from yesteryear. This allows us to observe how the role and function of primary-level political leaders differentiated. In addition to managing the affairs of the public, which they had traditionally done, now they are also engaged in business operations, using public assets as their resources. In the first role, whose beginning can be traced back to the people's commune era, they managed and controlled public services, and in their new role, their official titles enable and authorize them to engage in business undertakings. One place where this can be clearly seen are the changes in the "targets" local political leaders were supposed to meet since the 1980s.

> Through visits and observations, we were able to identify six targets that were important to village cadres: rank, promotion, job and privilege security, relative autonomy, economic gain for both the collective and oneself, and services for the villagers. It was possible to find exact benchmarks set for each of these indicators (see Table 2.1).[5]

Items 1, 2, 3 and 6 in Table 2.1 are not new, and have been targets since before 1980. Items 4 and 5, namely, relative autonomy (from superior) and gains for the collective and self were added later on. And the sixth target—services for the villagers—did not refer to the provision of public goods such as management or services, but rather employment opportunities created for the

Table 2.1 Targets and benchmark for village officials

Targets	*Indicators*
1. Rank; 2. Promotion; 3. Job and privilege security; 4. Relative autonomy; 5 Gains for the collective and self	Agricultural yield per *mu*; application of agricultural technologies; corporate profit for rural enterprises; value of fixed assets; personal income
6. Services for villagers	Job opportunities in nonfarm industries

[4] Chunlin Xia, *Image capital and the village cadres' strategy of status maintenance: Fieldwork in a village in Shandong province*. Master's thesis, Peking University (1998).

[5] S. Rozelle & J. Li, *The Economic Behavior of Village Leaders in China's Reform Economy* (Beijing: Economic Management Press, 1992), 23.

villagers (suggesting that insofar as cadres had the power to place farmers in corporate jobs, they must in some way, or indirectly, have served as the "boss" at these companies). These newly added targets reflected the changes in the overall targets primary-level political leaders were subjected to in their work. And the general direction of these changes, in my own opinion, was indicative of the development trend in the economic role for such group, whereby the power structure that formed gradually over the last few decades accrued superior economic capabilities for primary-level political leaders relative to other people.

As their role in economic operations grew, primary-level political leaders also become increasingly fiscally self-reliant, with more ways to raise funds than ever before to meet the needs of a growing budget.

Table 2.2 shows the marked increase in expenditure since the 1990s. Under the existing fiscal system, neither additional staff positions within the local government nor expansion of transfer payment from the central government was allowed, which of course meant only one thing: more spending could only be supported by vastly larger funds over which local governments had independent control. The existence of such a vast pool of money was the only way in which local governments could be weaned of their dependence on transfer payment from higher governments. So primary-level political leaders absolutely had to look for other sources of revenue. They could only be as fiscally independent as they were capable for finding these sources. And these "collectively owned" township enterprises that were established by these local leaders fit the bill. So in addition to transfer payments from the central government and miscellaneous service fees local governments collected, profits produced by industrial development at county, township, and village levels became another important source of revenue directly useable by primary-level political authority (see Table 2.3). One could hardly overstate the importance of this money to the local budgets and fiscal spending.

These changes in the composition of local revenue sources would suggest that local government payroll and the scale of its bureaucracy would grow during those years in which township enterprises performed well. Or in other words, greater economic self-reliance and reduced dependence on transfer

Table 2.2 Changes in town "TD" payroll size and spending, 1992–1996

Year	*Total spending*	*Salary and other allowances*	*In-kind benefits*	*Administrative overhead*	*Other expenditures*	*Total size of paid staff*
1992	17,775	5067	2538	2153	8017	12,327
1993	28,021	6151	2857	5475	13,238	12,730
1994	41,326	9206	6512	8486	17,122	13,325
1995	77,879	10,232	11,149	7323	49,175	13,476
1996	60,667	10,514	6024	5560	38,569	15,068

Unit: 100 yuan
Data source: Statistical bulletin for "TD" township

Table 2.3 Changes in the amount "TD" township collected in miscellaneous fees

Year	*Total*	*Household payment*	*Village enterprise payment*	*Township enterprise payment*
1990	343	19	67	257
1991	407	30	41	336
1993	1108	40	493	575
1995	1357	42	208	473

Unit: 10,000 yuan

Data source: *Compendium of Documents on Agricultural Economy of TD*, Nos. 41, 53, 49, 65

payment and miscellaneous fees effectively constituted the necessary precondition for growth of local government staff. But primary-level political leaders must exercise actual control over these enterprises if they are to be able to appropriate their profits to meet their fiscal objectives. Unless they are personally involved in the management and operations of these enterprises, financial support from these enterprises could not be guaranteed. Such control provides indisputable testament to the fact that primary-level political authority was steadily transforming into an economic interest group that specialized in the commercial management of public assets. Their rivals in this process were obviously other individuals in the community who also engaged in economic and commercial undertakings. But they had ways to ensure that they prevailed over their competitors both in how much control they had over these operations and in how great a share of the profit they can claim for themselves. The strategy is to assign each economic entity a place on an administrative hierarchy, and none receiving a higher place than what it reserves for itself.

One important thing we attempted was to establish at the township level an organization, namely, economic association, whose job it is to manage collective assets. We refer to this as agricultural collective asset management system reform. In the past, there was no such thing as economic association, and while people's commune and township government both represented the government, who was going to represent the farmers? Since 1992, we have found that a variety of independently operated economic concerns are no longer under township control, whose assets are, therefore, controlled solely by the independent operators. There was a great deal of tension between the government, which was in no position to run the economy, and these enterprises. When it came to running companies, the government lacked decision-making powers, and was completely at the mercy of these enterprises when it came to access to the enterprises' money. If they refused to hand over money to the government when the latter needed funds, there was not much the government could do. The chief executives had comparable ranking on the bureaucratic hierarchy as township government officials, and did not take orders from the government. Meanwhile, the headquarter of the newly established collective asset management company was under the direct leadership of the CPC committee, and entrusted with managing township collective assets on behalf of the farmers... At the village level, the economic cooperatives were expected to facilitate the collective economy, and after restructuring, they were

> allowed not only to collect annual fees from corporations – including fees for land use and for management, housing provident fund and the fund to support public interests – but also to disburse agricultural grants, while charging a nominal service fee.[6]

Obviously, the objective of such "reform" is to enable primary-level political leaders to lay claim upon what power other economic actors have to control [resources], to hold on to the power they have to manage collective assets, so as to maintain a reliable and steady source of revenue for them. This essentially amounts to using political means to advance economic interests. As we can see, as a result, these primary-level political leaders were able not only to rake in economic gains but also to secure fiscal autonomy.

At the same time, however, these changes also had serious political drawbacks: their engagement in economic activities means that primary-level leaders had to compete with the community over resources, market, information, capital, protection, among other things. This only worsened the misalignment between primary-level leadership and the community in terms of interests. Once primary-level political leadership became a body with economic interests, it would inevitably develop its own economic objectives, and enter into competitive relationships with other entities that are essentially commercial. This is obviously at odds with their default responsibility to serve the interests of the community as a whole.

There would have been nothing inappropriate about its competing with other entities had primary-level political leadership been purely an economic entity. But that is not what it is: it is also a political organ and is for that reason not on equal footing with its competitors in the economic realm. Because of its economic involvement, it has developed a special set of self-interests, has to compete for resources with other entities and groups, and deals with them on utilitarian terms, i.e., based on expediency. But as a political organ, it is expected to promote the public interest, distribute benefits, and provide services for all, that is, the exact opposite of special interest. While its political role facilitates its economic pursuits, the converse is not true. Its economic pursuits can tarnish its reputation, credibility, and integrity, and breach applicable code of conduct. This may eventually undermine trust in these organs, reduce compliance with orders they issue, and damage their overall credibility. The tension between these two roles could not be clearer.

These difficulties were lost on many of these leaders, however. In fact, they are trying to grab even more resources, so as to further "the collective interest". These efforts have only exacerbated the kind of tension described above. For example, there was the issue of whether only collectively owned enterprises should be eligible for loans from economic cooperatives. If so, it would mean that primary-level political leaders would be able to benefit, nominally on

[6] Transcript of the August 1997 interviews with the staff of the rural economic committee of Zhejiang province.

behalf of "the collective", from the profits these loans help generate. Another example has to do with the leasing of land. The collective collects rents on land it leases out, which constitutes a reliable and steady revenue source. But since lessees are always looking for the lowest rent, the primary-level leaders' involvement in leasing land clearly puts lessees (farmers) at a disadvantage with respect to land use rights. There were also cases in which collectively owned enterprises used the leverage they had to push down the price of raw materials. There were more similar cases.

All of these amount to profit-seeking activities, which also happen to be based on unfair competition, in which power was used to protect one party's monopoly. There is inherent tension between the advantages and privileges associated with a monopoly and the interest of the community. Economic gains and political legitimacy ended up undermining each other.[7] The foundation of the latter is the willingness and ability to act on behalf of and serve the community, while the former entails competition with other groups and entities in the community. This allows us to understand how the inherent tension between their multiple roles is the reason why primary-level political leaders always found themselves at the focal point of political and economic conflicts.

Given such inherent tension between their different roles and capacities, primary-level political leaders inevitably fall into political quagmire. Obviously, as a public organ, its unmatched political capital offers it not just a competitive edge, but even the power to coerce others or to monopolize resources, which undermines fair competition. When a public organ's advantages and privileges trump market selection, it seriously hurts other economic actors' chances of success. The credit needed to secure loans, leverage in pricing, qualifications to raise funds and control over assets, which are but some of the trappings of primary-level leadership, can often take other economic organizations years of hard work after entering the market to achieve. Such privilege did nothing to adjudicate the conflict between what is "public" and what is "private", all it did was to drive a wedge between primary-level leaders and the community.

For example, since it is so much easier to get things done with money that belongs to the collective, primary-level leaders became keenly aware of the importance of control over public assets to augmenting one's power, and were strongly in favor of developing the collective economy.[8] "Collective" property ownership effectively strengthened primary-level leaders' ability to exercise commercial control over public assets, and by derivation the profits generated therefrom. Naturally, in places that are relatively prosperous, this kind of control allowed more people to benefit. For example, in some cases contribution towards village reserve and township endowment and other miscellaneous fees were waived for villagers, education expenditure, old-age pension, and other welfare benefits for the villagers were increased. But as far as we can tell,

[7] Claus Offe, "The Attribution of Public Status to Interest groups," in *Organizing Interests in Western Europe*, ed. Suzanne Burger (Cambridge University Press, 1981), 123–158.

[8] Transcript of the August 1997 interviews with the cadres of TX county of Zhejiang province.

primary-level leaderships were by far the primary beneficiaries. From the point of view of those who did not enjoy such status, this is a kind of unfair pillaging by an entire group, which put others at a decisive disadvantage, completely unable to restrain that group. How can economic competition be unencumbered from such privileges and perks? How can public interest and private interest be distinguished from each other in official conduct? How can the legitimacy of political leadership be restored after having been infected by the conflation of and cross-contamination between public and private? How can the conflict between accumulation by a group and its legitimacy be resolved? All of these problems are exacerbated by primary-level political leadership's taking on different and incompatible roles, something that, it would seem fair to say, is the root cause of the increasingly acute predicament this group finds itself in recent years.

2.2 The Public Office as a Vehicle for Pursuing Private Objectives

One of the many ways in which the contamination of the public office by economic activities of the occupant manifests itself is how these positions have been turned into instruments for advancing their personal interests. Nowadays, primary-level political leaders expect from their jobs not only promotion opportunities, but also, and perhaps more importantly, the profits they can gain. This shift in incentives has serious implications for recruitment: primary-level leadership positions attract few candidates if they offer little by way of economic benefits, yet the competition can be fierce if there are economic gains to be had. Many departments have trouble filling their available positions because few people are interested. To address this, more perks and benefits must be offered, including such things as old-age pension, increases to allowances on top of basic salary, the opportunity to change one's status from farmer cadre to regular cadre, discounts on housing prices for township officials who want to purchase property in the cities, urban household registration, classifying primary-level officials who are veterans as central-government-level officials for purpose of job-related benefits, classifying village officials who had served as Communist Youth League Secretary for four consecutive years as "township-level officials" who are also eligible for permanent change of status, and so forth. All these offers were designed to make these primary-level leadership positions more appealing to potential applicants. But these benefits are not always enough. In some of the more affluent areas in Jiangsu and Zhejiang provinces, for example, these jobs attract very few young people native to these areas unless they bring substantial personal gains. The shortage is especially acute at the village level. In response, new recruitment policies have relaxed the eligibility requirement to "allow non-native graduates and veterans to apply".[9]

[9] Transcript of August 1997 Interviews with the cadres of TX county of Zhejiang province.

Another aspect of this for-profit transformation of the public office is higher turn-over. For many office holders, once they have acquired the qualifications, built connections, and accumulated the capital needed to operate a business, they no longer have any reason to stick around and serve the public interest, and would become preoccupied instead with the pursuit of personal gains. To many people, the status as an office holder and the experience that brings are a prerequisite to and preparation for what they will do in the private sector afterwards. One village in Hebei province, for example, went through three or four CPC secretaries within the span of eight to ten years. Each succession was considered "normal", in the sense that none of those who left the position had done so for disciplinary infraction. All of them quit voluntarily to focus on their pursuits in the private sector. But this was abnormal. These people would serve as CPC secretary for maybe two to three years, during which they would work on building up relationship with various departments and setting up their own company. Once they had done these, and completed all the necessary paperwork, they would quit their official positions and devote all of their time and energy towards running their company, whether it was an animal farm, a brick factory, or some other small business. When asked why they would "step down from their positions voluntarily", the unanimous answer was "being a public official diverts too much energy away from running the company".[10] Many incumbent CPC secretaries waste little time looking for a successor, which amounts to offering another person the opportunity to profit in the future from serving as a public official. This is in addition, of course, to protecting their own interests, and ensuring that they will have the space needed to focus on running their own businesses.

So why even bother spending several years serving as a public official at all? The answer obviously is that doing so can bring one things one would need to run a successful business, including bank loans reserved for "collectively owned enterprises", collateral and real access to public funds. Clearly, since public office brings privileges and perks not available to those who have not served in these positions, the experience of being a public official prepares one for more lucrative engagements in the private sector in the future. Such is the incentive mechanism by which these positions have been rapidly turned into instruments of personal profits. Conversely, some of those in charge of local economic entities have also found a fast track to these leadership positions, or been granted CPC membership, making public offices even more of a means to personal ends. For example, in early 1997, one township in Kaihua County, located in the mountainous areas of Zhejiang province, adopted a policy that included outstanding economic acumen and having for-profit development projects under one's name as qualifications for being a CPC member. Over the course of a year, fifteen people joined the CPC under this policy.[11]

[10] Survey conducted in a village in Hebei in the winter of 1997.

[11] "On the inappropriateness of denying Party membership to those who do not run a profit-making project," April 27, 1998, *Newspaper Digest*. Originally published in *Organization Personnel Daily* (April 23, 1998).

Another related phenomenon is people serving in multiple positions in the CPC, in primary-level political organs, and in economic organizations at the same time. Wearing different hats simultaneously—as CPC operative, as administrator, and as people heading economic cooperatives or enterprises—makes it all too easy for one to give themselves whatever favor they need in one position by doing something in another. In the village in Hebei province mentioned above, a number of people who served as CPC secretary managed to become the head of some enterprise or some farm while still in office. In Zhejiang province, the village council and the economic cooperative were in fact a "combo", and in many villages one and the same person served as the CPC secretary and the chair of the village council. Among the villages in XSH township, all but one had a village chief who was not also serving in another leadership or management position. The rest were essentially "three-in-one": the same person heading the CPC committee, the political leadership, and the economic team. This was the case in 60 or 20 percent of the 317 villages in that area.[12] Now if we include those who were "two-in-one", it would be no exaggeration to say that incumbent village officials control more than 80 percent of the village enterprises and agricultural trade groups. At the primary level, not only is this kind of personnel overlap not frowned upon, on the contrary, it is something to be flaunted. People would put their multiple titles right there on their business cards for all to see. You had the head of the village council also serving as the deputy CPC secretary, or the village council secretary also serving as the head of a village enterprise. These are so commonplace nobody would raise an eyebrow. Table 2.4 shows these crossover appointments among village officials in one township in Zhejiang province.

Unlike the recusal principle aimed at avoiding conflict of interest, crossover appointments are widely accepted and adopted in rural areas. One and the same person might be CPC secretary, member of the village council, and head of the economic cooperative, is in charge of human resources and makes nomination and appointment decisions about leadership positions, drafts policies, implements policies in the capacity of village council member, signs business

Table 2.4 Crossover appointments among village officials in one township in Zhejiang province

Category	*Number of people*	*Percentage*
Officials/cadres	89	100
Officials/cadres who hold multiple positions	64	72
Officials/cadres who hold more than three positions	37	42

Data source: Calculations based on "List of office holders in TD village"

[12] Transcript of the August 1997 interviews with the cadres of TX county of Zhejiang province.

contracts as representative of legal entities, oversees expenditure as either CPC secretary or some other senior leader (to prevent involvement of multiple authorities in decision-making).[13] This was considered "best practice" that should be widely emulated, a point that was often made at meetings where experiences were shared.

> In a new organizational configuration that is suited to the needs of a market economy, the village CPC committee, the village council and the economic cooperative effectively formed a tripartite that worked in concert to try to meet the local CPC committee's work targets. The village chief also served as the head of the silk fabric factory, and the deputy village chief and the manager of a clothing factory are one and the same person, while each one of the other five village officials is, in addition to overseeing agriculture and public undertakings, directly involved in the operations of an enterprise.[14]

As a consequence of such practice, not only were the three branches of power at the primary level, namely, the CPC committee, the village council, and the economic cooperative not clearly distinguished from one another with respect to function and purpose, but they are deeply entangled in their interest. Far from being seen as problematic, such entanglement was treated as best practice and encouraged by the system. Checks and balances, especially those that would help prevent conflicts of interests between the political and the economic arms, were not built into the institutional design for primary-level organizations. There is practically no recognition of the possible political consequences of such internal functional tension. "Crossover appointments", as far as the officials were concerned, were harmless to any of the parties involved and even helped to alleviate the burdens on the farmers.

The total number of officials could be kept under control when the same individual is appointed to multiple leadership positions, which could also alleviate the burdens on the farmers. Here, an average-size village would have five officials serving in all the positions across the three branches of power, and the number would be seven for slightly larger villages, where there would be three officials serving in each branch, and key village leadership positions must be filled by people who also served in other leadership roles.[15]

> In our area there were a total of 1980 people in leadership positions before the end of the last term. Since the start of the new term the number is 1869, a drop by 112. Most of these people hold more than one leadership titles, which helps to alleviate the burden on the farmers, prevent the number of officials from

[13] Transcript of the August 1997 interviews in Zhejiang province.

[14] Organization Department of Zhejiang Provincial Committee, 1997: 240, "A Survey into Dongbangtou Village of Dong County", Organization Department of Zhejiang Provincial Committee, (1997). (ed.) *Rural in-site research in a new period----Research on the construction of rural primary-level Party organizations with different economic types in Zhejiang province*, unpublished.

[15] Transcript of the August 1997 interviews with township cadres in Zhejiang province.

ballooning, and workload deflation. But while the number of village official decreased, the number of township officials has grown, because more staff members are simply needed at many agencies and departments to cope with an expanding workload executing rules imposed by higher levels of government. The township justice bureau, for example, used to have a staff of one person, and now there are six people. Other agencies that have seen similar payroll expansion include the family planning office and the tax department.[16]

One thing this widespread practice of allowing one individual to occupy multiple primary-level leadership positions illustrates is that, for both the villages and the townships, any change in the number of officials, whether it is increase or decrease, has significance only for administrative division of labor, and is politically inconsequential as far as social integration and economic cohesion of the community are concerned. In the townships, it is mostly public security and tax agencies, whose work involved substantial direct interaction with members of the community, that have seen payroll expansion. By contrast, in the villages, similar staff growth has occurred in departments and offices in charge of economic operations, where positions are reserved for veterans in the bureaucracy. This crossover is sometimes referred to by the villagers as "letting senior most official run the economy". In the vast majority of cases, township officials are enthusiastic supporters of village enterprises. The thinking is that the most important thing is to get these enterprises up and running, and if it takes money to do it then that's what one has to allow.[17] This is why in some places whoever who can get an enterprise off the ground, or even just to put together a concept for a company, would be rewarded with a leadership position. Meantime, a certain institutional complementarity between village leadership and township leadership was taking shape: profit generated by village enterprises benefits the township, while the township can be counted on to help address public security and other order maintenance issues in the village. Such interdependency effectively strengthened the political and economic connections between the two administrative levels, which in turn translates into the personnel mutual penetration between the two bureaucracies. The result is of course complex and inextricable web of entanglement of interests among the occupants of leadership positions.

Evidence of the existence of these webs of entanglements abound in the petitions that have been filed. These documents would typically dispose problematic behavior by an entire leadership group, instead of any one individual. Punishments either could not be carried out or did not produce the intended effects, or else could not be meted out to any individual because the entire cohort was collectively culpable.[18] All of this goes to show the degree to which

[16] Transcript of the August 1997 interviews with the organ cadres of TX county of Zhejiang province.

[17] Transcript of the August 1997 interviews with township cadres in Zhejiang province.

[18] Discipline Inspection Office of the Central Commission, *Transparency in Village Affairs and Democracy in Village Management* (Beijing: China Fangzheng Publishing House, 1997).

at the rural primary level political leaders were bound up with one another by shared interests. When there are built-in checks and balances among the different constituent organizations within a group, the individuals working within that groups do not have all of their interests overlapping one another's, and it would be highly unlikely for an entire cohort to be rule-breakers at the same time. But when the profit motive has become a common and inherent feature of primary-level leadership positions, putting the same people in multiple positions is a good way to protect people's gains. It provides some kind of institutional guarantee for solidarity among the leaders with respect to their economic interests, makes mutual support the most sensible strategy for all of them, and, just as important, safeguard the political security of the group, and by derivative, of each member thereof. So it would not be hard to understand why anybody who has left a leadership position would want to stay in close contact with incumbents by providing any economic or financial support possible. For once such ties are severed, these former officials would likely face the real prospect of being removed from their leadership positions at enterprises, and losing all the privileges and perks that these positions have brought them.

2.3 "Collective Ownership" and "Monopoly Control" of Land in Villages

In their capacity as "operator", primary-level leaders must have control over collectively owned assets, which, in rural areas, means first and foremost, having control over land transactions, i.e., the right to manage the land. During the people's commune era, the collective's control over land was simply a matter of course and not a source of dispute. However, since the land contracting system was adopted, things have become a bit more complicated. On one hand, the contractor enjoys legally protected right to use the land, while on the other, the monetary value of the land—measured either by the market value of its output or by the exchange value of the land itself—continues to grow each year. Meanwhile, the amount of land controlled by the primary-level leadership is decreasing, and these people's ability to derive profits from the use of that land is, therefore, severely curtailed. This is the reason it became a top priority for primary-level political leaders to devise rules that would effectively allow them to reinstate the power of control "the collective" once had over land assets. But this naturally led to competition between (private) entities that had leased the land and the "collective" (which is public). In many villages, such competition was an important cause of conflicts involving officials. In order to prevail, they brought to bear their legislative role in primary-level governance, stressing collective ownership of land, something primary-level leaders have "exclusive control" over. It becomes a lot easier to make sense of some of the local land policies once we place them within the context of officials' efforts to minimize the loss of exclusive control. After all, land policy adjustments afford a prime opportunity for retaining such control over this key asset.

In 1983, a village in Zhejiang province which we will refer to as W adopted, in compliance with township-wide requirement, a "dual land use" contracting system. But in 1990, important revisions to the system were introduced whose purpose was to "reduce the acreage reserved for growing food for household consumption while increasing the acreage reserved for leasing to contractors". Specifically, this was achieved by changing the formula used to calculate the acreage reserved for growing food for household consumption. The calculation used to be based on the size of the household, but now it also factored in the age of household members, allotting fewer points to the elderly and children. This change effectively downsized the amount of land used to grow food meant for non-commercial use.[19] While land policy revisions typically led to changes in who leased land and at what rate, more importantly, primary-level leaders used these occasions to reaffirm that the "collective" had ultimate control over this asset. Each revision could potentially strengthen that control by changing how much land would be set aside for contingency, who could lease land, contracting fees, or through the introduction of "economy of scale in agricultural production". All these measures could help the "collective" secure control over more land.

> Land used to grow food for household consumption is managed by the household, while management of responsibility land[20] is in the hands of contractors, which are usually factory-run agricultural workshops, agriculture service teams or crop growers with large plots of land. The right to use paddy field once leased to farming households would be transferred from them (in units of groups) to the village economic cooperative, which would then apply whatever pertinent standards to distribute it among farming households, who used the field for non-commercial purposes, and contractors, who use it to grow food for commercial purposes. In this way land distribution was no longer carried out along divisions among villager groups. Instead, each administratively-designated village would carry out its own uniform planning.[21]
>
> Paddy field, which was above and beyond land used for growing food consumed by the farming household would be leased by the economic cooperative either to the collective or to crop growers who had large plots of land. Only those who fully recognized and respected national interests, and the interests of the collective, and were committed to abiding by the contracts, and adhering to uniform central planning would qualify for such contracts.[22]

Otherwise, various preferential treatments would be implemented to boost people's incentives to engage in "collective" agricultural production.

[19] "Maintaining Stability in Land Contracting by Implementing Minor Adjustments", issued by WX village of Zhejiang province in 1990.

[20] Which refers to land used to grow food for commercial purposes. – Trans.

[21] "Implementation Rules for Promoting the Large-Scale Operation of Paddy-fields", issued by XL village of Zhejiang province (1994), 1.

[22] "Implementation Rules for Promoting the Large-Scale Operation of Paddy-fields", issued by XL village of Zhejiang province (1994), 1.

> Any economic cooperative or other types of public organizations that need to construct buildings for their agricultural production enterprise would have their land use fee waived once their land use application has been filed and approved by the government; Collective agricultural enterprises that operate on at least 30 *mu* of land and perform exceptionally well would qualify for tiered financial reward for concerned village officials, with 50 percent of the total amount reserved for bonus distributed among senior officials, while the remaining 50 percent among other village officials proportionally according to rank.[23]

With these targets having been instituted, the "dual land use" contracting system became an instrument for facilitating land transfer and capital flow, which help strengthen primary-level leadership's control over publicly owned assets.

> To affirm ownership rights, sustain contracting rights, optimize operational flexibility and improve management...land transfer mechanisms must be established, economy of scale promoted... and the collective's capacity for uniform operations and service provisions boosted.[24]

Policy adjustments such as these were invariably geared toward increasing the proportion of "collectively owned" land, which would augment the land operations capacity among village-level political leadership (as evidenced by increased receipts in contracting fees collected from contractors). As such, the operational process turns a piece of fixed asset into liquid asset, allowing primary-level leadership to enhance their operational power and ability to derive profit therefrom. Another piece of evidence is the fact that, despite continual decline in the acreage of contracted land for agricultural production over the years, the amount primary-level leadership has collected from contracting fees has grown each year (see Table 2.5).

Obviously, the state's and the collective's rights to own land and individual contractors' rights to use land (over extended periods of time) were bound to clash whenever these adjustments were enacted. For example, some villagers decided to turn land into cash by selling it. Some county-level land bureau

Table 2.5 Receipts from contracting fees in TD township in Zhejiang, 1991–1996

Year	*1991*	*1993*	*1995*	*1996*
Agricultural contracting fees collected	30	37.47	44	66

Unit: 10,000 yuan

Data source: "Collection of Economic Documents for Agriculture in TD Township", Nos, 53, 49, 65, and 46

[23] "Notice on Policies on the Development of Agriculture" issued by BB County, Zhejiang province (1992).

[24] "Opinions on Effective Implementation of the Second Round of Land Contracting and Responsibility System" (Second Draft), Zhejiang province (1997).

(which represented the state) passed legislation reverting the right to trade land to the government, claiming that all land is owned by the state, and no trade is permissible unless approved by county-level land bureaus. For their part, individual contractors lobbied to have a say in setting land price, in an effort to secure greater profits for themselves from trade. Meanwhile, enterprises that had been leasing land were now trying to purchase it, so that instead of paying rent they could become owners. All of this comes down to the fact that increasingly, user fee, rental fee, and contracting fee made up the bulk of the income from land for whoever operated it.

2.4 Augmenting Exclusive Control: Monetization and Capitalization of Assets

Transforming fixed assets into liquid capital offers another maneuver through which primary-level leadership can increase control over assets. The original purpose of collective ownership of land was to keep to a minimum the trading of land, which was believed to lead to asset "loss", i.e., the diversion of land from agricultural to non-agricultural (commercial) uses. In reality, however, putting the power of control in the hands of primary-level political leaders has had the opposite effect. Not only did it do nothing to curb the diversion of land away from agricultural use, it allowed primary-level leadership to keep whatever profit that such diversion yielded, thereby giving them an incentive to profiteer from land transactions. While land contractors did receive some compensation from these transactions, the entirety of the appreciation in land value that resulted from such transactions went to primary-level leadership and enterprises that rented out the land. Not only were individual farmers who contracted land excluded from price negotiations, they were not allowed benefit from land value appreciations. As the manager of "collectively owned assets", primary-level leaders were able to secure for themselves a reliable source of income.

> In one village in Jiangsu province a few *mu* of land was set aside for business people from the cities to raise crabs that would be sold to markets in Shanghai. All taxes and other in-kind payment obligations were waived for the farmers who contracted out the land, who would also receive 800 *jin* of grain each year in return. The deal had some appeal to the farmers, who planned to give the grain to the elderly in their families, abandon farming, and look for work in the cities. Each business person would pay the village 2000 yuan per *mu* of land each year (which would be more than 1,500 yuan in net income for the village after taxes and the cost of grain purchases are deducted). By the business people's own estimates, each *mu* of land could bring in at least 10,000 yuan. In a neighboring village, inadequate compensation for the farmers who contracted out their land (450 yuan per *mu* per year) gave rise to resentment among them.[25]

[25] CCTV, "Focus Interview," February 1999.

Even though land had already been contracted out to individual households, and at least in theory the terms of the contract would "remain unchanged for thirty years", in reality, however, land transactions and trades were taking place fairly frequently in the villages. And it was evident that, overall, it was always primary-level leaders and leadership bodies, not the farmers, who benefited from these trades. In village X in Hebei province, for example, over the course of eight years, a total of more than 200 *mu* of land originally intended for private residential construction was sold (for more than 900,000 yuan), the village brick factory leased more than 100 *mu* of land (for about 50000 yuan in annual rent), a total of 250 *mu* of sandy soils were sold (for 13,000–19,800 yuan per *mu*). These numbers allow us to perform a rough calculation of how much primary-level leadership bodies earned from land transactions.[26] In village W in Zhejiang province, "surplus land constituted the main source of revenue for the village, if the village had 100 *mu* of land, on paper it would report 80 *mu*, and the difference would be available for sale".[27] As profits from the monetization of collectively owned assets became increasingly concentrated in the hands of primary-level leaders, village residents grew resentful and suspicious.

> All of the money from land sales is received by the village, and all the necessary paperwork was handled by village staff. There were no rules about how much of that money the village could retain for itself. In some villages 5 percent is kept for common use, but typically the heads of villager teams would distribute the rest among the villagers. Since 1995, however, the village coffer would claim 20 percent of the money received from land sales, and later on, the village would be required by township authority to retain another 20 to 40 percent to cover management fees. Whatever that was left after that would also have to be kept by villager teams for public use, leaving individual farmers nothing more than the meager compensation for forfeited agricultural output.[28]

It is difficult, however, to enforce these rules, because farmers refused to cooperate unless they are paid money, so selling land always takes a lot of work.[29]

Due to the rising proportion of money from land sales that the "collective" keeps for itself, village officials have become *de facto* the largest beneficiaries. So it is of course natural for them to try to safeguard their control over the distribution of profit by exercising their right to decide on land contract-related matters and to justify this by citing the collective ownership of land.

> Those households that had let the collective keep what was owed them in requisition and resettlement payments, and who kept for themselves only the compensa-

[26] Petition documents prepared in relation to X Village, Hebei province in 1997.

[27] Transcript of the August 1997 interview with the accountant of W Village in Zhejiang province.

[28] Transcript of the August 1997 interview with Z, a clerk in the township finance department.

[29] Transcript of the August 1997 interview with the Secretary of the Party Committee of W Village.

tion for forfeited agricultural output were eligible for other land contracts. But those who had kept what they had received in requisition payment would not be eligible for other land contracts until and unless they first returned that money to the village. Farming households' refusal to turn requisition and resettlement payments they had received over to the village would be ground for revoking their land contract and reverting control over the land to the village. From now on, all such payments associated with land requisition by the state or other collective entity for development purposes belonged to the collective.[30]

In these land deals, the legal persons with whom the buyer or the party requisitioning the land are dealing are not the people who leased out land, but rather the government at either the county, township, or village level. This means that the people who contract out the land do not really have the right to transfer the land, and their involvement in these deals is in fact largely passive and involuntary. They stand to receive but a small share of the proceeds, have no say in setting the price, and lack the standing for taking part in the negotiations. It is common practice for the buyer to stipulate in the contract that the village council would be responsible for "reaching out to" the land holder and trying to preempt their backtracking on the deal, a possibility that clearly presents a genuine source of concern for the buyer. As such, it is the village political leaders who are the ones calling the shots in these land deals, from setting the price to the disbursement of payment. Some may even seize this opportunity and impose various conditions, such as demanding the buyer to pay village officials a "salary" indefinitely, and using the "land sales contract" as something of an insurance against threats to the source of funds from which the salary will be drawn.

Land Sales Agreement[31]

Party A: Township Brick Factory
Party B: Village W Village Council

Party A, for purpose of expanding the brick kiln and increasing production capacity, seeks to requisition (about 25 *mu* of) land owned by village W. To this end, it has, upon negotiations with Party B, entered into the following agreement:

1. In order to facilitate this requisition Party B must perform the necessary preparatory work, until completion of the land measurement.
2. Party B agrees to defray the costs of the requisition by paying village W officials 10,000 yuan per annum in compensation.

[30] See Article 4 of the document "Stability in the Contracting of Land with Small Adjustment", issued by W Village (1990).

[31] "Agreement on Various Issues", issued by W Village Committee (April 1995).

3. The payment is disbursed lump sum each year, at the end of the calendar year.
4. This agreement is produced in duplicate copies. Each party keeps one, and must abide by its terms.

Signatures of representatives of Party A and of Party B
Official stamps of both parties

April 1, 1995

According to the terms of this agreement, the requisition fee is set at 12,000 yuan per *mu*, the rate of compensation for land on which mulberry trees are grown is set at 2000 yuan per *mu*, and for land on which cabbage is grown it is 500 yuan per *mu*. In addition, 4500 yuan per *mu* would be paid to Party B for land that the brick factory had already been using, plus the pollution fee, the total came to 131,086.97 yuan, to be paid in two installments.[32] All the land lessors reached an agreement, to which they were signatories, where a portion of the money received in requisition fee would be handed over to the villager team, to be distributed among the villagers, and the buyer would be responsible for paying the agricultural taxes and contributing to the public funds.[33] In return, the villager team would pledge to the village council not to backtrack on the deal. It's worth noting that, in this land deal involving multiple parties, even though "the land belongs to the villager team", the amount of money the villager team received is not the same as what the village council received, with the difference being no less than 2000 yuan per *mu*, even without factoring the salary that the buyer has promised to pay the village official indefinitely. This is illustrated by the following agreement between this villager team and the [affiliated] village by administrative-designation.

Village Officials:

Three land lessors from this villager team have agreed to transferring the right to use 1.011 *mu* of our land through requisition, at the rate of 10,000 yuan per *mu*, for a total of 10,110, or ten thousand one hundred and ten yuan. This amount is to be drawn from the land requisition fee to be paid by the cement factory, and disbursed to this team in one single payment. It will be entirely up to members of the team how the money is distributed among them, and village [officials] shall have nothing to do with any of this ever in the future.[34]

Team leader signature
Signature of person who collected the cash
August 19, 1995

[32] "Land Requisition Agreement" (March 1995)", and "Land Rental Fee and Pollution Fee Record" of W Village (February 1996).

[33] Document with the collective handprints of all the land lessors among the villager team (natural village) of W village (August 13, 1995).

[34] Villager team leader's Notice of Receipt.

Thanks to the power primary-level leaders are able to exercise over land deals, they stand to benefit substantially and easily from them. But not only is this deleterious to their own reputation, it is also frequently the source of social conflicts. As to the nature of these conflicts, it often concerns how economic gains are distributed, and not whether the villager officials had the right to do what yielded the gains in the first place. As the case of village W clearly shows, even though the land belonged to the villager team, it hardly tried to impede land deal of any type. The only things they are concerned with are the price, how the proceeds are to be divvied up, and whether the deal would relieve them of the obligations to pay contracting fees and various agricultural taxes, and contribute grain. Selling the land, from their point of view, is just a quick and easy way to have these obligations lifted from them. One villager said that he wished that the land a factory was trying to procure through requisition included his plot, because not only would that have brought in some money for him but it would also relieve him from the financial obligations directly associated with the land, *mu* for *mu*, he had contracted.[35] This suggests that in some areas in southern Jiangsu province earnings from growing crops did not constitute the bulk of a household's income. Considering the costs associated with the land and the benefits it produced, it would have made more economic sense for these families to trade the land for cash instead. After all, they never actually owned the land to begin with.

Concerning land-related conflicts in rural areas, while "loss of land right" and "mishandling of sales proceeds" would, when cited as their cause, typically command the attention of higher authorities, for people on the ground, the real issues were more often than not the price and how the proceeds were divvied up. Land deals per se did not generate tension between those occupying different rungs on the social ladder, what people wanted was to receive a cut of the profit. This goes to show how collective (group) land ownership tends to create profiteering incentive. Yet it is usually the primary-level officials, who are directly in control of the land, who are best positioned to profit. When the villagers resisted what they did, these officials usually resorted to sharing the profits among a larger number of people, instead of halting the profiteering behavior out of, say, an emerging sense of responsibility. All these are the consequences of flawed institutions. Because the existing land tenure system creates profiteering incentive but not the corresponding sense of responsibility among the primary-level officials, land transactions became one of the major sources of income funding normal operations of the local government. Villages where this is the case are rather "well-off", but the same cannot be said of the village residents. This is why in Jiangsu and Zhejiang there is a certain type known as "village rich villager poor". By "village rich" is meant that the village and its affiliated organizations have vast amounts of disposable funds.[36]

[35] Transcript of interviews with farmers.
[36] "In-depth Field Investigation in Rural Zhejiang in the New Era".

Primary-level political authority, with its own budget and directly in control of the land, is obviously at an operational advantage. That is why it both actively pushes to turn assets into cash and stands to gain the most.

2.5 Profits, Capital, and Taxes: Blurred Lines and Accounting Loopholes

Primary-level political authorities have long been in charge of electric power distribution. In many parts of rural China, the department nominally responsible for this does not actually oversee day-to-day operations, nor do electrical substations interact with rural residents directly. Instead, it is the village political apparatus that is "authorized" to carry out the managerial tasks. So long as they receive regular payments for electricity, the electrical substations do not bother to inquire about rates and related matters, or take an interest in whether anybody has done anything to jeopardize their reputation. In fact, in order to provide village officials an incentive to collect electricity payments, the substations might even encourage them to make a profit from this exercise by offering them "a commission". But no limits to what they can do with it are built into this authorization, leaving the perimeters of the village officials' responsibilities poorly defined. The mandate only to collect fees on behalf of another organization is one thing, and the mandate to operate the electric power distribution system in rural China is quite another. But it has never been clear to anybody which one the village officials have. Some of them claim that the entire amount they collect in electricity payments is turned over, and they do this work for free. But insofar as the amounts in electricity payment collected from different villages within the same area differ, it suggests differences in income among the teams authorized to carry out the collection. Since the electrical substations charge a uniform price, electricity distribution at the village level cannot possibly be free. What exactly are the production costs of electricity for the substations? Why is it that the electricity rates differ from village to village? Why would village officials even be involved in the collection of electricity payment, work that takes a lot of time and energy and produces no benefit? And why, furthermore, would they be the one to designate the village electricians? Under the exorbitant monopoly price for maintenance and repair, how are the receipts distributed among the different organizations?[37] All of the parties concerned are either mum or cryptic on these questions, and opinions are all over the place when it comes to the role played by the village political apparatus. Here is what one insider told me:

> The [central] government invested in and built these high-voltage transmission network. But for counties and townships, their governments build the low-voltage distribution cables to meet their own electricity needs, pay for it, and own what they build. Electricity used by villagers and rural enterprises is delivered to

[37] Transcript of 1997 interviews with farmers of W village, Zhejiang province.

them over low-voltage power lines, which is why the owner (which is the investor) has the rights to operate, to control, and to collect financial returns. Therefore, it is commonplace for village officials to fold as many things as possible into operating costs, including management fees, repair and maintenance costs, investment, and fees that can be difficult to collect, such as salaries and bonuses for the cadres.[38]

Apparently the village leadership is by no means responsible for just electricity payment collection on behalf of some other entity, they are also the "property rights owner" and operator of the power lines connecting the village to the county substation. Since the county and the township governments also invest in these power lines, they are co-owners, which means the pricing process is also necessarily one in which decisions are made about how the benefits are to be divvied up among stakeholders. The large number of stakeholders, and of the times by which the total profits must be divvied up and subdivided to make sure each gets a cut, is one reason for the high rates of electricity. And the practice of conflating taxes and profits both in collection and in expenditure makes it possible for village officials to profiteer from their managerial rolel, not only to fund their daily operations but also to recruit more staff. So long as such institutional profiteering and payroll expansion continue, rural electricity management fees (and taxes) will continue to rise, indefinitely.

Officially there are supposed to be around thirty full-time county government employees, but now the real number has reached around 130. Each year as much as 300,000 yuan must be set aside by county and township governments towards salary for sanitation workers alone. In order to reduce workload, governments at all levels are hiring more staff, issuing directives calling for recruiting beyond official limits to staff size (yet without providing extra money). This means the fiscal authority has to figure out ways to come up with the money to pay for all this. And they try to do so by tweaking with the fees and charges. The rate for electricity went up by three cents per kWh last year, there was no other choice.[39]

Rural power supply is just one example, but it is typical of how things are handled by primary-level governments in a number of areas. They all have two key features in common: primary-level officials working as both service provider and [enterprise] operators, adoption of accounting practices that do not separate between taxes and fees (public money to be used to provide public services) and profits (available for private use by individuals or groups and exclusive of other purposes). Even though primary-level political apparatus is mandated to be a public service provider, and granted the authority it needs to discharge that responsibility, it nonetheless behaves like any other economic organization when it uses its property rights ownership towards profiteering purposes. Moreover, it distributes the profits among its own ranks (to pay for

[38] Transcript of 1997 interviews with the township cadres in WD village, Zhejiang province.
[39] Transcript of 1997 interviews with the township cadres of WD village, Zhejiang province.

staff expansion). As for the taxes, the receipts are used not just to fund public undertakings, but also to pay for things that are enjoyed by a small number of privileged individuals, including car service for officials, mobile phones for officials, motorbikes for officials, and payment towards apartment purchase for officials. As far as the villagers are concerned, for whatever the amount they have paid (some of it as taxes) that is used to cover village administration overhead, they did not get in return satisfactory public services; and for the part of the money they have paid that has gone toward capital accumulation, it was invested by village officials, and they will never see a penny of the return on that investment.

Similarly, the money collected in public service fees and charges is used toward a variety of purposes. Some goes to funding public goods such as schools, some is invested in agricultural infrastructure, such as canals and electric appliances, and some in building brick factories and setting up enterprises. But those who contributed were never granted the right to benefit from such investments, and still less able to exert control over the operators (the village officials) by either making choices or pulling out, because they never had the right to do so. For the operators, while their dual roles allowed them to capitalize on their position in the government to engage in economic activities, such privilege did not come with accountability in the case of failure. They faced no risk of having to pay compensation for losses. Yet in the hands of inexperienced operators, which many of the village officials were, more than a few of these enterprises generated no profit. A lot of the money the villagers had contributed had simply gone to waste. When you are coerced into paying fees and charges nominally for public services yet there is no guarantee you will actually get in return what you have been promised, little wonder why some villagers would respond by refusing to pay, filing petitions with higher levels of government, or even fleeing by moving to the cities.

These difficulties in collecting fees and charges have forced rural primary-level officials to continue to look for other sources of revenue. And one fund-raising scheme that became quite popular was selling off fixed assets. As a result, more and more of the rural fixed assets were turned into cash, and treated as "tax receipts", that ended up being used to cover administrative overhead for primary-level government. This is what land transaction, something that has become commonplace, essentially is. According to *The PRC Land Law*, land in the countryside is collectively owned. And the collective is embodied by the village council. The only entities with the standing to sign contracts on behalf of the village in land rentals, land sales, land contracting deals, and surface land sales are bodies that can represent the village formally. Obviously, selling land is, compared with collecting fees and charges, a much easier "tax collection" method. Consequently, to alleviate their fiscal woes, many villages have resorted to raising money by selling land. What land that remains unsold would then be contracted out as the officials see fit.

Another source of revenue are administrative charges. In addition to land transactions, money can be obtained from a multitude of sources, including fundraisers, fines, subsidies from higher levels of government, loans, disaster relief funds, payment from village enterprises, contract fees for orchards, money collected for government grain purchase, money supporting public works (such as water and power facilities, and schools) and miscellaneous fees collected for everything from processing military draft, residence registration, birth permits, marriage licenses, and other paperwork. Village or county government can at anytime launch a new project by issuing an official document that stipulates the methods to be used to determine the amount of money needed, and sets the fundraising target.

- As stipulated in *Opinion on Implementing Village-wise Electrification Drive*, any individual with local residence registration must contribute 10 yuan, and each household must contribute 20 yuan for each *mu* of water paddy they own, and 35 percent of the aggregate basic allowance disbursed to groups of household must be contributed towards the electrification fund.
- As stipulated in *Opinion on Implementing Grade-school Construction*, any individual with local residence registration must contribute 30 yuan, and each household must contribute 5 yuan for each *mu* of water paddy they own, receipts from payments of annual fees for supporting education and compensating for power station equipment depreciation already go into this fund, and no additional payment is needed.[40]
- For 1996, the town of DT collects a supplemental (agricultural) fee towards the education fund, in the amount of 24 yuan per person per year, with the target total sum for 16 villages set at 342,864 yuan.[41]
- As stipulated in the *Notice on Raising Funds for Public Safety and Comprehensive Governance* for the county of BB, upon deliberation, the county government has decided, for the first time, to raise funds for public safety and comprehensive governance, to make up for existing budget shortfall. See Table 2.6 for village-by-village breakdown of the amounts due.[42]

Every notice like this one includes the amount due set for the listed entities, and the figures are always some nice round number within a fairly limited range. These could not have been based on careful calculations factoring in the financial situation of these entities, and are entirely decided arbitrarily. Every entity or organization must contribute, even though the exact amount may depend on the location, the timing, the nature of the organization, and who is in charge. As to how the contribution is used, it is simply not reported to

[40] Document No. 24 of Village Committee of X village, Zhejiang province, 6-8, 40-43.

[41] "Notice on Collecting the '1996 Agriculture Education Supplemental Fee," issued by TD Township.

[42] "Notice on Implementing the Public Security Comprehensive Governance Charges, 1996" issue by BB County.

Table 2.6 Village-by-village breakdown of the allotted contribution amounts

Payer	*Amount (yuan)*	*Payer*	*Amount (yuan)*	*Payer*	*Amount (yuan)*
GJB Village	300	NF Village	400	XT Village	300
WL Village	200	SL Village	300	XSH Village	400
XD Village	200	BB Village	300		
Village enterprises					
Plastics factory	200	Metallic products factory	100	Automobile parts factory	200
Mechanics factory	200	Electric power company	1000	Battery factory	300
Insulation factory	300	Casting factory	300	Gas station	100
County enterprises					
Company No.1	10000	Company No. 2	5000	Company LD	2000
Company No. 3	6000	Company No. 4	2000	Factory No.2	3000
Public institution					
Supply and distribution agency	500	Agricultural power station	300	Tax collection team	200
Credit union	300	Agricultural science and technology bureau	200	Radio Station	200
Water company	300	Health clinic	200	Movie theatre	300
Pharmacy	100	Office of the factory	300	Granary	200
Post office	100	Veterinary office	300	Food distribution group	200
Hydropower station	300	Fish Farm	200	Agricultural product market	500

anybody. Some investigations have shown that in some places each village has its own accounting practices, and some of the money is kept off the books.[43] This is indeed corroborated by an accounting report from one county in Zhejiang province that we examined closely: in 1996, the government of the township of TD conducted a thorough review of the fiscal conditions of the villages under its jurisdiction, and it found that a range of accounting irregularities was widespread, including money that had been "received but had yet to be recorded in ledger", money that had been "disbursed but had yet to be recorded in the ledger", white-slip promissory notes, and discrepancy between what was on the book and the amount of cash on hand. Table 2.7 shows what these irregularities look like for village W mentioned earlier.[44]

[43] X village, Hebei province petition documents, 1996-1997.

[44] "Statistical Overview of Village-level Finances" (Table IV) prepared by the People's Government of TD Township, Zhejiang province, November 5, 1996.

Table 2.7 Accounting records for village W

Cash on hand	*Received but not yet entered into the ledger*	*Disbursed but not yet entered into the ledger*	*White-slip promissory note (piece)*	*Total amount on white-slip promissory notes*
241,743.72	700,827.85	697,046.41	42	192,560

Unit: yuan

Table 2.8 Credits and debits for Village W

Type of debtor/debit	*Debit amount (yuan)*	*Type debit*	*Debit amount (yuan)*
Individuals (122)	1,217,394	Enterprises	42,272
Cadres (6)	46,860	Total	235,849
Contracting fee	7770		

Even for what is actually recorded in the ledger, the discrepancy between what should be in the accounts and what the ledger shows is quite striking (see Table 2.8).[45]

These discrepancies provide further illustration of the way in which tax receipts and profits are not properly distinguished from each other in accounting practices. If primary-level political apparatus is an operational enterprise pure and simple, then both debts and failure to enter transactions into the ledger undermine efforts to monitor the business; but if it is a public institution, the discrepancy between the amount of what is recorded and in actual transactions means the absence of proper rules and regulations governing financial and fiscal matters at the primary level, and a fortiori, considerable arbitrariness in accounting practices. When something goes wrong, cadres' default strategy is to do whatever that would protect one another. By making sure benefits are shared among them and no information is disclosed to outsiders, in most cases they are able to effectively thwart both efforts by villagers to report malfeasance and those by their superiors to investigate: "So long as relationships among the cadres are well-maintained, and nobody blows the whistle, then nobody would know".[46] Currently, the only body that can perform oversight are higher levels of government. Besides penalty imposed by them, there is, in reality, no other societal monitoring mechanism in place. Even though some villages have set up financial oversight committees, they are mostly made up of cadres and accountants responsible for granting approvals and issuing permits for use of public funds.[47] They do not hold regular

[45] "Statistical Overview of Village-level Finances" (Table VI) prepared by the People's Government of TD Township, Zhejiang province, November 5, 1996.

[46] Transcript of the August 1997 interviews with township cadres in Zhejiang province.

[47] Membership list for the finance group and the oversight group of W Village.

meetings or engage in other regular activities,[48] and amount to little more than, thanks to the conflict of interest inherent to such a set-up, a group of people engaged in "self-monitoring". The democratic finance management teams had no mandate to grant approvals, audit accounts or decide on cases, and higher levels of government have adopted a modus operandi that is fundamentally predicated on the unscrupulous accounting practices that conflate tax collection and profit-making. Because they bend over backwards to avoid hurting either the image or the efficiency of primary-level political apparatus, they are excessively cautious and very highly inefficient.

These ambiguities and confusions in both ideas and institutional configuration have a direct impact on how farmers perceive and understand the nature of taxes and how they are used: "All are but different ways to pry money out of our pockets, how is anybody supposed to understand any of it?"[49] Therefore, they would refuse to pay "money" for anything, regardless of whether it is taxes, fees, rents (contracting fees), or fundraising contributions, and it can be very difficult to tell which are the legitimate ones and which are not. As a result, many villages end up not being able to meet collection targets for even taxes that are perfectly legitimate. Take Zhejiang province, one of the relatively economically well-off areas in the country, as an example. What I gathered from fieldwork across the province is that in some townships, some of the villages "went years without being able to pay anything at all to higher levels of government because they simply could not get the villagers to pay their due". And "later on, the township authority divided up the villagers into small groups, and imposed collection targets on each. But even then they were able to collect about 80 percent of the target amount". A large number of villages owed vast amounts of money in unpaid dues, sometimes for years. And collecting that money, village officials admitted, is "just about the hardest work in the village".[50] The lack of a conceptually and institutionally sound taxation system has also resulted in irregularities in how certain taxes are collected. For example, even though what villages must collect to finance the village reserve and township endowment are, by law, rural taxes, and they are typically not collected from individual villagers. And the amount due is not determined by villager's income levels (but instead by how easy it is to collect it, and how much profit village enterprises have made). Some villages with means do not collect these taxes from individuals at all, but instead either use money from the public funds to cover it, or otherwise ask village enterprises to pay. Villagers are only asked to pay when either of these other two sources of funds is unavailable or inadequate.[51]

[48] Transcript of the August 1997 interviews in W village.
[49] Transcript of the interviews with farmers.
[50] Transcript of the interviews with the cadres of W village.
[51] Transcript of the August 1997 interviews with village cadres.

All these practices suggest that village and township authorities can often make changes to who pays which taxes, depending on the situation at hand. And this is tantamount to making changes to the rights and obligations of members of the community in relation to the local political authority, a relationship that is largely determined by the tax system. More importantly, primary-level political authority does not have the legal mandate to make these changes. Yet they do in fact make these changes, and the practice has all but crystalized into an unwritten rule. What the issue about land shows us is that as far as village governance is concerned, "state ownership" of property is increasingly purely symbolic. In the absence of effective legislation and enforcement mechanism, such "ownership" has little substance. By comparison, while "collective" ownership often is able to produce substantial benefit for "the collective", insofar as the collective interest of primary-level political authority is what is at stake, the systematic failure to clearly separate profits from tax receipts makes the materialization of that benefit particularly onerous. It gives primary-level political authority the incentive to exercise its power of control in order to fill its coffer. The power of control, which now comes with the mandate local political authority has been given by higher levels of government, is now widely used for the pursuit of economic ends. Not only is this detrimental to the national interest but it also engenders among the public deep concern about the fairness of the system. Yet under the existing primary-level political apparatus no effective oversight is possible to prevent such lack of fairness, nor is it feasible for the central government to achieve meaningful control of [local] assets by revoking primary-level political authority's political mandate. I look into the consequences of these abnormal fiscal and tax systems in Chap. 4.

What all these phenomena indicate is that since the people's commune era, there has been a downward shift in who has control over resources in rural areas along the political power hierarchy.[52] Bodies and affiliate individuals on the lower rungs of the bureaucratic ladder have more opportunities to exercise control over (the allocation) of resources. Even as primary-level politics become less and less reflective of and bound by the national interest, they were not becoming more responsive to what is in the interest of the local communities either. The disappearance of the administrative oversight mechanism that had once been in place and the yet-non-existence of a mechanism for public oversight have created a vacuum in which primary-level political power has in effect become something of an autonomous and closely knit resource monopoly. Whatever advantages it enjoys is not the result of any competition, or their business acumen—if anything, government-run enterprises are more likely to fail than to succeed—but is owing to the *de facto* privileges it has as a matter of course under the old political *status quo*. The current system of ownership

[52] Scott Wilson, "Competing Claims to Village Property and the Gradual Clarification of Property Rights," presented at Property Rights in Transitional Economies: Insights from Research on China, Hong Kong, (June 1996).

provides safeguard for these privileges, and give those who have these privileges more space in which to exercise them. This not only allows primary-level political authorities to avoid having to rely on its constituents for support, it can even help them survive when what is in their interests is at odds with what is in the interests of their constituents.

2.6 Personnel Regime: The Support System on Which Monopoly Power Depends

The function of the personnel regime is to allocate the power of control among different actors in a society, and in rural China it plays a very important role in shaping the opportunity structures different individuals face. For example, when villagers are able to elect village officials, this gives them greater ability to make choices, and this allows them to play a greater role in who become a cadre, which in turn makes it more difficult for elected officials to pursue interests that are at odds with what is their constituents want. Obviously, when the electoral system is in place, cadres can easily find themselves out of office if they did not put their constituents' interests first. Moreover, pressure from competitors and rivals compels them to do everything they can to stay informed about the needs of the community by listening to the people. In this way, political authority and the public become institutionally connected, and political activities, which used to be confined largely to within the bureaucratic system, are now playing out in the society more broadly, and doing so more openly. Instead of building more relationship within the bureaucratic system, trying to win more votes became the primary preoccupation of these political authorities. This transformation can give political competition a sharper ethical edge and bring more sense and reason to the discourse, which is conducive to stability at the primary level. Therefore, it is important to recognize fully how significant a role the personnel system plays in distributing benefits and power in rural society, shaping political behavior, and determining how much space of action different individuals have.

Of course, the staff recruitment mechanism currently in place in rural areas does not even come close to this kind of electoral system. This has led many to the rather simplistic view that all personnel change decisions at the primary level in rural areas are made by higher government authorities. But this is not in fact the case. While higher governments do have the power to select, approve, and appoint village-level officials, the starting point of the recruitment process is at the primary level and few who do not get on well with people in that ecological niche can expect to survive long in their positions. Presently, primary-level officials typically nominate people with business acumen for village leadership positions, with an eye to boosting the value appreciation prospects for the resources controlled by the village. Moreover, ensuring the continuity of shared benefit of the village is a critical factor in nomination decisions, which is why people from within the village are overwhelmingly preferred and those who already hold leadership position elsewhere are not at all considered except when they are being offered short-term secondment appointments allegedly for "training" purposes. The current personnel change procedure, which has been in effect for many years, includes the following steps. First, the incumbents nominate candidates for their replacement (except for unusual cases, such as when no agreements can be reached about the nominees, in which case, the county or township leadership would nominate candidates). Then the county or township government would dispatch people to the village to vet the candidates (collect background information on the nominees and opinions on the nomination). Once the vetting process is complete and candidates are approved, election is held, the results of which would be delivered to the county or township government for certification and the winner announced. In fact, in such an electoral system the right to choose (nominate) candidates is largely concentrated in the hands of just two bodies, the village and the county governments, and village residents have very limited involvement in the entire process. Even though the township government gives the approval and makes appointment, the village incumbents often play an important role in the initial deliberation and nomination, and the final decision must be something that both groups can agree on.

As is shown in Table 2.9, "vetting" is a critical step in the nominating process. The team in charge would report information they have collected from the village to their superior, and the county and township government would make their "preliminary selection of candidates" on the basis of that. It is precisely at this stage that input from the incumbents can make a difference. Minutes from the first [CPC] subcommittee meeting in the village of XT show that the main item on the meeting's agenda is to draw up a prospective list of new members of the village council, and also to set out the division of labor among them. According to meeting minutes, the main objective of another meeting, where CPC leadership, members of the village council and of the village cooperative convene, is to announce the policy that incumbents must train and to identify qualified candidates, and to make sure all incumbents are on board.

Abstract of Minutes from Village Leadership Meeting[53]

Attendees:	Members of village leadership, village council and village cooperative representatives, task force from township government, nine total;
Duration:	Half a day;

[53] Minutes of the Meeting of the Three Leadership Groups of XT village Zhejiang province, 101.

Table 2.9 Village leadership election schedule

Stage	*Dates*	*Tasks*
Preparation	April 1- 30	1. Convening CPC leadership, village council and village cooperative, bringing all in line, announcing task assignments 2. Drawing up work plan, putting together election task force 3. Convening meetings for government officials, officials dispatched from higher levels of government, and CPC leadership, people's representatives and governmental officials other officials from exchange programs, mobilization 4. Preparation by task force of materials for information dissemination and raising public awareness of the election
Vetting	May 2 - 31	1. Vetting by task force, conducting background check on each incumbent 2. Collecting information from the general public, announcing democratically selected nominees for members of the three bodies 3. Convening meeting of the secretariat, task force reporting their vetting work 4. Convening meetings for CPC leadership, village council and village cooperative, settling on preliminary list of nominees
Finalizing Nominees	June 3 – 20	1. Convening CPC committee meeting to discuss and to decide on nominee selection 2. Village CPC subcommittee elections 3. Voter registration, posting voter roll on June 18 4. Submitting recommendation for first round of candidates, posting list of nominees on June 20
Election of subcommittees	June 21- 24	1. Convening meetings for CPC leadership, village council and village cooperative to discuss and determine the number of people representing economic cooperative, designate the representatives; deliberating, discussing. and deciding on the list of candidates for village council and village cooperative; discussing and deciding on electoral mechanism 2. Announcing village council member candidates on June 23 3. Training election workers
Election	June 25–26	Task force supervising election; organizing election of village council members and village cooperative representatives
Review	After the election	1. Amending village ordinances, drawing up three-year plan for new term 2. Formulating settlement policies for former cadres 3. Conducting review 4. Holding orientation for newly elected officials

Source: "Village leadership election schedule" issued by W Township government, Zhejiang province

Agenda: Making sure all are on board with respect to both the substance and the procedure for organizational capacity building for primary-level government; village secretariat giving remarks on their assessment of the election; township task force presenting comments on election, putting forward requirements; drawing up future work plans.

Key points of resolution:

1. All officials replaced in the recent election were of sound caliber overall, and the main difficulties they faced include: stagnant growth of collectivist economy and persistent public safety issues (petty thievery, rampant gambling); recently replaced officials occasionally showed a lack of focus, and did not work as closely together as a team as possible.
2. Recently replaced officials are responsible for putting forward guidelines for identifying candidates and training newly elected officials.
3. All must stay focused, and work together as a team at all times.

From what we could tell, township government's role in these elections is limited to performing oversight, organizing and facilitating execution, and to certify (approve) the finalized list of nominees. But the nomination is primarily within the purview of the incumbents, who decide such matters through majoritarian rule. The influence of the township government is most evident in setting the qualifications, such as the age and academic degree requirements. While the possibility of a replacement decision made entirely unilaterally by a superior level of government cannot be ruled out, it is much more common for the village officials and the township leadership to come to an agreement about the final list of candidates through some kind of "negotiations". In other words, when it comes to personnel decisions, the township leadership would not ordinarily choose to make an end run around village officials. And the candidates are not chosen hastily shortly before the election is held. Instead, incumbents would usually begin to look for qualified individuals one or two years in advance. They may even resort to assigning promising individuals to unofficial positions so they may receive the necessary training that would prepare them for candidacy when the conditions are ripe. These chosen individuals become "reserve cadres". Dossier submitted by these village incumbents to personnel departments contains detailed records on their "training targets", including which body (CPC subcommittee, village council, cooperative, Communist Youth League or Women's Federation, and so forth) these targets are most suitable for.[54] Moreover, most of the would-be cadres are from cadre families. For example, members of the village council end up in the CPC subcommittee, members of the economic cooperative end up in the village council, the deputy militia platoon leader ends up in the CPC subcommittee, Communist Youth League subcommittee chair ends up in the village council, the treasurer ends up in the village council, the accountant ends up in the CPC subcommittee, the head of the village factory ends up in the village council, villager association chair ends up in the village council. Of the 35 reserve village officials, only eight had been farmers (not already holding an office), less than a quarter.[55]

[54] "List of Village-Level Reserve Cadres" for T Township of Zhejiang province, (June 1991). 139-142.

[55] Ibid.

It took the different parties years to build just the right kind of relationship needed for a personnel system like this to work. Under such a system, on one hand, the higher-level government is able to maintain its authority insofar as it is responsible for organizing, consultation and certifying final results, and on the other hand, continuity of the village's economic operations is preserved since no one knows who is best qualified to further the economic interest of the village except village officials. Such a personnel mechanism helps to perpetuate the blurring of the line between the public service and profit-seeking roles of those occupying these leadership positions, and ensure that the monopoly interests of village officials are minimally affected by personnel changes. It is, therefore, a system that is acceptable to both the township government and the village leadership. But this also helps us better understand why many primary-level officials are quite concerned about the "village elections" called for in *Village Council Organization Law (Trial)*.[56] They are worried that there would be "more pushback from the primary-level officials than from anywhere else".[57] "Some primary-level officials urge township governments not to implement it, out of fear it would make it more difficult to get things done, and that even fewer people would want to collect fees".[58] Judging from some of the input the Ministry of Civil Affairs received from primary-level officials as it was undertaking to amend the *Village Council Organization Law*, there are important differences of opinion on this matter.

Upon review, we can identify four positions:

I. Village councils [should be allowed to] maintain their autonomy.
II. Given the enormous strain village councils are under as a result of the central government's imposition of rigid targets, the law should allow them a certain measure of administrative functionality.
III. The village council should be turned into a local office of the township government.
IV. The village council and the village public affairs office should be allowed either to co-exist or otherwise to do so nominally, while sharing the same staff.[59]

At the core of these suggestions is an effort to make sure the village council's administrative mandate under the old system is preserved, so that village leadership incumbents can still have influence over who replaces them. What "election" would do, however, is to expose them to other sources of influence,

[56] This refers to the "Village Committee Organization Law (Trial) of the People's Republic of China."

[57] Transcript of the interviews with the county-level cadres who oversaw the election.

[58] Transcript of the August 1997 interviews with township cadres in Zhejiang province.

[59] Zhenyao Wang, Pusu Tang, *Research Report on the Legal System of Village Committees in China's Rural Areas* (Beijing: China Society Publishing House), 1994.

thereby undermining what monopolistic control and interests they have long enjoyed as a group. This is why many of these officials would like to see their administrative mandate left intact as a way of protecting such control and interests. Furthermore, elections may weaken village primary-level officials' power over personnel decisions, thereby threatening the cohesion of their collective interests. When personnel changes cannot be predicted, the personnel system cannot be counted on to perpetuate monopolistic power and control. All of these, therefore, could potentially disrupt how gains and losses are distributed among stakeholders.

2.7 Instability in the Structural Foundation

Now we return to the question raised earlier. The foregoing discussion about ways in which different roles primary-level officials play can clash, and the institutional roots of such tension, allows us to begin to appreciate why rural primary-level leadership has become increasingly caught up in social conflicts. On one hand, these officials have become increasingly detached from the public they are supposed to serve, which has compromised its effectiveness as agents of political representation. Not only does this have deleterious effects on social cohesion and order in rural areas, but it also leaves local governments disconnected from the central government in their development plans and objectives, thereby threatening the functional capacity of rural primary-level officials. On the other hand, the evolving and increasingly ambiguous role of primary-level officials, as both (enterprise) operators and public servants, and the blurring of the line between tax receipts and profits have not only undermined primary-level officials' political credibility but also pitted them against the rest of the community.

In the modern era, there have been repeated attempts to overhaul the primary-level political system, almost invariably aimed at correcting this particular form of alienation. However, thus far most have focused on establishing bureaucratic hierarchy and strengthening top-down control, which have failed time and again to produce the intended results. Boosting primary-level politicians' power of control could not address their functional handicap as political representatives, even if, that is, it might help them become more efficient at the margins. It cannot achieve social integration through effective representation or communication of what is in the best interest of the community. The very institutional configuration at the primary level and the cleavage between what it wants and what the community wants converge to thwart primary-level officials politically. All of these reform initiatives have assumed the perspective of the central government or its bureaucracy, and overlooked the ways in which strengthening and cementing the rights and claims of the society or community can be conducive to the establishment and maintenance of social order at the primary level by restoring the organic bond between the people and their leaders. In other words, these initiatives have fallen far short of institutional overhaul, which is what is needed if the severed ties between leadership and the people are to be reestablished. Instead, measures intended to further empower primary-level officials have helped to deepen the alienation. Evidently, the basic structure of the primary-level leadership is relatively unstable.

The root cause of this instability is the structure's inherent tendency to engender conflict and its inability to reconstitute society, to forge balance between leadership and the people, and between the public and authority. On the contrary, it reliably creates political cleavages, driving a wedge between the interests of the authority and those of the village residents. This effectively compels higher levels of government to choose between the two sides, and whichever side is favored, the other side stands to lose. Moreover, personnel, fiscal and financial, and ownership systems in rural areas all tend to help perpetuate this alienation, even generating new forms of fissure.

The existence of political power that serves the public presupposes interdependence between the authority and the people. Ideally, primary-level political power is dependent upon and capable of communicating or representing the interests of the majority of a rural community; the very survival of the political power should depend on how well it is able to advance these interests. Its objectives ought to be the aggregation of the will of the people it represents, such that they would be willing to pay taxes in exchange for (i.e., "buy") public services. By this standard, rural China has never seen, at the primary level, genuine "body politic *that serves the public*". Rural politicians in the imperial era did not meet this standard, nor did rural gentry from the Republican era, nor did primary-level leadership in the years since. All of them have been overwhelmingly reliant on superior political bodies as the source of the mandate to rule, and the will of the community they rule have had little or no influence on their authority or behavior. Even when it did not derive its power entirely from authorization by the central government, it has often managed a kind of "autonomy" that leaves it essentially isolated from other parts of the national political ecosystem, an isolation that effectively makes it possible for it to defy any attempt to implement a uniform rule of law across the whole country. Therefore, the kind of social integration rural primary-level political authority has traditionally been able to forge is very limited in scope, and the principles of allocation and appropriation it adheres to are also rather antiquated. In the modern era, primary-level officials' increasingly important role as economic operators has been very consequential, insofar as it thrusts them into a conflict zone. The modernization of rural primary-level politics remains a work in progress.

CHAPTER 3

Village Rule and Governance: The Role of Covenants and Conventions

Ideally, the central government can play one of two roles in the establishment and maintenance of rural social order. First, this can happen through the legislative process, i.e., the passage and promulgation of laws [by the central government] that would serve as the normative foundation for social order in rural communities. In this scenario, the proper role for rural primary-level political leadership is to enforce these laws, and these officials should not have the authority to make their own laws (except when specifically authorized to do so). Their primary task is to make sure national laws are adhered to and implemented at the local level. Alternatively, the central government can be instrumental in the establishment and maintenance of rural social order by functioning as an arbiter. In this role, the central government is not directly involved in management and regulation in the rural communities, but is instead on standby, ready to arbitrate when problems arise. In the latter case, the local authorities enjoy considerable "autonomy" (albeit not enshrined in any law). Moreover, the central government's rules and regulations have only as much *de facto* authority as the rural primary-level officials are willing to carry out the central government's arbitration decisions. Of course, arbitration decisions are made on a case-by-case basis, and do not lend themselves to generalization across a broad range of cases. Still, primary-level officials tend to follow something akin to the *stare decisis* principle, and treat like cases alike. This means that while many of the rules governing how rural primary-level authorities govern and

This paper was presented at the Seminar on Law in China's Rural Society held at the Department of Law, Peking University. I received many helpful comments, for which I am grateful. However, for the sake of authenticity, I have reprinted here the original paper so that published commentaries shall remain relevant. These appeared in *Peking University Law Review*, 2000, Vol. 2, No.1. http://www.shehui.pku.edu.cn/wap/sz/content.aspx?nodeid=1534

J. Zhang, *Primary-Level Government*,
https://doi.org/10.1007/978-981-96-6209-8_3

decide cases are not laws promulgated by the central government, they have for the most part not been explicitly prohibited. That is to say, they enjoy tacit consent from the state authority.

In rural China, the second scenario is by far the predominant one. In this situation, the critical importance of primary-level authorities consists not only in its having been given the mandate by the central government to govern at the primary level, but also in the relative "autonomy" it enjoys, an autonomy that at times comes close to being monopolistic in its purview. More specifically, "relative autonomy" implies that in addition to enforcing national laws selectively, within their jurisdiction, primary-level authorities often enjoy *de facto* legislative and judicial powers they have presumably earned through years of legislative and judicial practices. These powers do not necessarily represent the state as such, but are no less a source of substantive authority than the latter. When it comes to enforcing national laws, primary-level authorities have considerable latitude, and can decide at their discretion when to "invite" superior level of government to get involved in handling a local case, and when not to. And "monopoly" entails that the legislative and judicial powers primary-level officials have are neither easily replaced by comparable powers of the national government, nor easily abolished altogether, even though, that is, both are theoretically possible. For what is theoretically possible may nonetheless be practically unfeasible when the necessary mechanism for its realization is absent.

All of the above forms an integral part of the foundation of rural social institutions. Together with other systems such as collective land ownership, and collective taxation, these institutions are instrumental in maintaining the administrative dominance of primary-level political apparatus [in rural China]. Even though recent development of non-collectivist economy has had some political implications, the primary-level political autonomy just described is, I believe, mostly intact. In particular, one outstanding feature of these social institutions worth noting is the fact that the legitimacy of such collective village undertakings as politics (elections), assets (profits), and social rights (to welfare) is traditionally based on little more than what is decided among the villagers and for the village. These decisions are made relatively independently of a constitution that applies more broadly, meaning that it is the village itself, and not the state, i.e., the central government, that is ultimately responsible for safeguarding the rights of the villagers.

Even though the national constitution is, in theory, superior to all local ordinances, and should therefore be the legal basis of the basic rights of citizens (village residents), in practice, however, such universal principles are often purely academic. It is instead the village authority that, so far as the individuals themselves, pertinent organizations, and even higher levels of government are concerned, is responsible for defining these rights of the village residents. Consequently, at the rural primary level, no clear line separates defining rights and enforcing them. Instead of having different agencies in charge of each, primary-level authorities are responsible for both. Should any resident leave the jurisdiction of the village leadership, they would have effectively forfeited all the rights associated with being a member of the village.

This may in fact go some distance towards helping us understand how it is that, despite the lack of public and community support, primary-level leadership is nonetheless able to maintain their political mandate? Obviously, we would be unable to make sense of this resilience if we focused only on the instability of the rural political machinery. Of course, observers sympathetic to the authoritarian framework might try to argue that after all such a regime can simply be sustained through the forceful exercise of power. But that would be inadequate as an explanation for how rapid development of the market has apparently done little to hasten the disintegration of such rural primary-level political regime. The question we ought to be asking is how it is that an institution that does not represent the interest of the community can nonetheless stay intact like this? What are the social institutions that are helping to prop it up, and perpetuating its role as one on which the community is critically dependent. In this chapter, my goal is to show that it is the rural political regime that establishes village residents' status as members of the society, and that status is what allows these individual to enjoy "rights" that they can actually exercise, and it is also the basis for those relationships that individuals can enter into with social and public institutions that make them eligible for participation in the community economy, public assistance, share of public goods, public services and welfare. In contrast, even if and when the rights of individuals can find theoretical basis outside the rural political establishment, in the absence of a set of institutions that can ensure their realization, these rights are no more than abstract ideas.

I have drawn mostly from both written and unwritten "covenants" and "conventions" in rural China from the contemporary era, and I have also recorded my observations of the powers primary-level authorities have within their jurisdiction, and how they wield it. It is my view that these documents and records do in fact provide a more or less accurate account of the basic institutional set-up within the jurisdiction of rural primary-level political authorities. Even though many of these covenants and conventions are meant to be taken literally,[1] the contents are often dictated by higher governments, to serve as the legal basis for village governance, and they are at best somewhat haphazardly enforced in practice. Still, we by no means underestimate their value for understanding the rural political regime we have been observing. After all, these covenants and conventions have for the most part been drafted by rural officials themselves, and reflect long-standing beliefs among the population about what goals governance should aim to achieve, and contain fundamental and widely if also tacitly acknowledged principles for the establishment of individual rights.

[1] Huang, *Civil Justice in China*. Huang's analysis of differences between representation and practice in China's institutional culture is particularly useful.

The central question I am trying to address in this chapter is how rural social order can be maintained despite the relative instability of the primary-level political system. To answer a question like this requires an adequate understanding of some of the other factors related to primary-level governance, especially what instrumental role its institutional foundation plays in mitigating the effects of that structural instability. I will end the chapter with a preliminary discussion of the implications for the issue of how a country's national political apparatus is built (and the scope of its jurisdiction expanded).

3.1 "Membership" Status for Village Residents

Textual evidence indicates that the registration of "individual resident" in rural areas has a long history in China, going as far back as the end of Western Zhou, when this was done to ensure ample supply of military conscripts.[2] However, later development of the household registration system apparently had much more to do with taxation: in addition to providing a basis for implementing the draft, the system also became a way to control and deter tax evasion. Traditionally, calculations for taxes, tax cuts, and exemptions had been based on the number of laborers and the size of the land, which means that household registration has invariably been linked with the registration of properties and assets, and "land constitutes the most important item among properties and assets, and residence does not count at all".[3] This indicates that so far as tax calculations are concerned, "properties and assets" are primarily determined by the size of land owned by a household. This is why it naturally falls on the body that has information about land and people to be in charge of registration, and nobody is better suited to undertake this task than the primary-level political apparatus.

Registering both assets and householders does more than linking household registration with taxation, it is also how a definitive relationship between the rural population and a certain "public-serving" entity at the primary level is established, insofar as such an entity must be responsible for recording, verifying, and making changes to household information in rural areas. In fact, such an entity does more than these, it also has fiduciary responsibilities toward the individuals on their registrar. For the village residents, should their affiliation with that entity keeping track of them cease, while they are relieved of their tax duties, they also will have lost any functional ties with that entity. When nothing is amiss, this may not matter much if at all, but when situations arise where an individual needs help from public-serving organizations, the level of protection afforded them may be very uncertain, for nothing prevents the people working for or in these organizations from refusing to provide assistance by declaring that it is "none of our business". Moreover, since it is typically the

[2] *Discourse of Zhou, Vol. I. Discourses of the States.*

[3] Mingguang Chen, *Taxation and Corvée Labor in Ancient China*, (Beijing: Commercial Press International Co., Ltd., 1996), 28.

responsibility of rural government to provide such benefits as education, welfare, and old-age care, not being on their list of eligible beneficiaries amounts to forfeiting these benefits (or, as people today like to say, to relinquish one's "rights"). Therefore, the household registration system does more than simply keeping track of who lives where. More importantly, it provides the institutional basis on which rural residents can establish their identity as members of the community and the society. Rural government is the form that institutional basis takes.

This form of population management within each locale is still very much in effect to this day, which helps to ensure the important role primary-level government plays in anchoring rural residents' functional membership in their communities. While some have suggested that linking household registration with tax collection in this way constitutes evidence that "state-building" has reached into the countryside, the fact is that one would be hard pressed to find record of rural residents in household registration records kept by higher level governments. This is because not only is the rural government responsible for registering local residents with boots on the ground, it also falls on the rural government to carry out verification, changes, and certification. Population and household records kept by the national government are only used for statistical purposes, yet welfare benefits for the rural population are neither supplied nor distributed by the national government, and taxes collected from the rural population do not go into the coffers of the national government either. At the local level, any task that falls within the purview of the rural government can only be carried out on the basis of verified and certified household registration records. This means that it is the rural government that gives household registration the significance it carries for the rural population.

Even though household registration functions as the basis for determining how allowances, subsidies, and other benefits are distributed among the rural population, it is incumbent upon rural governments to submit updates with some regularity, which in effect puts them in a position of exercising control over a ranger of matters related to taxation. Keeping track of the rural population through registering households has become so critically important that in some places the local authority has even established oversight mechanism. In the 1930s, one landlord in Fengrun, Hebei province, once declared ownership of 5 *qing* of land, half of what he actually owned, in order to evade land taxes. The false declaration was later exposed and the landlord punished for it.[4] And it was the local authority, not national tax officials, that was responsible for both uncovering and meting out punishment for the fraud. This case is testament to the fact that involvement of rural authorities in registering rural population and verifying and certifying their membership in the community goes way back, even though different groups of people have undertaken this task throughout history.

[4] Hongyuan Wei, ed., *Survey and Studies of Rural Society in Eastern Hebei Province in 1930s and 1940s*, (Tianjin: Tianjin People's Publishing House, 1996), 109.

As population mobility continues to grow, the significance of household registration also changed. However, the related systems and institutional configuration have not. In rural China, how much labor people contribute to the community, receive in welfare benefits, and pay in taxes are all determined by the size of the land registered under each household,[5] because ultimately land is publicly owned. In some areas, some farmers would go work as laborers in the cities and contract their land out to others to farm, and require the contractors to meet all the pertinent tax obligations, either in cash or in kind. In so doing, however, these farmers do not relinquish the right to terminate the contract and to work on the land themselves, an option they can fall back on in case things do not work out in the cities. On the outskirt of cities, many people with rural household registration opt out of changing their registration status to urban residency, for the very reason that retaining their rural residency status allows them to continue to be eligible for all the welfare benefits and other entitlements associated with it. For farmers who are not farming, while they are no longer subject to land-related taxes and duties, they are not thereby stripped of membership in the community. By parity of reason, land contractors do not become members of the community just because they farm a piece of land as contractors. All of this goes to show the role this social institution plays in rural China: people may try very hard to get away with paying taxes, at all or at least by themselves, but nobody wants to forfeit the wide range of rights, benefits, and privileges related to contracting land, starting a business and keeping property on homestead that come with being a registered member of the community. And even though greater mobility has made control of the registered population more difficult, that this basic connection between membership and rights and privileges continues to hold is self-evident, whether people realize or are willing to openly acknowledge it or not. Obviously, this means that the rural primary-level political apparatus continues to occupy a central place in the lives of rural residents, insofar as through it alone can they establish their community membership status, without which they have no entitlement. The primary-level political apparatus is irreplaceable in its ability to create these critical organizational affiliations for individual rural residents that form the basis for entitlements.

This is the reason why, with very few exceptions, all village covenants and conventions in China are by design exclusionary. Insiders and outsiders are clearly distinguished from one another. Visitors, even those who stay only briefly, must register with the village authority. The importance of this kind of

[5] On December 29, 2005, at the 19th plenary session of the Tenth Meeting of the People's Congress, a decision was passed that the *People's Republic of China Provision on Agricultural Taxes* was abolished as of January 1st, 2006. On the same day, then President Jintao Hu signed Executive Order No. 46 abolishing all forms of agricultural taxes ("Issues related to agriculture, rural areas and farmers" are now matters of the highest priority for the Party and the Government", www.cnr.cn. March 5, 2013).

differential treatment consists in the different rights and obligations different statuses entail. Village residents must be counted in the jurisdiction of a specific administrative body if their entitlements, rights, and benefits are to be officially guaranteed. In rural China, household registration status falls into a number of different types, each entailing different rights and obligations. Some people, such as teachers, are registered under the county administration. These people are paid a salary, and are therefore neither entitled to land allocation, nor required to volunteer their labor for the community. In some places, teachers with rural household registration are neither allowed to participate in village affairs negotiations nor eligible to vote. Among those registered as exclusively agricultural households, some have to meet their food needs by purchasing from the market (and for whom the village is not responsible for meeting their food needs), while others depend on food allowance given to them by the village (and for whom the village is responsible for meeting their food needs). People in the former category are to be distinguished from other, regular rural households, in that they are often believed to have other sources of income, and for that reason to be ineligible for the same entitlements to village resources as do the others. According to some village covenants, people like that who actually live in the village must be required to contribute toward a "welfare" fund. All these different rights, obligations, and welfare entitlements associated with different statuses are ultimately based on one's household registration status, which cannot be easily altered. Whether this is explicitly written in any official documents, people tacitly agree that unless one is formally registered as a resident in village, that person is not entitled to any of the public benefits that only come with such status. Short of having such status, other conditions may have to be met for one to be eligible for the same. For women who marry people with urban household registration, their entitlement to village benefits is automatically revoked.

Any person who is formally registered as a resident in this village has the following rights: all the rights provided for in the constitution, the rights to participate in village activities, to submit suggestions and criticisms, to perform oversight of the cadres; the rights to vote and to stand in elections, and the right to public benefits.[6]

Generally speaking, village residents' status changes with changes in their marital status, and with their death of course. And those who move away are subject to additional obligations.

> Any person who is registered in either agricultural or non-agricultural status in the village and whose move out of the village has been approved must contribute

[6] Dongguan Village, "Village Self-governance Charter for Dongguan Village, Jingshan County, Hubei Province", in *Documents, Regulations and Rules of Village Committees in the People's Republic of China*, ed. Village, Primary-level Governance Office of the Ministry of Civil Affairs (Beijing: China Social Publishing House), 435.

toward a welfare fund. Those who are not native to the village are required to contribute 500 yuan per person, and the amount for those who are is 200 yuan per person. Those who live here but are registered as residents elsewhere pay half of what local residents do, as a prerequisite for getting registered locally. No refund will be given to those who change their place of registration from the village to elsewhere.[7]

Rules such as these are necessarily evocative of the body responsible for providing public services. In theory, it should be a local body representing the central government that "manages" the collective needs of the village residents. But in fact, except in emergency situations such as natural disasters, the central government has no such responsibility towards individual members of rural communities. While it does address requests brought before it by organizations or jurisdictions, matters related to private individuals or households are customarily the responsibility of primary-level political authority. So a registration log for village residents becomes a critical source of information for establishing eligibility for "public" services. Primary-level political authority has the power to set the eligibility requirements, e.g., residents who marry non-locals are struck from the registration roll and non-locals who marry local registered residents are themselves added to the registration roll, depending on resource availability and demands. But settlers from elsewhere must still have their qualifications verified before they are granted local registration. These qualification requirements are, however, subject to change. For example, to meet the village's need for technicians, village authority may try to attract qualified individuals by offering them local residency registration status and related welfare benefits. Eligibility criteria for local residency status are set by primary-level political authority. Even though in theory village officials must seek approval from township government before they can finalize any residency registration-related decision, in practice, since the materials to be reviewed by the township government are prepared by none other than the village officials, the approval process is mostly just a formality.

Since the primary-level political authority gets to decide who can be given local residency status, and how, some have turned this into a business opportunity. If you are a "village outsider", it means you are not entitled to benefits, such as homestead, registered village residents are entitled to. Your only option would be to buy land at exorbitant prices, pay more for land contracts, renting houses and electricity. Nor can you vote in elections or participate in village affairs consultations, or enjoy a range of other benefits enjoyed by registered village residents. However, none of this exempts these individuals from the same duties and obligations their registered counterparts have. This "unfair" treatment offers yet another illustration of the inherent limitations of both the membership status and the mechanism and the organization by which it is

[7] Buxi Village, "Village Self-governance Charter for Buxi Village, Zhangqiu County, Shandong province" in *Documents, Regulations and Rules*, 376.

established. Within the framework of such localized and differential identification status, and given the distinction between those who are "insiders" and those who are "outsiders", there is no mistaking of the different ways members of China's rural population are treated.

No. 61 The following individuals are eligible to settle in Taiping: Those who are married to registered Taiping residents, those whose biological parents are registered Taiping residents, those who have made extraordinary contributions to Taiping, those who invest in start-ups in Taiping, and all other individuals whose qualifications have been reviewed by the village council and approved by higher-level people's government.[8]

Distinguishing clearly [those who are and who are not registered village residents] entails either affirming or denying any individual "membership" status in the village. Only "those who are officially registered as village residents" enjoy the same rights.[9] Official members are only those with permanent residency status, and those who stay only temporarily do not have the same status. These differences in status are reflected in differences in their rights, safety, and security guarantee and welfare and benefits. For example, village residents enjoy priority and discounts for land contracts, homestead land allocation, and land allocation for growing food for household consumption, pay-outs from collective profit earnings, free education for their children, allowances and subsidies, the rights to vote and to run for public offices, to participate in village governance and other affairs, to submit comments and suggestions, to perform oversight, the right to take part in decision-making related to major issues in the village, and the rights to a range of public goods and services in the village. In contrast, "outsiders" are not entitled to these things, unless they have either "made extraordinary contributions to the village" or paid a fee of a specified amount, which is usually more than what is required of village residents. Still, even then, they are subject to a rigorous vetting process before they can be accepted as "members with full rights" as all the others.

No. 46 Anybody who is not a registered village residents must pay 35 yuan for each square meter of land they want to use for building a house;

No. 55 Removal of any individual from the roll of registered residents must be recorded diligently according to pertinent rules, and all de-registered individuals must pay all dues in full (fees, contributions and loan repayments);

No. 56 In principle registration of new residents will be discontinued, except in special cases, such as for individuals with special skills hired by

[8] Taiping Village, "Village Self-governance Charter for Taiping Village, Xiumei Town, Linli County, Hunan Province", in *Documents, Regulations and Rules*, 466.

[9] Bao'angang Village, "Village Self-governance Charter for Bao'angang Village, Guangdong Province", in *Documents, Regulations and Rules*, 471.

local enterprises, key senior leaders in organizations with special significance, family members of senior leaders. These cases are subject to a review process at the village council, and approval by the township authority. No one would be registered unless these conditions are met.

No. 57 Newly registered individuals are required to pay 500 yuan in registration fee. This fee may be reduced or waived for individuals that meet certain requirements. This decision is made collectively, and takes into consideration the contribution of the individual.

No. 58 With the exception of individuals who possess superlative abilities and skills or who have made extraordinary contributions to the village, those who were registered after 1981 are not eligible for job placement services, housing allocation, adjustment of household registration status from agricultural to non-agricultural, or free education for their children.[10]

The rationale behind these rules is not just to regulate resource allocation, but also to make sure that each member is clearly identified as falling under the jurisdiction of a specific organization or entity. Much like permanent registered residents of cities, members of the rural population do not exist as un-attached and un-affiliated individuals. Any such individual would have no access to any protection that could only be provided by an organization and on the basis of one's affiliation with it. The existence of members of the rural population, therefore, must be "confirmed and verified" by the primary-level political authority, and these organizations serve the function of establishing people's membership status, and certifying their rights associated with that membership. To change one's organizational affiliation, a village resident needs a "letter of introduction" issued by primary-level political authority that refers them to that other organization, otherwise no organization would either be willing or obligated to take on the associated responsibilities. This individual would then be at risk of falling outside the reach of any organization capable of offering them protection, and of being subjected to discriminatory treatment. Many a conflict involving primary-level authorities demonstrate this very fact.

In 1988, one Mr. Xue from Changcun village married Ms. Wang, who is from the neighboring village, and they had a son. Due to deterioration of the relationships between them, and also between Ms. Wang and her mother-in-law, the two divorced in 1991. Local customs call for both Ms. Wang and her son to be officially removed from the registration roll of Changcun village. Not only did she resist and stay on in Changcun, she remarried someone from outside, who then came to the village to live with her. Mr. Xue also remarried, and had another son. A land dispute subsequently broke out between the two families. Ms. Wang

[10] Dongguan Village, "Village Self-governance Charter for Dongguan Village, Jingshan County, Hubei Province", in *Documents, Regulations and Rules.*

> considers herself a registered resident of the village of Changcun still, and believed she should not have to return the land that had been allocated to her and her son. She sued, claiming it was unlawful for the village authority to demand her to return the land. The court sided with her, on the basis of household registration, and ruled that Ms. Wang and her son are still entitled to the 4.86 ***mu*** of land that she was allocated when she married [Mr. Xue]. Despite this, following local customs and village ordinances, the village council regards Ms. Wang as somebody who is about to move away from the village and who should have her residency status terminated, and decides on account of that to reclaim the land they had been allocated, to give it to Mr. Xue's new wife and their son instead.[11]

In this case, the village council was instrumental in establishing a person's status as a formally registered member of the village. We saw that not only is this mandate exercised at the primary level, just as importantly, once a determination has been made, it is not easily invalidated or trumped by any other law besides these customs and ordinances. Ordinarily, the approval process for establishing membership status takes place at the village level, with the full knowledge and approval of the community, and is as such completely legitimate. This also means that when the village and higher-level government legal bodies decide differently, the public sides with the former. As far as the village residents are concerned, only village membership officially recognized by the village authority in the form of formal registration gives one the right to partake in the village's collective benefits. But when the customs and village ordinances "do not recognize" an individual's residency status, then that provides justification for depriving the individual in question of their "legitimate rights" to occupy land. In the above case, even though the court has already issued its ruling, unless the village's own registration system corroborates it, odds are poor that the ruling would override local customs and village ordinances. So if the power to establish an individual's village membership ultimately rests with primary-level political authority, which follows its own rules instead of those followed by the courts, there is little reason to believe that the individual in question is being afforded protection under the law. Some drafters of rural covenants and village ordinances are aware of the possibility of conflict and make provision for it by stipulating that "when decisions made based on local rules are at variance with those called for by the law of the state, the latter trumps the former", in practice, since primary-level authority's interpretation of rural covenants and village ordinances is not subject to check by another party, no case would be referred to the courts unless it has been decided that no solution is possible using the local rules. In a village in Sichuan, where a similar dispute took place, the village council "vetoed" the court's ruling, and collectively ruled against allowing two women originally from other places,

[11] Chenghu Yang, *Elites in the Villages in the Institutional Network: Motivation and Power Limit of China's Rural Communities.* Master's Thesis, Peking University (1998). Changcun Village is located in Dali County, Shaanxi province.

once married to and then divorced from local men to keep either their resident status or their entitlement to land compensation. They justify their ruling by saying that this is meant to protect village's public property from covetous desires of greedy "outsiders".[12]

3.2 Eligibility Requirements for Enjoying One's Rights as Village Resident

Historically, where a person lives has always served as the criterion for determining if that person is an "insider" or "outsider" relative to a particular village. However, primary-level authority does have the power to deny any individual insider status. Therefore, in many rural covenants and village ordinances we see provisions about when the failure to perform certain duties would lead to one's being stripped of rights. Obviously, there is nothing necessary or inevitable about these rights as defined by the covenants and ordinances, and they are not in effect until and unless they are ratified by the primary-level authority.

> All those between the ages of 18 and 55 who are officially registered residents of this village must perform volunteer labor or be subject to a labor draft. People who are exempt from the requirement are: public school teachers, kindergarten staff, students, those who live in any one of the five household categories eligible for special public assistance, in very low-income households, people with disabilities, and wounded or disabled veterans. In principle this requirement must be fulfilled through the performance of labor. However, cash contribution may be accepted instead, at the rate of 5 yuan per unit of labor. Labor performed for projects that are not organized by the village cannot count towards the volunteer labor requirement.[13]

> Each registered village resident has the duty to (1) comply with village legislation, and abide by the rulings and decisions passed at resident conferences, village people's congress, and the village council; (2) complete tasks assigned by the village council in a timely fashion; (3) get along and be in solidarity with fellow village residents, treat the elderly with respect, and the young with care and compassion, protect the collective interest of the village, and resist and combat efforts to undermine it; (4) facilitate efforts to uphold high moral standards and promote ethically sound cultural practices.[14]

Failure to perform these duties would result in one's being stripped of their "rights":

[12] CCTV Report, (1997). "*Shehui Jingwei* (Society)," No. 65.

[13] Dongguan Village, "Village Self-governance Charter for Dongguan Village, Jingshan County, Hubei Province", in *Documents, Regulations and Rules*, 435.

[14] Buxi Village, "Village Self-governance Charter for Buxi Village, Zhangqiu County, Shandong Province", in *Documents, Regulations and Rules*, 375.

> No rights without duties and no duties without rights. Anybody who has not met their obligations towards the village of Taiping has not the rights and cannot enjoy the range of economic benefits to which registered residents are entitled... All village residents can share the village's collective benefits and participate in public activities, except those who have not fulfilled their obligations.[15]

Villages that include these requirements in their covenants and ordinances must also have the capacity to enforce them. This means that they must be able to provide the things that are specified in these rights declarations, lest there is nothing dependable the village residents can lean on. Meanwhile, village authorities must be able to mete out punishment, so that rule breakers understand the nature of what they have done, and what consequences they would face if they continued. The village's asset system plays a role in both these requirements. The assets of a village are mostly made up of fixed assets, asset management in rural areas now primarily consists of efforts by village officials to make sure assets stay fixed, are not traded (contracting does not count, as that amounts to land leasing), or are only allowed to circulate (through transaction) with their approval. This effectively prevents non-residents from competing for these assets and facilitates closed and collective management of the same, resulting in sharp reduction in economic trade, which is based on individual property right, and the economic opportunities trade could generate. This creates just the right condition for the village as a collective to act as an economic monopoly (with absolute command of economic opportunities). Indeed, the village authority is capable of meting out "punishments" for noncompliance with local customs and village ordinances precisely because of its monopoly position. It can easily put in place the conditions needed for village residents to discharge their duties, because these assets allow residents to create economic opportunities. Sometimes, to ensure that village residents would fulfill their obligations, the volunteer labor requirement is literally included in the rules governing the management of land contracts. For example, refusal to contribute volunteer labor or comply with labor draft might become an issue (in relation to one's rights) when one tries to contract land.

> A more sound management system for volunteer labor and labor draft is in order. The village council shall incorporate the requirements into the management system for land contracts, in order to make sure they are met.[16]

The mandate to stipulate not just the conditions for exercising one's rights as village residents but also the consequences of failing to meet those conditions is at least as binding as any other law, and often trumps them. And this is

[15] Buxi Village, "Village Self-governance Charter for Buxi Village, Zhangqiu County, Shandong Province", in *Documents, Regulations and Rules*, 464.

[16] Huojiacun Village, "Village Self-governance Charter for Huojiacun Village, Lishu Township, Lishu County, Jilin Province", in *Documents, Regulations and Rules*, 5.

a mandate that the village political authority grants itself. In the eyes of the officials themselves, local customs and village ordinances are not inferior to any external laws in terms of their legal standing, and may even surpass them. This very fact is endlessly reiterated in the covenants and ordinances themselves, lest residents should be unaware of it.

> Cases that are already handled by relevant government agencies and that also fall within the purview of local rules and ordinances may be subject to both sets of rules. [However], any violation of the law or breach of discipline that is local in scope, for which local rules and village ordinances are applicable, it would then be up to the village council to implement the rules and ordinances, and to issue interpretations of these rules.[17]

> When and if the village council deems necessary, it may file a request with a relevant government agency to have future actions taken against those in violation of village ordinance, including suspension of business license, shutting down business operations, removal from office, formal citation, among others. For those who are particularly recalcitrant, on top of whatever punishment meted out by the government's judicial departments and/or based on local rules and village ordinances, the village council may authorize additional measures such as: (1) having the perpetrator admonished publicly over the village's PA system; (2) fining the perpetrator no greater than 200 yuan; (3) having the perpetrator fired from their jobs at village enterprises and (4) having their entitlements to collective benefits temporarily or permanently revoked.[18]

While some more cautiously worded local rules and village ordinances do include provisions about the defendants' right to appeal the verdict, the vast majority simply state that "punishment shall be enforced as decided". Such punishments are essentially unofficial, and are only meted out to those perpetrators whose wrongdoings do not amount to criminal offence according to national laws. The provisions setting out the punishment can be very detailed and specific, or very brief, leaving the enforcer with broad latitude.

> For those who committed acts that resulted in limited damage to industrial and agricultural production, if the damage is not so severe as to break the law of the nation, the punishment will be a fine in the amount of 100–200 yuan, or of 500 yuan if the damage is serious; For those who acted in violation of pertinent rules that resulted in damage to public property or disruption to public order, the perpetrator must pay a fine of 10–30 yuan if the damage and disruption are fairly limited, or 50–100 yuan in more severe cases, in addition to compensation; tree thieves would be fined 5–10 yuan, and have their tools confiscated; those who caused harms to trees or forests are fined 5 yuan; those who commit tree decapi-

[17] YJZH Village, "Village Self-governance Charter for YJZH Village, Zhejiang Province", in *Documents, Regulations and Rules*, 12.

[18] WX Village, "Village Self-governance Charter for WX Village, Zhejiang Province", in *Documents, Regulations and Rules*, 9.

tation are subject to a fine of 5 yuan; fruit thieves are fined 5–10 yuan for each *jin* of fruits stolen, and the fine would be 5–10 yuan for fish thieves, 3–5 yuan for peanut thieves, and 2–3 yuan for each stick of sugar cane stolen; individuals who steal production implements, provided the amount stolen does not warrant prosecution under the national law, are required to return what they have stolen, and pay a fine of 20–50 yuan, but no more than 100 yuan, for each infraction; bamboo thieves are fined 50 yuan for each infraction, and have their tools confiscated; bird thieves are fined 5 yuan; gamblers are fined 30–60 yuan, in addition to being referred to the public safety bureau for further action. The exact amounts of these fines listed above may be subject to change upon consultation with the public.[19]

In more rigorously worded covenants and ordinances, some of the other benefits to which village residents are entitled, such as eligibility to compete for outstanding performance awards, to join the army and be hired by certain institutions are linked to how well or poorly they have done in relation to the requirements stipulated in these covenants and ordinances.

A personal file system should be set up in the village. A personal file should be opened for every resident when they turn 16. Detailed records of how this person has done, including both contributions and infractions, qua resident would be kept in the file, and the information would serve as the basis for excellence award competition, army recruitment and job placement.[20]

But it would be wrong to believe that rural covenants and village ordinances contain only penalty and do not offer protection. In fact, punishment and protection for insiders are connected to each other. Yet even when it comes to protection, a distinction is made between insiders and outsiders. In other words, whether something is right or wrong is one criterion, and a person's status relative to the village community is the other. For example, in the Shaanxi case in which a husband poured acid onto his wife's face, the village officials supported and helped the husband in bringing his wife, who had been a migrant laborer working away from their home village, and been unfaithful, back to the village so she could be punished. The underlying rationale was to adhere to the tradition of protecting the "standing and honor" of local male residents, and punishing those women who did not keep their chastity. Had it not been for the deliberate inaction on the part of the village community, this resident would not have been so emboldened as to dare to defy the law. That defacing through acid attack was allowed to go on in broad daylight, instead of being forbidden, owes largely to the tacit consent by rural covenants and village ordinances. Little wonder, then, that even though the perpetrator is already behind bars, he nonetheless continues to believe that somehow village officials can pull

[19] Baoan'gang Village, "Village Self-governance Charter for Baoan'gang Village, Guangdong Province", in *Documents, Regulations and Rules*, 476.

[20] Baoan'gang Village, "Village Self-governance Charter for Baoan'gang Village, Guangdong Province", in *Documents, Regulations and Rules*, 9.

strings and get him out of prison and send him back home.[21] Such confidence is based on his understanding of the way rural covenants and village ordinances work, and his own experience with the people and the organizations that enforce them. Regardless of legal merit of this kind of protection, what is significant is the fact that no other organization is capable of doing the same for member of rural communities, and this guarantee alone is sufficient to create a sense of dependency among the rural population.

In people's everyday lives, when conflicts arise between national laws and rural covenants and village ordinances, the latter would, if supported by most of the village residents, more often than not prevail. These rules and conventions are, after all, built into the very social fabrics that shape and structure the lives of these people, they provide the justification for both the protections they enjoy and the punishment they suffer. Many measures justified on the basis of these local rules are, as far as officially appointed cadres are concerned, legally dubious from the point of view of the nation's legal system. But to the local officials, the laws of the land just do not really count in these places, among people who are not familiar with, do not recognize, or even know about them.

For example, sometimes local rules call for stripping of people of their rights who run afoul of rules and regulations, as a form of "lawful" revenge. Such practice cannot be justified by the nation's laws, yet as far as rural conventions are concerned, the concept of inalienable rights does not function as a basic premise. The efficacy of social control trumps the principle of rights that is fundamental to law. No punishment is more severe, in these conventions and ordinances, than having an individual's name struck from the registration roll of a village (expulsion). As to whether an individual, regardless of their registration status relative to a village, has certain rights that are guaranteed simply because they are citizens, that is entirely outside the purview of these local rules and conventions. "Experiences with the enforcement of rural conventions and village ordinances show that, as far as China's rural population is concerned, if one was not a 'resident' of 'a particular village', it makes no sense to talk about the rights of citizens. In other words, to be a citizens (with the full set of rights all citizens are entitled to[22]), one must first be an accepted member of a rural community",[23] especially in the eyes of the primary-level officials.

> Village residents are entitled to the following rights and treatment: (1) priority in job placement in [local] enterprises; (2) allowances; (3) exemption from mandatory contribution and labor draft; (4) free education from pre-school to university; (5) house construction subsidy provided the house is in compliance with all building codes; (6) dividend calculated according to tenure at Taiping enterprise, title, and contribution.[24]

[21] Lu, *Great Country, Weak People.*

[22] Added by the author.

[23] Zhiyu Shi, *Chinese Culture and Chinese People* (Taiwan Fengyun Forum Publishing Co., Ltd.,1997), 195.

[24] Buxi Village, "Village Self-governance Charter for Buxi Village, Zhangqiu County, Shandong Province", in *Documents, Regulations and Rules*, 375.

If an individual is considered an "outsider", i.e., one who is not formally registered as residents in a village, that person's rights to any such benefits are not protected under these local rules and conventions. A fortiori, the penalty they would receive would also be more severe. That is to say, for the same infraction, harsher punishment is meted out to perpetrators who are "outsiders". For perpetrators who are registered members of the community, the punishment can often be reduced or commuted, but the odds of that happening to an "outsider" perpetrator is extraordinarily small.

One early evening in February of 1992, in the village of Zhongling in the mountainous region of southern Gansu province, hundreds of villagers surround the home and the adjacent yard of the Xia's. A few dozen among them hurled eight packets of home-made explosives, incendiary devices and rocks they had prepared into the yard. Members of the Xia family, along with two merchants visiting from other cities were crawling out of the building that had been destroyed in the explosion. But the gate had been blocked, and other village residents bludgeoned them to death with stones and sticks. The bodies were then tossed into the burning building to be destroyed. Over two dozen village residents were directly involved in the violent attack, which took place overnight. In addition, there were more than two hundred spectators, and more than seventy villagers who provided materials including explosives, kerosene, gasoline, among others. Tensions between the Xia's and other village residents and the cadres of Zhongling village went back many years. Before 1980, Xia had been a senior village official in Zhongling. After retirement he left and village and made a lot of money running a brick factory he contracted in another town. He hardly hung out with other villagers, and largely kept to himself. As a result, other villagers accused him of being selfish, niggardly person who thought of nobody else despite all the money he had made. He deserved, in their eyes, divine retribution. Everything came to a head when rumor began to spread that the Xia's had been selling the bile they extracted from the hogs in the village. That was what triggered the violent incident.[25]

The Xia's had not been covered by the village's protection system. Meanwhile, there was no ready alternatives to which they might turn (unless they illegally set up their own private underground organization). That proved to be a dangerous combination. It is quite clear that what the differential treatment for insiders and outsiders such as codified in rural conventions and village ordinances actually does is strengthening solidarity within the village. And the center of gravity, as it were, around which the cohesion took effect was the body that afforded protection, which in most cases was the primary-level political establishment. If a village resident needed a formal residency status and the rights and protection such status would afford, they must enter into the protective system through proper channels, such as by birth, immigration, marriage, and inheritance. Alternatively, one must engage in activities approved

[25] Xiaoyang Zhu, "Rural Society: Punishment and Transition," *China Social Sciences Quarterly*, Vol. 21(1997): 4.

by the organization, in order to qualify for its protection. It stands to reason that in rural China, in the absence of other protection systems, or other protection systems that are nearly as effective, entering into the *de facto* one must be something of utmost importance. Certifying people's residency status in a village makes the village political establishment a level-one organization with real power. It is responsible for protecting residents from harm, making sure they are safe and can enjoy welfare benefits, and for executing administrative powers related to registration, identification, and certification. The village political establishment coordinates village life, and ensures its orderliness, and it is only natural for those who are protected to acknowledge and to help preserve that order. The protection is not unconditional, and the condition is an individual's willingness to put the interests of the community before their own.

Demonstrably, members of rural communities have as many rights, and as much freedom to exercise those rights, as the village to which they belong would allow and support. The village is essentially an executive entity, with respect to both the granting and the implementation of rights. All villages do not have the same set of rights codified in their local rules and ordinances, or the same conditions for exercising these rights. But what they all have in common is an emphasis on the conditionality of these rights: one has them only insofar as one has not done anything in contravention of the rules. Obviously, village officials' legitimacy and authority are critically dependent on their ability to safeguard these rights. Currently, this is made possible largely by village officials' control of the tax system under the "collectivist" economy. Where such control is weak, whatever rights local officials provide their constituents are merely nominal and lack substance, and as a consequence, these officials' authority is compromised. For example, this was true of those Zhejiang villages that we studied, where the village was poor while the village residents rich. Where and when tax revenue is insufficient for funding public services, village enterprises must make up the shortfall. As to the performance of these enterprises, and whether they would answer to the demands of village officials, these are importantly a function of these enterprises' standing in the system.

One issue raised by the differential treatment of insiders and outsiders is the absence of a public sphere in rural China. The scope of rural conventions and village ordinances is coterminous with the village, what an individual does outside their own village either falls into an administrative no-man's-land, or is referred to the village to which they do belong for processing. Ordinarily, different conventions and ordinance apply to different constituents, and those who venture outside a jurisdiction and enter "public spaces" can expect to be claimed by no organization. Therefore, for all intents and purposes, rules that apply to "public spaces" that are beyond any particular jurisdiction are simply non-existent. That is to say, in those kinds of spaces members of rural communities are left exposed, i.e., without any meaningful protection. Even the most basic of rights would be merely nominal in the absence of an organization charged with guaranteeing their realization. In rural China, the rights of unaffiliated individuals are constantly at risk of being violated, precisely because, as noted earlier, being outside any institution's jurisdiction, those individuals are the responsibility of no organization, and easily become the target of discrimination. They are not, for the most part, treated equally as their counterparts who do enjoy institutional protection.

Take land contracts as an example. There are usually two prices, one for registered village residents, and another, the "market" price, for residents who have moved in from elsewhere but are not formally registered locally. Also, various fees unregistered residents are required to pay, such as contribution towards the housing provident fund and management fees may be substantially higher than what registered locals need to pay. Still more common is for outsiders and insiders to have uneven bargaining powers in negotiations. Any such contract, even after it has been agreed to and signed by both parties, may be declared null by the insider at any time. And if revenue generated by contracting fees turns out to be substantial, the village may go so far as to go back on the expiration date and the amount set for related charges, and threaten to take the land back unless the other party agreed to an increase to the contracting fee. This means that even after a contract has been signed and notarized, the right of the insiders to nullify or revoke a contract can be exercised, aided and abetted by primary-level officials and their mandate, at practically any time. In these cases primary-level officials are acting at the behest of village residents, whose interests alone they purport to represent. To safeguard these interests, they are determined to prevent outsiders from being able to lay claim to or otherwise benefit from local resources.

Huanguang Wang and his brother contracted 162 *mu* of land in Houshamiao county. According to the terms of the 18-year contract they signed, the contract fee would be 100 yuan no matter the price of grain. After the contract was notarized, the two brothers began working on the land, and took out some loans to grow crops. Their hard work began to pay off after several years, the loan had been repaid in full, one payment at a time, and the land yielded surplus grain. At this point the village council decided unilaterally to reject further payment of rent, took the land back and contracted it out instead to local farmers. The Wang brothers turned to the courts and the notarization authority for help in their efforts to sustain the 18-year term of the contract. However, even a court certification could do little to stop the village council from taking the land back.

Yongxing Guo and his wife contracted an orchard in the village of Luocun under a 14-year lease, at the rate of 2000 yuan per annum. In 1993, Luocun's village council "notified" the Guo's that the annual contracting fee had been increased to 4000 yuan. The Guo's protested. At the end of the autumn harvest season, just as the family was preparing seedlings and fertilizer for the next growing season, a group of villagers, led by village officials, barged into the orchard and cut down trees, openly in defiant of warnings from the forestry bureau that cutting trees down is punishable by a fine.[26]

[26] China National Radio, "Xinwen Zongheng" News, (December 20-23, 1996).

In both of these cases, outsiders' rights were trampled upon essentially because they fell into an institutional limbo that left them vulnerable to abuse and without recourse to any organizational protection. On one hand, they were not officially registered residents of the village whose land they had leased, so were not covered by the protection offered by the local rules and ordinances; yet on the other hand, they were beyond the reach of the political authority in the place where they were officially registered residents, and could therefore not be effectively supported by them either. So despite the fact that they had acted in accordance with the nation's laws and were eligible for legal support, within the jurisdiction of any particular village, the national's laws do not readily apply, not if local officials choose not to invoke them. Outside of all the clearly demarcated jurisdictions, if an individual finds themselves in a public, open space, they must, at the appropriate time, find an authority that would claim them as their charge, and such an authority are invariably primary-level (i.e., village) political officials. In theory, laws that apply in public and open spaces have a broader scope of application. But in point of practice, at the village level, there is simply no such thing as a public open space that is somehow above and beyond the jurisdiction under particular local rules and village ordinances. Neither can the laws universally applicable abolish local rules and ordinances, nor can the existence of the former invalidate or deactivate the latter. Local rules and ordinances have primacy, and within the village system, they trump rulings based on the nation's laws, thereby thwarting the laws' ability to offer protection to individual citizens. But for those individuals recognized by a particular authority as being a legitimate member of a rural community, the protection it provides is solid, thorough and decisive, so much so that it is not unusual for such protection to become a source of tension or conflict.

3.3 Coordinating the Individual-collective Relationship

The efficacy of local rules and village ordinances presupposes the existence of the village as a (collective) entity. While these rules and ordinances can be brought to bear in adjudicating conflicts among individuals, they are first and foremost designed to coordinate the relationship between individuals and the collective as a whole. Based on a review of the local rules and ordinances we were able to collect, it is clear they have provisions on such subjects as moral persuasion, deterrence, value inculcation, public properties, and public interests, encouraging mutual assistance in matters of economic production and daily living. While the distribution of benefits is mentioned, there are rarely any mentions of protection of either the property rights or any other privileges of individual members. As far as individuals are concerned, these local rules and ordinances are long on laying out the duties and obligations of community members and short or altogether silent on their rights. By contrast, as far as the village collective is concerned, the primary commitment of these local rules and ordinances is to the protection of its public property and public interests. This has led us to conclude that these local rules and ordinances are first and foremost designed to manage the relationship between individuals (the private) and the village collective (the public) to which they belong.

> Registered village residents must be committed to safeguarding the reputation of the village of Taiping. Saying or doing anything, no matter where or when, that might tarnish the reputation of the village of Taiping is forbidden.[27]
>
> Our mantra is: My personal fortune and reputation rise and fall with those of the village.[28]

Correspondingly, provisions in these local rules and ordinances that pertain to the protection of property apply mostly to public property: including funds, land, production tools, and fixed assets, and not much if at all to private property. Unlike provisions on other matters, where there is considerable variation in detail, on that of land, the language is remarkable consistent. All of them proclaim that land is collectively owned by the village as a whole. Land, therefore, offers a strikingly clear illustration of where these local rules and ordinances stand when it comes to the individual-collective relationship.

> Each household has the right to use the land, including contracted land, land allocated by the collective, and land on which one's ancestral home stands, but not ownership of that land. Any use organizations or individuals in the village make of any land must be in compliance or otherwise consistent with overall planning and adjustments... If land that has been contracted by households is needed for public works in the village, the village council should draft a plan, present it to the households concerned, and try to negotiate a deal, and the households concerned should be strongly supportive of the project. If the negotiation does not reach a deal, it is up to the village council to render a decision on the matter.[29]
>
> Under the contract responsibility system, the land is still collectively owned, and the collective has the right to make plans, and to change them... If and when the collective lays claim on land meant for growing food for household consumption, adjustments are made accordingly in the allocation of contracted land and surplus land of other households. When these adjustments are made, the trees lining the plots of land being reallocated are also reassigned. Planters shall receive no compensation for the trees that are dug up by others as a result of reallocation. These land adjustments take place every year before the fall.[30]

[27] Taiping Village, "Village Self-governance Charter for Taiping Village, Xiumei County, Linli County, Hunan Province", in *Documents, Regulations and Rules*, 464.

[28] Dongyao Village, "Village Self-governance Charter for Dongyao Village, Chaoyang District, Beijing", in *Documents, Regulations and Rules*, 269.

[29] XJZH Village, "Village Self-governance Charter for XJZH Village, Zhejiang Province", in *Documents, Regulations and Rules*, 4-5.

[30] Oujiacun Village, "Village Self-governance Charter for Oujiacun Village, Zhaoyuan Municipality, Shandong Province", in *Documents, Regulations and Rules*, 395.

"Collective" ownership of land is both absolute and relative. Relative to representatives of even higher authority, village officials' review and approval are preliminary, and not final. In theory the review and approval process for land use involves multiple levels of government. The primary-level officials would submit paperwork to superior government departments for final decision. Yet the very fact that the "collective" at different levels of government is involved in this process, loopholes and blind spots emerge. The different levels of government would spar, but in the end it turns out who is in charge of what is poorly defined for any level.[31] This ambiguity has in fact made it a lot easier for primary-level officials to execute the management of rural land. The rapid growth in land trade in rural China has only been possible because most of the trading decisions are made at the primary level, and other nominal "owners" have had very limited if any role at all in that process. The co-existence of the central government's attempts to curb land transactions and the active involvement of primary-level officials in trading rural land provides ample evidence for the critical role the latter play in these transactions. Besides, it is stipulated in rural conventions and village ordinances, albeit in somewhat ambiguous language, that land is collectively owned. In land transaction and contract deals, key decisions are usually made by primary-level officials. The original user of the land up for contract may try and even succeed in securing for themselves a cut in the land requisition fee or some other form of compensation, thereby checking the extent to which economic returns from land deals are concentrated in the hand of the "collective". But villagers are not otherwise involved in decision-making in relation to land deals, or how benefits are to be distributed. In Zhejiang province, most land-related petitions filed by villagers are complaints about the price and the way the yield is distributed. Very few petitioners take issue with the power and authority primary-level officials have in relation to these deals. In fact, some people in rural areas want the land they have contracted to be requisitioned or transferred to others: "nobody actually owns the land, but whatever money one gets belongs to oneself, not to mention having one's grain contribution obligations waived".[32] All of this constitutes incentives for primary-level officials to get involved in land deals. In fact, in point of practice, *de facto* endorsement from most people of primary-level authority's role in land management means the legitimacy of that involvement is simply taken for granted.

Even though this is not usually made explicit in the rules and ordinances, we can glean from long-standing practice a number of areas covered by the mandate of primary-level authority: approving land sales, and acting in its capacity as legal person to sign contracts; making changes to existing land allocation according to demographic and other changes in contractual relationships; making distributive decisions regarding economic returns from the contract, sale,

[31] Roy Prosterman, "Some Proposals on China's Rural Land System Reform," [in Chinese], *China Reform*, August 1995 (with Hanstad and Li).

[32] Transcript of the summer 1997 interview with the residents of YJZH village, Zhejiang province.

and leasing of land; and making decisions about surplus from these returns. This makes it almost inevitable that the "collective" enjoys much greater earnings than any other entity or individual in rural China. And there are very few checks built into the fiscal and monetary system on this power primary-level officials have to made this distributive decisions. In this sense, there are striking similarities between how primary-level authority manages the collectively owned land and how, in the old days, the senior members of a lineage managed the land owned by the clan on behalf of all its members. Furthermore, if the economic returns are invested into land management, then primary-level authority would also be functionally akin to the landlord group in the old days. Within a group, each member still has the right to decide how economic returns generated by the land would be distributed. While the amount of those returns may be greater than before, village officials can no longer keep it all to themselves.

The most conspicuous manifestation of the kind of power the collective has with respect to land is the frequent reallocation. As for the individual, their power is limited to the implementation of the egalitarian principle. Almost all of the village officials we interviewed told us that the egalitarian principle is what drives all the land reallocation decisions. Except those cases where somebody is allowed to keep returns from a privately negotiated contract, every time land reallocation is scheduled is when the need arises to mitigate allocation inequality caused by demographic shifts and employment status changes. This is testament to the widespread acknowledgment among the rural population that land, as a basic need and a public good, must be equally distributed. This principle is behind the frequent land reallocation in some places.

Q: How often does land reallocation take place?
A: About every five years.
Q: When do you decide to reallocate land?
A: When villagers request it. People think they see inequality, and when a large enough number of people complain, we reallocate.

Even though in the nation's Land Law it is also stipulated that land is public property, I have noticed that the notion of "collective ownership" such as is used in rural conventions and village ordinances does not mean quite the same thing. For registered village residents, it signifies the need to make payment to "the collective" for the use of land.

> Any contractor or business operator engaged in economic production or natural resource exploration is required to pay a fee to the collective for the use of any collectively owned production materials and facilities, including land, hills and forests, uncultivated hills, surface water, mines, agricultural machinery, factory plants and equipment, transportation vehicles and storage facilities.[33]

[33] Changgang Village, "Village Self-governance Charter for Changgang Village, Yanmenkou County, Jingshan County, Hubei Province", in *Documents, Regulations and Rules*, 425.

In the minds of registered villager residents, what "collective ownership" means from the outside is that they are all entitled to sharing the benefits. And as far as contracts are concerned, "collective" ownership comes down to the equal right to make use of and to benefit from the use of resources. If extending the term of a contract contravenes the egalitarian principle, village residents would usually let them dismay known. The right to use and the right to own, at the primary level, are not clearly separated from each other, since returns from public land are usually fairly evenly distributed, something that is typically built into a community's *modus operandi*. In southern China, land intended for growing food for household consumption is tax-exempt, so is in high demand. But since land intended for growing commercial crops is often subject to disproportional tax rates, people are always eager to offload them, in exchange for the right to engage in nonfarm activities. For example, in return for putting one's land up for contract one can obtain a place in labor recruitment quota or cash payment, so different opportunity sets are available to those without land than to those with land. By contrast, farmers in northern China are much more strongly dependent on their land for survival, so to them egalitarian distribution is of enormous importance. Long-term contracts make it difficult to ensure equitable distribution of increases in marginal return on investment in the land, so even though they provide protection for the rights of the contractors, villagers who believe they ought to be able to share those benefits would demand land reallocation. Therein lies the crux of *de facto* control of land by primary-level officials.

> All the land in this village, including land occupied by ancestral houses, land for growing crops, and forests are collectively owned by all the village residents. The village council is, with consent from all villagers, in charge of its management. Land contractors and other lawful users of land enjoy only the right to use, but not ownership of the land. Within the term of a land contract, provided concerned village residents operate in accordance with the terms of the contract, and do not file special request for reallocation, no change shall be made. But where public opinion calls for redress, based on the principle of majority rule, and without changes to the fundamentals to the contract system, just enough and no more adjustment shall be made to meet the demand for redress.[34]

> Land intended for contingency use shall from now on be allocated every three years, adjustments must be made after each change in somebody's registration status, including to land intended for contingency use. No more than 30 percent of all land should be reserved for contingency use, and if it exceeds that proportion the production team must correct it. Land occupied by ancestral houses and land intended for growing food for household consumption is to be reallocated every three years.[35]

[34] Huojiadian Village, "Village Self-governance Charter for Huojiadian Village, Lishu County, Lishu County, Jilin Province", in *Documents, Regulations and Rules*, 3.

[35] Minutes from the village council meeting of a certain village in Zhejiang province.

The reason unequal allocation of land tends to generate pressure associated with "discontent" has to do with returns. But it is also importantly attributable to an indirect tax at a flat rate for all. In rural areas, the various taxes and contributions farmers are liable for are not paid directly to the government's tax departments. Instead it is the primary-level authority that acts as an intermediate "tax collector". The formulas they use to calculate how much any household owes in taxes and contributions have stayed the same for years. It is based on two things: household size and the amount of land a household has. The allocation of land entails the approximation of equal distribution of tax burden, which in turn is based on the presumption that each farmer invests the same amount into the collective's land, and therefore is entitled to the same return.

> Land tax would be collected at the rates of 14 yuan, 15 *jin* of wheat and 20 *jin* of corn per *mu*. Each household would be taxed according to the amount of land registered under their name.[36]

Most rural conventions and village ordinances do not specify the amounts residents must pay in taxes, which are determined each year at the senior official meeting. Meeting minutes show that the amounts vary from year to year, mostly in the form of moderate increase. Cuts and exemptions are given to the elderly, those unable to work and those with disabilities or illnesses. But in the main the calculations are based on household size, the number of able-bodied, the amount of land registered under each household, and the egalitarian principle.

> Calculations based on the size of the paddy field: for each *mu* the amount of contribution is 5 yuan, for monocrop mulberry fields the amount is double that; calculation based on the number of able-bodied laborer: the contribution amount is 16 yuan per laborer; criterion for able-bodied laborer: aged 18–55 [for male] (18–50 for female) as recorded in household registration (in accordance with rural conventions and village ordinance).[37]

> Hog contribution requirements: 40 percent based on household size, 60 percent on area of paddy field registered under household; paddy field, lighting charge calculation: 10 yuan per *mu* of paddy field, lighting charge is 20 percent increase from the year before; housing provident fund contribution is 3 yuan per *mu* of land, and 4 yuan per able-bodied laborer aged 18–55 (decided at the village official meeting).[38]

> The amounts of mandatory contributions are in principle a function of the size of a household's contracted land, household size and number of able-bodied laborers in a household. Such contributions go toward housing provident fund, public

[36] Changgang Village, "Village Self-governance Charter for Changgang Village, Yanmenkou County, Jingshan County, Hubei Province", in *Documents, Regulations and Rules*, 425.

[37] File No. 94-28 from the village archive for one village in Zhejiang province.

[38] Minutes of a village cadre meeting in one village in Zhejiang province.

welfare fund and management fees. Contribution toward housing provident fund is calculated based on contracted land area, at the rates of 10–15 yuan per *mu* of paddy field and 20–30 yuan for monocrop mulberry field; contribution toward public welfare fund is calculated based on household size, at the rate of 10 yuan per individuals with a rural registration status; contribution toward management fee is calculated based on the number of able-bodied laborers in a household, at the rate of 30 yuan per fully able-bodied rural laborer. Contribution towards rural education fund is based on the number of fully able-bodied laborers in a household (aged 0–55 for male and 0–50 for female), at the rate of 20 yuan per person. Contribution towards military draft fee is based on the rural population, at the rate of 7 yuan per person (as per county government's guideline).[39]

To ensure these taxes, contributions and fees are properly collected, they are, by stipulation, classified as public property in many rural conventions and village ordinances. Special emphasis would be placed on such status.

Farmers' contribution liabilities refer to all other fees they must pay *in addition to* regular taxes, in-kind contribution per central government requirement, contribution toward village coffers and county coffers. Their contribution toward village coffers goes toward housing provident fund, public welfare fund and management fees.[40]

"Other" fees is a very broad term, and its invocation means that the collection of just about any charges and fees village or county officials wish to impose would be mandated by the rural convention and village ordinances. Exactly what these charges and fees are for is not usually explicitly specified, and is subject to change at any time, without discussion or consultation. This in effective gives primary-level officials a great deal of latitude and discretionary authority in deciding what to do, at least within their own jurisdiction. Economists have noticed how inefficient and costly such historical legacy of a management system is, and that its management budget is not subject to the control of government at higher levels. But at the primary level, people are not nearly as concerned about management costs as they are with other things besides efficiency, such as the politics of resource control. Principles of egalitarian (re)distribution of land and tax burdens have *de facto* strengthened primary-level official's mandate, insofar as implementation of these principles constantly calls for the active involvement of an organizational authority capable of issuing policy guidance. While the process of formulating this policy guidance does have drawbacks, including its prohibitively high costs, overly simplistic management approach, and tendency to generate inequitable outcome, it is able to ensure that every rural person has land to farm on.

[39] "Advice on Making Sure the Proper Execution of All Work Related to Collecting Village Reserve and Township Endowment", issued by Haiyan County of Zhejiang Province", 2–3.

[40] Changgang Village, "Village Self-governance Charter for Changgang Village, Yanmenkou County, Jingshan County, Hubei Province", in *Documents, Regulations and Rules*, 425.

Primary-level officials' mandate to and capacity for managing collective property are therefore established in the minds of the rural population. This is why in most rural conventions and village ordinances collective property and private property could not be treated more differently.

> Animals raised must be closely watched, and grazing in collectively owned orchards or on collectively owned wheat fields is forbidden. For each tree damaged or destroyed the perpetrator is fined 50–100 yuan. In addition, five trees must be planted in replacement, and survival of the seedlings must be ensured. Grazing on wheat field is subject to a fine of 20 yuan per grazing animal, in addition to compensation for associated economic losses.[41]

However, the same rural conventions and village ordinances would apply very different principles to treat damages to private property.

> The legal aid office's responsibilities include providing arbitration in cases of conflicts among private individuals arising from either work-related or non-work-related activities. The primary objective is de-escalation, and helping to make sure peace and social order are maintained.[42]

Some rural conventions and village ordinances do purport to give equal weights to collective and private properties, evincing a willingness to afford equal protection to both. But there is little doubt that collective assets would still enjoy priority.

> [Village residents ought to], of their own volition, maintain public order and safety, avoid doing anything to undermine public order, or to obstruct professional activities of civil servants; stealing, blackmailing, mobbing and grabbing state-owned, collectively-owned or privately-owned assets are strictly forbidden; care must be exercised in handling public property, no one should do anything that might cause damage to water conservation, transportation, electric power supply and communications facilities; logging in forests owned by the state or the collective is prohibited, digging up dirt on roadside near crop fields is prohibited, causing destruction to crops, vegetables, fruits and other agricultural products is prohibited, farmed animals must be prevented from grazing on young plants, contaminating water by putting poison in ponds is prohibited; unlawfully imposing constraints on other people's personal liberty or unlawfully trespassing on other people's residence is prohibited; one must not keep, destroy or open other people's private correspondence.[43]

[41] Ximafang Village, "Village Self-governance Charter for Ximafang Village, Yangfang Township, Changping District, Beijing Municipality ", in *Documents, Regulations and Rules*, 263.

[42] Ximafang Village, "Village Self-governance Charter for Ximafang Village, Yangfang Township, Changping District, Beijing Municipality", in *Documents, Regulations and Rules*, 263.

[43] Xitun Village, "Village Self-governance Charter for Xitun Village, Zhuoli County, Linyi County, Shanxi Province", in *Documents, Regulations and Rules*, 281.

Rural conventions' and village ordinances' commitment to protecting the collective is also clearly seen in the priority they accord the collective over the private whenever conflicts arise between the two. When the collective has decided to requisition something or to take back some asset, the individual involved is usually at a decisive bargaining disadvantage.

> No compensation shall be provided to those affected by land reallocation within the area covered by the master plan, and if the reallocation involves land that are functionally comparable. In cases where newly allocated land is substantially different from the previous plot with respect to productivity and crop variety, the affected household is entitled to compensation in amounts no greater than 1000 yuan per *mu* of dry field and no greater than 500 yuan per *mu* of paddy field. For those who obstruct or interfere with efforts by the collective to execute residential housing building plans, the following actions might be taken:
>
> 1. Since land is collectively-owned, the village council has the authority to reclaim the land and redistribute contracting or use rights;
> 2. If the individual is employed by a county, county or village enterprise, they are to be terminated from their job;
> 3. Building report request shall be denied;
> 4. Certification documents shall not be furnished;
> 5. The individual will not be entitled to old-age pension.[44]

Since buildings are not classified as collective property, conflicts involving them are usually resolved without resorting to these harsh measures. More often they are adjudicated by means of written "agreements" reached through negotiations.

> Agreement
>
> Through negotiations, the Jin family and the Zhu family have agreed to the following:
>
> The Jin family had built entirely on their own in 1995 the asphalt road they would use, prior to commencement of construction they ran the plan by the Zhu family, who indicated that they would not be using the road for either entering or leaving. During the construction, the Jin family noted that the dirt road to be paved over had been only 50 centimeters wide, so with a Shen family in the same village as witness, the Jin family asked to trade fuelwood with another Jin family for 70-centimeter width of land. At the end of 1996, the Zhu family asked to be allowed to use this private road for entering and leaving, and agreed to have a sidewalk opposite the Jin residence relocated to land registered under the Zhu family, and to leave room for a 50-centimenter wide road when building a wall around their residence.
>
> Signed by: Zhu, Jin
> Arbitrated by: Shen, Gu
> 1997

[44] "Provisional Decision Regarding Village Development Master Plan" (Textual archive), anonymous village, Tong county, Zhejiang province, 60.

This kind of interpersonal agreement is quite common in rural areas. It indicates, we believe, that different principles are applied to address conflicts among individuals and those between the individual and the collective. While negotiation and discussion are used for the former, punishment is used for the latter. Even though this does show that in rural conventions and village ordinances protection of collective assets takes precedence, it does not necessarily mean that the kind of protection collective assets is afforded is more effective than what is given personal assets. The importance rural conventions and village ordinances attach to collective assets is an indication of two things. First, it reflects the fact these documents, insofar as they are created by primary-level officials, are functionally akin to legal codes representing the authority to rule a collective; second, it is a reflection of a particular set of facts in relation to collective assets: (1) nobody is held accountable for what happens to them; (2) people generally expect public property to be universally shared; (3) the large quantity of unowned assets; and (4) the neglect they are often subjected to. Of course, what is even more important is the fact that, while rural conventions and village ordinances try to protect collective assets from destructive actions of individuals, they are toothless for protecting these assets from the same actions by primary-level officials, and wasteful use is widespread.

Furthermore, rural conventions and village ordinances are not the only "agreement" between the collective and individuals. When money is involved, it is not uncommon for the collective to act on behalf of individuals in deciding what to do with their assets, e.g., by selling them to other individuals, and in signing the agreement.

Housing Transfer Agreement

Party A: Village Council
Party B: Village Resident surnamed Zhang from group 11

Ms. Yao, a recipient of Five Subsistence Allowances, was admitted to the county's assisted living facility at the end of 1995 upon approval by the village council. Ms. Yao's residence, assets and land have since been repossessed by the village and become collective property. Based on a review of the conditions of the house, the village authority has decided that the three rooms Ms. Yao lived in (including use rights to the land on which the house sits and the surrounding trees) would be transferred to Party B's name. A flat transfer fee of 800 yuan is to be paid in full to Party A. This agreement is effective upon being signed by both parties.

Two copies of this agreement have been furnished, each party retains one copy for their record.

Seal of Party A
Signature of Party B
April 1, 1996

And when a collectively owned enterprise needs land that has been leased to individuals, the village can sign a lease [with that individual] to use that land. But in regard to the amount at which the contracting fee is set, the expiration date, or the other terms contained therein, the agreement obviously favors Party A.

Land Lease Agreement

Party A: Village Council
Party B: Village resident surnamed Wang

In order to meet the development needs of village enterprises, Party A intends to lease land from Party B, under the following terms of agreement.

1. The land to be leased is the mono-cropping mulberry field to the east of the Education Building, the area to be determined through on-side measurement.
2. The term of the lease is temporarily set at 10 years. Upon expiration of the lease the two parties shall negotiate the terms of the renewal. Until then the fee shall remain unchanged regardless of fluctuations in the price of agricultural and derivative products.
3. The fee will be 2000 yuan per *mu* per year, which includes compensation for forfeited crop yield.
4. The area of land leased is one *fen* and five *li*.
5. [Party A is to] make a one-time payment in the amount of 3000 yuan to Party B.
6. Party B shall have their agricultural tax liability associated with the leased land waived. Central-government imposed contribution requirement and village-imposed contribution requirement will be paid by the actual user of the leased land.
7. Three copies of this agreement have been furnished, the village enterprise, Party A, and Party B will each keep one.

Seal of Party A
Signature of Party B
April 9, 1995

We can see here that provisions in rural conventions and village ordinances, written or otherwise, tend to have much more to say about matters related to people's private lives than those of the country's formal legal codes. These conventions and ordinances are expected to serve as an instrument for maintaining public order in rural areas. As a matter of principle, these documents place the interests of the collective ahead of those of individuals. Notably, not only does this principle apparently enjoy universal tacit consent, nor has it been cited for incommensurability with the nation's formal legal codes, which only apply to administrative units above the county. Even though most of these conventions and ordinances are not couched in terms of "rights", the use of terms such as "prohibited" and "allowed" and the severity of the punishments meted out to perpetrators leave little doubt that essentially what they are doing is allocating "rights" among different parties. It is just that since these documents are drafted and passed (unilaterally) by village officials, they would end up with a favorable share of rights as a matter of course. Rural conventions and village ordinances are mostly used for addressing internal affairs. When the interests of village residents are at risk of being hurt by actions of outsiders, these conventions and ordinances can offer protection to individuals qua "members of the collective". Most village residents endorse this principle. As we saw earlier, when outsider contractors have reaped financial gains that are too substantial for village residents to feel comfortable about, the village council would often unilaterally decide to terminate the contract in order to safeguard the interests of the village residents.

The differences between rural conventions and village ordinances on one hand and a nation's formal legal codes on the other are quite clear. The protection offered by the former to "public" assets and undertakings is rather limited in scope, since what is "public" is largely coterminous with the village community. Rural conventions and village ordinances do not concern themselves with the protection of whatever that is public but exists outside the village community. When they are used to adjudicate conflicts involving these kinds of public assets, these local rules would usually call for applying different principles. Rural conventions and village ordinances are not designed to coordinate the relationship between public and private interests that obtain beyond the confines of the village, and they are meant to be useful only for purpose of regulating the collective-individual relationship within a self-standing rural community, specifically by declaring the "overarching objective of safeguarding the collective interests of the village, and overall orderliness".[45] The underlying philosophy may well be a long-held belief in traditional Chinese society, according to which mutual dependency defines the basic mode of existence, and so the individual should rely on the collective for its own survival.[46] This philosophy entails that rural residents' primary "duty" is to obey and comply with the rules of the collective, "to safeguard the collective interests, and to fight against anything that might harm the collective interests",[47] even though it is rarely made clear in these documents in what exactly "collective interests" consists. Even though, by design, these documents, once drafted, must be approved by the village delegates, since most people who serve as "delegates" are in fact village officials, who are also the people who worked together to draft these documents, it is not hard to see that not only is it not quite accurate to regard these

[45] Qicai Gao, *On China's Customary Law* (Changsha: Hunan Publishing House, 1995), 76.

[46] Francis L. K. Hsu, *Americans and Chinese: Passage to Differences*, (Honolulu, University of Hawaii Press, 1981).

[47] Gao, *On China's Customary Law*, 10.

documents as "covenants" involving the people, in fact, their primary raison d'etre appears to be the protection of public safety and security. Insofar as these documents are sometimes called "covenants among the people", that is no more than an indication of the fact that both their creation and their implementation take place at the very primary level of Chinese society.

3.4 The Nature of Rural Convention and Village Ordinances

A careful examination reveals some broad commonalities among all rural conventions and village ordinances.

Exceptionalism

Exceptionalism is the idea that people belonging to an in-group are somehow exceptional, and are to be treated by a different set of standards from those that apply to people excluded from this group. The scope of every rural convention or village ordinance is confined to a relatively independent and self-standing rural community. By "dependent" is not meant complete insulation from one another, but is meant instead to underscore the fact that they are not under the jurisdiction of some centralized authority, but are ruled under a decentralized system of power. There are both similarities and dissimilarities among these documents, but regardless of the specific provisions they contain, the bodies that promulgate them are relatively independent of one another, even if, that is, these bodies shared the same name or report to the same superior authority. Around the world, we have seen different substantiations of this community prototype, in the forms of family clans, lineages and settlements, and in all of them only their members are meant to be "served by" the conventions and ordinances they have adopted, whose applicability is confined to these communities proper, beyond which either their effect is significantly curtailed or they are not recognized all together. Contemporary rural conventions and village ordinances have strayed little from tradition in this respect, granting the right to share common resources, such as the rights to contract land, to favorable prices, to recruit workers, to work, and to have a say in matters involving salary and bonus, only to insiders, while adhering to stringent criteria for who can be considered an insider. It is very common for these documents to adhere to the principle of differential treatment for insiders and outsiders, especially in relation to their ability to lease, make use of and profit from village resources. Should village residents object to a particular arrangement, even notarized contracts or the nation's laws could do little to protect the rights and interests of the outsiders. Whether an individual is an insider or outsider relative to a particular community matters not only to what rights they do or do not have, but also to (especially when conflicts arise) whether they are eligible for any protection at all offered by these locally applicable rules. This has the effect of breeding dependency on the collective among the individuals, and of perpetuating the idea that the safety and security of the individual are inextricably linked with the fate of the rural community to which one belong, and not of the country as a whole.

The Primacy of Collectivism and Absolutism

The primacy of collectivism and absolutism refers to the presumption that the interests of an internally cohesive collective must always serve as the ultimate criterion in any practical deliberations. A good number of these rural rules requires strict conformity to an absolutist set of moral norms, and mete out a range of punishments to violators, including moral condemnation, rebuke broadcast through the public announcement system, and denial of opportunities and/or entitlements. These rural conventions and village ordinances cement the idea that certain conditions must be satisfied if one is to have and maintain good standing as a member of a rural community, i.e., they must be ideologically committed to that community and be willing to abide by the shared values. There is a certain symbiotic relationship between these rural conventions and village ordinances on one hand and village officials on the other, such that even while the latter are effectively given the mandate to draft, implement, change, and interpret these local legislation, they are themselves hardly ever bound by them.

Ambiguity and Non-Formalism

Ambiguity and informality are features of codes of conduct that either predate or exist in parallel to formal laws, that allow a considerable degree of latitude in their implementation, depending on who is involved, what is at stake and the timing. In the majority of cases, the member on the village council in charge of politics and law (who usually also serves as the arbitor) must be present when an agreement is reached, in order to ensure the agreement's credibility. However, the agreement does not have to be consistent with precedence, or be rule-based. How similar cases in the past had been handled can have little if any irrelevance to how the current one would be, and there may or may not be a discussion of what principle should apply. Consequently, since the stakeholders all believe and want different things, the solution can be very different in different cases. Not once did I see the words "according to rural conventions and village ordinances" in all the rural conflict resolution agreements that I have reviewed. Quite obviously, in these interpersonal disputes, it is up to the two sides to reach an agreement about how the conflict is to be resolved.[48] This

[48] Zhiping Liang called this "a stable state in which the demarcation between rights and facts is poorly defined, a state that is characteristically incapable of being captured in terms such as property rights, rationalization, rights, or institutions" in his June 1998 keynote speech delivered at a sociology and anthropology seminar at Peking University. I find this idea quite interesting, but I prefer to use "non-formalism" to describe these features of customary law. Here is why. The distinction between "rights" and "facts" in an idealized state seems to be difficult to understand, as it

procedural *ad hocness* means the search for some underlying "principle" is often futile. In rural China, there is no necessary correlation between the existence of rural conventions and village ordinances in writing and the quality of governance. Even when these documents do exist, they rarely function as the normative criteria by which things are decided. In fact, these written documents have increasingly taken on the style of "reports", and are not meant so much as a source of practical guidance for village community members but more as a way for local officials to meet perfunctorily the requirements of higher-level governments. To use the transfer of the rights to land slated for building residential housing as an example. Despite explicit prohibition against trade land in both rural conventions and village ordinances, and the country's formal legislation, primary-level politicians, and sometimes higher-level officials, are the very people who have the motive, the opportunity to engage and land trade and routinely do so.

Examples abound of rural conventions and village ordinances that contain provisions supporting this way of handling village affairs, especially interpersonal relations. In village DT in Zhejiang province, for instance, its village ordinance stipulates that those who fail to care for the elderly members of their family are compelled to do so, no matter what. However, according to the terms of a formal "agreement" settling a similar case, support for the elderly is conditioned upon the elder's agreeing to help care for their grandchildren.

Agreement Concerning Brothers YY and YK's Financial Support and Care for Their Elderly Parents:

(1) Per discussion between the two brothers and both parents, the parents would undertake the responsibility to care for the children of the two brothers. During the busy season YY's mother [alone] would look after the children (during off-peak season the two grandparents share the parenting responsibilities), in addition to cooking for the families of both YY and YK (during off-peak season the two families would do their own cooking).
(2) Each of the two brothers would supply 70 *jin* of rice to their parents each month, and when the two parents no longer have any viable source of income, the two brothers would pay their parents' 14-yuan monthly living expenses.

appears to presume that certain "nominal rights" do not in fact obtain, and some facts do not cohere with boundaries defined in terms of rights, or have such import. This is inconsistent with how "right" is ordinarily defined. In my understanding, rights are more than nominal claims. They include all the elements that would allow their realization, i.e. ingredients that would turn them into reality. Rights in real life are institutions abstracted from facts that mark the *de facto* limits to people's action. They are likely to be unwritten and unspoken and the term "non-formalism" reflects this. What the term also conveys is the idea that factual limitations intrinsic to social norms essentially amount to limits to rights. I will not be discussing those rights here that either cannot be realized or have yet to be realized (i.e. rights that lack a factual foundation) because they do not yet form part of the social (behavior) norms. I am inclined toward the view that whatever their form of expressions, and whether they are explicitly acknowledged or not, all social norms are basically ways to describe rights (justified behavior) and systems for allocating them.

(3) All three parties have agreed to the above, should any one party breach the terms of this agreement, village officials shall be called up to show up in person to enforce compliance.[49]

In another agreement, real estate is used in exchange for exemption from providing financial support to one's elderly parents, which is in blatant violation of village ordinance. Yet the agreement is recognized as a valid document.

> Per agreement reached among three brothers, HH would gift his real estate property to his two brothers in exchange for them agreeing to provide financial support for their elderly parents. The said property would be evenly divided between HJ and ZH.[50]

These cases give us reasons to believe that rural conventions and village ordinances are not primarily used to adjudicate interpersonal conflicts. In practice its function is to provide a basis of coordinating the relationship between individuals and the collective with respect to both rights and benefits. In particular, it serves as a foundation for the establishment of village officials' mandate to rule and govern on behalf of what is "public". These rules give these primary-level officials ample space in which to exercise the powers given to them, the powers to draft codes of conduct, to arbitrate, to implement the rules, and to determine how the rules are to be interpreted. With the exception of rules that blatantly contradict national legislation and have been accused of doing so in a lawsuit, there are hardly any limits to the powers primary-level officials have to introduce local rules, enforce them and adjudicate cases on the basis of them. Basically, whatever the rules say, the officials can enforce it, and the "degree" of the enforcement would be entirely at their discretion, depending on the "seriousness of the case". Such built-in ambiguity and informality make ***ad hoc***ness and arbitrariness prominent characteristics of the way primary-level officials carry out their official duties.

Metastasis

Here metastasis refers to the phenomenon where punishment for a breach of rule expands in scope and impacts other areas of the perpetrator's personal life. For example, in disputes between the collective and an individual, the individual is most likely placed at a decisive disadvantage, at risk of being terminated from their enterprise job, having their applications for official certifications and verification (such as those related to their marital status, their residential registration status, and so forth) denied, and even their entitlement to old-age pension payout may be cancelled altogether. The effectiveness of rural conventions and village ordinances does not consist so much in how widely endorsed they

[49] Dispute Mediation Registration Form (No. 1) of Residents of TD County (August 7, 1986).
[50] Dispute Mediation Registration Form (No. 3) of Residents of TD County (August 7, 1986).

are among the rural population but more in how easy it is for primary-level officials to carry out the punitive measures, which can in turn be attributed to the expansive "law" enforcement powers they have. Such powers allow them to go beyond the misconduct for which the perpetrator is supposed to be punished and target the punishment also at just about any other rights and interests the person has had in the past, has now, and will have in the future. This means that the binding force of these rural codes of conduct is not a result of popular support for the provisions contained therein, but a reflection of the kind of administrative power brought to bear in enforcing them. Since the rural population is utterly dependent on their village "membership" status being in good standing, and on the benefits such status entitles them to, in the absence of viable alternatives to being the member of any one particular village, the cost of carrying out punitive measures in that village, by enforcing its own rules and ordinances, would be very low, making these rules highly efficacious. The efficaciousness of any one village's rules would likely be somewhat diminished should people have the freedom to choose to become residents of other villages.

Localized Applicability

Local applicability is the idea that rural conventions and village ordinances have their distinct principle of governance and jurisdictional scope, even though the influence of a country's formals laws on their precise contents has also become increasingly evident. Rural governance and national governance are related to each other but at the same time clearly different in important ways, and the relationship between them is by no means a simple one. Apparently the two complement each other, and connections between them exist wherever necessary, however, care is taken to make sure neither encroaches upon or interferes with the other in practice. When such interference does happen, it is usually a result of a request by the side being interfered. In his study of rural China a century ago, Arthur H. Smith, a Western scholar, also found evidence for such a tradition. He noticed that the central government's governing power was anything but welcome in the countryside. The examples he brought forth illustrate the way in which the central government and its bureaucratic institutions were typically treated as a kind of back-up, or last resort, used more as an instrument of threat than anything else. Primary-level officials bluff their constituents into believing that somehow whatever they did was stamped with central government approval, but few if any of them really want to be subject to any central government supervision.

> When the head of the family returned, it was to find that the headmen had already left the village on their way to the District city, to enter a complaint against him, as one who refused to pay his just dues to the defence of the village. A lawsuit begun upon such a basis meant nothing less than a calamity greater than any flood that was likely to overtake him, so the distracted father hastened to pursue the headmen with offers of adjustment, made through third parties. By dint of an

immense amount of talking, the headmen were induced to return to the village, without entering the city and making a formal complaint.

The father of the offending lad then appealed to certain friends living in another village, to come and intercede for him with the outraged guardians of the welfare of his own village. In the course of the next forenoon, the persons who had been entrusted with this difficult task, made their way to the village, and had interviews with some of the headmen. It was impossible to get all of these men together at any one time, but one set was first seen, and then another, until the matter had been thoroughly discussed in all its bearings. These conferences, including plans of adjustment offered, modified, rejected, amended, and afterward brought up again and again, actually consumed the whole day, and all the next night until the crowing of the cocks announced the dawn, and it was not until daylight on the second day, that the weary and disgusted "middlemen" returned to their own village, having at last succeeded in securing a reduction of the proposed fine, which was to have been an exemplary one, to a merely nominal amount.[51]

Little surprise then to see that, about a half a century ago, the central government attempted to impose some measure of constraint on the rural conventions and village ordinances in northern Zhejiang. What had motivated such action, apparently, was the central government's concern that rural officials there had been trying to augment their power by means of adopting increasingly expansive local rules and regulations.

The Eleventh Month of the Thirty-Fifth Year of the Republic of China

Judiciary Department, Bureau of Social Affairs, Chongde County

Per the Public Affairs Office of all counties and townships, and meetings of the People's Delegation at all levels:

Most meetings of county and township people's delegation in this county have made only their minutes available to this office, and there have been few cases of discrepancy between what is recorded in these minutes and what is in our own record. From now on, no separate request shall be issued for each individual meeting, a separate report must be filed of the motions and decisions slated to be voted on at each such delegate meeting. Until we grant approval, all those rules and regulations that are inconsistent with the country's customary laws shall not be approved. Any approval would be considered lacking in legal merit, and ineffective, and the heads of countys and townships are prohibited from enforcing them.[52]

All such evidence points toward but one thing, which is that rural codes of conduct have long been very distinct from the country's laws and statutes. But the difference between them lies not so much in their underlying principles of

[51] Arthur H. Smith, D.D., *Village Life in China: A Study in Sociology* (Fleming H. Revell Company, 1899), 324.

[52] Judicial Division of the Bureau of Social Affairs of Chongde County (Today's Tongxiang, Zhejiang province), (November, the 35th year of the Republic of China or 1946), Tongxiang Archives, dossier 295; Catalog 6; Case 19. Punctuation added by the author.

governance as in their jurisdictional scope, i.e., who the people are whose hold on power is strengthened by their enforcement. In fact, there are ways in which these local codes of conduct and a country's formal laws are compatible, which creates space in which the two might learn from each other, especially what the other does best. But there are also aspects of the two that are simply not on the same wavelength. In those aspects, the two systems tend to apply in different domains and neither would want the other one to encroach upon its own jurisdictional turf. Still, this does not alter the fact that both have a need for the existence of the other, especially for purpose of either complementing or supplementing it where its own power is most wanting. For example, the legitimacy and credibility of rural codes of conduct are buttressed when endorsed by the central government, while the central government is dependent on these rural rules and regulations to establish and maintain order in those faraway places its own judicial powers do not or would not reach. From the point of view of superior levels of government, the primary objective of local rules and village ordinances ought to be imposing constraints on the rural community and must not be establishing power monopoly. They should especially try to avoid contravening laws enacted by higher government authorities, or evade oversight. To ensure compliance, higher governments have often required rural officials to submit their local rules and village ordinances for review and approval. As a result, rural officials have adapted these rules according to the standards of higher governments, so that are increasingly like a set of "public safety" rules, and have shed much of the language that was once used to lay out social norms. The growing influence of national laws on the objectives set out in these documents has been unmistakable. The report below, prepared by a county-level cadre, offers a window onto what people like him think about rural conventions and village ordinances.

> (The goal is to make sure) each village drafts its own Charter for Villager Autonomous Rule and Village Ordinance that are legally sound, democratic and binding. These documents should be used to encourage compliance among village residents with their duties and responsibilities. With regard to recalcitrant individuals who refuse to comply, and resist persuasion, they should be dealt with according to the type of the alleged violation, and prototypical cases shall be referred to the justice system for judicial processing.[53]

Yet, the state has nonetheless not deemed it necessary to set up a separate law enforcement and oversight mechanism in order to supplant primary-level authority as the *de facto* legislative, enforcement, and judicial body. The traditional model of rural governance has, therefore, been left largely intact. Especially pronounced in the primacy of local authority over higher authorities. Under this model, rural communities are allowed to draft their own rules and regulations by which local affairs are managed. In the wave of rule-based rural

[53] Research report by a county committee on rural primary-level organization (July 1998).

governance, the creation of these kinds of normative documents has apparently been encouraged by the central government. Another feature of this model that has changed little over the years is the role primary-level authority plays in conflict arbitration. Therefore, despite the fact that courts at the local level, a critical institutional component of the contemporary national political system that needed to be built afresh, are supposed to be an integral part of a bureaucratic hierarchy with the high court as its center, they have never properly fit into the rural political apparatus and operations, nor have they ever enjoyed autonomy from primary-level control. This means that not only can these institutions not be counted on to perform functions that what similar institutions in the West have historically performed, namely, extending the jurisdictional reach of the national bureaucracy, reigning in local self-rule, and replacing fragmentation with uniformity in the country's governance structure, they have instead helped to strengthen primary-level authorities' hold on power, and become an instrument for repelling the central government's efforts to bring them to heel.

The two cases mentioned earlier in this chapter (in which the village council unilaterally nullified a land lease and an orchard contract) illustrate how little weight the country's *Contract Law* carries at the rural primary level relative to rules and regulations created by primary-level authorities. Documents prepared by the courts, the Agriculture and Forestry Bureau, and the Notary Offices were summarily ignored, because while such behavior allegedly ran afoul of the *Contract Law*, they did not violate the traditional rules in effect in the local community. In these two cases, the village cadre noted, when answering questions from reporters, that because of widespread resentment among the public, they felt compelled to step forward to ensure that justice was done, i.e., that local residents received their fair share of the benefits. Such "justice" was essentially what had long been accepted as the "rule of the land" in these communities. And at any rate so far as the village council was concerned, terminating the land and orchard contracts before the end of their terms was not a breach of common practice. Obviously, this is a different kind of "justice" than the one the country's *Contract Law* was intended to defend. The former is based on the principle that collective benefits yielded by collectively owned assets belong exclusively to insiders, while the latter upholds the principle that the rights of parties to a legally binding contract (either individuals or collections of individuals) must be protected. Given the limited amounts of materials we were able to access, at this point we are yet unable to provide a complete picture of all the rules that might be supported by this parochial notion of "justice". Still, what we can already offer is evidence in the form of the following record, pertaining to Northern China, excerpted from *Investigation Report on Common Practices in the Handling of Commercial Affairs in Rural Areas*:

> Within rural communities the leasing of land and real estate may, or may not, be subject to a definite term, and each location may decide on the matter as they see fit. Normally, land leases expire in either the spring or the fall. Since much prepa-

> ration is required for the planting season, in the absence of a definite date by which the term of the land lease is up, the chances of the contractor having to revert the land after having already invested considerably towards the preparation, and thereby suffering associated economic losses increase significantly. This kind of practice with respect to setting the term for land contracts is not only commonplace across much of the country, it is also often applied in other kinds of contractual relationships, such as those between contract farmers and their landlords.[54]

This record shows that customarily land leases are for one year, but it seems that the date by which the land must be reverted to the landlord is usually not specified. Had the tenants known when that would happen, why would they prepare for the planting season? Or, it may be that even if such a date has been specified, changes can be made around the time of spring or fall. Starting with the basal ratio by which the yield is split between the landlord and the tenant farmer (which has typically been 2:8, 3: 7, 1:2, or 4: 6), and assuming that the landlord has decisive bargaining power over the tenant farmer,[55] the former may raise the rent, or decide to terminate the contract, full-term or pre-term, and the tenant cannot object.[56] The landlord may also haggle *ad hoc* to jack up the rent when the amount specified in a valid contract is considered too low. Therefore, according to such traditional notion that how yield is divvyed up may be subject to change depending on the harvest, there seems to be nothing wrong with the actions in the two above-mentioned cases. After all, as far as customary law is concerned, the village council is supposed to represent the interests of local residents (as opposed to those of tenants from outside). To justify their breach of contract, the village council reiterated the imperative to reclaim the land so as to be able to make it available to local residents. These are collectively owned assets, a share of which these residents are entitled to, and why should they be prohibited from doing to rectify the situation when others are reaping benefits instead? Obviously the two sides are not even playing with the same set of ground rules. To the extent rules are used only to protect those on one's own side instead of for establishing equal treatment of "others", it is natural that conflicts should have persisted till this day.

Given their exclusive focus on distinctive features of individuals instead of events and occurrences, and with the absence of universal principles that apply equally to different groups of people (insiders and outsiders), there can be no dispute that rural covenants and village ordinances can only function as an

[54] Ministry of Justice of the Republic of China, ed., Investigation Report of the Civil and Business Common Practices (Taipei: Jinxue Bureau, 1969); cited in Zhiping Liang, Customary Law in the Qing Dynasty: Society and the State (Beijing: China University of Political Science and Law Press, 1996), 53–55.

[55] Yuanlian Zhou, Zhaohua Xie, "Lease system in the Qing Dynasty." Cited in *Customary Law*, 100, 105, 114.

[56] Guozhen Yang, "Land contracts in the Ming and Qing Dynasties". Cited in *Customary Law*, 99.

instrument for maintaining order in a social structure that is premised on exceptionalism. And even when and if complications arise that may be difficult to settle, instead of turning to external authority for help in adjudicating possible conflicts, the expectation is for everybody to get behind these local and parochial norms. In other words, the only condition under which the legitimacy of other authorities may be acknowledged is if they endorse these parochial rules. In this sense, other legislations and norms are competitive with these rules. It follows that there is little interest in or tolerance for national statutes, which are hardly ever voluntarily invoked by primary-level authorities.

So when do cases get "referred to the judicial organs for processing"? In general, there is nothing in customary law that requires "immediate referral" of cases to the government's judicial authorities. Instead, all cases are by default "processed locally first". In fact, the village authority's mandate to apply local codes as a first resort is acknowledged by the central government, which "prohibits turning to government judicial authorities as a first resort".[57] Rural covenants and village ordinances in the modern era count "referral to the government's judicial authorities" as a form of punishment it can mete out. In the eyes of members of the rural communities, if a case is given this treatment, it is sure sign that the measures available to the local authorities to investigate, to set the penalty or otherwise to arbitrate are no longer deemed adequate. Whether a case is handled locally or referred to higher judicial authorities depends not only on how the different relevant legal provisions are interpreted, but also on the nature and turpitude of the alleged misconduct, and how much the defendant is willing to pay to defend themselves. On a deeper level, referral signifies having everything done strictly by the book, according to the letter of the pertinent legal codes, leaving little room for using such forms of capital as personal relationships to influence the final outcome. So it is only natural that people would do everything to avoid or prevent it. People prefer having misconduct and disputes handled locally, applying parochial legal codes, and being able to influence the outcome by maneuvering their personal networks, which would also in effective increase the level of control primary-level officials have over how cases are decided. Indeed, this is something that the 1899 case described earlier and these later cases have in common.

Lack of Alternatives

There is no other way. Rural covenants and village ordinances stipulate the membership relation between individuals and the village community, and the former have the rights that they do thanks entirely to this relationship. Without this relationship, they are not entitled to the support, supplies, and guarantees that they depend on the community to provide them with, including allocation of land for homestead, the rights to lease land, real estate, fish ponds, mountain forests, and the use of electricity, water, and agricultural instruments. That is to

[57] Gao, *Customary Law*, 78–79.

say, rural households are not granted these rights abstractly by the central government or on account of the constitution. Instead, they are, for all practical purposes established by the rural authority with which these households are in close contact on a day-to-day basis. Rural officials and their power over rural communities constitute the immediate setting for the lives of their members, and the rights relationship established through the constitution are only the intermediary setting for the rural population's lived experiences. That these rights the rural population enjoys are primarily existentially dependent on rural authorities and only secondarily on state bureaucracy is widely accepted in society at large. No other organization or set of norms, not even the constitution itself, powerfully symbolic as the supreme law of the land as it may be, can substitute for rural authorities in that capacity. We may reasonably conclude, therefore, that rural officials constitute a unique political force that functions, with "consent", as the *de facto* proxy for the constitution as a safeguard for the rights of the rural population.

Such an institutional setup is fundamentally predicated on constraints on the rights of the individual, and their ability to choose their organizational membership or affiliation. In the countryside, one may enter into such a relationship through birth, inheritance, or marriage, and thereby obtain the rights necessary for survival. For the average person living in a rural community, unless they are able to secure membership in some other social institution by such means as academic achievement or promotion through bureaucratic ranks, they cannot freely choose their organizational affiliation by, say, finding a job outside their hometown, unless, of course, they are willing to forfeit these rights and privileges altogether. A rural resident's identity and rights are necessarily, therefore, bound up with an organization that is at once a Hobson's choice and irreplaceable. This organization alone has the right to decide how to interpret these rights, and when women marry people from outside their hometown, and when people become old, sick, and die, it is again up to that organization to revoke their rights and privileges, so that [the things they had rights to] become available for trading, reversion to collective ownership, or transfer to others who are qualified. The bottom line is to prevent anybody who is not a member from being able to profit from local assets. Insofar as rural political apparatus occupies this position in deciding cases and adjudicating disputes, it is little wonder that it shapes the order of rural life more effectively than does the court system. Not only does it decide which rights and privileges members of any rural community enjoy, but it also has the power to either allow or deny these people's ability to actually exercise these rights. As we already saw in the case discussed earlier, in which the village council notified one resident surnamed Xue that the court's ruling notwithstanding, it would, instead of doing what the ruling required, reclaim the land from Wang and reassign it to Xue. This illustrates the way in which, in the social order under which rural residents live, the village authority trumps the court system, and rural covenants and village ordinances trump the country's statutes. This supremacy provides guarantee for a number of mandates for the village political apparatus, including the right to decide how residents' property and assets are reassigned, the right to interpret residents' membership claims, and the right to act as an arbiter in cases of dispute. As we saw in another case already mentioned, the village officials enjoy the indisputable rights to take back real estate or land and to trade them. The previous holder of the rights to these assets is not at all involved in negotiating whatever that passes for an "agreement" about these transactions. The village authority alone, in its capacity as both the rightful owner and the recipient of the proceeds, gets to decide who the buyer would be. All of these rule and customs help cement the standing of rural officials.

That special importance is attached to the collective in rural conventions and village ordinances may have to do with the role "family bylaws" or "household codes of conduct" from which they evolved once played. These rules had been designed to strengthen a rural community's political standing, maintain internal cohesion, and make sure the community as a whole had full control over collective assets. Obviously, some form of organization is needed to realize these goals, some public organ with the authority to control various institutions. So it is imperative for rural conventions and village ordinances to strengthen the authority of these public organs, even though the exact form these organs have taken has continued to evolve over time. In China, growing importance and influence of social institutions with administrative functions have been the general trajectory of this evolution in modern times. But as the old social units were gradually being displaced by the village as a social unit per administrative designation, especially during the period in which both co-existed, the basic principles of lineage self-preservation and defense against threats that had been operative for centuries were preserved, in the form of rural convention and village ordinances. For example, roughly corresponding to a rule in a traditional family bylaw that says violators "would be referred to the judicial system for legal actions, expelled from the community, and denied admission into family temples and entry in genealogical records", among other punishments,[58] you have a rule in rural conventions and village ordinances that says "select [violators] would be publicly reprimanded over the public announcement radio system, required to submit confession and repentance in writing, or otherwise admit to wrongdoing in public, required to pay fines and compensation (including expenditure on movie screening and performance troupes), expelled and exiled, and even referred to the judicial system for legal actions".[59] These punitive measures were clearly designed to uphold the order of public life, maintain cohesion and solidarity, and the body that was charged with exercising this power was none other than what we refer to today as rural primary-level authority.

[58] See *Li Lineage Bylaws*, compiled in the 28th year of the Daoguang Reign in Qing Dynasty by the Li lineage from Taiping County, Ningguo District, Jiangnan. Discussed in Yong Zhu, *Study on Patrilineage Laws in the Qing Dynasty* (Changsha: Hunan Education Press, 1987), 215.

[59] Primary-level Governance Office of the Ministry of Civil Affairs, *Documents, Regulations and Rules*, 1995.

What we can draw from the above analysis is that it is not so much the rural conventions and village ordinances themselves that lend credibility and strength to these local authorities but a kind of social system that these bylaws represent. According to common practice in rural governance, primary-level authority has the mandate to decide if an individual has formal membership status in a village community. With such status come a myriad of rights for the rural population, including political rights (to participate and to vote), economic rights (to employment, to a share of collective assets and protection), and social rights (welfare entitlements and education). Behind these rules and ordinances is an entire social system that determines not just what rights people have but also how rights can be exercised, and this is true even though the codification of the system is not ostensibly couched in terms of "rights". While having membership status in a village community does not guarantee that one can exercise one's rights, at the very least it establishes a necessary precondition, and it is the primary-level authority that executes this crucial step. This basic fact does more than shaping the position of authority these individuals find themselves in, it is also instrumental in determining the kind of relationship between them and the people in their jurisdiction, namely, the rural population. This simply follows from the axiom that any system for deciding what rights a particular group of people enjoys, whatever its specific structural features, is also the institutionalization of the relationship between those who grant the rights (primary-level political apparatus) and those who are granted the rights (the villagers).

From the perspective of the overall social order in the village community, the various features of rural conventions and village ordinances still cannot be equated with "a collective or organization made up of individuals who congregate in the name of a certain set of norms, and are willing to abide by it", because what results is not quite an orderly group of equals or equivalents.[60] However, nor can it be compared with a dictatorial political system in which the authority issues absolute commands. It is rather a set of norms whose main purpose is to, in the interest of the public, allow primary-level authority to step in when and where necessary to prevent the abuse of private power. The task of maintaining defensive order puts the arbiter in a position of relative passivity, in which they do not seek a highly specialized (and differentiated) form of arbitration authority that allows them to determine which principles to apply and how these principles are to be interpreted, and to act as a kind of third-party authority capable of transcending the parties in a dispute. Instead, the arbiter's task is to capitalize on the broad discretion and latitude they have and find the right balance of interests among the stakeholders, with the aim of preventing tensions from escalating and threatening the status quo.

One consequence of this has been the institutional laxity of social norms. This means that, under such a system, the appropriateness and justifiability of

[60] Terada Hiroaki, "Contract in the Legal order in Ming and Qing Dynasties", in Shiga Shuzo, *Civil Trials and Civil Contracts in the Ming and Qing Dynasties* (Beijing: Legal Press, 1998), 153, 159.

social acts are primarily contingent on the actor's own desires, investment, and agency, that is, it is left to their own discretion. As such, rules lack rigidity, i.e., are non-binding, and everything simply "depends". Unpredictability and uncertainty are the norm, and *ad hoc* special treatment is commonplace. In fact, the level of erratic capriciousness can reach such a point that few except those working on the primary-level frontline have much of an idea what is going on. It is possible that the high costs associated with this model of governance help explain why the power to provide interpretations of the applicable rules always lies with primary-level organizations. Even though rural conventions and village ordinances have undergone textual revisions, some of which significant, what these documents say about the relationship between primary-level officials and members of the rural community, between what is public (the collective) and private (the individual), have remained largely unchanged over time. Nor have these revisions ever amounted to anything like a call for reflecting on the basic framework of local political apparatus and operations. The occasional resource reallocation is as far as these revisions have gone.

There is little reason, therefore, for us to see rural residents as equivalent to citizens in the modern sense of the term, since citizens are granted their rights by virtue of the constitution under whose jurisdiction they choose to fall. According to this sense of citizen, rural residents ought to be citizens, people for whom the state functions as the entity that decides what rights they have, what these rights entail, and how these rights are to be exercised. For citizens, so long as they are within the government's jurisdiction, their rights can be exercised no matter where exactly they are. In particular, the principle of the same rights for all is universal. But in fact, the situation of rural residents is rather different. A "rural resident" exists first and foremost as a member of a fairly small and self-contained collective entity. While they might also be part of an even larger political unit, such as a state, national legislations neither provide the normative framework for their lives nor offer them protection for their rights. As we have seen from the numerical examples of rural conventions and village ordinances, a country's legal codes cannot simply supplant rural codes of conduct and ordinances, nor can the central government become directly involved in rural governance. Given this, how does "state-building" manifest itself? So far as routine affairs are concerned, the continued coexistence of two sets of legal codes and judicial practices means rural governance is primarily based on traditional codes of conduct and the country's court system (which does not effectively replace local systems of arbitration even when local courts have been established since their operations are invariably under local control) still has limited scope of application. A uniform and all-encompassing judicial order for the country is far from being realized. Primary-level authority's role in deciding cases, the inherent imprecision and non-rigidness of the rural conventions and village ordinances on the basis of which it performs that function, and the central government's functional irrelevance continue to be the basic features of rural governance.

In the last century, the state (central government) has grown increasingly aware of the dangers this situation can pose to its authority, insofar as it might undermine its power basis. However, attempts to increase its own practical influence in rural communities have apparently been largely unsuccessful. What makes this a particular challenge, in my view, is not so much that a country's legal codes are "modern" while rural conventions and village ordinances are "parochial", or that the former is formulaic while the latter natural (conventional). Rather, it is because the two sets of legal norms, which are in important ways quite *similar* to each other, compete for turf, i.e., sphere of influence and application. And until now, the question of how far each reaches, and where the reach of one ends that of the other begins, has not been properly settled. Indeed, this is exactly the problem that European countries have been trying to solve over the last several centuries through "state building".

CHAPTER 4

Rural Fiscal and Taxation Systems and their Political Implications

In each of the first three chapters I have alluded here and there to tax-related behavior among primary-level officials. While these give us some idea about the space in which these officials carry out their activities, they do not provide an adequate account of the rural taxation system, an important instrument for resource allocation that is hugely politically consequential. In this chapter, I examine how this system works in rural communities, and the range of social effects it has on them. In particular, I consider the role the tax system plays in fiscal empowerment of primary-level officials, and the ramifications of the absence of constraints on such power.

4.1 Historical Legacy

A great deal of evidence of many features of today's rural tax system can be found in economic historical documents and materials. What is surprising, however, is how little has changed over many centuries both in the underlying rationale of the design of the system and in its implementation. Clearly tracing the historical roots of present-day rural tax system will help us better appreciate its rich legacy, and why it may be so resistant to change.

Studies of tax system of the Tang dynasty have shown that the principle of egalitarianism featured prominently in both the *zuyongdiao* system (the tax and corvée system)[1] and the two-tax system.[2] Under both systems tax rates were determined, as they had been for centuries before, by applying that principle to different denominators: land, household, individual, and even township. What available historical documents, including the relatively little studied documents

[1] The zuyongdiao system combines "zu", which refers to grain tax, "yong" which is labor corvée, and "diao", which is cloth tax. – Trans.

[2] The two-tax system includes two tax categories: household tax and land tax. These are collected twice a year and paid in coins. – Trans.

J. Zhang, *Primary-Level Government*,
https://doi.org/10.1007/978-981-96-6209-8_4

excavated at Turfan, show is that a range of taxes, including land tax, householder tax and poll tax, had two underlying principles in common. The first is equality in distribution, and the second recording and reporting tax receipts for administrative units only in the aggregate. Even though an adjustment was made later on (in Tang dynasty) based on household classification, according to which households are divided into nine brackets based on their assets, with different tax rates for each bracket, such adjustment was more of a measure to mitigate inequality in land allocation and did nothing to challenge the formula used to calculate tax burden. This is because "household classification based on assets" is still predicated on the idea that household asset is determined solely by the amount of land a household has, rather than in monetary terms, a much more abstract concept of valuation. The scheme assumes that labor input from the farmers makes no meaningful contribution to household assets. Yet not only would a monetary valuation be capable of reflecting differences in land ownership but it would also be able to distinguish among contributions to the final output from management, labor, and operations. The asset valuation produced using this method is more comprehensive and more accurate. Therefore, I am inclined to agree with those who argue that "household classification based on asset" was introduced in order to "mitigate wealth inequality within the general framework of tax egalitarianism, rather than to abolish tax egalitarianism altogether".[3]

D.C. Twitchett, in his study of financial administration during the Tang dynasty, also noted this particular issue with a fixed tax rate. According to Twitchett, the *zuyongdiao* system, far from being perfect, is a complex kind of poll tax based on fixed rates. Since it is predicated on the presumption of equal land allocation to each eligible taxpayer, it fails to reflect economic reality or variation among individuals and regions. In fact, smallholding peasants, who were taxed at a fixed rate regardless of output or productivity, bore the brunt of the tax burden under the *zuyongdiao* system.[4]

Another feature of the rural tax system was that tax receipts for administrative units were recorded and reported only in the aggregate. This has enormous implications for the evolution of tax system in modern times. According to researchers who study China's tax history, tax records from the Tang dynasty often contained only sum totals, and included no taxpayer names, so the amount of tax collected was often filed under the *lizheng*, the head of a basic administrative unit in rural China.

> As for records on the tianjiuerfen tax, except the one place where it was noted "33 *shuo* and 6 *dou*", which was not a round number, all other numbers were round numbers. Grain contribution was recorded under the names of taxpayers, including the amount. But for seeds, the amount is recorded in the aggregate

[3] Minyi Qu, "Research on equalitarian land allocation in Tang Dynasty," Cited in Jinxiu Li, *Financial History of Tang Dynasty*, Vol. I, Book II. (Beijing: Peking University Press, 1995), 451.

[4] D. C. Twitchett, *Financial Administration under the T'ang Dynasty*, cited in Jinxiu Li, *History of Finance in the Tang Dynasty* (Vol. 2), (Beijing: Peking University Press, 1995), 452.

> only, for the township, so only the name of the township appears. For tianjiuerfen tax, the grand total is recorded, without the name of the township from which the tax was collected. At the time of Tianbao land tax was two *sheng*. But land owned by households was scattered all over the place, and sizes varied, so if the tax paid by each household was individually recorded and then aggregated, the total could hardly have been such a nice round number. We can infer from the above analysis that the taxes received by the *lizheng* were then aggregated by the county government, and subsequently delivered to the provincial government. So *lizheng* receiving taxes paid by individuals would be step one in the tax collection process, and step two would be the transfer of that money to the county government.[5]

Ample evidence exists for *lizheng*'s role as the smallest unit of identifiable taxpayer under this tax system. Not only does the *lizheng* issue the tax invoice called "*chao*" and the tax receipt "county *chao*" (available at both the county and the town levels, in possibly a superior tax filing system to what is in place in some places today) to individual taxpayers, but the *lizheng* is also listed as the "joint signer" on ledgers and registrations, effectively making him the treasurer. There is also a vast body of historical documents that suggest that "the town is merely a nominal administrative division, and management of the town's fiscal affairs falls de facto on the *wuli*[6] instead"; "land allocation is administered by the county chief and the *lizheng*, without the town being involved"; "both tax collection and bookkeeping are the responsibility of the *lizheng*, who is effectively the chief financial officer of the town"; "Verifying and updating household registration, making sure planting is done on time, investigating violation of rules, collecting taxes and enforcing military draft encompass the full scope of rural primary-level fiscal administration".[7] Obviously, in their capacity as "household registrar" and "treasurer" the *lizheng* plays a crucial role in rural households' payment of taxes. "Since the national budget must be based on household registration and ledgers, formal government documents specifying the budgetary requirements are passed down from the central government to primary-level authorities through a series of official channels, which helps to ensure that the amount collected and the amount laid out in the budget accord with each other".[8]

Even though historians who study fiscal administration contend that local officials "do not tend to have a lot of power"[9] when it comes to tax collection, the collection process described above seems to suggest that, as far as the relationship between taxpayers and tax collectors is concerned, the practice of aggregate tax filing may well have created loop holes that allow the collective to game the system and take unfair advantage by misrepresenting such things

[5] Li, *History of Finance*, 113.
[6] The lowest administrative division. – Trans.
[7] Qu, "Equalitarian Land Allocation", in Li, *History of Finance*, 1995, 105–7.
[8] Qu, "Equalitarian Land Allocation", in Li, *History of Finance*, 1995, 105–7.
[9] Li, *History of Finance*, 1995, 115.

as household registration, tax evasion, damages caused by natural disasters, availability of in-kind contribution, inequitable tax burden distribution, and late payment. Aggregate tax filing also encourages group responsibility, whose establishment requires standing in a community as a person of authority. Yet it suppresses the development of personal or individual responsibility, and overlooks the ways in which people may behave very differently in discharging their responsibilities. The system gives local officials the incentive to milk their relationships with other people for their potential to yield benefits to themselves through unfair and undisclosed deals. Such behavior may in turn cement these individuals' standing in the community as holders of power and authority. When private dealings are always a possibility, those who must pay taxes could have their tax reduced or waived altogether if they know how to make a deal with the right person, and those who should not have to pay taxes may end up having to pay, possibly even a considerable amount. The strong and universal urge to avoid uncertainty leads people to do what they can to get into the good graces of people in power.

There is yet another vestige of the traditional tax system that has created even more opportunities for this kind of behavior. Studies of the fiscal administration and tax system during the Tang dynasty done in the 1930s and 1940s found that "[outside the centralized system] there existed a kind of assignment system under which particular officials or government organs were authorized to take charge of specific funds, in-kind contribution, land or individual taxpayer, which then became a special source of income on which these officials and government organs relied to support themselves".[10] Historians call this *zike*. Obviously, this was a form of local income that existed beyond the parameter of the official tax system, somewhat akin to what we would today call extra-budgetary income. *Zi* refers to the coins paid, in lieu of labor service, by a special group of people who worked as support staff in a range of positions either in the government or for particular government officials. These positions included *xunsanguan*, *sanwei*, *gongjiang*, *yushi*, *guanhu*, *zahu*, *sanyue*, *yinshengren*, and others. Those who must pay *zi* enjoy special status and must possess certain required skills, which are primarily determined by the needs of the government. *Ke* refers to the coins paid by low-ranking auxiliary staff—such as baizhi, zhiyi, fangge, shupu, qinshi, and zhangnei—of government officials, that exempt them from labor service. The coins they pay go into the personal coffer of the government officials these people work for.[11] The importance of *zike* consists not only in the fact that it helps reduce government expenditure but also because it is special, *ad hoc*, and arbitrary. Those features make *zike* even "more significant than labor covee" to fiscal administration.[12] More importantly still, individuals who paid *zike* occupied different positions on a

[10] Attributed to Qingyuan Ju, cited in Li, *History of Finance*, 531.

[11] Li, *History of Finance*, 539, 541.

[12] Li, *History of Finance*, 531.

hierarchical ranking of titles,[13] and the way *zike* was collected was similar to private contracts insofar as both were "arbitrary".[14] This suggests that how much was collected was determined by how much happened to be needed by the local government given its expenditure and staff size. There was otherwise no predetermined target.

All these practices were developed to make it easier for primary-level officials to "expend" as they wish free from any meaningful constraints, and for those bodies that enjoyed such freedom to exploit aggregate accounting for their own survival. Since these people did not have access to tax receipts over which it could exercise control, they resorted to milking as much out of *zike* as they could to meet their spending needs. Lacking capital of their own, they built up capital by exercising the right to collect *zike*, and then squander it as they wished. In all of this fiscal legacy there is no trace of any mechanism intended to check "expenditure". Instead, all we can see are efforts to establish money collecting bodies not accountable to anybody and collection methods—such as designating special sources of income—that maximally met the whimsical needs of primary-level officials. Since *zike* income was inherently decentralized, pegged to the budget needs of local governments, and did not count towards the central government's aggregate income, it received little public attention. Yet its ubiquity is known to all. Not unlike extra-budgetary income at the primary level today, its political significance trumped its fiscal importance. Primary-level officials' total control over from whom to collect it and on what to spend it meant that outsiders had hardly any way of ascertaining accurate information related to it, or exercising meaningful oversight. And of course, insofar as it is either formal or informal action by a political body, it is inextricably linked to some kind of public organization. After all, the "target" for collection is determined by the "expenditure" (needs) of some particular public organization. This cannot be done by somebody without power, so it cannot in itself improve the moral quality of that power. Indeed, the converse is true: it tends to breed the abuse of power.

With regard to these problems, researchers who study the history of fiscal administration have asked by how much both the budget and tax receipts would have needed to increase in order to meet these spending needs had this special source of income not been there? That is a question about how to balance the budget, but what deserves more scrutiny is the issue of political consolidation given the ineffectiveness of checks and balances on power as such. When changes to the tax system are entirely dictated by the arbitrary needs of tax collectors, taxpayers have no say whatsoever in how the system works. The act of paying one's taxes does not entail, under this system, rights, responsibilities, oversight or demand for accountability. Paying taxes is conceived of as nothing more than a kind of voluntary contribution. This illustrates not only

[13] Attributed to Chunrun Li, cited in Li, *History of Finance*, 533.

[14] Li, *History of Finance*, 533.

how the impact of tax practices on both private property and collectively own property but also the proper relationship between the public and the private have historically been understood. In particular, the way we now understand how privately collected taxes should be purposed towards public use is very different from what it has historically been. Today, we think of paying taxes as (an autonomous act associated with an individual's rights claims) one form in which private resources are channeled toward public use and management. And because taxpayers are ultimately the consumers of publicly supplied goods and services that are paid for with tax money collected by the government, and it is their "needs" that are the engine of the tax machine, they not only have a say in how and on what that money is spent but are also allowed to exercise oversight. All of this is indicative of the power relationship between the tax system and different groups of stakeholders. Obviously, "a tax system that is less than fully satisfactory" such as described above helps to protect the interests of primary-level officials (who have the mandate to collect taxes), and in this lies the key to why little progress has been made in tax reform for a very long time.

In his study of Song history Professor Ray Huang also finds evidence that powers related to taxation are in the hands of primary-level officials.

> Expansionist policies of the Tang dynasty (of the Li lineage) were continued in the Song dynasty. While replacing the *zuyongdiao* system with the two-tax system may have seemed to amount to comprehensive reform, in reality it was no more than forced abandonment of something that had stopped working, and reluctant acceptance of reality. In fact, even the two-tax system was not exactly a central government policy. It had long fallen to the military garrisons themselves to set the tax rates and design the collection procedure. This meant that military officers enjoyed autonomy in levying taxes, which they used towards meeting the needs of troops under their command. As a consequence, the garrisons became entitled to the land they occupied until perpetuity... When the Song dynasty (ruled by the Zhao lineage) unified the country later on, the central government simply took over the military garrisons' control of military affairs and tax administration, instead of implementing comprehensive reform of the entire social system.[15]

Despite many rounds of tax "reform" throughout history, the basic interests of primary-level officials, and the institutions instrumental for protecting these interests have never faced any meaningful threat to their existence. In Europe, where such threats did occur, they tended to originate from two sources. One were the taxpayers, who organized themselves around the growing awareness that they, as property owners, should have the rights to make certain decisions for themselves. They became an important countervailing force in the society, and worked to make sure that different aspects of taxation—its structure, decision-making process, scope, uses, and efficiency—were legitimate and justified. "No taxation without representation" became the rallying cry for

[15] Ray Huang, *Expanding on the Historical Vision* (Beijing: China Social Sciences Press, 1998), 65.

advocates for taxpayer control because it signifies the satisfaction of the social consent condition. The other source of threat is the very process of "state building". While its aim was to strengthen the power of the state to exercise direct control [over society], oversight by the public helped shape a new, "public role" for state agencies as managers of public assets. This meant that as state-building continued, the role and function of the state and the state's relationship with society were also changing. With respect to taxes, the public role (of the state) and the monarchical role (of the royal lineage) differed fundamentally in that the former manages public assets and provides public services while the latter manages private assets and pursues private gains for the royal lineage (a group) by capitalizing on the private assets. In France, tax reform, an undertaking of great importance in the country's history and that was carried out concurrently with the process of state-building, offers a telling illustration of the structural changes European societies were undergoing throughout the fourteenth and fifteenth centuries. In a critical shift, indirect tax collection was abolished and semi-independent tax collection agencies emerged.[16] The former gave the king unprecedented power to levy taxes directly from his subjects, which effectively established a political body that took charge of managing public assets that was beyond the control of the individual fiefdoms but also had greater authority. This necessarily led to a decline in the political standing of the heads of the fiefdoms. The latter, for its part, helped take the control of the tax collection process out of the hands of the local authorities, which turned them into entities that were semi-autonomous but also answerable to the higher political authority of the state.

The significance of these two developments lies not only in the way in which they boosted the state's tax revenue and taxation power, or extended the downward reach of state power into rural communities, but also in how they laid the foundation for a modern constitutional political system. Tax reform necessitated the transformation of state agencies from institutions that served the monarch to institutions that served the public. The royal family's private assets, the uses that would be made of them, and the principles governing how they yielded benefits would have to be clearly distinguished from public assets and how these are to be managed. The separation of the interests of the royal family from the role of protecting the interests of the public, which is facilitated by the establishment of a public management oversight system, is what is needed to earn the public's approval and trust, and for the political power of a modern public authority to be cemented. Therefore, tax reform is about far more than fiscal balance or centralizing benefits, it is closely related to a host of important issues and changes in society, including the role of the state (its public responsibilities) as a modern political entity charged with administering public affairs, the establishment of state management agencies, political institutions (tax policymaking and oversight mechanisms) and their relationship with social interests. This is why in Western societies debates about the tax system

[16] James B. Collins, "State Building in Early Modern Europe: The Case of France", *Modern Asian Studies*, no. 31, (1997).

are often essentially about politics, i.e. whether taxes are justified, and whether they have the consent of the public. Throughout human history, time and again revolution broke out when, in the absence of a legitimate tax system, people resorted to violence to resist paying or when other tax-related problems occurred. So not only does the establishment of laws governing taxation make it easier to oversee taxation matters, it is also able to turn the potential for violence into an interest in debates about the tax structure. What kind of tax system a society has, therefore, has consequences for its stability.

From a political-sociological point of view, tax reform has never been a singular event, or one that is simply about fiscal and financial matters. It necessarily takes place against the backdrop of the struggle over the institutional distribution of power. In such context, the optimal fiscal structure is in fact a function of the way fiscal powers and responsibilities are distributed among different entities: the wider the coverage of a particular form of public goods is, the larger should the administrative unit be that is responsible for providing it, or in other words, the responsibility for providing public goods with larger numbers of beneficiaries should fall on higher levels of government. In ascending order, therefore, we would have the district government providing public parks services, the municipal government providing firefighting services, the state government providing judicial services, and the central government providing legal protection, education, and national defense.[17] Against this backdrop, tax collection and expenditure signify the distribution of power between the public and the private sectors, which has important consequences for the limits of resources flow. Tax collection, after all, is essentially the transfer of resources from a property rights holder to an institution that represents the public, and expenditure is decided by the market rather than by the collective through administrative decree. This obviously raises the question of where the reasonable limits should be to both the powers and resources of either public institutions or individuals. Consent by the society must be fashioned through "constitutional constraints" in order to prevent inequity in either tax collection or expenditure (such as certain special interest groups being disproportionately benefitted). Therefore, the key in choosing a tax system lies not so much in what the most reasonable tax structure is but more in the decision-making process itself, i.e., whether it is able to reflect the preferences and values of all individuals and institutions that enjoy the same rights.[18]

We know that these essentially political issues related to the fiscal and tax systems have not always been salient throughout Chinese history. We might surmise that the very fact that these issues have yet to be resolved on an institutional level is the reason for the perpetual threat facing rural primary-level government. I will now turn my attention to rural finance and fiscal systems in

[17] Jiandong Wen, *Public Choice School* (Wuhan: Wuhan Publishing House, 1996), 115.

[18] James M. Buchanan, *Public Finance in Democratic Process: Fiscal Institutions and Individual Choice* (New York: Liberty Fund, 1999), cited in Wen, *Public Choice School*, 206-8.

contemporary China. It should become obvious to the reader that many similarities exist between many of the problems we see now and some of the problems we have been looking at that we have inherited from the past.

4.2 "Collective Accumulation": Setting Targets and Reaching Them

The system of collective accumulation has its origin in the socialist commune system, and has always been taken very seriously by governments at all levels. The term "collective accumulation" encompasses an entire system of fiscal accounting, tax collection, transfer, savings, and expenditure that is carried out at the village level. Closely associated with "collective ownership system" in rural communities, collective accumulation has two main sources. One is money collected from individual households that goes into "village reserve" or "township endowment", the other is money that households pay that is deposited into the so-called "agriculture development fund", which includes taxes and fees paid by rural proprietors, and user fees required for such production materials as land, sand, electric power and transportation, and management.

Decisions regarding the collection of money for village reserve and township endowment are explicitly laid out in writing. According to the rules, before March of each year the village economic cooperative must announce both the spending plan for previous year's village reserve and current year's budget, submit them to the village council for review and approval, and another copy to the township government as record. However, in practice, the economic cooperative is not a separate and distinct entity from the village polity. In fact, most members of the former are village officials. In the places where I conducted fieldwork, the head of the economic cooperative was in most cases also the head of CPC village committee, while delegates that make up the village council were usually people who headed villager teams. Therefore, decisions regarding collective accumulation were in effective made by officials at the village and township levels. This means that at the "village council meetings" where the budget was supposed to be reviewed for "approval" often turned into meetings where specific collection targets were announced and assigned.

The exact targets set for the village reserve and township endowment varied from year to year, and changes typically reflected the following factors.

(1) The percentages set by superior levels of government.

According to rules set out in the *Provisions* promulgated by the State Council, the amount of the village reserve and township endowment should not exceed 5 percent of net rural income from the previous year. For the current year, that proportion is set at 3 percent; and it is 2 percent for the village reserve and 1 percent for township endowment; contribution toward rural education (aged 0–55 for male and aged 0–50 for female) and military draft is collected from each person, at the rate of 1 yuan per person.[19]

Around 40 percent of village reserve goes toward the Housing Provident Fund, the amount each household must pay is a factor of the size of the land they have under contract. Around 30 percent of village reserve goes toward the Public Welfare Fund, and the amount each household must pay is a factor of the number of people in a household. The amount collected from each household for management is calculated in the same ways as Housing Provident Fund.[20]

(2) The ratio is only useful as an abstract point of reference, and in fact, the binding collection targets came in the form of specific amounts set by superior levels of government.

The target amount for the village reserve for the current year is 281,123 yuan, for the minimum production cost is 238,122 yuan, shortfall from previous years is 12,593 yuan, so the grant total to be collected is 531,838 yuan.[21]

Each town and township enterprise employee is required to pay 3 yuan each month to the village as contribution towards the Industry Subsidization of Agriculture Fund, which is subsidiary of the Rural Agriculture Development Fund. The payment is collected by each enterprise, and is separate from what the enterprise has to pay towards the agriculture development fund in corporate tax. Rural self-proprietorships with taxable income are required to pay 2.5 percent of their revenue toward the village reserve, and the rate is 7 yuan per month for self-employed truck drivers, 3 yuan per month for those who work for over 6 months in accumulation out of a year in nonfarm jobs such as housebuilder. Village officials are charged with collecting the above taxes. Fees for land use and river network project water use are to be collected in accordance with pertinent rules.[22]

(3) Increases, reductions, exemptions, and extensions granted to accommodate special circumstances. For village officials, the collection of village reserve and township endowment is mentally demanding work. In the words of many township and village cadres, "few tasks are more difficult than" collecting money, and that "it is even harder than enforcing the family planning policy". This goes to show that even though collective accumulation has long been a long-standing practice, the

[19] "Regulations on the Implementation of Several Specific Policies on the Rural Areas", issued by BB Township, Zhejiang province.

[20] "Notice on Further Improvement of Rural Collective accumulation System", issued by BB Township, Zhejiang province.

[21] "About the Issues of Collective Endowment and Substituting Fees for Labor Service Fees of the Township Job Center", issued by BB Township, Zhejiang province.

[22] "Regulations on the Implementation of Several Specific Policies on the Rural Areas", issued by BB Township, Zhejiang province.

work faces many uncertainties and there is never guarantee it would be completed without incident. Before each collection season, decisions are made and passed at the village official meeting. In the event of projects for which fundraising may be particularly difficult, either a CPC committee meeting or a villager delegation meeting would be convened to mobilize the public. But what happens at these meetings is not decision-making, but execution and implementation. That is where influence is used to get results, and these meetings are resorted to when buy-in from CPC members and cadres is needed. When it comes to matters related to village reserve and township endowment, village officials have to follow orders. They do not get to decide the amount to be collected, their role is strictly to meet the targets set by the township government, and sign contracts with rural households. Cadres are evaluated for how well this work is carried out, with consequences for promotion prospects. The only discretion village officials have is in redirecting funds, such as diverting money that had been meant for village enterprises or other subsidies to make up for the shortfall. Villages that are simply too poor to meet the target have no other option than asking for an extension. In fact, because of the widespread poor performance of village enterprises, plus poor management, failure to meet targets on time is commonplace in the countryside.

According to statistics released by one government agency in Hunan province, the total amount of debt owed by rural communities had reached 5.93 billion yuan. As much as 88.4 percent of all townships and towns were in debt, owing an average of two million yuan. The amount of debts owed by villages is just as astonishing. Statistics show that the city of Changde owed a total of 880 million yuan, or an average of 210,000 yuan per village. The number of villages in debt was 480, accounting for 83.4 percent of the total.[23]

Because of this, around the same time each year township governments would issue official documents to lower levels of government urging them to try different things that might help them meet the village reserve collection target. These include imposing financial penalty, such as withholding certain subsidies from the township government, on villages that do not collect money for the village reserve,[24] financial reward for villages that deliver good results in the form of increased remuneration for the village cadre, and finding multiple fundraising models.

To facilitate collection, we propose setting the amount of remuneration as a proportion of the amount collected. The specific proportions are as follows. For villages that have collected 95 to 100 percent of the target amount, 0.4 percent

[23] *China Comment* (published by the CPC Central Committee Information Office), "Observation and Reflections" column (1998), 23.

[24] "Advice on Building up Collective Accumulation," issued by BB Township, Zhejiang province.

of the receipt would be set aside toward remuneration; 0.3 percent for 91–94 percent; 0.2 percent for 85–90 percent, 0.1 percent for 80–84 percent. And for villages that fail to collect at least 80 percent of the target amount there would be not remuneration. Those villages that complete the collection process by the end of April will be rewarded with a 10 percent bonus. In theory only those individuals who took part in the collection would be eligible for remuneration. Disbursement can be made lump-sum at the end of the year or in two installments – one in the spring and one in the fall.[25]

In recent years collecting money for village reserve has met with challenges, and more effective and more diverse fundraising models will be explored this year. First, households are encouraged to pay their due by the deadline. Alternatively, village cadre can go door-to-door to collect payment. The second option is to task designated grain distribution centers, industry and commerce bureaus, fiscal and taxation bureaus, and transportation bureaus with collecting corporate contributions.[26]

Designated collection agencies are usually those normally in charge of matters most directly and closely related to different aspects of people's everyday lives. So when people visit these offices to try to get something (paperwork) done, they would be told they can get what they need on condition they make the required payment towards village reserve or township endowment. However, on the whole practices like this have done little if anything at all to boost collection efforts. After all, if and when people choose to avoid coming into contact with these agencies in the first place, they become rather useless as collection agencies, too. For example, several villages in one township in Zhejiang experimented with letting household accounts to be debited for the amount they owe, then credited with the difference if what they are owed from selling grain to the government exceeded the amount of the debit. As a consequence, in order to avoid having their accounts debited, peasants no longer want to sell grain to the government. Instead they sold excess grain on the open market. By doing so they made an end run around grain stations, which managed grain purchase on behalf of the government, and the refusal to sell grain to the government became widespread. So, soon enough, the practice was abolished by the township government. Among rural officials, the widely shared worry remains how to make sure money (taxes) is collected. It would be fair to say that in not just the last few decades, but indeed the last several hundred years, this problem has not been solved for good, and scarcely any change has taken place at the institutional level. So, in the country, it is common to have households' unpaid dues recorded in the village ledger. That amount

[25] "About the Issues of Collective Endowment and Substituting Fees for Labor Service Fees of the Township Job Center", issued by BB Township, Zhejiang province), and "Adhere to the Collective Endowment System, Improve the Double Management System", issued by the suburban area administration bureau of the JX city.

[26] "Advice on Building up the Collective Accumulation," issued by BB Township, Zhejiang province.

would then be deducted from what households would otherwise receive in benefits or funding program. Of the repayment records that I reviewed, including those for land requisition, almost all had a column titled "outstanding balance paid through deduction". While this may be an indication of how common unpaid balance had become, the root cause is a deeply flawed and inefficient tax system.

The second source of collective accumulation—agriculture development fund—has three components: money collected from the village, from the township and from the county. All the money is then aggregated and appropriated by the village and township governments. Money collected at the county level includes outlay from the county government, which is made up of the following: the amount of taxes collected for use of farmland retained by the county government, 6 percent of land fee collected by county-level land management bureau, 25 percent of the compensation paid for land transfer that goes into government coffer, a portion of the profit earned by the county-level enterprises, such as silk factories, that use agricultural materials, the live pig stability fund, the piglet fund. Money collected at the township level includes township and town enterprises' contributions toward the supplemental agricultural fund, the portion of land use fee retained by the township government, kiln and stone processing plants' payment toward resource utility fees, 20 percent of the user fee for land designated for residential housing, payments towards supplemental agricultural fund from state-owned enterprises, large-scale collectively owned enterprises, joint ventures (either investment or operations) and foreign enterprises, and enterprises operated by educational institutions, a portion of the 10 percent of pre-tax revenue of township and town enterprises that is slated for expenditure towards social causes, 10 percent of the amount of township and town fiscal revenue in excess of the basal contract target. Money raised from the village would include contributions from village enterprises, privately operated enterprises and individual workers toward the supplemental agricultural fund, 20 percent of dividend received by workers that work for state-owned enterprises, joint ventures (either investment or operations) and foreign enterprises, and enterprises operated by educational institutions, contributions toward supplemental agricultural fund from those who are self-employed in either commercial or agricultural enterprises; resource fees paid by village-owned stone-processing plants, craftsmen's contributions toward the supplemental agricultural fund; 40 percent of user fee for ancestral land; 10 percent of contribution enterprises make from their profits towards the village cooperative, and so forth.[27]

Contributions towards the agriculture development fund are much more closely related to [village] resources than do village reserve and township endowment. And for that reason, it is easier for primary-level authority to gain control over them. Even though where the money comes from is clearly

[27] "Notice on Regulating and Improving the Agriculture Development Fund System", issued by a county government in Zhejiang province.

recorded in the books at the county and township levels, at the village level, how much village enterprises actually contribute is largely determined by the measure of control primary-level authorities have over them. Conversely, we might say that it is determined by how dependent enterprises are on primary-level authorities. This affects the structural relationship between the two sides and their respective positions in negotiations. As a result of the confluence of these factors, the fundraising capacity differs significantly from village to village. Given the relatively primitive state of institutionalization of accounting work, village officials are often unaware of the amount of profits enterprises generate. In order to attract contracting enterprises, and to facilitate their management, most villages would set a fundraising target, say, 100,000 yuan per year, based on estimates. But since these estimates typically are rather independent of and unrelated to enterprise profits, more often than not they come nowhere close to the ratio requirements set by the county and township governments.

In order to sustain these revenue sources, a key task for primary-level authorities is to establish a personnel system that would allow them to use interpersonal (even personal) relationships to make up for the lack of institutional trust. The way it works is that one member of the cadre would be tasked with taking on dual identities (representing the collective and also the enterprises), so that people running enterprises would be sure to discharge their obligation to contribute fund towards the collective. But while this individual may be dependable, insofar as they are able to see to it that the village receives the money it needs to raise, they are not necessarily best suited to run a business. In those villages that have, for one reason or another, opted out of this practice, the relationship between the cadres and the local businesses is often fraught. However, since all local businesses must use those resources that can only be provided by the collective, including the electric power grid, "collectively owned" land and buildings, bank loans, collaterals for credits and other things any start-up would need, that is, since they cannot "buy" these things on the market at comparable prices, they have to come to terms with their dependency on the "collective", even though they are vexed by the unlimited demands it makes on them.

When it comes to the amount of contribution towards the collective coffer, those who must pay always wish it was smaller, and those who must collect it always wish it was bigger. As far as primary-level authorities are concerned, the amount they are able to collect for village reserve, township endowment, and the [agriculture development] fund always falls short of what is needed. This explains the existence of an alternative form of collective accumulation that is not monetary, namely a supplemental contribution in the form of labor corvée.

> All males aged 18–55 and females aged 18–50 (including those who have moved to a city and not dependent on government grain allowance, but excluding non-tenured rural primary school teachers, students, cadres who have been specially

recruited by the government, soldiers on active duty, and those who are unable to engage in productive activities due to disease or disability) are subject corvée labor ...at the rate of 12 labor credits per person per year.[28]

The required number of "labor credit" changes from year to year, in some years it was 15, in others 10, depending on demand. While labor corvée primarily assumes the form of actual labor, "monetary equivalent" can also be accepted in lieu of labor, from those who are either unable or unwilling to perform the labor. The exchange rate between labor and money may be based on established rules (five to seven yuan per credit), or "set according to what is actually paid in remuneration for the labor performed". This largely depends on the kind of labor, since the labor demand for some types of work, such as carrying rocks used for road construction on one's bare back into the mountains, goes unmet no matter what the stipulated remuneration rate is. Since decisions about how much "labor" is needed are based on demand (and made by the village officials at the start of each year during planning, with the amount owed in remuneration settled at year's end, following the principle of clear separation between the village and villager team for accounting purposes), and also, and more importantly, the monetary value of each unit of labor is determined by village officials, the value at certain locales sometimes became so exorbitant the peasants could not afford them. Even demands issued by superior authorities could not make these payments meant to be a substitution for labor materialize. In theory, the money collected for these payments ought to be used to fund public works, such as repair and maintenance of agricultural fields, flood prevention and emergency response, tree planting campaigns, transportation development, projects in the public interest, water conservation projects, public welfare, and so forth. But in fact, what actually end up getting funded this way depends largely on the thinking of village officials. For example, some villages have long suffered from the lack of paved roads, yet when members of the community express their desire for these to be built and their willingness to contribute their labor towards the construction, more often than not they would receive little if any support from the village officials. The result is a good idea that was nothing more.

4.3 Township and Village Governments' *De Facto* Power to Set the Tax Rates

Since village reserve, township endowment, and corvée labor are the three main sources of collective accumulation, there are, in theory, definitive and clear rules about each one of them on the books. In practice, however, the collection of these contributions is not based strictly on individual obligations, but rather on collective obligations or obligations related to collective account settlement. This is reflected in the practice among village officials to decide

[28] Labor Contribution System of XT Village, Zhejiang province.

what fund to be purposed towards tax payment. For example, enterprises' operating funds might be drawn upon to pay taxes, i.e., to count towards tax contribution, without any regard for and completely independent of responsibility of individual taxpayers. Not only is this commonplace among rich villages, they see this as a source of pride. The township governments apparently do not see anything wrong with this practice. That are far more concerned with the amount actually received in tax payment, and if it allows them to meet the target. Indeed, more than a few village cadre hold the view that there is nothing objectionable about repurposing enterprise operating funds toward tax payment, and that is a form of welfare benefit provided by the village. In fact, in many prosperous villages, it is common practice to draw on the collective fund to cover taxes and fees that should be paid by individuals, and to finance public services with contributions extracted from profitable enterprises. [In these villages], money is directly from the villagers only when the above practice is not financially feasible. Since the tax target is set at specific amounts, while the percentage requirement does allow some latitude, households who cannot afford to pay are often cut some slack, as it would be useless to exercise coercion. These non-paying households would be subject to no action except a notation in the village ledger indicating that they "owe money". Village cadres would want as few people to know about such cases as possible out of fear of copycats.

According to our observation, farmers' actual tax burden far exceeded the three types of taxes and fees just discussed, and decisions about the additional obligations were mostly made by village and township leadership. Since there were no existing rules that could be cited as justification for the collection of these fees, these decisions were typically made after a brief discussion among a few cadres, who based their decisions on little more than the fact that other villages had done the same thing. Tables 4.1 and 4.2 show a Henan farmer's record of what they had been required to contribute in the spring and the fall of 1997, of which the amounts that went toward village reserve, township endowment and labor corvée account for but a relatively small percentage.

Table 4.1 Fees due in Spring 1997

Category	*Amount*	*Category*	*Amount*
Agricultural tax	2601	Family planning fund	273
Specialty product tax	1652	Road maintenance	452
House provident fund	1134	Capital and asset fund	172
Public welfare fund	566	Rescue for humans and animals	171
Management fee	1134	Old age home fund	172
Education fund surcharge	1747	Social and public interest causes fund	783
Local militia fund	181	Total	11,219.00
Special allowances	181	Per capita	147.62

Unit: yuan

Table 4.2 Fees due in Fall 1997

Category	*Amount*	*Category*	*Amount*
Village reserve and township endowment	10,377.40	Hybrid species seeds	1702
Jiuqigou	403.80	Newspapers, magazines, science and technology	249.60
Building roads in the mountains	814	Total	14,347.3
Wheat and rapeseed fund	799.5	Per capita	188.8

Unit: yuan

Data source: GW Village, Henan province, "Notice on contribution requirement for village residents", 1997

> There are 99 people in the brigade, including a few who had formally changed their registered source of food supply from cultivation to the market, and 78 who were registered as rural residents. Of these 78, two had no tax liability because unmarried, leaving 76 as the total number of people who had to pay taxes. With a total of 111 *mu* of land, leaving aside what was used for road construction, per capita land allocation was 1.25 *mu*.

The amount in each category of contribution would first be set down in documents issued by the county and township governments. This would be followed by calculations aimed at arriving at an average by factoring in such things as the size of the land, population, and the type of labor individuals engaged in. Usually, the pre-set figure would fall within the ballpark of the correct numbers. But it looks like, judging from the table above, that contributions toward the housing provident fund, the public welfare fund and the management fee (collected in the spring) in effect duplicated the contribution toward village reserve (collected in the fall), since it is made clear in quite a number of government documents that the village reserve covers exactly these three items. Furthermore, contributions toward "local militia fund, special allowances, family planning, road maintenance and education fund surcharge", which were all slated to be collected in the spring, were exactly what would be covered under "Five Fundraisers", which is collected in the fall. Conventionally, "Five Fundraisers" raises money for the following: building rural schools, special allowances for veterans and families of fallen soldiers, family planning, training local militia, and building roads in rural areas.[29] Obviously, villages must make sure that everything looks perfectly reasonable and justified on paper, yet the villagers have little knowledge about what exactly is in the records. They are never consulted, nor is their permission ever sought. This way, village officials get to decide how much money to try to raise, how to raise it, entirely at their own discretion.

XT Village fundraising methods for electrification of public facilities:

[29] See "Adhere to the Collective Endowment system, Improve the double management system", issued by the suburban area administration bureau of the JX city.

- Each registered resident of the village is required to contribute 10 yuan.
- Each household must pay 20 yuan per *mu* of paddy field they are contracted to farm as according to the official record, and any sub-contracts among households are to be factored in to make sure no land is unaccounted for.
- 30 percent of the base amount each village team pays each team member household.
- The contract team head is responsible for collecting the contribution, no less than 50 percent of which must be in cash.
- For those households who owe utility payments, measures must be taken to collect the money.
- Collection is to take place between December 2nd and December 5th, and must be completed no later than December 25th.[30]

That village officials should have such vast discretion in tax-related matters has more than a little to do with the presumption of justifiability what primary-level authorities do has historically enjoyed. Thanks to this presumption, these officials are unencumbered by the need to ensure that what they do have basis in the law. In the minutes we reviewed for meetings where village officials discussed money collection there was no trace of concern about whether they had the legitimate right to make such decisions. Nor did we see attempts to establish their legal mandate to collect fees. Indeed, it is explicitly stated in *Instructions for Implementation of the New Tax System* that "with regard to the system of agriculture tax collection, local authorities have a certain measure of discretion".[31]

As for the reason for such wide latitude, it can, in my view, be traced back to the long-standing tradition of allowing *de facto* spending need to dictate collection target. For example, when, in 1994, the central government delegated the power to collect slaughter tax to sub-national governments, Zhejiang provincial government announced that their purpose for collecting this tax was "to ensure that the local government could raise the funds it needed, to facilitate the work of collection entities, and the implementation of examination and quarantine measures".[32] In one document issued by one township government, it was stated that "all units (villages) must base the total amount to be raised on their actual needs, and notify residents of the amount due as early as possible, and to avoid collection in installments let residents feel that they are being asked to pay again and again".[33] Evidently, according to this way of

[30] Minutes for the village meeting, "Opinions on the Electrification of Our Village".

[31] Zhejiang Provincial Bureau of Finance and Taxation. (n.d.). (ed.) *Practical Manual of the New Tax System*, "Chapter 8: Agricultural Tax System", unpublished, 359.

[32] Zhejiang Provincial Bureau of Finance and Taxation. (n.d.). (ed.) *Practical Manual of the New Tax System*, "Chapter 8: Agricultural Tax System", unpublished, 291.

[33] "Notice on Further Improvement of Rural Collective accumulation System", issued by BB Township, Zhejiang province.

thinking, the legitimacy of the source of the tax revenue has little to do with the rights of the taxpays, and much to do with the fiscal needs at the primary level as the officials see them. Determining how much to collect on the basis of expected expenditure, exploring ways to expand the tax base in order to meet actual needs and language such as "to ensure that the local government could raise the funds it needed" all go to show how this long standing basic principle ultimately helps explain the *de facto* mandate of primary-level authorities when it comes to tax-related matters. Under this principle, the collective does not need to abide by the tax law when setting the tax rates, and the tax law itself need have no organic relationship with stakeholders' rights to bargain, their consent or common understanding. Such summary dismissal of taxpayers' rights, and their role in the drafting of the tax law, is why no attempt has been made to establish relevant institutions that would clearly define the relationship between the two parties. In this may lie the reason why collecting taxes has always been so difficult, as has resorting to the law in addressing non-compliance and other irregularities.

Such difficulties notwithstanding, primary-level officials' power to set tax rates remains unchallenged. People are somehow convinced, erroneously, that the *status quo*, and perhaps even allowing primary-level authority to have still greater tax-related powers, is what is needed to solve the collection problem. As for these officials, they would rather deal with that problem year after year than giving up their prerogative and allowing others to also have a say in tax-related matters since after all the *status quo* helps perpetuate their power and dominance. Whenever it sees fit, township government has the full discretion to raise funds for practically anything, whether it is to build roads, install power lines, water pipes, build primary schools, or even to demand village residents to sell raw materials at ultra-low prices to local enterprises (such as what happened when villagers were asked to either supply ducks to the duck processing plants for free or sell them at below-market prices, as a form of local "tax"). As for the village government, it might require handicraftsmen or people who make a living doing odd jobs to pay agricultural tax retroactively, regardless of whether they turn a profit or receive welfare benefits villagers are entitled to. Their very livelihood is by itself enough to subject them to these taxes. For example, somebody who has purchased a tractor would be required to pay agricultural implementation usage tax, regardless of what the tractor is actually used for and how much it has contributed towards the bottom line. Similarly, if somebody slaughters a pig, unless it is used for observing a small number of festivals or as required by ethnic religions, they must pay slaughter tax whether they sell the meat or consume it themselves.[34] This is not unlike the system governing how village-operated enterprises pay taxes. Rarely would the details be laid out clearly and completely when the contract agreement is being negotiated.

[34] Zhejiang Provincial Bureau of Finance and Taxation. (n.d.). (ed.) *Practical Manual of the New Tax System*, 291.

Rather, either of two things that are polar opposites to each other would happen: the enterprise having to pay whatever amount village officials demand of them based on their estimate of how much needs to be raised, or not being asked to pay anything. The former is by far the more common scenario, which would explain the existence of reminders like this: "The village cooperative should consider not only how much they really need, but also what enterprises can afford, and try to keep the amount of required payment to no more than 30 percent of an enterprise's profit".[35]

While it issues these reminders to the village officials, the township government demands even more of those township enterprises run by it.

> In order to make ensure payment of asset usage fee, and also considering uncertainties in corporate performance, starting in 1991, said fee shall be collected in two installments. The first one would cover usage of assets, while the second one proportional contribution based on corporate net profit. The total should not exceed 40 percent of net profit. The enterprise department would calculate and ascertain the amount and notify each enterprise.[36]

Here the first installment essentially amounts to a rental fee for the assets, while the second one a tax. The first one is set in advance, and stays the same regardless of the profit. Therefore, not only does whoever that becomes a member of the governing body at the township or village level become the *de facto* legitimate collector of the rent, but they also can set the amount at whatever level they want.

> The amount to be paid in the first installment, i.e., the asset usage fee, is set forth in a binding agreement, such that if the enterprise suffers losses, then it must meet its payment obligation by drawing from funds it would otherwise use to pay staff salaries. The guaranteed minimum to be paid in salary would be lowered to 340 yuan per person, and the amount for construction materials enterprises would not exceed 1260 yuan. This payment is to be made on a quarterly basis. The account would be balanced every year, and the result would be one indicator used to evaluate the job performance of the head of the enterprise.[37]

As for the other things toward which enterprises are expected to contribute, it is up to the different departments of concern to set the exact amount.

- Operational costs: Industry, transportation, and construction enterprises must contribute 0.5 percent of their sales revenue; the amounts for commercial enterprises are 2 percent of sales revenue totaling more than five million yuan, and 1 percent if total revenue is under five million yuan.

[35] "Regulations on the Implementation of Several Specific Policies on the Rural Areas in the Year 1993", issued by HYBB Township, Zhejiang province.

[36] "Opinions on the Implementation of the Township Enterprise Contract Responsibility System", issued by HYBB Township, Zhejiang province.

[37] "Opinions on the Implementation of the Township Enterprise Contract Responsibility System", issued by HYBB Township, Zhejiang province.

- Management costs: Industry, transportation, and construction enterprises must contribute 0.5 percent of their sales revenue (or revenue from projects); commercial enterprises and restaurants and food retailers must contribute 0.3 percent of their sales revenue.
- Special purpose fund: Paper material fee is collected from each staff member on enterprise payroll, at the rate of 0.5 yuan per person. And for those from whose monthly paycheck union membership dues are automatically deducted, no separate payment is necessary. Training and education costs are covered by monthly contribution from enterprises in the amount of 0.05 percent of sales revenue. Pension is collected each month from each staff member on enterprise payroll at the rate of 5 yuan per person, to be handed over to the pension fund for township and village workers. Technology development fund: enterprises must contribute one percent of their monthly sales revenue; supplemental agricultural fund calls for a 3 yuan per employee contribution from enterprises. The base salary on the basis of which the amount of contribution towards each of the three types of fund is calculated is an average of 80 yuan per person a month.[38]

Even more demanding requirements are reserved for sole proprietors and small business-owners, who have no say at all in setting these requirements.

> When individuals submit their applications to set up private enterprises, they must make a one-time guarantee payment (in cash) to the office in charge. The amount for regular enterprises is 500 yuan, and for textile factories it is 500 yuan per spinning machine. Besides taxes, electricity bill (collected in accordance with pertinent regulations enforced by concerned agencies), private enterprises are also liable for contributions towards a number of funds:

- Agriculture development fund: 3 yuan per payroll staff member per month, 6 yuan per spinning machine per month
- Education surcharge: 1 yuan per payroll staff member per month, 2 yuan per spinning machine per month
- Family planning fund: 1 yuan per payroll staff member per month, 2 yuan per spinning machine per month
- General use fund: 2 yuan per payroll staff member per month, 5 yuan per spinning machine per month[39]

The amount to be collected for many types of taxes and fees is set on the basis of the type of work involved and fixed tax rates, and regardless of differences among workers in salary and productivity, everybody is liable to pay the same amount. This practice does not take into consideration fluctuations in

[38] "Regulations on the Required Contribution by Enterprises and Related Financial Issues", issued by the Industrial Office of HYBB Township, Zhejiang province.

[39] "Regulations on Further Improving the Management of Private Enterprises (Trial)", issued by the Industrial Office of HYBB Township, Zhejiang province.

salary, so while it appears to be egalitarian, in fact it is not equitable. Because it treats people at different earning levels alike for tax purposes, who must shoulder the same burden despite these differences. Not only does this do nothing to remedy inequities in income, it exacerbates them by adding to the strain low-income individuals are already subject to. The inequity becomes even more egregious when we factor in the uses towards which the tax money is put. Most of it goes towards agriculture (investment, maintenance), instead of public undertakings, most of which anyway has its own fundraising regime. What this essentially does is to evenly spread out the burden of financially supporting agricultural development among individuals who earn different incomes, and who do not benefit, both actually and potentially, from these investments to the same degree. Most importantly, investors cannot make choices on the basis of return on their investments, or exercise any kind of control or oversight over who are in charge of these investments and how they discharge their duties. In this sense, investment becomes coerced. This gives tax collectors the incentive to levy taxes not only arbitrarily but also discriminately (such as applying different rates to collectively owned enterprises and private-owned enterprises). Arbitrariness contributes to unchecked expansion of payroll and expenditure increases; while discrimination turns tax collection into a means of robbing some people of their resources and handing them over to others.

With regard to personal matters with public service relevance, such as old-age care, healthcare, insurance and family planning, there usually is no room for people to make their own choices, so any mechanism for encouraging competition among entities responsible for allocating public resources is non-existent. In the countryside taxes in these categories are currently under monopoly control, collected exclusively by concerned government agencies, an arrangement that still feels very much like a form of coercive fundraising, and can easily generate resentment among the rural population. Resistance takes the form of widespread coordinated non-payment, something that is abundantly borne out by checks conducted by primary-level financial officers. The mandatory nature of these requirements is also manifested in the fact that these tax collection "targets" are essentially set through administrative decisions, which are based on conventional practice and experience, instead of taxpayer incomes. The "targets" are determined without any knowledge of how much people actually earn, and no ceiling is set. The larger the payment amount the better, and the size of the payment by an organization is positively correlated with the amount of monetary reward its senior leaders receive (see Tables 4.3 and 4.4). The question of the legal justifiability of collecting so much money apparently is never given any thought.

Evidently, the design of the rural tax system revolves around how much can be collected, and is relatively unconcerned with how to win public's support for the tax structure, that is, the question of its legitimacy. Still less attention is paid to the issue of how to make sure the money collected is used towards providing public services, and taxpayers accept their tax liability as something reasonable and justified. Such lack of societal support and the involvement of

Table 4.3 County government departments tax collection performance evaluation form, 1997

Department	*Target (10,000 yuan)*	*Amount collected (10,000 yuan)*	*Bonus for officials with full ranks (yuan)*	*Bonus for officials with deputy and vice ranks (yuan)*	*Penalty for officials with full ranks (yuan)*	*Penalty for officials with deputy and vice ranks (yuan)*
Culture and education	2.4	21.8	800	600	N/A	N/A
Commerce	1.3	8.7	500	300	N/A	N/A
Construction	9.3	25.2	1100	800	N/A	N/A
Resources	23	56.73	2000	1400	N/A	N/A
Agricultural Machinery	50	103	3200	2200	N/A	N/A
Agriculture	1.5	2.67	500	400	N/A	N/A
Foodstuff	12.1	19.31	800	600	N/A	N/A
Transportation	64.6	76.33	2600	1800	N/A	N/A
Civic affairs	2	2.3	500	400	N/A	N/A
County	123	124	3000	2400	N/A	N/A
Feed factory	10.2	10.3	700	400	N/A	N/A
Engineering	53.8	60	1000	800	N/A	N/A
Commerce	20.6	20.54	N/A	N/A	500	300
Trade	308.4	183.33	N/A	N/A	2600	1700
Management	22.4	11.9	N/A	N/A	500	200
Corporation management	174.9	83.82	N/A	N/A	2000	1900
Planning	13.2	6	N/A	N/A	500	200
Fuels	31.5	27.07	N/A	N/A	2000	1300

Note: Money needed to pay the bonus must be raised by each department, penalty must be paid before February 25 at the government office.

Table 4.4 Township tax collection performance evaluation form, 1997

Name of township	*Annual target (10000 yuan)*	*Amount collected (10000 yuan)*	*Bonus for CPC committee secretary (yuan)*	*Bonus for chief of township (yuan)*	*Bonus for deputy chief of township (yuan)*
ZHB	242.6	256.6	5000	5000	5000
SHZ	470.8	484.8	5000	5000	5000
QT	737.4	757.4	5000	5000	5000
TG	321.4	321.4	5000	5000	5000
LC	214.5	214.5	5000	5000	5000
BZH	375.3	375.3	5000	5000	5000

Note: Money needed for the bonus is to be raised by each township

Source of data: "Fiscal Affairs Bulletin, 1997", SHZ township, Hebei province (February 1998)

stakeholders in the decision-making process is the key reason for the collection difficulties primary-level authorities face. Without the participation of those who pay the taxes and fees in the whole process, there can be no broad-based societal consensus on the legitimacy of the system, and no way for the preferences and values the individuals and organizations that have been given equal rights to be fully expressed. As a result, coercion must be resorted to to carry out the collection, necessarily generating tension and conflict between reluctant and resentful payers on one side and determined collectors on the other.

4.4 The Absence of Procedural Constraints

While the existence of "a budget and fiscal spending review and approval system" is common in the rural areas, the primary concern of such a system is balancing the budget, following the principle of "spending within one's means, avoiding overrunning the budget".[40] There is nothing in it about giving taxpayers any control over the process. The budget is drafted by "the leadership through a deliberative process", which amounts to a group of people talking about how much of other people's money they plan to spend.[41] These people have complete discretion over how to collect money and how much to collect, and it is not difficult to imagine the consequences of that. Rural fiscal management includes two parts: revenue and expenditure. Sources of revenue include money collected from enterprises, public institutions, rural households, agriculture development funds, and others. Expenditure includes investments in various projects, spending on social welfare programs, procurement of fixed assets, and others. There is nothing like a dedicated committee tasked specifically with overseeing all these details. On the contrary, primary-level officials typically encourage putting control over this entire process in the hands of the one person chiefly in charge of township or village affairs, i.e., a kind of "stroke of a pen" review and approval system.

> Spending decisions concerning village collective accumulation shall be made strictly either in accordance with the stroke-of-a-pen review and approval system or when signed by the chair of the village council and countersigned by the CPC secretary. The CPC secretary must review each spending decision that was made personally by the chair of the village council. Accounting staff may refuse to execute a payment request if it has not been reviewed or not been reviewed properly.[42]

The likely rationale for rules like this is to prevent multiple departments from being able to make spending decisions, and expenditure from getting out

[40] Financial System of Budget and Final Accounts of TD Town, Zhejiang Province.

[41] Milton Friedman & Rose Friedman, *Free to Choose: A Personal Statement*, translated by Qi Hu, Xueyuan Xi, and Qiang An, (Beijing: Commercial Press, 1998: 119)

[42] "On Strengthening the Financial Management of the Village-level Collective Funds", issued by the SHZ County Party Committee in June 1998.

of control. However, such a rule also belies the failure to appreciate the fact that the one person that ought to be subject to restraints is the person who holds the power of the purse. Indeed, the absence of procedural constraints is a notable feature of just about every aspect of fiscal affairs management in the rural areas.

Despite of prohibitions in accounting rules and regulations "against the practice of appointing either key village officials themselves or their close relatives to the position of village accountant", such appointment does happen because it is practically impossible to prevent rule-bending in one form or another. The village accountant is on a par with all other village officials when it comes to "salary and other fringe benefits". In fact, more often than not the position is held by a village official. The appointment is made by the village leadership, with which the accountant maintains close ties and have some common interests. This means that if and when accounting rules come into conflict with orders from village officials, it is in the interest of the accountant to follow the latter over the former. After all, the mandate of the accountant is given to them not by the system but by individuals who run it. There is no autonomy to speak of for the accountant. The relationship between this person and superior government departments (township fiscal managers) is not like those between subordinate and superior, or those involving dispatch or even direct supervision. This person answers instead to the village leadership. Nor is the accountant answerable to the village delegates, still less to the financial management team. The only people the accountant has to answer to are those in the village leadership. And even though it is expressly stated that the accountant "has a range of rights, including the right to give suggestions to their own employer, its parent organization, and public institutions on matters related to the raising and use of funds and the management of assets, the right to perform oversight by issuing orders to curtail production, the right to report the financial situation of village cooperative organizations to superior authorities and other concerned departments, the right to disclose issues and problems in financial management, the right to decline to process either receivables or disbursement that run afoul of existing financial rules, the right to demand that such violations be halted and corrected, and reported to superior authorities for further disciplinary action",[43] apparently, this individual is not acting as a professional, nor is he answering to the demands of a professional body. Instead, this person is first and foremost trying to answer to the needs of political authorities on different rungs on the bureaucratic hierarchy, and whenever an executive order is issued to him by his superiors, he has no choice but to do what is asked of him.

More unusual still is the fact that more often than not the accountant is also a village cadre. This allows him to have a say in the appointment, promotion, and demotion of subordinate accounting staff, and be able to attend various

[43] Refer to the accounting system of the village-level economic cooperatives in TD town, Zhejiang province.

village meetings that discuss production, operations, and management.[44] When he does these things, he is discharging his managerial responsibilities in his capacity as a village cadre. The accountant enjoys no autonomy in relation to the village leadership, and nobody—in the form of either a superior financial department or some kind of villager association—exists that is specially positioned to provide the accountant with support. There is no such thing as a set of "institutional rules" that is independent of the orders of the village leadership to which the accountant is expected to answer. While such tension is an extremely rare occurrence, when it does occur, the accountant's delicate position compels them to play it safe, by, say, keeping their mouth shut, refusing to provide certain information, or cook the books when asked to by orders from the village leadership. Whenever the accountant decides to report something to their superior or village delegate, which sometimes can happen, it is usually due to conflict over power. But if things do come to a head like that, cooperation between the accountant and the village leadership effectively come to an end, and only one of the two parties can stay where they are. The following document filed in support of an appeal to a disciplinary decision handed down in one XNB village in Hebei province shows that a "fall" awaits an accountant who agreed to let somebody who had filed a complaint to "review the ledger".

> WGM, a member of the Communist Party of China, and a person of loyalty and honesty integrity, has served as the village accountant for many years. The decision by MJP, the Secretariat, to remove WGM from this position is completely unjustified. When asked why he had done this, he replied that since he was the CPC committee secretariat, he gets to decide who he wants and who he does not what for any job.[45]

Because the accountant has access to critical information, and because of the absence of any legal channel through which that information can become publicly available, it makes it all the more difficult for them to be neutral. Whoever who gets their support would *ipso facto* be able to access the ledger information, which would effectively give them an edge. Therefore, whenever a dispute regarding financial matters arises, all parties involved seek to secure influence over the accountant (as can be seen in the case about resettlement in relation to the construction of the power plant in Sichuan discussed in the chapter on village politics) in order to get whatever material that would support their own case (while prevent the other parties from doing the same), manipulate the books, and "protect the evidence" or otherwise "protect their reputation from being tarnished". When the village leadership gets hold of the necessary financial documents, the complainant, denied of what they need as evidence for their case, would usually file one appeal after another tenaciously. But if it is the complainant that has got hold of the documents they need, most

[44] Friedman & Friedman, *Free to Choose*, 1998: 119.

[45] See the support materials prepared in 1998 by several CPC members in XNB village, in Hebei province, for their petition.

often this would lead to escalation of the situation, and "damaged reputation". For this reason, village leadership rarely if ever encourages allowing the complainant themselves to look at the ledger. Instead, they would appoint an investigation team to do it, while making sure no other individual has access to the information (as can be seen in the case in Shandong discussed in the chapter on village politics), and that any report to be made public is only released when everybody involved has agreed to speak with one voice. However, if and when the investigation team arrives at the conclusion that "after multiple rounds of review no irregularity has been found", even though this may put an end to the appeal and petition, doubts and suspicion will linger. From the point of view of the village leadership, investigation by themselves would be able to "uncover the truth that the public is seeking and prove that members in their own rank are innocent of any wrongdoing".[46] But by contrast, village residents see such behavior as no more than efforts by village officials to cover up for one another so nobody is caught for anything that may be deleterious to their collective reputation. After all, if superior government officials come to know what village officials have done, there can be serious consequences. Ultimately, this form of "self-audit" offers a solution to such web of conflicts.

> There is this one village in our township, after one of the former village officials left office, he convinced several village residents to write a letter together asking the township authorities to audit the village's books. So that is what happened, but nothing amiss was discovered, and some efforts at clarifying things were made. But the people who wrote the letter were not convinced, and proceeded to write another letter, this time addressed to the city government. A number of people from the city's agriculture and commerce committee came to the village on a fact-finding trip; township authorities told them nothing is amiss with the village ledger, but the committee people from the city insisted that township authorities stepped up and do another check. So the ledger was brought over, and examined by a number of people, and then an announcement was made in the village that everything was in order. This time village residents kept quiet, but were they convinced?[47]

Another kind of organization where the applicable procedural rules imposed constraints on its functions was villager (democratic) "financial management team". What the team does is to make publicly available, albeit within certain limits, some portions of the ledger, for the purpose of preventing collusion among cadres.

> The democratic financial management team comprises five members, who are nominated by the villager delegation. Members can include a village delegate, an accounting staff and the chief of finance and head (of the economic cooperative), with the chief of finance serving as the team leader. The democratic financial

[46] Financial Audit Report of JX District, Zhejiang province, 1997.

[47] Transcript of the July 1997 interview with the township cadres in charge of finances in TD township, Zhejiang province.

> management team has its own official seal, which is kept by the team leader. The team is tasked with keeping track of account balance in cash, securities with market value, capital and assets, checking the financial propriety and soundness of each debit and credit, and correctness of every calculation by the accountant. In addition, the team is responsible for reviewing all original documentation submitted for processing reimbursement, putting its seal on those that are deemed legitimate and proper and issue recommendations about further actions for those that are questionable or objectionable, and send the latter to the agriculture and commerce bureau for further review.[48]

As the number of problems related to rural finances grew, the mandated responsibilities of the democratic financial management team also expanded.

> The democratic financial management team has a membership of five to seven people, who are chosen by the village delegates through election. Members can be village delegates or CPC village committee members in charge of disciplinary inspection. One person would be the head of the team. The team oversees compliance with financial rules and regulations, and looks especially closely at spending plans, earnings allocation plans, how money from the housing provident fund, the public interest fund, and welfare payout is withdrawn and disbursed, how the salary for the managerial staff is set, how well contracting and other economic agreements are executed and enforced. The team has access to everything from cash, bank deposits, assets, products and the ledger, and any attempt at obstructing the team's work is prohibited.[49]

Compared with the 1992 rules, those from 1996 included certain concretely specific "right": nomination was changed to election, and instead of stipulating outright who the team leader would be, the rules called, albeit in cryptic terms, for the "emergence" of one. In addition, the rights mentioned in the 1992 rules mostly pertain to checking and verifying outcomes, while the 1996 rules mandate examination of financial and distribution plans. These changes should be considered progress.

However, the progress was on paper only, since there was no real way for these rules to be implemented, due to faulty design of the power structure of the team. For example, the head of the financial management team is the head of the economic cooperation, yet the person who serves as the head of the economic cooperation is usually also the Party secretariat, and the Party secretariat, who possesses centralized power to rule on applications, is hierarchically above the member of the CPC village committee in charge of disciplinary inspections. The financial management team also includes an accountant, and this person is answerable to the team in the same way they are answerable to the Party secretariat. In some villages the financial management team is made

[48] "System of Democratic Financial Management and Fiscal Transparency" issued by TD town in 1992.

[49] "System of Democratic Financial Management and Fiscal Transparency" issued by TD town in 1996.

up primarily of village cadre or people who have been nominated by the village cadre. Other villages would submit team membership information to their superior simply for the sake of appearing to have provided this information, yet the team never actually meets or does anything. Furthermore, if the seal of the team is kept by the "team's head" (cadre), it would mean that him putting the stamp on something amounts to the same thing as the team itself doing that. Basically, from an institutional and structural point of view, the "financial management team" is essentially inseparable, in terms of both power and interests, from those individuals whose behavior [the team's head] is supposed to oversee. It is unclear who the people are this person is responsible for, and whether it comes down to either self-regulation or regulation by one's subordinates, where would the incentive to do it come from at all? Moreover, the power with which the financial management team is entrusted is reactive in nature, in the sense that their work is only in the form of checks and investigations *ex post facto*, and does not involve monitoring or review for approval prior to a transaction. So the existence of the team does nothing to prevent illegal tax collection or spending. Any investigation of possible wrongdoing must be initiated by the team's head, but why on earth would this person want to have people look over transactions on the books that they themselves have approved? This means that even though nobody "attempts to obstruct what the financial management team is charged with doing", built-in structural impediments make it both undesirable and difficult for the team to carry out its duties. In other words, whatever "mandate" they appear to have is effectively unactionable.

In some places the awareness of the risk of the village cadres exerting undue influence over the accountant has led to deliberate efforts at building necessary distinctions into the institution, i.e., by requiring the financial management team to be answerable to the township government. But instead of putting the power of oversight over financial matters into the hands of the village residents, this requirement has made it that much easier for township and town government to watch over village cadre, but now with the help of people from the primary level. Because what this requirement really does is to put more financial regulatory power into the hands of the "officials in charge of agricultural and commerce" at the county or township levels, and not in the hands of village delegates, those who represent the people who actually pay the taxes. Essentially, this primary-level financial regulatory model is still largely of the traditional kind, characterized by oversight by superior government organs (that is, people who rule those who pay taxes, instead of those who represent them).

> The village shall set up a collective asset management team, headed by either the CPC committee secretariat or the village chief. Different individuals will serve as the bursar, accountant, and supervisor. Close relatives of village cadres are not allowed to serve in any of the positions related to financial matters, and the team's head is answerable to the county agriculture and commerce bureau, as well as the

> township agriculture and commerce authorities... The village shall set up a democratic financial management team, whose five to seven members shall be individuals who have some familiarity with financial matters and are fair-minded who have been elected by the village delegates. The membership list is submitted to the township agriculture and commerce authorities to be kept on file, and membership serve three-year terms, with no term limits. Key members of the village leadership are barred from serving on this team.[50]

Such a guiding philosophy entails that the purpose of setting up the democratic financial management team is not so much to allow village delegates to become involved in oversight, but rather to facilitate monitoring by superior government organs by making it easier for them to obtain the necessary information for conducting audits. The "mandates" given to the financial management team is not the power to "make decisions" but the power to "report things to superiors". And insofar as the team does discharge its regulatory responsibility over-spending, it complies not with the demands of the village residents but those of the superior financial authorities.

The responsibilities of the democratic financial management team are:

(1) monitor and perform oversights over financial activities of collective economic organizations and the village council;
(2) collect and report to superior government bodies complaints and suggestions from members of the public;
(3) check all items of income, and deny approval to spending that are inappropriate;
(4) provide assistance to the agriculture and commerce authorities as they perform oversight over collective accumulation;
(5) any other responsibilities stipulated by the villager meeting or village delegation meeting.

Ad hoc spending items shall be subject to strict scrutiny, as well as extra-budgetary spending in notable amounts. Those that are deemed genuinely necessary must be approved by the village delegates after a deliberation process. Further approval from the agriculture and commerce authorities is needed as well.

> The power to approve budgetary expenditure in amounts under 100 yuan for non-production purposes and under 500 yuan for production purposes rests with the team's head alone; the power to approve budgetary expenditure in amounts over 100 yuan for non-production purposes and over 500 yuan for production purposes rests with the democratic financial management team, and any approval must be certified by a stamp with the team seal.[51]

[50] "Opinions on Strengthening Financial Management in Rural Areas", issued by SHZ County, Hebei province in June 1998.

[51] "Opinions on Strengthening Financial Management in the Rural Areas", issued by SHZ County, Hebei province in June 1998.

So it is easy to understand how the power the financial management team had did not come from either the stipulation about it being "answerable to villager delegation meeting" or from tax-paying village residents but from superior government financial organs, which had given that power to the team. This is why, indeed, that the financial management team cannot get anything done without the backing from superior government.

> Anything from budgets, production plans, public interest project plans, infrastructure construction plans, fiscal and spending plans to eligibility requirements for contracts across different sectors must be discussed and approved by the democratic financial management team before they can take effect. The team is accountable to the villager delegation meeting, and is required to discharge its responsibilities diligently. The villager committee must subject itself to oversight and regulation by the democratic financial management team, do what it can to make it easy for the team to do its work, and refrain from engaging in any behavior that might be obstructionist.[52]

Not unlike the way the financial management team is set up, the villager delegation meeting is practically inconsequential in relation to financial matters at the village level even though it is, according to the law, supposed to impose procedural constraints. In the rules for these meetings it is common to see specifications of the types of matters that can be "formally discussed". They mostly cover finance and accounting management, budget and review of spending, expenditure in excess of 500 yuan for non-production purposes, and expenditure in excess of 3000 yuan for production purposes, various spending decisions and public interest undertakings, village reserve, fundraising, the signing-up, arrangement and deployment of corvée labor, and major issues with significant impact on the interests of the village residents.[53]

Yet, even in model villages where compliance with bureaucratic norms is strong, the subjects brought up for discussion at the village delegation meetings tend to be confined to gathering feedback to proposals already submitted by the village officials, as in discuss, raising concerns, stating opinions and attitude.[54] The primary objective of the village delegation meetings is to provide a space for attendants to express either support or opposition to decisions that have already been made. It may deny approval to a decision (which would lead to the village officials making a different decision), or choose one from several, but it does not make decisions of its own, and only ratifies those that have been made by primary-level officials. In Huojia Village in Jilin province, for example, statistical records show that villager delegation meetings were convened 14 times in 1992, where 21 proposals from the village council were discussed and

[52] Friedman & Friedman, *Free to Choose*, 1998: 119.

[53] "The Village Delegation's Functions and Responsibilities", in *The Village Delegation System in Rural China*, ed. Primary-level Governance Research Programme (Beijing: China Social Publishing House, 1994), 77.

[54] Friedman & Friedman, *Free to Choose*, 1998: 119.

voted on, in which nine did not pass and the other 21 did.[55] However, a review of records of the 37 times the villager delegates met between 1992 and 1998 suggests that even in such a model village with respect to the operation of the village delegation meetings, genuine oversight through "discussion" of receipts and disbursements is rare (see Table 4.5).

Most frequently on the agenda of the village delegation meetings in this particular village are actions related to decisions issued by the village officials, including discussing them, declaring one's stance on them, publicizing them, implementing them and passing them. With regard to financial matters, if they concern some project in the village, or something that involves the collection of fees, something that requires fundraising, for either all or part of the amount that is needed, village delegates can have meaningful participation in the process. For example, how much each person would contribute toward road construction was decided (at the tenth meeting of the third delegation, held in July 1997). Other topics were on ways to exercise discretion while trying to comply with requirements issued by county and township governments. For example, it was decided (at the eighth meeting of the third delegation, held in November 1996) that monetary payment in lieu of labor input is acceptable as a form of contribution toward public works projects that take a long time to complete, and an increase was approved for village reserve and township endowment (at the seventh meeting of the third delegation, held in May 1996). What these topics of discussion had in common is they were all concerned with the receipt of incoming funds, and "approval" would have made it easier to raise funds or collect fees, but otherwise there is almost nothing to suggest that the village delegation meetings placed any restrictions on either the village budget or expenditure. Expenditure in very small amounts does not have to be brought up for discussion by the village delegates, especially if it concerns administrative overhead at the primary level, including the costs of routine activities and the budget. Things that are brought up for discussion tend to concern production projects, i.e., whether to partner with Heihe to build a brick factory, and whether to build an outer wall and a gas station. Yet these discussions are confined to the question of "yes" or "no" to the project in question, and do not concern either the review or approval of budgetary spending. What this means is that if and when village delegates approve a particular project, this amounts to giving village authorities the license to make use of and manage the fund for the project in any which way they see fit. As a consequence, the rule that says "approval by the village delegation meeting is required for disbursement in excess of 1000 yuan" has become, in practice, a requirement for projects that are projected to cost more than 1000 yuan to be approved by the village delegation meetings. And once a project is approved, even though the delegates' right to continue to monitor its progress has not been suspended, much of the usefulness of such a right has been lost. Such an institutional configuration ensures the delegates' inability to exercise meaningful control over the use of funds.

[55] *The Village Delegation System in Rural China*, 1994, 78.

Table 4.5 Huojia village villager delegation meetings agenda

Date	*Agenda*	*Date*	*Agenda*
Jan. 11, 1992	Presentation of village cadre personal mission statement	No. 29, 1994	Brick factory contracting, setting compensation standard for land use
Jan. 12, 1992	Election of village council member candidates	Dec. 7, 1994	Mobilization for election of new delegates
Jan. 15, 1992	Election of village council chair and vice chair	Dec. 14, 1994	Out-going village delegates presenting their personal mission statement
Jan. 28, 1992	Agricultural production, enterprise development, land use by brick factory	Dec. 22, 1994	Setting schedule for next election
Jan. 29, 1992	Compulsory education, salary for corporate employees	Dec. 29, 1994	Certification of candidates for general election, set scheduling for run-off election
Feb. 17, 1992	Terms of return of land by brick factory	Jan. 3, 1995	Selecting candidates for village delegates
Feb. 21, 1992	Corporate managerial staff reorganization	Jan. 12, 1995	Inaugural address by newly elected delegates
Feb. 23, 1992	Election of corporate managers, personal mission statement by newly-elected corporate managers	May 16, 1995	Education spending, examination for recruiting reserve cadre
March 31, 1992	Setting up food processing plant, management of volunteers	Oct. 15, 1995	Issues related to agricultural machinery use in land tillage
June 15, 1992	Contract workers, setting standards or land usage fee, farm land restoration	Jan. 18, 1996	Establishing measures for disease prevention for farm animals
Aug. 12, 1992	Different models of operation, recruiting talents, policy incentives	April 26, 1996	Mechanization in agriculture, development of rural enterprises
Sept. 16, 1992	Establishing brick factory, establishing livestock market	May 25, 1996	Discussing target for village reserve set by the township government
Oct. 22, 1992	Plans for economic development zone	Nov. 17, 1996	Staff streamlining
Dec. 30, 1992	Review of 1992 work performance, announce work plan for 1993	March 3, 1997	Brick factory offering stocks to employees, defining cadre job duties
Feb. 5, 1993	Promoting market-oriented thinking, planning for agricultural, industrial and derivative industries	July 9, 1997	Examination of road repair plans
April 23, 1993	Establishing a brick factory in Heihe, hog farm plans	Aug. 5, 1997	Job performance evaluation of CPC committee, solicitation of comments and suggestions
Jan. 16, 1994	Review of 1993 work performance, announce work plan for 1994	Sept. 11, 1997	Decision regarding labor input-monetary contribution exchange rate for public works
June 30, 1994	Economies of scale, private enterprises, plan for new village	Feb. 10, 1998	Enforcement of agricultural tax cut and exemption
Aug. 9, 1994	Mechanization of agricultural production, upgrading farmland and forest network	June 23, 1998	Setting the timeline for the fourth election
Oct. 6, 1994	Work plans for late fall and early winter		

Note: Based on Huojia Village, Jilin province village delegation meeting minutes, 1992–1998.

In the absence of procedural constraints that might have been imposed by the village delegation meetings, review of and decision on financial matters at the village level end up relying on either "the stroke of a pen" or reciprocal reviews and approvals among the cadres. This means that how the system works hangs entirely on the moral caliber of a single or at most a small number of cadres. In other words, the [legitimacy of the] system is wholly predicated on the presumption that the person wielding that "one pen" is absolutely fair-minded and just. However, judging from testimonies from village residents, the "stroke of a pen" system of review has little credibility.

> Even within a household you cannot imagine not discussing matters related to family expenses with the wife and children, how is it that in a village, which can easily spend anywhere between a few hundred thousand yuan and a few million yuan a year, can be allowed to put all the decision-making power in one pen, i.e., the hands of the one person holding it? But such being the rules set down by superior government, nobody in the village has the audacity to raise concerns, not village officials, who would rather not let the Genie out of the bottle, and still less the residents.[56]

In fact, even results of official monitoring, such as the yearly checks conducted by the county task force on village financial affairs, indicate that the "stroke of a pen" review system has very low regulatory efficacy. In official reports, there is ample evidence that many spending decisions approved under such a system that were recorded in official documents were haphazard. Any constraints that might have been expected from such a system is non-existent.

> Since last year, we have in this township declared illegitimate and revoked eight documents related to the collection of agriculture-related fees, including multi-channel fundraising to finance education, rolling loans, distribution of rat poisoning and iodized salt, universal voluntary collective self-defense and others. Another 13 charges deemed to have weak justification were also dropped, including fundraising through land development, insurance for students, family planning deposit, single child birth permit, school uniform, ancestral home land size measurement fee, voluntary collective self-defense, and others. All this amounts to an estimated saving of more than 600,000 yuan for local residents.[57]
>
> Judging from the results of the clean-up, several issues with the way village finances are managed stand out. First, cash flow is poorly monitored. Among the 28 pilot villages, there were 1,446 cash payouts totaling 2.1876 million yuan for which there was neither an invoice nor any other form of official record. Of the 1,446 disbursements, 225, amounting to a total of 3,007,000 yuan had not

[56] Keshu Wang, et al, "Strengthening Financial Management Is an Important Way to Increase Villager Autonomy", in *Compendium of Documents on the Transparency of Village Affairs*, ed. Primary-level Governance Office of the Civil Affairs Ministry (unpublished, 1997), 182.

[57] Wenzhi Wang, "Rural primary-level organization construction in QT township in Hebei province" (a speech), July 1998.

undergone any review and the purpose for the use of fund could not be accounted for. As a result of the audit and clean-up the aggregate value of the net assets for the 28 pilot villages dropped by 8.22 million yuan, and another 4.69 million-yuan worth of assets off the books was uncovered. In GT township the village CPC secretary alone took out loans totaling 230,000 yuan, and the village accountant took out an unauthorized loan in the amount of 23,000 yuan to pay for a motorcycle. Everybody treated the collective fund as if it was their own piggybank. Secondly, financial documents are significantly inaccurate. Fix assets are not regularly appraised, and material properties are not regularly inventoried, making discrepancy between what actually exists and what is recorded on the books inevitable. There were 11 pieces for which no official record exists, valued at 908,200 yuan. There were another 27 pieces of material assets, at an estimated value of 1.40 million yuan, that did not exist at all despite there being record thereof. In 1992, an office building was built in XZH village. Yet the accountant could find no construction contract, no cost estimate or budget, and certainly no proof of asset transfer. All we have is a slip of paper on which it was written that the village committee chair has taken out 206,000 yuan. Thirdly, the line was blurred between the debtor and the collector, and too many accounts were not in good standing. Village enterprises easily got away with not paying their due, and little was done to collect the money. In AX township alone 558 individuals were identified as owing money, with the amount of money totaling 906,500 yuan. In QT township 18 pieces of public property, worth 4,300 yuan, had been in the private possession of nine individuals. In some villages, due to poor management of land requisition fee it is not uncommon have the money divvied up illegally among the cadres and residents. For example, in GT township, the money collected in land requisition fees was gobbled up so quickly practically every household in the village had at least 10,000 yuan in their account overnight. Fourthly, expenditure for non-production purposes was massive. According to data collected for 17 villages for the 1992–1995 period, management fee alone for the four-year period reached 3.144 million yuan, accounting for 29 percent of four-year aggregate village GDP, and 84.4 percent of the receipts of the three agricultural taxes combined, which came to 3.726 million yuan. Out of the management fee expenditure on reception alone was 558,800 yuan, which accounted for 5 percent of village reserve. In DY village, 24,000 yuan was spent on reception in 1994, averaging 2,032 yuan a month. Auditing of the books for JL village shows that not only did the village CPC committee secretary spend lavishly on meals on public's dime, but he also pocketed another 4,100 yuan in reimbursement for restaurant. In addition, the head of the brick factory, who also serves on the village CPC committee, has failed to report any money he has received since 1994, embezzling more than 30,000 yuan in public fund.[58]

We can easily see from these documents that notwithstanding the existence of procedural oversight on paper—any budget and changes to one must be passed by the village delegation meeting before it goes into effect—such rule has no teeth due to the absence of any meaningful distribution of power. Village delegates are people who also serve as village cadre and in leadership

[58] "Report on Village Finance" of JX Town, Zhejiang province, December, 1996.

positions in the (natural) village, and are mostly expected to carry out and relay orders. Therefore, they tend to have little knowledge about receipts or spending, and are poorly qualified to veto on fiscal matters and the budget. Furthermore, since the village delegation meetings are convened by the village council, a body that lacks any independence because it has numerous ties and shared interests with village officials, there is no reason to suspect that the meetings can perform the regulatory function purportedly expected of it. And it is precisely because a vote by such a body carries no weight at all as a resolution and is only useful for purpose of information gathering, it has never been taken seriously by the village delegates, who mostly regard it as little more than a kind of notification, not unlike whatever announcements made by the village in the form of tables drawn up on the public announcement bulletin board. In practice, budgets were rarely discussed before they go into effect. Usually it only shows up in the year-end report. So even if and when problems are detected, there is no way it can be "addressed in a timely fashion", since it will already be at the end of the year in question. Besides, thanks to their growing technicality matters related to the budget are inaccessible to the ordinary folks, who more often than not would lack the kind of training needed to master them. In reality, fiscal management at the primary level is hardly ever done "preemptively".

4.5 Self-regulation

The only entity that might be able to place any kind of limits on spending at the village level would be superior government bodies, and not "democratic financial management team" or "village delegation meetings". This would explain why the intended reviewer of the following application is neither of the latter two, who represent taxpayers, but rather somebody in the township government, whose approval is what is being sought.

> Township CPC committee, the government,
>
> The CPC committee, cooperative and villager committee of this village hereby request approval for tripling of the year-end bonus for key village cadres, at the amount of 1,650 yuan. We have arrived at this decision after reviewing the performance evaluation of key township CPC and government leaders for 1992, the state of the village for this calendar year, and considering the average bonus for the two CPC committee members at the village enterprise (550 yuan), and careful discussion of the matter among committee members.
>
> Thank you for your consideration.
>
> Salute.
>
> BB Township XT village CPC committee
> Economic cooperative
> Jan. 6, 1993

[Reply]

A decision was reached by the township CPC committee and the government after joint consultation that the year-end bonus would be tripled.

(Signature)

Feb. 4, 1993

The reason behind this is that the salary for village official is set by superior governments, and usually no consultation is needed with either the financial management team or the village committee. While in principle there are rules on the books that require "the salaries and months covered for village officials at all levels to be determined on the basis of the income of the village residents and the officials' workload",[59] the right to "set" these number was obviously not granted to either the village delegates or the financial management team, but instead to the cadres. Moreover, official documents issued by government bodies at comparable level clearly indicate that the exact amount of annual incremental raise in cadre salaries is clearly specified in township government documents. Nowhere in these documents does it say anything to the effect that the amounts "have been approved by township people's delegates", leaving one to wonder whether this was forgotten or whether no such procedural constraint was deemed necessary.

(In 1984), the monthly salary for the three key members of village leadership is 40 yuan. When title-specific allowance, and performance-based supplements are factored in, the total may exceed what others in the village receive. The salaries of other village cadres are drawn from village management fee, and the number of cadres must not exceed three, whose monthly base salary would be kept in the 30–38 yuan range.

(In 1991), the monthly salaries for all village officials throughout the entire township are as follows: the base salary for those in senior leadership positions is 60 yuan, the merit pay is 70 yuan; the base salary for deputies is 50 yuan, and the merit pay is 60 yuan. The salaries of other officials are to be set by village officials.

(In 1994), the monthly salaries for all village officials throughout the entire township are as follows: the base salary for those in senior leadership positions is 200 yuan, the merit pay is 100 yuan; the base salary for deputies is 180 yuan, and the merit pay is 100 yuan. The village CPC committee members and the village accountant are treated as deputies for purpose of salary calculation.[60]

Government documents specify not only how much village officials receive in salary but also how the salaries are paid for.

(In 1984), salaries of cadres are drawn from the revenue of village enterprises, but the cadres are not otherwise eligible for any other benefits enterprise employees

[59] "Opinions on the Implementation of Several Specific Rural Policies", issued by BB Township, Zhejiang province.

[60] "Opinions on the Implementation of Several Specific Rural Policies" for 1984, 1991, and 1994, issued by BB Township, Zhejiang province.

> are entitled to. Fifty percent of the fixed portion of the salary (20 yuan) is paid for by the township, which is used toward management, while the salaries of other cadres, including the deputy director, must be drawn from the management fees.
>
> (In 1991), all village officials not engaging in frontline production, including those in senior leadership positions and deputies have their salaries drawn from the revenue of village enterprises, which will allocate the money to the village. The salaries of other cadres will be drawn from the management fee or the portion of the profit that enterprises contribute.[61]

However, the rules of the township government only apply to the base salary, which is but one component of the earnings of village cadres. In some of the villages that are doing quite well financially, it is entirely feasible for them to pay cadres extra in the form of bonus or remedial allowance. Based on a review of minutes of village cadre meetings I have collected, incomes that fall into these categories are decided at village cadre meetings, in other words, these people are effectively making decisions about their own major source of income.

> Grain contract labor remuneration, for the eight cadres involved, five of them would receive 111 yuan each, the other three 50 yuan each. For the year-end bonus, each would receive 700–750 yuan (XT village CPC committee expansionary meeting, 1987).
>
> Annual incomes for cadres at different ranks:
>
> Cadre No. 1: Eleven months (825 +44+430+200) yuan
> Cadre No. 2: Ten months (756.5+40.50+360+180) yuan
> Cadre No. 3 Ten months (812+43.20+380+200) yuan
> Cadre No. 4: Nine months (611.50+37.60+270+150) yuan
> Average: 1,723 yuan per person
> Accountant, vegetation custodian (five people, detailed calculation omitted): average 100 yuan per person.
> Nursery teacher year-end remedial allowance: 120 yuan per person (XT village CPC committee expansionary meeting, 1989).
> Remunerations for village officials and cadres at different ranks are as follows: the salaries for CPC leadership, people's delegates and government officials, and the accountant would be paid in accordance with government documents, the salaries for all other personnel would be set at 40 yuan. The discretionary portion of the income would be: 40 yuan each for two individuals, 35 yuan each for three individuals. Cadres who own a gas range would receive 10 yuan each month in coal supplement (XT village CPC committee, 1990).

These meeting minutes also contain information about other receipts and expenditure, including allowance for the five types of households experiencing special hardship, assistance for applicant for hardship registry, work-related expenses for village officials, allowances for veterans and social welfare, among

[61] "Opinions on the Implementation of Several Specific Rural Policies" for 1984, 1991, and 1994, issued by BB Township, Zhejiang province.

others. We may infer from this that a large number of decisions related to receipts and spending are made by village senior leadership, albeit in accordance with official guidelines such as laid out in government documents. This means that any oversight on expenditure at the village level would have to come from superior government bodies, instead of representatives of village residents, the taxpayers. Yet we already saw how ineffective government oversight actually is. As for the reason for this, not only is the government unable to receive adequate information and in a timely fashion about how villages fill their coffer and how they spend the money they have, but even with the limited information it does receive, superior government bodies are reluctant to subject lower levels to stringent rules because of the former's dependency on the latter for tax collection. The township government is at once the body charged with performing oversight over financial administration at the village level and the body that sets tax rules. But since compliance with these rules depends entirely on the village officials "implementing" them, if they do not, the township would face enormous difficulties in collecting taxes.

> The county government deploys rural residents to work on major projects as laborers, and this incurs costs of labor, machinery, equipment, and other things, and cost overrun is the norm rather than the exception. Moreover, rural residents have their own businesses to operate, and if they spend too much time away working on these public works, their business income suffers as a consequence. Therefore, 41 village delegates jointly filed a signed petition seeking to be able to make monetary contribution towards these county-level public works in lieu of labor.[62]

> With the aim of strengthening this township's capacity for public safety management, building up its security force, increasing the role of the public in public safety, lifting up the moral caliber of the society, creating a favorable social environment for advancing both the material and the spiritual culture in the township, ensuring that village enterprises, public institutions, and the self-employed are able to operate normally and that all local residents are able to pursue the good life as they see it, this government has, upon careful deliberation, resolved to start charging, for the first time, a fee for integrated governance. The fund raised for public safety and united self-defense must not be diverted for other purposes. This is expected to redress underfunding in public safety (at the township level).
>
> All concerned parties must see to it that these are properly implemented.
>
> BB Township People's Government
> March 26, 1996[63]

In the appendix to this document the "public safety fundraising plan" is presented, which lists the amount of money each concerned organization must raise and contribute. The targets for township-operated enterprises, for

[62] Minutes from the village delegation meetings in Huojiadian village (1992-1998).

[63] "Notice on Implementing Overall Management of Public Safety and Governance Funds," issued by BB Township government, 1996.

village-operated enterprises, for villages, and public institutions, and the self-employed are 28,000 yuan, 2800 yuan, 2400 yuan, 700 yuan and 50 year each, respectively.[64] These new targets have not been voluntarily agreed to by taxpayers or organizations that demand public safety services, but are set, after "deliberation", by the township government based on its understanding of the funding "shortfall". When the government sets its tax collection target on the basis of central-government-imposed budget, it can hardly count on voluntary tax payment, and must resort to coercive measures that can only be executed with the help of primary-level officials. For such efforts to succeed the mutual support between the township and the villages is crucial: without assistance from the primary level, the township would have a hard time collecting even a single penny. This means if the township government watches what officials at the primary level do too closely, and draws resistance from them, it would hurt its chances of having its own targets met. This structural relationship ensures the township government's inability to perform meaningful "oversight" over the way officials at the village level exercise their power.

Moreover, since both regular audits and personnel shuffles, which are the government's main tools for carrying out oversight, are only last resorts, they might jeopardize a few expenditures here and there but do nothing to address the root cause of the problem. The township government has its hands tied behind its back and is unable to put the principle of taxpayer oversight to practice, because doing so would undermine its ability to meet its self-imposed "new fundraising targets" and to make use of the funds raised. Authority is instrumental to any government, allowing itself to be subjected to oversight undermines that authority, leaving the only option: self-regulation. The ineffectiveness of self-regulation is why reigning in tax-collection behavior at the primary level has been a perennial challenge.

The documents presented above illustrate how problematic primary-level tax system is with respect to its underlying philosophy, principles, organizations, and oversight structure. These problems are revelatory of the institutional causes of long-standing issues of late-payment, non-payment, and collection inefficiency, namely, a flawed fiscal and tax system that provides perverse "incentives" to both taxpayers and tax collectors. Moreover, these problems also lay bare the political ramifications of an unsound fiscal and tax system, that is, its tendency to give rise to social conflicts.

In addition, in terms of people's basic beliefs about fiscal matters and the tax system, we found widespread ignorance among taxpayers about the principle that public taxes ought to be used toward providing public services. As a result, a large amount of tax money is invested in economic production-related causes instead of the provision of public services, conflating investment with public service provision, allowing tax collectors to shirk their responsibility towards the public while hurting the interest of taxpayers. For example, if a fund that

[64] "Notice of Implementing Overall Management of Social Security and Governance Funds," issued by BB Township government, 1996.

has been raised is invested towards production, people who have contributed are effectively investors, and should therefore be entitled to a share of the return on their investment, and be given the right to make decisions about their money based on their own assessment of that return. By contrast, a tax should have basis in some kind of principle, and the people who collect it ought to provide corresponding public services, and the people who enjoy these services have an obligation to pay that tax. But what we saw on the ground was that people are required to pay the same taxes regardless of whether they enjoy public services. When "tax" and "investment" are conflated, tax collectors come out as the big winners, while the degree of control taxpayers have over what they get in return continues to decrease. They are unable to benefit from what their tax contribution makes possible, since much of that benefit flows towards tax collectors, whether it ends up generating profit for them or is altogether wasted through misuse.

In terms of the principles behind the design of the tax system, the following practices have become the *de facto* norm: setting the collection target based on the spending needs (making up for shortfall as needed), collective accounting (at the village or organizational level), creating tax categories outside the purview of the law (exploring new sources of tax revenue), allowing conflicts to be resolved through arbitration (reaching compromises and settlements privately), the absence of procedural constraints (tax collection departments at all levels having the discretion to decide whether and how much taxes to collect, and to make changes at any time as they see fit).[65] There is nothing in these rules that provide the basis for clearly defining either the rights and duties of both taxpayers and tax collectors or the proper relationship between the two. Neither can those who pay taxes make claim on certain rights they should have because of the fact they pay taxes, such as the rights to public services and to have a say in how the tax money is used, nor can tax collection departments mete out punishment to those who dodge or evade taxes in accordance with the law. This means that *both* those who pay taxes and those who collect them are operating under poorly defined and ill-understood rights and duties. On one hand, the lack of a clear definition of the scope of taxpayers' rights makes it difficult to establish a system of tax-related oversight and monitoring, and the lack of a clear definition of the scope of their duties creates more space for tax evasion. On the other hand, the lack of a clear definition of the scope of tax collectors' duties manifests itself through the absence of any pressure (sense of obligation) on them to provide public services, while the lack of a clear definition of the scope of tax collectors' rights hamstrings their ability to comply with rules and regulations. All of this has the effect of exacerbating two problems that tend to go hand-in-hand. On one hand, tax dodging and evasion are rampant in rural areas, since it is in the perpetrator's self-interest to do so, and the odds of

[65] Rong Tao, "On the Non-legal Characteristics of China's Agricultural Tax System", in Judicial Research Center of the Law Department of Peking University, *Proceedings for the "Laws in China's Rural Society" Seminar*, unpublished (1990).

getting caught are minimal, so more and more aggressive measures must be used to collect taxes. On the other hand, public services at the primary level are of poor quality, and the use of tax money involves significant waste and abuse.

Customarily, tax is collected by primary-level agencies instead of professionals working for tax collection departments that are directly under the supervision of the central government and that interface directly with both individual and institutional taxpayers. This has had the effects of putting more power in the hands of primary-level authority while giving them less incentive to abide by ethical codes of conduct. The result is growing distrust, decreasing willingness to work together, growing reluctance to interact and increasing mutual resistance between primary-level officials and their constituency. Since they never had a say in determining the tax rules, or consent to the ones that are imposed on them, they have no other way to express their discontent besides refusing to pay. Trying to change the tax policy by submitting suggestions and other orderly means of political activity is simply not an option. There can be little doubt that all these have contributed to conflicts and tension at the primary level. Such a system does not necessarily produce more gains for primary-level officials than might a tax system that does not have all these flaws (and may indeed be less restrictive), since collecting taxes under such a system has become a major headache and challenge for the people who have to do it, who also have to deal with the political risks brought by the antagonism between them and the taxpayers, including constant resistance, complaints, and petitions. These are the social fallout of an unsound tax system. Not only has it done nothing to ameliorate and mitigate conflicts of interests or to promote policy revisions, it has in fact done much to breed tension and instability at the primary level.

CHAPTER 5

Personnel Changes and Organizational Support

5.1 Mixing Administration and Politics

One important issue on which Chinese and overseas scholars who study rural self-rule have focused their attention is how, and what kind of authority emerges. There are two analytical approaches to studying this issue, one is from the point of view of administration (rise through the bureaucratic ranks), and the second is from the point of view of politics (competition over interests). Historically in China, rural authorities fell beyond the scope of the hierarchical system of bureaucratic officialdom, and never received subvention from the central government to defray administrative overhead. For that reason, for many scholars, local officials were no more than parochial in stature, and most of the people who served in these positions were influential members of some prominent local dynasty. The contrast between such a parochial system of authority and the bureaucratic officialdom (through the ranks of which one might rise) "could not be starker".[1] So can we discuss matters related to rural authority from the point of view of bureaucratic officialdom? Generally, the bureaucratic officialdom is essentially a personnel system, and falls within the purview of administration. By contrast, the emergence of rural authority is a political process, which can only happen, in most cases, when there is a support system consisting of shared or joint interests. Within such a system, the rights possessed by the person(s) of authority are born of their ability to exert influence on it. Such influence would allow the person(s) of authority to have control over the distribution of wealth, while the support system has implications for the emergence of authority and the allocation of power, which are in turn a reflection on the level of organizational maturity of the system itself. Along this

[1] Zhongan Chen & Su Wang, *A Study of Bureaucratic Officialdom in the Han and Tang Dynasties* (Beijing: China Book Company, 1993), 258–9.

J. Zhang, *Primary-Level Government*,
https://doi.org/10.1007/978-981-96-6209-8_5

line of thinking, most researchers have treated rural authority figures such as heads of lineages, of neighborhood blocks, village seniors, rural gentry and elites as falling outside the scope of bureaucratic officialdom, based on the presumption that the assumption of these positions by particular individuals follows a certain kind of political logic—defined by the relationships between local elites and wealth, education credentials, family organizations and even local militia—instead of a kind of administrative logic.

However, the situation has become immensely more complicated in the modern era. The first reason for this development is the growing trend among the local gentry to operate and behave like government bureaucrats, and the second reason is the increased presence and influence of state apparatus at the primary level as a result of constant regime change. This amounts to "the subsumption of politics under administration" (to borrow from Yeo-Chi King's description of Hong Kong).[2] On one hand, the emergence of rural authority was profoundly influenced by state activities. For example, the process of state-building itself helped spawn the bureaucratization of the structure of rural authority, and as Western learning made more inroads into the imperial examination system, the number of rural gentry that left their hometown looking for more development opportunities in the city grew, creating greater space in the countryside for parasitic business operators who monopolized power of control. During the Land Reform Movement, those who had been born into families with politically proper credentials and lineages became officials, while during the Great Leap Forward, it was farming virtuosos who were elevated to leadership positions in the villages, and then when getting rich by going into business was in vogue, many successful rural entrepreneurs were appointed to these positions. Evidently, the criteria used by higher-ups to fill the ranks of local leadership shaped its make-up. In many studies, this observation was cited to support the claim that state apparatus was "penetrating more and more deeply into the rural political environment": after all, shifts in prevailing state ideology underpinned the pattern of leadership changes at the primary level. Whether it was promotion, departure, opportunities and fortunes and misfortunes, it was all inextricably linked to what the state expected of its rural officials. Seen in this way, the placement of primary-level cadres was an administrative exercise, and the needs of the state given its prevailing ideology and its bureaucratic dynamics were the main variables in the determination of who took on rural leadership positions.

There is, of course, another aspect to this. Abundant historical evidence exists to suggest that the developments described above failed to turn primary-level officials into *bona fide* agents of the state who faithfully carried out state policies. In fact, primary-level officials' lackadaisical performance in executing state policies was a perennial problem, as was the threat posed to state finance by tax revenue shortfalls. At the same time, studies of "elections" throughout history demonstrate that at the provincial and prefectural levels, designation by

[2] Ambrose Yeo-Chi King, *Chinese Society and Culture* (Oxford: Oxford University Press, 1992).

superior government officials of individuals to fill the ranks of primary-level leadership, i.e., the "top-down recruitment model", not only did little to make local leaders more responsive to the needs of the central government, but it actually had the effect of "improving and strengthening local control".[3] This is perplexing, and one cannot help but wonder just how effective this "top-down recruitment model" was, and how much the model was able to do to incorporate primary-level cadre into the system of bureaucratic officialdom with the central government as its core. Obviously, the administrative recruitment mechanism does not explain what we have observed. After all, if the co-existence of two parallel political operating systems throughout much of Chinese history was the reason for the limited influence the imperial courts had on rural politics, that changed in the modern era, when the "state apparatus reaching deeply into the fabrics of rural communities" should have, at least in theory, made a difference, especially given how widespread the top-down recruitment mechanism became.

For example, primary-level cadres who excelled at carrying out orders and policies from above (such as by raking in large amounts in tax revenue) often got promoted, apparently illustrative of the way in which the central government exercised influence on and control of primary-level cadres. Yet if this was in fact true, then we still need to explain why the state felt the need to promote "self-rule" in the countryside, i.e., the villages: why would election of the village council be proposed as a way to strengthen allegiance among primary-level officials to the central government and their acceptance of the latter's objectives if these had already been achieved through the implementation of the top-down recruitment mechanism?

In fact, it was not people at the primary level who initiated this push for "self-rule", nor was the campaign set in motion by any particular interest groups trying to maximize their share of power. It was set in motion by the state, more specifically, certain high-level state agencies. The main objective was to mobilize rural populace to become involved in monitoring the behavior of primary-level officials, as there seems no other way to explain the widespread reluctance among rural residents to take part in these elections, or why the rate of vote by proxy was so high, or why sometimes cadres had to literally take the ballot box to the homes of rural residents to get them to cast their vote, lest the rate of participation would be too low, and why some rural residents even demanded that their participation be conditioned upon "openness and transparency in village governance". The two main concerns that fueled the campaign to mobilize rural residents to get involved in performing oversight over primary-level officials were "the deteriorating relationship between primary-level officials and the community"[4] and the central government's inability to

[3] Gengwang Yan, "Administrative system of the Han dynasty", cited in Hehuai Hong, *Election Society and Its End* (Shanghai: SDX Joint Publishing Company, 1998), 92.

[4] Chih-yu Shih, "Comment on Rural Self-administration and Base-level Elections", in Chong-pin Lin, ed., *PRC Tomorrow* (The National Sun Yat-sen University, 1996), 144.

effectively reign in primary-level officials. If the qualifications used in the "top-down recruitment model" are properly implemented, why couldn't that address these "concerns"? And why would local "self-administration" be considered necessary? Obviously, the central government realized how little it can by itself do in terms of monitoring, and that the criteria it had adopted in recruiting rural officials has not had the intended effects, so it had to turn to resources outside the state establishment to execute monitoring. This made it possible to deploy (political) means that are distinct and separate from administrative measures to tackle problems at the primary level.

Yet out of concern for social stability, politically instituted monitoring tends to be subject to management within the administrative domain. Even though this "subsumption" of politics under administration can curtail political interference from outside the administrative domain, it can also spawn competition and rivalry over economic and other gains within the administrative domain. In terms of hiring decisions, such subsumption triggers a slide toward an organizational structure that features internal networks, in which cadre appointment is affected by where one stood in the system, whether it is on the supporting or the opposition side, which effectively undermined the uniformity of administrative standards and their implementation. The area in which the intersection and tension between the logic of politics and that of administration is felt most strongly in the nomination process: in order for any nomination to comport with the political interests of a particular group, that group would have to be able to provide the kind of organizational support needed to "facilitate" the emergence of authority, which, of course poses a threat to both uniformity and neutrality of the administrative domain. A combination of the need to make sure that the nominating process is not interfered with by forces external to the administrative domain (such as family influence) and a desire to adhere to the top-down recruitment model effectively puts the power to nominate candidates for government positions in the hands of a small number of incumbent officials. This in turn can cause conflicts and rivalry within that group to escalate.

The paradox that requiring rural officials to be nominated by local administrative incumbents has not strengthened the uniformity of administrative norms and practices as had been hoped could only have been observed with reference to the mutually obstructive forces necessarily inherent to the flawed structure described early. Administrative efficiency is hampered by infighting within the administrative ranks over competing interests, and it would not be possible to eliminate these interests in the administrative establishment, simply because it has for a long time been the norm for both the power to make nomination for candidates and the power to decide on these nominations to be concentrated in the hands of people who work inside the apparatus. While this institutional setup may be helpful in preventing frequent political challenges from reaching crisis point, it makes it more difficult to achieve the uniformity of administrative norms and practices, to improve administrative efficiency, to protect the system from the deleterious effects of schism, and to ensure that information flows unobstructed. But if one was focused only on the nomination process in relation to administrative positions, all these issues would simply go unnoticed.

According to a widely held and rather representative view, the above problem is of little research importance within the Chinese context. The argument is that for the longest time officials at different levels of the bureaucratic hierarchy have always been appointed by superior governments and elections have never played an active role and always been something of a formality, and nobody ever expected them to be a substantive form of engagement. This view presumes that not only is this form of top-down control highly effective in shaping what happens at the primary level but that it is also exemplary of what could happen during the transition in state governance. The idea seems to be that primary-level officials share the objectives of the central government, which is the state, and they have been placed in their positions by the state, so therefore as a group they are entitled to a share of what interests the state receives. We are yet to subject this conclusion to careful analysis. In fact, the idea that state bureaucracy and primary-level officials are *in sync* with each other in terms of goals and objectives is really an ideal, and is mostly a presumption, rather than something that has been established empirically. Vast amounts of documents exist that show that just the opposite has been true.[5] Now to the extent that primary-level officials unrestrained by the central government's efforts to control them were no rarity, we need to discuss to whom they own their loyalty instead, i.e., who they are serving, and how and from

[5] We may draw upon two pieces of evidence to show the exact opposite. In the article entitled "Governing through Contracts" (presented at the Conference on Laws in Rural China held in January 1999), Xiaoli Zhao made a number of findings after reviewing documents related to tax receipts, village reserve and mandatory contributions in one township in Qianyang, Shaanxi province, including: "agricultural taxes were still being collected according to targets that had been set at the People's Commune era", "the targets for grains, cereals and edible oils had changed little over many years", "with respect to the distribution of proceeds from contracted land, the formula used to calculate agricultural taxes and targets for grains, cereals and edible oils, and the amounts that must be collected are clearly laid out, and stayed largely constant from year to year. By contrast, village reserve at the township and village levels, especially when it comes to labor corvée, household assignment, contract fees, collection targets and collection dates were wildly arbitrary". The second piece of evidence comes from Zili Yang's "Notes from Fieldwork in the Countryside" (posted on Yahoo discussion board on February, 10, 1999), in which he recounts his visit to one township in Zhao County, Hebei province in 1994. "The chief of the township tried again and again to explain", writes Yang, "that some are done to comply with county policies, some are done because there were no other choices, and others still were altogether denied by anybody. He opened up the ledger and I could see in it words to the effect that Dongxiang Village had a per capita net income of 2,400 yuan. Under taxes and fees only two items were listed, contribution to village reserve and contribution to township reserve, while agricultural taxes and contribution toward fundraising campaigns were left out. Agricultural taxes are collected by the central government and were not particularly hefty, and accounted for no more than ten percent of total taxes, and by comparison, involuntary contribution towards other miscellaneous projects was far more of a source of financial strain". These documents collected from research sites offer evidence that increases in peasants' tax burden were for the most part neither due to increases in central government taxes nor properly recorded in central government tax revenue.

where they get support. My goal in this chapter is to cast doubt on the absolute conclusion mentioned above. By examining the difficulties facing the top-down cadres recruitment mechanism and the consequences its implementation over the years has had, I want to show the extent to which the interests of primary-level authority figures have been institutionalized and how much impact "elections" that have been heavily promoted in the countryside have had on these interests. It is particularly important when we are trying to make sense of the paradox described earlier to assume the practical inseparability of the logic of administration and of politics.

5.2 Personnel Changes at the Primary Level

Throughout Chinese history, there has always been some kind of examination system in place for selecting qualified individuals to serve in the government. Yet, despite this, "recommendation" or "nomination" by incumbent officials has always been an integral part of the selection process, even as the examinations waxed and waned. The widespread existence of this practice meant that only a tiny number of individuals are ever involved in that process. And since it rarely touches on questions related to the legitimacy of an existing regime or policy changes,[6] people would tend to see these processes as essentially apolitical: after all, they allow people on the higher rungs of the government bureaucracy to pick whoever they want to fill positions at lower levels, using criteria they had settled on, so as to ensure that incumbents can always be replaced. However, the very fact that recommendations and nominations have become a normal part of the selection process does have some rather extraordinary political ramifications. For example, when an individual is discovered by chance by some incumbent official who recommends them to a particular position, that tends to lead to that person's subsequent rise through the bureaucratic ranks. This person will likely end up building a network of people who are specifically loyal to that higher-up, thereby creating a sizeable system of support.

While things like this were commonplace at all levels of government, when such recommendation or nomination, either by a body or by a representative thereof, was a normal and integral part of the selection process, which is the case at the primary level, it is particularly noteworthy. In the past, who became an authority figure at the primary level had very much to do with people's wealth, education and reputation, and getting involved in the affairs of the public meant one had to build a public image for oneself, and perform tasks akin to what might be done by the public media. However, in the modern era, as primary-level officials behave more and more like government bureaucrats, qualifications, such as wealth and educations, have also changed with the times. But rather than reducing the number of people who qualified, these changes actually led to an increase. Meanwhile, as the size of the production unit in the countryside decreased, so did the amount of public activities, and the number

[6] Hong, *Election Society*, 1998, 4.

of people who partook in them, making it increasingly difficult to find qualified individuals to fill government positions. Primary-level officials have lamented that it has been years since there were any young people suitable for such jobs, and in general very few people have any interest at all in the affairs of the public, leaving them with no other choice but to let the same people serve term after term. In some villages the same people have served as cadres for years and years, while in others the eligibility criteria have been relaxed to allow individuals who have demonstrated outstanding abilities in generating private profit, whether it is for enterprises, or in manufacturing, herding or agriculture, to be recruited for these positions that serve the public interest.

Roughly speaking, we might call this a process by which "bureaucrats" are chosen by "officials", one in which the officials set the criteria while the bureaucrats chosen are at their service. Still, it would not be entirely correct to assume either that this selection process is underlined by unanimity among the officials, or that the chosen bureaucrats are subject to effective control by the officialdom as a whole. In fact, the process is beset by many difficulties attributable to what happens within the officialdom (schism, fractions and competing interest groups), which prevent administrative standards from being fully implemented. As a consequence of these political goings-on within the administrative domain, the bureaucrat selection process could not stay politically neutral, people, instead of institutional rules, became the deciding factor in who got picked. A recruitment process that should have been standardized has been turned into an instrument for trading favors and displaying loyalty. People seem to think of this as the proper way to fill the administrative ranks and speak approvingly of it. Yet whether people admit it or not, much of what happens in rural politics has to do with competitions in personnel decisions. While such competition mostly takes place within the officialdom, the need to consolidate power and garner support can lead to such fights spilling over into the larger community. Political activities can give rise to unique systems of trust that are distinct from what one typically associates with the bureaucratic regime, including special channels, secrecy, excluding candidates from outside one's own fractions, blocking efforts to evaluate candidates for competency and moral caliber, and obstructing development of information transmission channels. Under these conditions, if the only source of information regarding potential candidates for superior officials is whatever subordinate officials "report" to them, naturally incumbent bureaucrats are first in line to make recommendations and nominations. Thanks to the chronic absence of any systematic regulation on what kinds of relationships are permissible between the subject and the object of recommendations or nominations, favor trading has become the norm at the primary level.

The proper selection procedure calls for cadres already in reserve to be the candidates. Members of the reserve cadres receive customized training designed to prepare them for future service as officials. Such practice is notable for its anticipatory logic: the preparations for "cadre recruitment" are done well in advance, when decisions about the "naming of reserve cadres" are made.

"Naming of reserve cadres" is essentially a process in which future candidates for positions in primary-level government are put through training specifically customized for them based on their own background and the needs of the position they are being groomed for, then placed in a variety of positions for internships. The number of reserves must be greater than that of incumbents by at least two. These decisions are made with some regularity, and evaluation of the performance of each individual is recorded and kept on file. In fact, this constitutes the bulk and the primary part of the personnel selection process, and is a highly reliable mechanism.

> To address the aging of primary-level officials in the countryside and the shortage of successors, better planning and preparations for the training of reserve cadres is imperative. Both the teaching of theory and practical training must be given proper weight. Make sure to cultivate the trainees to improve their caliber, to put them through exercises to build their capability, to offer each individual training tailored to their specific strengths, to monitor the situation and make adjustment as needed, and to be flexible and respond to changes quickly. It is important to establish a system of rules governing the recommendation and the probationary training of reserve cadres. Candidates recommended by village officials for reserve cadre are to report to different positions in the village leadership for probation, and a record-keeping system must be put in place to make sure all aspects of the training are properly recorded.[7]

The reserve cadre system is not intended to address the issues of power sharing or distribution. Instead, its purpose is to make sure that incumbents always have successors. For this reason, the whole process has been overseen by administrative bodies, executed with great care, and insulated so very few people are involved. However, the qualifications have remained largely the same for years: priorities are given to those who have had formal schooling (typically junior or senior high school), the desire to improve themselves, some life experience, and are morally upright. These conditions have been reiterated so often they have become bureaucratic boilerplate. Despite this, the people who end up occupying leadership positions at the rural primary-level come in all different types and sizes. Apparently these qualification requirements do little more than describing a general perimeter, and may be more useful as a guide for what kinds of characters to rule out than as a one for telling incumbents who to recommend. In point of practice, the two things who gets recommended most importantly depends on are: (1) Who are the (group of) people who are doing the recommendation, and what are the things they care about.

This in turn depends on the method used for deciding who becomes a reserve cadre. While an organizational procedure for this does exist, which primarily involves the submission of materials prepared by lower levels to superior levels along the bureaucratic chain, unlike promotion decisions for cadres, it does not require consultation with a wide range of concerned parties. While

[7] Report on various types of villages in JX region, Zhejiang province.

reserve cadres are essentially serving in a back-up capacity, they are one step shy of cadres in full position, and who get to serve in this back-up capacity is decided by cadres of the same rank through deliberation and consultation, which are instrumental in subsequent decisions about who are promoted to full position. Judging from experience at the primary level, the most important step in the designation of reserve cadres takes place at the primary level, when incumbents at the same rank (village level) or one rank above (township level) make recommendations. When the two parties are from the same production unit, have shared work experience and such, the recommendation carries particular weight. In many places in the countryside there is a widely held belief that "village officials are appointed by township authority", this is most likely because not only are statistics on reserve cadres collected at the township level, and documents are released and policies are announced by township authority, but also that the village is not officially recognized as an administrative division. This is why township authority is often assumed to be in charge of "appointment", creating the false impression that reserve cadres and incumbent officials in the villages somehow have nothing to do with who the next crop of fully appointed officials will be. In fact, the first step is village incumbents nominating individuals for reserve cadres, this is followed by the submission of the nomination to the township authority for the official records. Then candidates are required to complete workshops and training sessions, and some may be placed on probation in non-essential positions.

Therefore, what incumbents think of potential successors is of critical importance. The following factors are typically considered: having earned the trust of key superior officers, agreeing to let current distribution pattern of interests and benefits stay unchanged when they assume office, agreeing not to pass up future opportunities for gain for current incumbents, and so forth. These criteria, it might be noted, bear little resemblance to the criteria village officials are required to adopt by higher government authorities, i.e., they deviate appreciably from the criteria typically used by officials to select bureaucrats, but these are the ones that everybody in rural China is familiar with. Ordinarily, within the bureaucratic hierarchy, there are only promotions and never demotions, and it is only when a promotion opens up a vacancy that somebody new is brought in to fill it. This means that the incumbent cadres who recommend the next crop of officials of full position have been slated for promotion, immediately or in the near future. So they are effectively picking their own subordinates. But at the village level, for purpose of official statistics only a small number of people may be allowed to rise through the ranks and reach leadership positions at the township or even the county level. Most village officials face the prospect of serving in their positions for a very long time, and do not retire until and unless age and health prevent them from staying on. By contrast, township-level officials are replaced much more frequently, because of the age limit. Since conventionally village-level officials serve for extended periods of time, when somebody's job performance is sub-par and superiors want them replaced, it poses a particular challenge. Superiors have to come up with

Table 5.1 Cases of normal succession

One village in Anhui province		*One village in Zhejian g province*	*One village in Hebei province*
Former village CPC secretary No. 1	*Former village CPC secretary No. 2*	*Former village CPC secretary*	*Former village CPC secretary*
| | |Son Current village CPC secretary	| | |Nephew Current village CPC secretary	| | |Nephew Current village CPC secretary	| | |Cousin Village enterprise manager

Data source: Interviews with village residents

some justification for removing that person from their position, especially since they will typically not have perpetrated any easily identifiable infraction (this was the reason for write-in ballot only election in Jilin).[8] So this is when recommendations for individuals to serve as the next crop of officials are made not by officials who are themselves about to be promoted but by those who are about to retire. Indeed, this is by far the more common practice in personnel selection in rural China, especially before election became widely adopted. So in order to make sure that one's interests will still be protected even after one's retirement, out-going officials will seize this opportunity to recommend the people in their fold, and in the countryside, this would usually be somebody in the same lineage. Based on documents we collected in different locales, the majority of candidates for offices who gained their candidacy through normal means (where "normal" means anything other than non-standard mechanism such as competitive election or removal of an incumbent due to disciplinary violations) are known to be some "relative" of key village officials. In some villages, the number of close relations of the number one or number two top officials, such as their sons, sons-in-law, younger brothers, and other people related to them through marriages, who end up succeeding can be considerable (see Table 5.1).

Obviously the recommendation and nomination system for filling village leadership positions deviates somewhat from the administrative principles governing how officials should select bureaucrats. It is therefore inevitable that the system should have a political tinge in point of practice. At the core of the system is the idea that the only people who would be recommended and nominated are those who can be trusted with maintaining the existing distribution pattern of interests and benefits. This means that the administrative principles imposed on primary-level officials by superior government bodies are usually just ignored. Still, this is not to say that township officials have no influence whatsoever on leadership selection at the village level, it is just that whatever influence they might have can only be realized when officials at both the village

[8] Yuejin Jing, "How write-in ballot only elections came to be," *Open Times*, 1999, 3.

and the township levels have arrived at some kind of agreement, whether it is explicit, implicit, or tacit. To the extent that township officials are involved in keeping track of, monitoring, training and appointing village officials, their roles in deliberation and veto power are not entirely naught. And no newly appointed official can afford to forfeit or ignore what support township administration might offer them, especially under extraordinary circumstances.

> In 1987, I retired from military service and returned to my hometown, and started teaching middle school. The job did not suit me since it required me to basically read off prepared scripts. In 1983 order came down that I would be transferred to a different position, to serve as the deputy district chief for Chengguan district, which is in the township. Since the village where I was from is of some importance, personnel decisions are never taken lightly. But superior officials wanted me to undergo some training, and gain some practical experience working in rural areas, so I would be prepared to assume leadership responsibilities in the future. In 1984 superior officials met with me and said that Gucun village faced serious aging among its senior leaders, making the village unable to meet the demands of reform and opening-up. They wanted me to return to Gucun, and succeed the long-serving CPC secretary, and help bring some much needed changes to the village. After that meeting I returned to the village and became the head of the brigade, while also serving as the deputy secretary of the CPC committee. In 1985 all the long-serving senior leaders retired, and I took over formally, and became Gucun's CPC secretary.[9]

In the case of this particular cadre, he was treated by township authority as an up-and-coming young leader, and it was quite clear which position he was being honed for, which was the CPC secretary, succeeding the long-serving incumbent. But this kind of situation tends to take place in villages where there is a shortage of suitable candidates, or where for one reason or another the selection of a suitable candidate poses a challenge, or when the concerned township official has been transferred to another position, and their replacement needs to find someone who sees eye-to-eye with them on important issues, and is younger so would be able to get more work done. Regardless, if village officials object to a particular nomination, township officials cannot just override that objection. It is especially rare for them to appoint somebody to a village leadership position who is an "outsider". The example above involves a retired military service personnel who was originally from the village, who later became a teacher in the village after retirement.

While township officials do have the authority to make leadership appointments, they rarely appoint officials for full positions. Mostly they appoint people to deputy positions or other positions for purpose of probation. This allows them to see if the performance of these individuals is satisfactory to village officials. If it is not, then these candidates will be kept in the probationary positions for longer, possibly indefinitely. A good many village cadres with impressive educational credentials who came up the ranks under careful tutelage never earned the full acceptance of peers. Of course, in the event that candidates with the backing of

[9] Chunlin Xia, *Image Capital and Village Cadres' Survival Strategy: Fieldwork in a Village in Shandong Province* (Master's thesis, Peking University, 1998).

> township officials do encounter resistance from the village, township officials would do what it takes to help them overcome the resistance. The CPC secretary mentioned above is a case in point. His competitors repeatedly went to higher-ups in an effort to marshal support for their own candidacy for the CPC secretary position, but never succeeded. He even got township officials who backed him to attend the CPC member meeting where the election for the CPC secretary was to be held. Still he was unable to get the results he wanted, because in the end the source of the strongest support for candidates is people inside the village.
>
> Who gets CPC membership is decided by the secretary, and all members are now within the control of the incumbent secretary. Who is going to get Q elected? At the time a township deputy secretary in charge of election was also involved. After Q was defeated, this deputy secretary started talking, and said that the results were no good, and that the thinking of others is biased, and that in the interest of the brigade people should reflect on the situation and agree to a rerun. But it turned out he didn't get wanted he wanted even with the rerun. In fact, the CPC secretary and the team leader had already come to an agreement earlier on, each of them would secure three votes...[10]

Evidently, support from township officials is important as a matter of course. But usually it is insufficient to tilt the balance of power. What is most important is what incumbent village officials and other supporters in the village think about a nominee. If a cadre does not enjoy full endorsement (lacks support) in the village, support from the township authority is of little help. Only when support from village officials and support from the township officials are combined can the successful appointment of a candidate be secured. The current procedural rules governing recommendation and nomination provide ample space for the joint deliberation and consultation by officials in the village and in the township. For example, village cadres can, in their capacity as "institutional recommender" meet with people in the township to present the qualifications of their preferred candidates and let people know about their moral caliber and competency. And township cadres can, for their part, visit the village and meet with a meaningfully sized group of CPC members to collect their opinions. But it is up to village cadres to decide who can (and would be notified to) attend these meetings. And in most cases, village cadres would also be in attendance. All of this is out of reach for people who are not part of the administrative establishment. With the close working and operational relationship between incumbents and concerned departments in the township on the one hand and the standing of the person who made the recommendation on the other, the nominee's status as a solid candidate is all but guaranteed. This is what allows public office and private associations to mix, and what is laid down in official documents and the *de facto* influence of the interests of

[10] Xia, *Image Capital*, 1998.

different parties to work in conjunction. But all of these machinations are explicitly prohibited by existing bureaucratic rules governing personnel selection and appointment.

Moreover, insofar as nominated reserve cadres must undergo "targeted training", it allows even greater discretion in their selection, and makes it easier for those making the recommendations to exercise control over what happens in key leadership positions in the future. For example, they can plan somebody's rise ahead of time (direction, e.g., secretary, director, member of the women's affairs committee). Once it has been decided who is to be recommended, they would be monitored and trained. This is to ensure they attain all the qualifications such as required for purpose of official statistics, including courses they need to take to get the necessary education credentials and connections with the right fractions. As far as township officials are concerned, all they need to do is to follow orders, complete assigned tasks and make sure all the statistical targets specified in official documents are met. But at any given time, these statistical targets are only of secondary importance. After all, information such as a candidate's education background and age can easily be obtained from the official statistical records, but when it comes to whether they are suitable for a particular position, whether it makes good sense to appoint them, it can only be clearly explained by people familiar with them and who would actually "say something". Even if a candidate possesses all other qualifications, if they are spoken of in unfavorable terms, it could seriously hurt their prospects. At the very least, it would not bode well for future cooperation between said candidate and others in the same village.

One other area in which the influence of village officials over personnel selection is especially pronounced is their ability to create vacancies *ad hoc* to accommodate somebody new. Alternatively, they might appoint somebody to the position of "assistant". While the qualifications for selecting candidates are set by township authority, the issue of trust is not easily addressed at that level. Township authority may be able to assess village officials' suitability for higher offices, but when it comes to first-time office holders in the villages, former incumbents' approval and favorable evaluation are the most important sources of their credibility. Therefore, while township authority does make "appointments", it does not quite follow that they have a decisive say in personnel matters, it must work in concert with village incumbents for a nominee to prevail eventually. And of course, just because somebody's name is on the list of reserve cadres it does not necessarily mean they will be promoted, since they are after all only the back-up.

> Of the 35 reserve cadres in the township, 25 are serving in one leadership position or another, such as the Youth League secretary or committee member. Ten of them are not serving in any leadership position, and who are either engaged in farming or working in village enterprises. Twenty-four of them are male, 11 are

female; 22 are between the ages of 20 and 30, 13 between the ages of 30 and 37; 20 finished junior high school, and 13 finished senior high school. The numbers of CPC members, Youth League members and the unaffiliated are 7, 13 and 15, respectively. In terms of prospective leadership position, 8 are being honed for the CPC committee, 19 for the village committee, 2 for the economic cooperatives, 5 for the women's affairs committee, and 8 recently started in their new positions.[11]

5.3 The Network of Village and Township Officials

Except in extraordinary circumstances, governments above county level do not get involved in village elections, and it is also rare for village residents to get involved. These two groups of people might be asked for their "opinions", or be allowed to listen to reports, but these consultations are meant only to provide information that might be used in decision-making, and do not amount to a change in who has the power to make decisions. Even though many village residents are under the impression that "whoever is wanted by higher-ups will end up in leadership positions", this would be inaccurate if by "higher-up" is meant government authorities above the county level. In the majority of cases, whether or not names are submitted to higher authorities for the official record, village official decisions are made jointly by village- and township-level officials. Incumbent cadres play a critical role in the initial selection of candidates, while the influence of township officials is largely limited to monitoring, consultation, issuing approval, and reviewing. This means that in the old days, when it came to the selection of both "candidates" and "winners", village officials and township officials each had the right to nominate candidates and to review and issue judgments, veto power is shared by both parties. So by convention, the candidates for village leadership positions are jointly selected by village- and township-level officials after deliberation and consultation. Influential people in the village act as sources of information.

Neither the county government nor village residents have any involvement in this deliberation and consultation process. Over the years, as this system becomes more cemented, village governance is increasingly dominated by the intricately close working relationship between village officials and township officials. These close relationships include both those that are public in nature and those that are private ion nature, and form the basis of a tight-knit network. This network is instrumental in maintaining the relative power positions of both the village and the township. On one hand, they support each other, in order to boost their own standing and protect the interests of those within the network; On the other hand, it is powerfully exclusive, barring any outsider from getting involved, whether the outsider comes from above or below. Primary-level power configuration is unalterable by anything that village residents might do. While some complaints filed by village residents might, once

[11] Master List of Reserve Cadres for TD Town, 1991.

fact-checked and validated, result in the removal and replacement of some village officials, or even an entire cohort of them, such actions do nothing to alter the village-township power structure as a whole. In the end, the personnel selection process stays intact, and there is little village residents can do to effect changes.

For its part, the network forged with some combination of public and private affairs tends to shield village political operations from interference from above, effectively creating something of a "buffer zone", insulating matters at levels below the county and the township. If governments above the county level wish to have a good grasp of conditions in the villages, and address the talent shortage that has hampered village governance, they would often need to dispatch some "cadres" to the village communities to assume the position of secretary in economically underdeveloped villages. But the people who are stationed in villages are from the township, and officials from the county or municipality will go no further than the township, where they would be temporarily placed in some leadership position nominally to undergo "practical training".[12] These temporary placements do connote "practical training", but they are no walk in the park and can be hard work. The only people who are chosen for these stints are young people who recently joined the workforce, for whom this would provide an opportunity for them to be observed, trained, elevated, and burnished with the right qualifications. Its short-term effectiveness is especially pronounced, which also means that these people usually have a hard time forming long-lasting bonds with the locals. So in general, the transmission of routine information about their performance still largely depends on the "screening" done by township officials operating inside the "buffer zone", and this is also why the activities of primary-level officials are often able to evade monitoring by superior government authorities. Furthermore, this buffer zone has also contributed to the alienation between the county government and village residents. Except in cases such as petitioning by those with special grievances, there is very little contact between the two, which limits the number of possible channels through which county officials might collect information about what goes on in a village that do not involve village cadres. In fact, the county government is more accurately described as having been tightly "surrounded by" officials from the village and the township. Unless a large number of petitions compel them to intervene, they have very little incentive or reason to get involved in village affairs directly. They rarely try to breach the existing management order that features bipolar control by township and village officials. On the contrary, they are not only heavily dependent on primary-level officials for meeting a range of performance targets but even rely on the "protection" afforded by the buffer zone from distractions and disturbances caused by public discontent. For their part, incumbent village officials have also figured out through their experience how to parlay this kind of information

[12] Survey report on the strengthening of village-level party organizations in different types of villages in JX Regions.

blockage into a shield from crises while at the same time building solidarity within their own ranks. All of this helps to solidify the pivotal role township and village officials play in village personnel selection and leadership succession.

Basically, these standard practices ensure that any nominee supported by people (or organizations) outside the ranks of village cadres would be excluded. The reason why these nominees would raise concerns is that not only do they have supporters, but at times of need they might even become forces of resistance. By contrast, the standing (i.e., right) of cadres to make recommendations and the criteria they adopt facilitates the entry into administrative establishment of people who share their general outlook. These people are not joining the leadership ranks representing some outside interest group, nor are they subject to the neutrality requirement that applies to administrative personnel. In other words, if they do not already have the trust and confidence of incumbents prior to the start of their terms, it behooves them to establish all kinds of interest and organizational connections with older incumbents as quickly as possible once they start in their new positions. Failure to do so would result in their losing the confidence of these older incumbents. Should this person divulge information they have access to thanks to their connections to older incumbents, who know way too much, it could conceivably cause grief for the entire leadership. A lot of village matters are handled according to the village's own *ad hoc* rules that lack basis in official legal codes. These cover things such as bonuses for cadres, electricity bills, contracting fees, fees associated with land transfer and requisition, and the use of and contracting fees associated with land reserved for contingency. Faced with the temptation of power and opportunity, self-restraint can be a challenge for these cadres. So is blocking the transmission of information among members of the leadership. The only way to prevent information leakage, therefore, is to gag the entire leadership. And this cannot happen unless all the cadres agreed to bind themselves through solidarity, mutual trust, and shared interests. Withholding information from superior officials can help primary-level officials deal with punishments and disciplinary measures, while withholding information from the public can help mitigate the pressure from public opinion. Withholding information is instrumental for maintaining solidarity and mutual trust, and all of this works in concert with the practice of recommendation and nomination, further strengthening cohesion within the ranks of village and township officials (mutual support, mutual dependence).

Cohesion among village and township leaders has one other benefit in terms of allowing people to hold more than one position simultaneously. This practice allows village and township officials to become ever more closely linked with one another, effectively creating an information circulation loop. In the countryside, village leadership is made up of the CPC committee, villager delegation, the economic cooperative and affiliates, including the Youth League committee, women's affairs committee, and the local militia regiment. At the core is the CPC committee, while the villager delegation and economic cooperative function as the "foundational structure", and the affiliates as "auxiliary", forming an "organic whole". It is commonplace for village leaders helming different bodies to cross-serve in multiple positions. As can be seen in the multiple appointment chart for village officials in TD township, the CPC committee secretary usually also serves as the head of the economic cooperative, as well as the advisory officer of the local militia regiment; the village committee chief typically also serves as the deputy secretary or member of the CPC committee, and the deputy head of the economic cooperative, the Youth League committee secretary usually also serves as head of the local militia; and the head of the women's affairs committee is usually also a member on the village committee, the head of the committee on culture, education and health, and the head of family planning commission. Village committee members and CPC committee members also serve in positions in charge of security, arbitration, and welfare. Of the 1381 village committee members in TX county, 13 committee heads also serve as the CPC committee secretary, and 68 committee heads also serve as the CPC committee deputy secretary, 74 committee heads are the same person as the head of the economic cooperative, and 206 committee heads are the same persons as members of the CPC committee.[13]

Multiple appointments across different departments effectively link up departments in charge of different things. It would not be difficult to notice that insofar as there is division of labor among the village cadres, functional division (decision-making power) does not exist. Whatever the nature of the matter at hand, the final decision rests in the hands of the superior officer of concern, or must be arrived at through "group discussion". This makes the superior officer of concern the person with the final say. Other than this, there is no place for the professional opinion of any specific department specializing in some area or another. All that staff of any such department can do is to carry out orders once a decision has been made by either the superior officer or the leadership as a whole.

As far as finance and fiscal matters are concerned, the common practice of multiple appointments was originally intended as a way to "reduce the number of cadres and to provide economic relief for farmers". Yet the key problem lies in the low level of professional division of labor within the institutional structure. Despite ostensive division of labor among the cadres, multiple-appointments blur the functional distinction among the different departments, which seriously overlap in purposes and objectives. It also makes it possible for leaders of different organizations to move around through these positions liberally, so that the accountant will one day become the Youth League committee secretary, and the head of the factory the village committee head, and the local militia head the dispute arbitrator, and so forth. This effectively turns everybody working in departments with special functions into a clerk or administrative assistant. Everybody from the CPC committee, the village committee and the democratic finance management team is involved in the

[13] Table IV based on the survey report on the strengthening of rural primary-level organizations in TX County.

decision-making for all different matters in the village. For the individual cadres, multiple-appointment and being shuffled around apparently do not present any difficulty with respect to work "experience" and capacity. It would be great if one had experience, but whatever one does not already know one can learn. As a matter of course few of them feel strongly about any tension that might exist between the purposes and objectives of the different organizations in whose leadership positions they serve.

> When the village committee head also serves as the CPC committee deputy secretary, it makes it easier for them to take part in decision-making. When the secretary also serves as the head of the economic cooperative, and people in CPC or government leadership roles also serve in village enterprise leadership positions, it makes it easier for them to oversee economic matters. Without us, the enterprises cannot get off the ground (cadre interviewee).

Q: As an individual entrepreneur and an operator, you are profit-oriented, but in your capacity as the CPC committee secretary, you are supposed to consider what is in the interest of the public, aren't the two in conflict with each other?

A: There is conflict in terms of time use. Now family members have taken over business operations, and I am consulted on important matters (village CPC committee secretary interviewee).

5.4 Vying for Internal Support

The normal process for selecting new leaders indicates that the allocation of leadership positions is heavily dependent on the institutional support provided by the administrative establishment in the village and in the township. Typically this support system forms not before but after the candidates have been chosen. Once the support relationship is in place, the supporting organization can proceed with whatever it needs to do to support their preferred candidates in an orderly fashion, including notifying all the senior CPC members in the village to secure their endorsement, and tailoring the proposed qualifications for the new leader to suit their preferred candidates in terms of age, educational credentials and fractional affiliations, so that "it is obvious for whom it is meant" (village resident interviewee). Arrangements can also be made for their preferred candidate to enroll in the county Party school, where they can learn new knowledge, meet other officials, and make new friends. This becomes the basic logic of the leadership succession competition: internal support is what matters, not support from the outside, i.e., from the larger community, and the strategy for ensuring success is not to challenge incumbents, but to try to cater to their needs. So earning trust is far more important than displaying one's competency and capabilities. Without such a support system, a lone contender left with their own devices would unlikely prevail even if they had the support of village residents (the voters). The two cases below illustrate the contrast.

Case I

After graduating from the College of Finance and Economics, Guilin Fan, aged 26 and originally from the countryside, tried to make something of himself. Every time he returned to his hometown, the poverty and the poor management of village finances saddened him. So in 1998, he decided to go back home and stand in the leadership election, hoping to become the next village committee head, and help bring about much needed changes to his hometown and improve the lives of the residents. When the election results came in, seven of the ten village resident groups backed Fan as their preferred candidate for the village committee head, and Fan and an incumbent official were the two finalists. After he spoke at a rally, Guilin Fan devoted much energy toward meeting with village residents, visiting senior CPC members and retired village officials, in an effort to hear what they had to say, share what he planned to do, and win their support. In the end, he got 701 votes, the incumbent got 635 votes, neither had reached 50 percent of the votes, so they had to wait for superior government to designate a winner. Fan went to the county government and exposed inequitable, unfair, and illegal practices in village finance, and election irregularities such as the other finalist appointing the head of the election committee and letting his relatives serve as part-time poll workers. According to town officials, it is difficult to investigate infractions, nor is it easy to deal with them, and even if there is election misconduct, if people don't support you, even if you try to fight the system, it will come to naught. Given how complicated the situation is, it would be best if you pursued a different path. You are still young, and ought to show deference toward the older comrades.[14]

The young Fan's decision to stand in the election brought hope of change to the village residents. However, because he had been away for a long time, for school and for work, he obviously had not established the necessary connections with the interest group and organizational network in the village. Despite his effort to "pay courtesy visits" to as many people as possible, with the aim of building up a support group expeditiously, such efforts are no match against what his rival is able to pull off. So even though he is the favored candidate to a large number of villager groups, that is no guarantee for success, "almost feeling ominous". And so far as we can tell from the "rumors" going around in the village, what support system he does have most likely has something to do with the network of relatives (lineage): words are going around that he intends to have relatives run the coal mine. These rumors indicate that his competitor has been alarmed by his supporters, who are mostly his relatives. While Fan is trying to consolidate favorable conditions by tapping into his relatives, his competitor is trying to achieve the same goal by tapping into the

[14] Guilin Fan, "Village Chief Election," *Southern Weekend,* (February 5, 1999).

familiar administrative network. While the resources being utilized by both of them are readily available, the latter clearly has greater power of control, and in addition enjoys the trust of superior government officials. So despite Fan's competitor receiving slightly fewer votes, because the support system tilts in his favor, his success is all but guaranteed.

Case II

At the end of 1998, a township in a remote area in Suining, Sichuan province was holding a direct election for the head of the township. It came down to a showdown between two finalists: Tan and Cai. Tan was the incumbent township CPC committee deputy secretary, and the only person backed by current leadership and bypassed all earlier rounds of the election, Cai was the incumbent village chief for Village No. 10. The election rules allow two methods by which candidates are chosen: either they are nominated by the election district-wide leadership conference, or they are nominated by the CPC and the government, civic groups, and civil organizations. After losing in the primary, Tan, who had been backed by incumbent township leadership, felt the weight of the expectations from his colleagues for his stellar performance. Tan came well-prepared, and the pledges he made drew attention from village delegates. But Cai was born and raised locally, deeply familiar with rural issues, and could rattle off ready answers to any question one might put to him. In addition, Cai is member of a prominent lineage in this township, boasting north of nine thousand people, accounting for more than half of the total township population, and a source of influence one underestimates at their own peril. In the campaign debate, he noted his credential as a native who grew up drinking the water here, eating the grain grown locally, and was ready to serve his fellow residents. To this Tan replied by asking: do you mean to suggest that non-natives have made no contributions to the township population? What you are doing is to play on these folks' feeling to corral votes for yourself. On the eve of the election, Tan and his motorcade entourage made campaign stops all over the township, but Cai was only able to rally some primary school students, and gave a talk at their school.

The challenger Cai had hoped to build a support system by tapping into the fellow feelings of the township folks, but Tan managed to thwart his plan, causing Cai to lose whatever edge he had in garnering support. Cai was once again reduced to a solitary candidate, and Tan's support system and its constitutive relationships were unbreachable, and in the end Tan prevailed.[15] Who cast ballots was another important factor, but the article cited above has not much to say about this. Apparently this was not something that was deemed important, and their attention was focused exclusively on ballot casting for candidates in "direct elections", making it difficult for us to obtain similar kinds of documents. But what we are able to conclude is that it is no coincidence Tan won. The support he was able to secure from the leadership cohort was sufficiently powerful to outgun the support system surrounding a prominent lineage (Cai), and it is what makes it difficult for outside interest groups to make inroads. In 1998, when

[15] Jianguang Tang, "Direct election of the town magistrate," *Southern Weekend*, (January 15, 1999).

leadership election was held in Lishu, in China's northeast, some village officials became alarmed by vote corralling within a lineage, concerned that rivalry would begin between candidates supported by different interest groups and the administrative establishment.

> That is how things are in rural areas, if the leadership does not take control proactively, people might take advantage of the vacuum and try to corral votes. Otherwise, how is it that someone with no work experience, and a complete unknown when it comes to their job performance can receive so many votes? Some people collude with seedy characters from other villages to try to corral votes, disrupting the normal process. These people do nothing to serve the people, but instead spend all day partying and engaging in morally dubious activities. It would be ruinous for the village if these people were elected leaders.[16]

In election campaigns, vote corralling by individuals is considered improper collusion. Proper campaign activities include meetings of village officials where campaign situation is discussed, getting ballots in place, mobilizing voters, and rallying support for incumbent candidates. After all, incumbent leaders have legal standing to engage in such campaign activities. Depending on who is doing it, the same thing may be either legal or illegal. When an individual lacks support from the establishment, no matter how much widely scattered support they receive, it is still inadequate. Fan's case above demonstrates once again that the leadership qualifications set out on paper, including being young, well educated, having a broad vision and horizon and being professionally committed, are not really important. What matters more than anything is the connection between the candidates and supporters, and the kinds of support that can be marshalled. This is an illustration of the political nature of the process by which authority is forged in the country. It is by no means purely a matter of administrative personnel. But for historical and institutional reasons, the most powerful power brokers are inside the village administrative establishment, and not everybody can avail themselves of it.

One other function of the cadre support system is initiating routine "fine-tuning" of the allocation of leadership positions. The terms of village cadres do not all begin and end at the same time, so normal succession and strategically timed fine-tuning take place at the same time. Decisions about fine-tuning may be made at the village level (requiring review and approval by higher authorities), or at the township level (with consent from village leadership). In some villages, there are rules that permit incumbent leaders to be impeached if they are the subject of "widespread complaint from the public". To initiate the process, more than one fifth of the delegates must file a joint petition, which must then either be approved by the village delegate meeting[17] or at least two thirds of the commune delegates.[18] Yet the mandate to impeach is not the same as the mandate to submit requests, the choice of candidates is made by the CPC committee through discussion.

[16] Transcript of the 1998 interviews with Lishu township cadres.
[17] Charter for YJZ village.
[18] Charter for XT village.

The CPC committee has decided that HL Zhang would take up a job at the commune brick factory, and GR Zhang would serve as the CPC committee secretary and oversee the entire operation. SL Shen would serve on the village committee and be in charge of agricultural production.[19]

Decisions about changes in who occupy auxiliary positions are also made by village leadership. For example, according to the by-laws of the economic cooperative in XT village, in the event cooperative management committee members are impeached or added, the committee has the discretion to make allocation decisions regarding subordinate positions (in this village the incumbent CPC committee secretary PL Zhang was once appointed the head of the office of enterprise services).[20] As for members of the village CPC committee, the village committee and the democratic financial management team, these cannot simply be appointed by village leadership, even though it can make recommendations and submit nominations, as well as keeping records of replies to written requests and other related documents. So obviously this way of promoting people is also deemed legitimate.

The former commune chief had been reassigned to another position, so in accordance with township government procedural protocol, the village CPC committee has nominated SHM Zhang to be the next commune chief. The nomination was put to discussion at the commune delegate conference, and a vote was cast by a show of hands. The result was unanimous. We hereby notify the relevant authority of this process. Please advise as to whether everything has been done properly.[21]

Township officials also have some sway over decisions about shuffling people around in leadership positions. They can, shortly before a general election, remove some officials from their posts, and reassign others, while filling vacancies with people they have hand-picked from among the reserve cadres. These reshuffling can cover the CPC committee, the village committee and the economic cooperation and other leadership positions. In one notice regarding changes to the make-up of village leadership, township officials made a point of noting that "these [changes to] leadership positions in the village committee will officially take effect at the next general election".[22] Obviously these reshufflings take place before a general election, and are meant to prepare reserve cadres who are already on the books for assuming leadership posts.

Mid-April this year, the township CPC committee performed a comprehensive review of the leadership positions in the 12 villages by administrative designation and made some changes. These included placing four people in alternate leadership positions temporarily, and removing three others from their posts. Of the eleven reserve cadres who were promoted, six were non-CPC members, seven had retired from military service and two were women. Their average age is 29.8. Four of the eleven were put in charge of operations of the village committee, two were appointed to the position of deputy secretary of CPC committee, one was appointed membership on the CPC committee, and two assumed leadership

[19] Minutes of the meeting of the YJZ Village Committee on personnel changes.

[20] Report on the new personnel appointment for XT Village Economic Cooperative.

[21] Report on Personnel Change and Transfer for XT Village.

[22] Notice of the Announcement on the Appointment of Comrade TBL.

positions in charge of women's affairs. In the two months since, most of the eleven reserve cadres have performed their jobs competently, and the township organized job training tailor made for them, with the aim of helping them better prepare for their careers, and the general election scheduled for next year.[23]

We can see from these maneuvers that the standing of village and township officials and their prerogative to act as they see fit mean that replacement and succession of leadership became a choreographed process. Even if the appearance of a black horse costs somebody a win at the ballot box, that person would probably end up being appointed to some other position, in anticipation of the next general election. For example, in the fourth general election for village committee members held in Lamasi Village in Hebei province, Yongliang Chen and Yongsheng Chen, both candidates for the position of village director, were defeated in the final round by Jinwen Zuo, who had not been a reserve cadre. After the election, Yongsheng Chen received a promotion, and became the head of the township electric power station. Yongliang Chen, for his part, was allowed to continue to serve as general manager of the "village enterprise". After Zuo became the village director, however, it became more difficult for Yongliang Chen's enterprise to secure loans from the village, something that was once easy, since Zuo announced that [such decisions] must be approved by the village delegate meeting. But it also became harder for the village committee, now with Zuo at the helm, to demand contributions from enterprises. Since the two Chens were previously working in leadership positions in either full-appointment or probationary capacity, they had already built close ties with officials both above and below, rapport with township officials, and been able to garner support from the cohort of village and township cadres. Despite the fact he was appointed to his post by the township authority after having received more votes fair and square, Zuo ended up facing one hurdle after another throughout his career. For example, his CPC membership application was never approved by village officials, most of his supporters were individuals unaffiliated with the administrative establishment, and he relied mostly on private actions to build his credibility and reputation, including intervening to fight injustice when he saw it, and helping to adjudicate conflicts by serving as an arbiter (mediator). Once he even brought a few village residents with him to help thwart a land transaction between village officials and township enterprises, earning him a reputation for "being courageous" among the residents. But he was always rejected by the village and township officials.[24] Whether it was the way Zuo built his reputation among the village residents, or how he tried to secure support by tapping into social forces, he operated in ways that deviated markedly from the competitive behavior prescribed by the conventions. The introduction of elections brought the contrast between the two

[23] Report summary on the changes in TD township leadership.

[24] Beijing TV Station, *Village Election* (documentary), n. d. and the transcript of the interviews with the producers of the documentary.

different support mechanisms into still sharper relief, and the role of interests and gains grew increasingly pronounced. For instance, some of the residents later expressed "regret" for having supported Zuo, citing the fact that after taking office he "did not get water pipes installed for us".[25]

5.5 Rural Elections: The Institutional Transformation of Social Interests[26]

Whatever the original intent behind the introduction of rural elections may have been, it has led to increased use of political means in turning social organizations into special interest groups, and pitting organizations with different interests against one another. The only difference is in the extent of these changes and the scope of the mobilization. Among villages where the elections are held, one quickly notices how much interest there is among the residents. Uncharacteristically, they often congregate in large numbers in public places such as schools and the village committee office as if surveilling. Dogs owned by rural households could sometimes be heard barking at two or three o'clock in the morning, indicating that some visitors have been in and out "corralling votes". Peasants, known for their reluctance to speak their mind openly, have been uncharacteristically vocal, seeking out opportunities to meet with reporters and researchers visiting from outside and share what they know about goings-on in the village. Even though elections are fraught with problems, without elections such coalescence among residents who otherwise tend to mind their own businesses and have little shared interest would have been unimaginable. There is, of course, some ways to go. Now most villages have already instituted an election system, and the number of candidates standing in these elections has grown from one to two (albeit both individuals being picked by the establishment). Admittedly, these institutional changes have had very limited effects on the workings of the organizational support systems, these effects can be ratcheted up a notch or two when "write-in ballot only election", which had been invented in Ping'an Village in Lishu, Jilin province, is tried (the third village leadership general election, held in 1998). In these one can begin to see signs of meaningful change.

In 1998, the county enacted election reform. New rules called for "putting the right to elections entirely in the hands of voters", and for write-in ballot only elections in all the villages in the county. "Voters would cast ballots in direct elections for the village director, deputy director and village committee members". The rules also stipulated that "superior government departments or the village CPC committee would refrain from setting the tone, setting the

[25] Beijing TV Station, Village Election interview.

[26] This section previously appeared in my article "Observations on the fourth election in Lishu County," *21st Century* (China University of Hong Kong, December 1998).

parameters or nominating candidates".[27] The new rules made provisions for direct elections: ballot secrecy, individual voting, rank-choice voting, and transparent vote counting. If none of the candidates receives more than 50 percent of the votes in the first round, then the two who received the most votes would be the candidates in a second round. Once the counting is completed, the candidate who has received more votes would be immediately declared the winner and the next occupant of the leadership position, without the decision having to be authorized through a process of reporting, review, and approval. Two rule changes are particularly noteworthy: (1) the candidates who enter the final round were people who prevailed in the first round; (2) the result of the final round constitutes the "authorization" of the winning candidate's assumption of the leadership position. These rules clearly reflect a greater respect for the vote count and greater trust in the voters. Admittedly the election process is by no means flawless, nor is control over the process what it should be. After all, it takes time for cadres at different levels, incumbent candidates, non-incumbent candidates, and voters to learn and become familiar with the new rules. Still, the introduction and the implementation of these rules and their implementation demonstrate not only represent a new social governance philosophy that values greater openness, greater inclusiveness, and embraces transparency, due process, autonomy and the will of the public, but it has also already, despite how briefly it has been in practice, demonstrated its political and social significance, and helped to bring about discernible social change.

Township and village officials' traditional prerogative to recommend and nominate candidates for election was the first to be challenged by the introduction of rural elections. Many cadres have noticed a decline in the level of control they have over leadership succession, and begun to feel uneasy about it.

Q: How do you feel about elections?

A: We follow orders, but we do have our own opinions, and hope you will report them as truthfully as you can. Working as a village cadre means you are inevitably going to offend some people, which can hurt your odds of winning in an election, so this is really difficult work. These days people who can become cadres are hard to find, after all the investment you have made toward preparing somebody for a career in rural politics, they end up losing. Those who have won lack work experience, know little about how things work, are on rough terms with township cadres and the village CPC committee, and just generally have a hard time working with others, and in the end job performance has to suffer.[28]

This crisis arose largely because the support system once in place has been eroded. First of all, it had a limited scope, and included only incumbent village

[27] Article 20 of the "Electoral Methods for the Village Committee of Lishu County" (hereafter "Electoral Methods"), July 1998.

[28] Transcript of the July 1998 interviews with a village-level CPC secretary in Lishu County.

leaders, a number of villager group heads, and some CPC member. Their total number was dwarfed by the number of "voters", of whom there could easily be one to two thousand. So that is why these small number of people now needed to "hold over-night meetings" to discuss and strategize, and come to an agreement about whom to back, and ask each villager group head to "secure three votes", and so forth. But even with these efforts, they could not achieve the "sense of certainty" about how the vote would turn out the way they used to.

Q: Are you confident about winning?
A: I feel OK about my odds, but it's really hard to say. People might tell you they will vote for you, but you don't know how they will vote, and all the ballots are mixed together, how can anybody tell?
Q: So why do you feel OK about your odds?
A: I check most of the boxes when it comes to basic requirements: I graduated high school, (my opponent) only finish grade school and junior high; I am only forty, but he is pushing sixty; I have already worked as a village official for several years, and have gained some experience, whereas he has been out of the leadership loop for years, and has had no involvement in village affairs. He is not on good terms with incumbent leaders in the village, and is convinced they were responsible for ousting him, so township and village cadres are all backing me.
Q: Why don't you go out and corral votes, as your opponent is doing?
A: I am currently serving in a leadership position, and also a candidate, so it would be unbecoming for me to do these things myself, we have an election task force, headed by [village committee director], and it would be more appropriate if they went out to do that.[29]

Obviously, this candidate is still hoping that the personnel mechanism and operating rules that once prevailed would work again this time, and that the older support system would deliver for him. He fails to recognize, however, that his opponent is not relying on **the same** support system he is, and whatever it is his opponent is doing to try to beat him is helping an alternative support system grow rapidly as an institution. Elections have effectively created opportunities for the village population to (even if only briefly) come together and speak with one voice. In the face of this emerging force, what incumbent cadres can achieve through their campaign activities begins to show signs of waning. As for the elections in Lishu, they often produced winners that were not the most qualified when judged against "criteria set by the township authority". Similarly, candidate Zuo in the Lamasi Village election succeeded in parlaying support from outside the establishment into a win at the ballot, undermining the support system associated with it, reducing its influence over

[29] Transcript of the July 1998 interview with a candidate (an incumbent cadre) for the director of a village in Lishu County.

personnel matters, and dealing a blow to the old model of electioneering. Small wonder then why the cadres would have been "disconcerted".

Secondly, now candidates in leadership elections would not be hand-picked by township and village officials. Unlike under the old system, reserve cadres are no longer the *de facto* candidates, and they have to earn their candidacy at the ballot box. This shrinks the space within which they can use elections as a means to building networks, cementing their power and maintaining the existing benefit distribution pattern. After Zuo was elected in Lamasi, the plan of the cousin of one former village official's to convince the government to invest in his business was thwarted (Zuo responded by saying that it was not something he could decide by himself and "approval" by the village delegate meeting was required). These shifts are even more pronounced in the elections in Lishu, which put more power in the hands of the voters, and made voting actually count in leadership changes. Insofar as voters actually do care about how these process would affect their own lives, this would inevitably affect what new cadres do to get and maintain support. It would make no sense for them to focus on nothing else than trying to get inside the old boys' network, and to get to know the right superiors. They must also try to build solidarity with the village population. As some newly elected cadres put it, "being elected" puts more pressure on them than "being appointed", since while there used to be one group of people (their superiors) to whose needs and demands they must answer, now there are at least two, and while there used to be only one kind of expectations (those of their superiors) they must try to meet, now there are many. This shift from being picked by township officials to being favored by the voters can be analogized to the marionette puppet whose movements were once controlled by the pulling of a single string but are now controlled by the pulling of many strings. This helps to align the interests of the cadres with those of the population, and weakens the incentive to please higher officials either primarily or exclusively, and erodes the control the old boys network can have on newly elected officials

Thirdly, the impact of these changes can also be felt at the county level. For example, in Lishu county, election planning is carried out by officials at county or higher levels, who also are the only people who can offer interpretations of the plans and rules. This not only makes these people the *de facto* "leaders", but also put them in the position to offer consultation over election-related matters and to adjudicate election-related disputes. This allows county officials to be even more deeply involved in mediating and arbitrating primary-level disputes. By contrast, in the old days most village disputes were handled by village and township cadres. Today, the county civil affairs bureau would be responsible for receiving and processing complaints and petitions, offering interpretation of the rules, collecting evidence, certifying (or declaring null) election results, making them an increasingly trusted government body (within the existing institutional configuration), and one that voters would be willing to turn to for protection of their voting rights. Neither township nor village officials enjoy such standing. In fact, more often than not they are the ones being targeted or implicated in these complaints and petitions. What little they still try to do to influence the elections easily become the targets for complaint, and much of such effort ends in failure, where "there is nowhere to exert influence". In one of the villages I visited, after round two in an election, the election task forces dragged with their vote counting, because they feared the prospect of somebody they did not like winning, beating the incumbent village committee director. So village cadres and township cadres got together and tried to declare the election null before the counting even started, and order a rerun. However, under the new rules, there are simply no procedurally justifiable ways to pull off something like that. So in the end, their scheme to marshal their administrative capital in order to influence an election was thwarted. A few hours after county officials ruled that there was "insufficient evidence to support nullifying the election results", counting began. Delayed but not aborted. When the counting was completed, what township and village officials had feared did not come to pass, their favored candidate received more votes, and won fair and square.

Fourthly, as a result of elections, what guarantee for future promotion being a reserve cadre used to provide has largely diminished. Some of those who had already built up the necessary connections for themselves increasingly felt that these "relationships" cannot be relied upon anymore, and being on the "reserve" gives them little sense of security, now that everybody has to go through an election. Whereas before they might have complained that somebody tried to suppress them, now they could not blame voters if they do not vote for them. Whatever "tacit agreement" they had had with incumbent cadres could no longer provide them with guarantee, and they must now play by the new rules, trying to answer not to other cadres, but to the voters. We see this in the complaint aired by one reserve cadres who lost at the ballot box.

> I was confirmed as a reserve cadre five years ago. Since then I have served for a few years as the Communist Youth League committee secretary, joined the CPC, and attended the county Party school. But the cadre who put me on this track has since retired, and has not got much of a say in elections. So somebody in the village seized this opportunity to undermine me, trying to persuade them not to vote for me. That person even personally went to the polls, claiming that voters were illiterate, and needed somebody to help them mark their ballots. But the name that was written in was not mine. Whether you are a reserve cadre matters little now?[30]

However, candidates who won after receiving more votes feel differently.

> Elections are better than appointments, [it means] the cadres have the trust of the people, and they can more easily get things done, and their words are taken seriously. Voters elected me to do this, and if you resist, you are really opposing the

[30] Transcript of the July 1998 interview with a village resident who tried to expose election irregularities in a village in Lishu County.

voters. The numbers are clear, how could you possibly prevail? Had it not been for open and transparent elections, people would cast doubt on our legitimacy, suspecting that it is either bribery or some other shady dealings that got you to where you are. If people doubt your legitimacy, they don't do what you want them to, that would be difficult for us to stomach, wouldn't it? But after an election, everything can be clearly accounted for, everybody has taken part, and it is visible to all.[31]

In the past, whoever who got picked by higher government officials to serve as the village committee director got the job, so whenever [that person] wanted to get something done or make a case for something [they] always felt something was missing. Now it is the voters who elected me, fair and square. So long as the people support me in my work, whatever we want to achieve for the village will be done. If I fail, just remove me.[32]

Under the appointment system, responding to poor job performance with removal was a thorny problem. These are superiors and subordinates who have worked together for years, and in the name of preserving a façade of amicable relationship alone people would be greatly reluctant to take one of their own out. But under the new system, cadres receive their mandate from a difference source, and that problem is readily solved. It has been reported that the reason write-in ballot only election was first introduced in Ping'an village in Lishu had more than a little to do with the problem of people simply "not having the heart to replace somebody". Township officials found the job performance of some long-serving cadres to be unsatisfactory, and wanted them replaced, but constrained by these intricate personal entanglements among the people concerned, they could not bring themselves to nominating somebody else, so they resort to secret ballots, so nobody had to take the risk of making enemies. But after all, carrying out the "reserve cadre" system was made technically trickier because the new rules stipulated new ways of exercising power and included new institutional constraints.

Many people, some cadres included, were ill prepared for these changes in the distribution of power and control. Here is what happened in another village. There one candidate in the election for the position of the village committee director was not somebody township and village officials were enthusiastic about. But according to *Election Rules*, anybody was free to enter the race, so they could not really make this person drop out. They cudgeled their brains and finally came up with an excuse to bar him: unless he resigned as the head of the township office of production, he was not eligible to stand in the election. However, the list of candidates had already, as the rules required, been made public, so people in the village already knew he was going to be in the race. In the end, even though he was not granted permission to deliver a

[31] Transcript of the July 1998 interviews with the elected cadres of a village in Lishu County.

[32] "The inauguration speech of an elected village committee director of Lamadian Town, Lishu County" delivered in April 1993, in *Stories of Village Autonomy in Lishu County*, ed. Leadership Group of Primary-level Regime Construction of Lishu County, unpublished.

campaign speech, he received the most votes, without any incident. When we queried a county official about this, he consulted *Election Rules*, and glibly pointed out that the provisions do not allow what the township officials had done, because the head of the township office of production is not a formal position, and the person holding it would still be registered officially as a resident in the village, and so would be eligible both to vote and to stand as a candidate in village-wide elections.

In Lishu county, township and village officials do not have the final say on whether an election is valid, and in almost all cases in which an election was nullified, that ruling was made by a county official. Township and village officials clearly were not above the law, and their actions could not replace the ballots. Any complaints, including those filed by these officials, would need to have supporting evidence sent to the county civil affairs bureau for investigation and verification. This effectively augmented the county's ability to influence how village affairs were handled, whether this was intended or not. Its role as the mediator facilitated direct contact between the county and the village voters. We found that when people had questions about elections, they would bypass township and village authorities and go straight to the county civil affairs bureau, making these voters the "eyes and the ears" of the county on the ground. County officials were now able to learn about goings-on in the village directly from the information provided by the voters, effectively building something of a united front between the two groups, thanks to these elections.

So it makes perfect sense that any resistance against the write-in ballot only system would come from township and village officials, which are the people who make up the "support system" earlier described that reign at the primary level. County officials acknowledge the existence of this resistance, which is why they have to work really hard to promote the election system, require rule compliance and monitoring. In fact, township and village officials themselves are not entirely above acknowledging it in interviews. The following is fairly representative, even though the wording is cautious and somewhat diplomatic.

> It ought to be stressed that we are accountable to the establishment organizations, and leadership should be strengthened, so that unwholesome characters do not get elected, for that would make it difficult to work together later on, these are indeed things we worry about. The village committee director should not be entirely focused on what would be good for the local population, and forget they must also serve the interest of the country. The rural population is still rather uninitiated on many things, and should submit themselves to the leadership of those who are more progressive.[33]

As a letter sent to the office in charge of handling complaints and petitions shows, such worry is shared by some cadres in the village. In it, the person who

[33] Record of the July 1998 interviews with a township cadre of a village in Lishu County.

penned it noted that since being a village cadre means you end up making a lot of enemies, they are easily toppled under the write-in ballot only system, which can be taken advantage of and infiltrated by seedy characters going around corralling votes. So there ought to be some kind of entry requirement in terms of institutional affiliation. In a worrying tone, this cadre wrote:

> Cadres are assets of the state, so unless they have run afoul of rules, they should be the last people you want to mess with. Maintaining stability of primary-level leadership is important, and it should be achieved through a combination of democracy and centralized power, and cadres should not be left feeling as though their future is wildly uncertain. It would help to have some clear qualification requirements to follow. Whoever qualifies would be nominated by the CPC committee, subject to review and approval by higher authorities. And then they can be ranked by voters in an election. This would be a better approach, otherwise things would get out of control.[34]

This letter, written in 1992, reflected how ill-adapted some cadres were to the write-in ballot only system. They saw rule change as "things getting out of control", and wanted a return of the older more familiar rules that were also easier to navigate. But none of this weakened decision-makers' belief in these new rules. In its reply, the office in charge of complaints and petitions said that the qualification requirements mentioned in the letter "were the opinion of one person, the qualifications requirements for candidates were drawn up in accordance with the *Organizational Law of the Village Committee*". Not only did such a response uphold the new rules, it also helped to lend support for compliance, for letting higher-order rules and norms trump *ad hoc* rules introduced by primary-level officials, and for limiting discretion in rule implementation. It seems obvious that as entities ranked higher on the bureaucratic hierarchy replaced lower ones to take on the responsibility for making law, interpreting the law and enforcing the law, indeed enhanced the impact the state's legal codes can have on primary level governance. In other words, election threatened township and village officials' traditional role as the "maker" and the interpreter of the law.

Fifthly, elections also threaten to destabilize the cadres network at the township and village levels. As we can see in Table 5.2, over the course of the four elections that took places between 1988 and 1998, voter participation rate increased continuously, even as the number of incumbents who were re-elected decreased continuously, and the number of non-incumbents who won increased continuously. In the 1998 election in Lishu, in one township a whopping 50 percent of those who were elected village committee directors had not previously served in a leadership position.[35]

[34] Petition letters in a village in Guojiadian Town.

[35] Election data compiled by the county-level Civil Affairs Bureau and the transcript of interviews with local cadres.

Table 5.2 Results of four village committee elections

Year	*Voter turn-out (%)*	*Number of directors who were not re-elected*	*Number of deputy directors who were not re-elected*	*Number of committee members who were not re-elected*	*Newly elected villager group head who previously held no office*
1988	93.1	13	72	196	34
1991	94.3	41	119	285	221
1994	95.1	51	133	337	292
1998	98	113	14	128	825

Data source: Election statistics compiled by the county civil affairs bureau (August 1998).

The decline in re-election rate is an indication that the one factor crucial for the stability of the primary-level cadre network, namely, people working together for extended periods of time, is not readily present anymore. High turn-over within the leadership ranks seriously eroded the effectiveness of the network, making it harder for power brokers at primary level to collude. And that is what was meant when the village official cited earlier said that things "would get out of control". This explains the widespread failure to understand and to adapt to these new control mechanisms among primary-level officials. Having had the old order and the interpersonal support it sustained taken away from them, primary-level officials lost some of their clout and influence. No longer did they have awesome powers they could flaunt, and they must now follow the same processes everybody else follows, dealing a blow to whatever "autonomy" and "legislative discretion" they once enjoyed. What all these associated changes did was to undermine both regional fragmentation of the law (legal exceptionalism) and the normalization of ***ad hocness*** (discretionary implementation at the primary level). In Lishu, some primary-level officials expressed concerns about the duration of the term of office. Three years, they argued, was too short if one wanted to "get some things done" or "cement the foundation".

> It would be good if the term could be extended from three to five years, otherwise, when you take out the first year that is spent on settling in and the third year on preparing for the next election, really you've literally got about one year to try to get something done.[36]

In the Zhejiang area, what they tried to do is introduce reform of "supplemental income and insurance" for retired officials, in an effort to provide stronger guarantee for their standard of living post-retirement.

> Only those who retired from leadership positions above certain rank are eligible for these retirement benefits. These positions included village CPC committee

[36] Transcript of the July 1998 interviews with the elected cadres and the members of the Party branch of a village in Lishu County.

secretary, head of the brigade, CPC committee members, deputy head of the brigade, deputy head of a factory, and above. Whether other retired officials can enjoy these benefits depends on their financial conditions of specific locales. The benefits fall into four tiers: 8 yuan a month for those who served for 6–9 consecutive years in a full-appointment capacity, 6 yuan a month for those who served for 6–9 consecutive years in a deputy capacity; 12 yuan a month for those who served for 10–15 consecutive years in either full-appointment or deputy capacity, and 21 yuan for those who served for more than 21 consecutive years in a full-appointment capacity, and 17 yuan for those who served for more than 21 consecutive years in a deputy capacity. Those who are entitled to these benefits must have left their position in a normal succession process.[37]

A Pension insurance would be set up for all retired full-appointment and deputy officials who served for more than six consecutive years: those who had served in either full-appointment or deputy positions are entitled to 80 yuan a month, and all others to 60 yuan a month. The insurance fund is made up of money from three sources: 40 percent comes from village operating budget, 40 percent from the collective, and 20 percent from individuals. Villages that are experiencing collective fund shortage may, upon deliberation, explore other ways to raise money for the fund. Imposing mandatory contributions from village residents is prohibited.[38]

Elections amount to a shift in how those in power get their power. They replace a model in which leaders are given power by those who recommended or nominated them with one in which leaders are chosen by voters at the ballot box. Elections also mark the transition from decision-making behind closed doors to decision-making based on open competition. Contrary to what had been feared, such a shift did not weaken these new officials' mandate, or fill them with "trepidation about making enemies", but in fact became the wind in their sails. In Lishu county, for example, the 1998 election drew a large number of candidates who were incumbent village officials in senior positions trying to become the next chairperson. Within the parameter of the current primary-level political apparatus, power is not one of the things they lacked. However, it makes a meaningful difference, even if only symbolically, whether their power had been given them by the establishment or by the people. In one case, they have won among a relatively small group of people, while in the other, they were chosen by the entire village population, and so that amounts to a difference in how widely recognized they are. As one village CPC committee secretary who once served as the village committee director said:

In the old days all we ever wanted was to complete the tasks given to us by higher governments. That certainly doesn't work anymore, and you have to make sure the needs of both sides are addressed, otherwise village affairs would be

[37] "On financial assistance for retired cadres" prepared by one town in Zhejiang province.

[38] "Notice on Implementing the Village-level Cadre Pension System" prepared by one town in Zhejiang province.

unmanageable. You have to build rapport with the village committee director based on equality, and proceed with caution, and try to strike a balance.[39]

If the CPC committee secretary thinks this, so too must the village committee director. The public's new role as the source of their power places enormous pressure on officials, forcing them to realize the importance of the ballot box. If you want to win, you have to actually put in the hard work that it takes to get things done for [the voters]. Such realization has translated into an increase in pledges made in earnest to the voters, and a decrease in "cliches" and "talking points".

My pledge to you is that, using the 1998 level as a baseline, I will cut the economic strain on farmers by 5 percent in the first year, 10 percent in the second, and 15 percent in the third. If these targets are not achieved, I will resign from this office.[40]

First and foremost, be clean, upright and disciplined. Stay away from money that is not yours... and hold yourself to high standards at all times and under all circumstances. Do not covet what others have or to claim as yours what is not. Work hard to serve the village population, to share their concerns, their worries and to do what they want to get done, and always keeping their interests in mind. Stay committed to village self-rule, uphold the principle of transparency, and village delegation system, so that people are the real masters.[41]

As a result of this change in the source of officials' mandate, decision-making on village affairs became more cautious and more pragmatic. More people got involved, and the issue of procedure was being taken seriously. Decision-makers were realizing that their power was not unlimited, and an increase in such awareness marks important progress in social systems. As far as village cadres are concerned, their power is limited not only by oversight from above, but also by oversight by the voters, who can stop a decision from passing if they object to it. In one village in Shizipu township, Lishu county, the cadres there had planned to invest 100,000 yuan toward a turning tool factory and sulfuric acid battery factory, they had spoken of this plan in glowing terms, saying it is so good "you couldn't find something like it even if you were holding a lantern". However, despite its popularity among the cadres, the plan did not pass at the village delegation meeting. Delegates cited as their reason for rejecting it that neither of these two kinds of products had a market. These days turning tools are made of alloy steel and last up to eight–ten years, and there is no need to buy new ones. Sulfuric acid batteries were already being phased out, and people in the cities are getting rid of them. After investigating the matter, the cadres verified these claims. Had it not been for the restraint imposed by the

[39] Transcript of the July 1998 interviews with elected village cadres of a village in Lishu County.
[40] July 12, 1998 campaign speech by a village cadre in Lishu County.
[41] Speech given by a village committee director in Lishu County on July 20, 1998.

village delegates, the money that would have been invested toward these projects would certainly have gone to waste.

This case helped village cadres realize that "limited" decision-making power is not necessarily a bad thing, as it can tighten the space in which bad decisions can happen. And experience shows that the shift in the source of their power can bring about the kind of tightening just mentioned. In some of the institutionally better developed villages in Lishu county, the village delegation has shown a growing awareness of and willingness to impose limitations on cadres' discretionary power in deciding what taxes or fees to collect. For example, the agenda for one village delegation meeting in Huojiadian village included the following: review and evaluation of the village reserve and township endowment targets set by the township government, and those that are legally unjustified shall not pass, and village cadres must, therefore, not carry them out. According to the minutes from the meeting, the village delegation passed the following resolution in 1996 after reviewing the township government's targets for village reserve and township endowment:

> Given continual growth in rural household income, in accordance with pertinent provincial, municipal and county rules, collecting a reasonable amount towards township endowment and village reserve, and even increasing the amount by certain margin, would be permissible, and affordable to the farmers. The village delegation has voted to pass these collection plans. In addition, the village delegation has also passed a resolution calling for issues related to farmers' tax burden to be addressed and voted on by the village delegation. The outcome would be announced to the public, and any unjustified taxes must be resolutely objected to.[42]

While these restraints have yet to become permanent and still have room for improvement, and they tend to vary from village to village, their very existence is significant to rural governance, for they are a sign of village delegation's growth in both self-determination and self-rule capacity. They began to demand veto power over unjustified "burden", to have a say in some village matters, to learn how to exercise oversight, to take seriously and to exercise the power to decide whether to grant approval, and resist unconstrained selfish acts that involve the abuse of power. Village delegation has become not only a tool advocating for and celebrating due process but also a shield against forces that try to exploit the village. Such power would simply have been unimaginable had it not been for the shift in the source of the officials' mandate to rule. More specifically, this new-found power of the village delegation comes from the *Organizational Law of the Village Delegation*, in which the scope of this power is clearly delineated, and its legitimacy is built on its codification in the law and consent of the people. As a result, the village delegation's influence over village affairs was augmented. Another incident that also lent support to the conclusion was the subject of a piece of reporting on Sichuan Television. According

[42] Minutes of the May 25, 1996 Huojiacun village delegation meeting.

to the report, in one recently concluded election, two township cadres acted on their own to remove from the ballot box "null ballots", with the aim of reducing the total number of votes cast, thereby increasing the odds of one of the candidates ending up with "more than half" of all votes cast. However, this action never achieved its intended objective because it was declared invalid by election officials. Evidently, even when faced with the shift in where they got the power that they had, some of the township cadres failed to recognize the limits to their power, and continued to follow the old playbook and tried to run roughshod over the village delegation. In the end, such action was met with resistance and rejection.

5.6 Self-Rule Through Representation Versus Self-Rule Through Authority Figure

It is, however, easy to overstate the changes discussed above. After all, the persistence of many structural constraints means that those who cast a ballot still fall short of the full status of individual voters. For example, many of them are dependent on others for the land they work on as their means of production, and have little choice in the matter, and insofar as they are village residents, they do not yet stand in relation to the country's system of legal codes as citizens to the law (see Chap. 3 for discussions about how, in reality, the state is responsible neither for defining the scope of the rights of the rural population nor for ensuring that these rights are honored). Other factors that hinder the development of self-rule through representation include the lack of regular contacts between the administrative unit (voting district) and other social entities and institutions, and voter representatives' lack of independence and practical ineffectiveness. Until voter representatives actually become involved in managing the affairs of the village, are endowed with rights by the village population, and subject to their oversight and restraints in the exercise of these rights, that is, until these institutions grow more mature, elections can make but limited contribution to the development of rural constitutional politics. Even though it has been some years since rural "elections" first began to be held, and these have helped to create a method for recruiting leaders that is different from the appointment system (based on recommendations and nominations by township and village officials), how leaders who are chosen actually govern remains a problem. With but a few exceptions, in the vast majority of locations, institutions have had limited impact on preventing the abuse of power, despite these elections. "Elected" officials have had to govern by following the old *modus operandi*. In other words, while elections have helped to boost the legitimacy and credibility of the new leaders, they have not led to systemic transformation of the relationship between primary-level cadres and the rural population. The result is "self-rule" through authority.

Together, self-rule through authority and the township and village cadre network has made it difficult for either the village residents or superior governments to get involved in the primary-level personnel recruitment process. On one hand, official rules regarding cadre qualifications are either haphazardly followed or openly flouted. For example, to tamp down on factional tendencies, the government has instituted rules requiring "rotation" and "mixing" of cadres aimed at removing those who either "follow orders from superior blindly" or have been given their job by superior governments by pushing (including "voting") them out. But these rules have very little purchase at the primary level, and the further away from the central government you go the less relevant they are. The "Yang Dong Incident" (in which a joint petition signed by all township cadres calling for the removal of Dong, a township cadre himself, forced him out of office), in Henan province offers a good illustration.[43] The challenges facing many cadres in integrating into the establishment have led many who are not from where they are serving to treat these leadership position essentially as a "jumping off point" for getting the right packaging and obtaining short-term practical training. Their main objectives are to score quick job performance points, achieve rapid promotion, and then moving on to other places altogether. And even though in theory primary-level officials are government officials like any other, their loyalty is divided between the central government and the local cadre network. Forged of working relationships formed through day-to-day interactions, and held together by shared interests and reciprocity, this network constitutes an administrative environment with its own operational logic that is distinct from that of the central government. This led to a lack of uniformity, and inconsistency, in their administrative conduct. And due to the political nature of this compartmentalization, none of the theoretically available means to mitigating its adverse impact through administrative measures, including streamlining staff, paperwork reduction, and nomination of leadership candidates, has had notable effects. On the other self-rule through authority has effectively shielded those in power from societal oversight or any checks and balances. Governing, which is what comes after elections, is still firmly in the hands of a small number of people.

The key to transitioning from self-rule through authority to self-rule through representation is the redistribution of power through institutional processes and procedures. And these would not be processes and procedures that apply directly to elections. In the 1998 election held in Lishu, some of the village residents decided to "boycott" it, and demanded, in response to being asked to turn out to vote, that they would not unless the accounting books were made available to the public. While such a demand seemed at first blush to have been targeted at the election per se, in fact, it expressed broader concerns about the need for institutional reform more generally. It did not focus narrowly on the election under way, and encompassed issues such as the residents' right to know (openness) how the village is run and to exercise oversight (check and balance), which were integral aspects of institution-building. Yet these demands have not been made with a loud enough voice, and failed to

[43] Reports on villager autonomy on *Southern Weekend*, October and November, 1998.

garner favorable responses from the leaders, and only a paltry number of people would even bother to get involved. During my fieldwork, I noticed that a good number of village residents in Lishu county had but lukewarm interest in elections since they were skeptical these would lead to meaningful changes post-election. Not many village residents bothered to attend campaign speeches by candidates (though many did engage in below-the-radar mobilization), few questions were openly put to the candidates (even though there was no shortage of private conversations and discussions), and the number of abstention votes was alarmingly high in some village elections (exceeding 200), and surrogate voting was common, many villages resorted to mobilizing and even ordering people to evade election monitoring by superior governments. The lack of interest among village residents in village elections clearly had to do with how confident they are that their future interests were actually at stake, and it is a reflection of how little they trust the rules and regulations in place at the primary level. When I asked some of the residents why they were so uninterested in elections, they told me: "It matters little who get these jobs, they are there to profiteer, so why bother voting?" This made me realize that what people want is a fair and just system that would ensure that those who are elected do not end up profiteering from their jobs. Without the support of a system of institutions, elections themselves would be but a mission not yet accomplished. It is only when village residents get to choose not only who their leaders are but also how these leaders govern can there be said to be a genuine system of checks and balance. And until this happens, the rural population, even with their newly established right to vote, would still not know how to push for progress or what progress really looks like.

Institution-building essentially poses the question of how, outside elections, village self-rule through representation might be realized. If the goal of self-rule is to allow village residents to administer, regulate and manage themselves, then there is no getting around the issue of how to institute a mechanism that would support collective decision-making, whether it is through direct voting or voting by delegates who are themselves chosen by the residents. Even though the villager delegation system has been established in many villages, in most cases, they have had little to do besides preparing for and setting up elections. In the words of some villager delegates, "once the election is over, your title as the delegate expires, too". Evidently, the system has yet to become a fully integrated part of village self-rule. It plays but a very limited role in the day-to-day operations of the village. While the rules say that the village committee is the body that carries out collective decision-making, it is largely unclear how much power the committee and the delegates actually have. What can they actually do in the daily operations of the village, what are the things they can make decisions on, what are the limits of their veto power, and what can they push for, how is power distributed, and how can functional division of labor help improve the effectiveness of mutual restraints? All of these are not only practical issues in village self-rule, they also raise questions about the place of functional division of labor in both legislation and organization. On one hand, demarcating the scope of self-rule and guaranteeing that these powers can be exercised through passing legislation is part of institution-building. On the other hand, putting in place rules that allow different organizations to be able to perform oversight on one another, so there is no overreach, is part of organization building. Both of these have direct consequences for the development of post-election self-rule through representation.

Elections have also underscored the importance of deliberation procedures and protocols, which is a necessary component of an either direct-voting or indirect-voting collective decision-making mechanism. Deliberation procedures and protocols are the processes that yield decisions and rulings. They encompass procedural norms governing how collective decisions are made, and should be agreed to by all. If these rules are defective or incomplete, a good many decisions will be made beyond the scope of the collective decision-making process, without the knowledge or the consent of the residents. Obviously, this could engender conflicts and tension, and have deleterious political consequences both in terms of social cohesion and social order. Currently, the common practice is to allow the villager delegate to deliberate on a decision once it has been made by senior leadership. While this is an improvement, it still does not give village delegates a great deal of power or control. They might be able to introduce certain restrictions or limits either after a decision is already passed or, in some cases, a measure has gone into effect, but there is typically little they can do either to *prevent* bad decisions or to set the parameters *before* a plan or a budget is drawn up. If the deliberation procedures of the village delegation have teeth, and if no action can be taken until and unless it has been approved by the body, and if the approval can actually be implemented by a competent body, then deliberation would cease to be a mere formality.

How to establish reliable bodies to carry out arbitration or mediation is another issue raised by the introduction of elections. In the 1998 election in Lishu, many observers noticed that as the ability of primary-level administrative apparatus to effect integration and solidarity among different stakeholders continued to wane, kinship-based social networks and their ability to achieve cohesion began to grow. In particular, the ethical bonds among kin and relations turn out to be a valuable resource for establishing an institutional framework for managing the public's interests. As a countervailing force relative to the web of interests internal to the administrative establishment, such resource often becomes something that is readily available and much needed to newly elected rural officials. It does, however, have its limits. It can escalate existing conflict by effectively making a primary-level cadre the *de facto* representative of a particular clan or lineage, thereby not only costing them the ability to effect integration and cohesion among a larger number of constituents, but also damaging their reputation as a person who serves the public. This is obviously not helpful toward the sound development of self-rule through representation. Self-rule through representation requires rural leaders to transcend the divisions among different interest groups and stakeholders and answer to the needs of everybody. This puts the establishment of neutral, third-party organizations that have the trust and confidence of all stakeholders on the agenda. These organizations would be tasked with adjudicating conflicts, arbitrating and mediating, and curtailing leaders' ability to cater selectively to some groups at the expense of others. Priority should be given to ensuring delegates are committed to representing (the interests of) all impartially, and establishing independent organizations to carry out investigation and arbitration. (To be truly independent, these organizations would need to have no direct or indirect financial entanglement with any interest group, and do not stand either to gain or to lose from any particular election outcome. They would be entrusted with handling complaints and petitions, conducting investigations, and producing supporting evidence for rulings by the village delegation.) Presently, these tasks are performed by government agencies at different levels, even though they are not included among these agencies' primary responsibilities. Not only has the large number of visits from constituents everyday caused serious disruption to their normal operations, more importantly, the situation constitutes a breach of the principle of organizational non-interference. Insofar as the county government depends on lower-level officials, especially township officials, to gather the evidence needed to reach a ruling in any particular case, the interests of township government and of village cadres are inextricably linked, and county government's hands are tied when it comes to influencing village elections, it creates the perfect condition for illicit collusion and favor trading.

Therefore, whether the transition from "self-rule" through authority to self-rule through representation can be successful hangs even more on the establishment of institutions and systems that can allocate rights evenly than it does on the process by which leaders are chosen. What distinguishes the kind of "systems" we are discussing here and the kind currently in place in some rural locations is that the two have different underlying principles. Under self-rule through authority, the leaders make the rules with the aim of regulating things. However, since the leaders are not themselves subject to these rules and regulations, they are fickle, and are susceptible to being co-opted to advance the interests of some special interest group. Obviously, these internal tensions within the system hinder effort to establish a rational order. What is now needed are systems that the public can consent to and that are permanent.[44] "Consent of the public" means that the rules must be created and acknowledged by the village residents, and permanence means they understand the consequence of either compliance or non-compliance, and are prepared to act according to that understanding, thereby creating basic order in society. While elections cannot create these systems, they have brought the acute problems elections have exposed to the fore, bringing them the attention they deserve.

[44] Friedrich Hayek, *The Constitution of Liberty* (Chicago: University of Chicago Press, 1998).

Systems exist to allocate and demarcate rights, and optimal allocation of rights is of foundational importance to social stability. Optimizing allocation calls for imposing constraints on the powers that might be used to expand these rights. These constraints are designed to maintain the balance of power. And in essence, political progress is replacing conflicts and competition with peaceful, open, and manageable processes by building a structurally balanced system of power. I believe that the success of village self-rule will depend on whether we have the wisdom needed to promote social integration and cohesion by institutional and organizational means, i.e., by clearly assigning rights, responsibility, and obligation. But more importantly, it will also depend on whether we can realize that the only correct direction of our endeavor to build new rules for primary-level governance is toward the broader goal of village self-rule through representation that is based on constitutional politics and the rule of law.

CHAPTER 6

Observations on Rural Politics

6.1 Background

We have learned from a large body of research in social history and cultural anthropology that, similar to modern politics, many activities in traditional rural societies, such as ancestor worshipping, lineage tracing, parades and memorial ceremonies carry symbolic significance insofar as they are capable of spreading ideas, mobilizing, organizing, cementing power and internal cohesion, among others. The basic function of these activities is to uphold the power of the authority within a clan and to preserve ancestral inheritance. As such, written records passed down through the generations in the form of tombstone epitaph, family code of conduct, rural conventions and ordinances, and customary laws should be regarded not so much as covenants among members of a lineage but more as a set of promulgated rules about governing. They help strengthen control at the primary level, and sustain shared interests, mutual dependency, internal cohesion, and vigilance. The link between the interests of the individual and the survival of the whole, once established, is etched into people's consciousness. The traditional family clans play an important "organizing" role in maintaining rural social order. Driven primarily by a commitment to maintaining unity and security, a clan holds its individual members morally responsible for its own integrity and wellbeing. These are the moral norms on the basis of which the clan has been able to build centers of social cohesion that are outside the scope and independent of the state's organizational structure. In Francis L. K. Hsu's view, this type of organization is so widespread in traditional Chinese society that there were few kinds of sub-national yet non-local organizations strong and powerful enough to pose a challenge to the clan organization.[1]

[1] Francis L. K. Hsu, "Chinese Kinship and Chinese Behavior," in *China's Heritage and the Communist Political System*, Eds. Ping-ti Ho and Tang Tsou (Chicago: University of Chicago Press, 1968), 579–608.

J. Zhang, *Primary-Level Government*,
https://doi.org/10.1007/978-981-96-6209-8_6

These descriptions capture the "local" and "social" dimensions of rural politics, and suggest that they most likely first emerged in response to local conditions. Rural politics originated in the activities of local groups and individuals, and the resources that are brought to bear, including organizations, culture, central figures and participants are all from the local area, and its basic objective is neither to become involved in national politics nor to establish relationship or to ally with outside groups, but to maintain monopoly control over a specific locale. Because rural politics are relatively insular and have little in common with the rest of the country in terms of ideas, objectives, interests and motives, even though they are inevitably influenced by what happens politically in the country as a whole, national politics is of little value to our efforts to understand local politics. Essentially, political conflicts at the local level are borne of local events, or as Daniel Little understood it, local events were causally inherent and fundamental, while the broader context was causally non-fundamental.[2]

However, opinions diverge on the questions of what it is we are seeing in the Chinese society in the late modern period. One view holds that the traditional social model is still in place, and

> peasants participated in these Revolutions without being converted to radical visions of a desired new national society, and without becoming a nationally organized class-for-themselves. Instead they struggled for concrete goals – typically involving access to more land, or freedom from claims on their surpluses. Such goals were entirely understandable in terms of the existing local economic and political circumstances in which peasants found themselves.[3]

However, many other scholars believe that the situation described in the passage above has undergone serious transformation in modern China. And a key mark of this "transformation" is the fact that around mid-twentieth century, rural politics began slowly to become integrated into the national political structure, and has even been largely replaced by national politics with respect to substantive content. For example, it is well-known that the various "revolutions" reached deep into the countryside, changing both the composition and the role of rural elites, and creating a new breed of local political leaders who are driven just as much by national political objectives. These new leaders were able to become what they did because they possessed two qualifications. On one hand, they had the moral qualities rural communities expected of their leaders, on the other hand, they fit the profile of people the state believed would be capable of skillfully navigating the rural social landscape.[4] This would suggest that rural politics was already much changed from its earlier mode, in which it was independent and self-contained, and was beginning to establish a

[2] Daniel Little, *Understanding Peasant China* (New Haven: Yale University Press, 1989), 169.

[3] T. Skocpol, *States and Social Revolutions* (Cambridge University Press, 1979), 114.

[4] Richard Madsen, *Morality and Power in a Chinese Village* (University of California Press, Ltd. 1984).

presence in national politics. This "presence" may have started much earlier, such as indicated by a range of changes. Reforms to the fiscal system and tax collection in the countryside were already a part of the process of state-building,[5] *guanhua*, or the official language of the government, was introduced and increasingly widely adopted among the rural population,[6] ideas that make direct references to the country as a whole were broadly cited in decision-making processes, a national history and national logic became the central theme around which otherwise fragmented memories of the rural population were constituted into a coherent whole, and national political events and upheavals left indelible marks on peasants' lives, shaping their basic contour and forming their underlying structure.[7] Correspondingly, the model of social organizations in the countryside also underwent changes. Expansion of the political apparatus of the state led to the overhaul of the rural leadership configuration, introduced a different prototype for rural authority and new policies. Indeed, the collectivization movement of the 1950s "created a perfect congruence between the unit of taxation, the ownership of land and the structure of authority. Collectivization fulfilled state-making goals just as much as economic and ideological ones".[8] As one would expect, new forms of social organization—the production brigade, then the village by administrative designation—would gradually replace the clan organization to become the entity responsible for organizing village residents,[9] and cadres took over control in the village by virtue of their serving as the sole nexus between the local community and the state.[10]

Seen from this perspective, the basic function of all the administrative units and organizations set up by the state was to subsume rural life under a larger context. Within this explanatory framework, local political activities and events would be seen either as things engineered by local cadres that became a part of larger national political movements, or as a reflection or simulacrum writ small of what was going on politically in the country as a whole. This helps to explain why so many literary works about this historical period link the destiny of individuals with the ebb and flow of the history of a "country" or a "nation".

It clearly follows, then, that after these "transformations" just described, rural politics beyond the reach of the state can no longer be said to exist. Now rural politics was driven not by what rural communities saw as their own interests, but reacted and responded to conditions and events outside its own

[5] Prasenjit Duara, *Culture, Power and the State: Rural North China, 1900–1942*, (Stanford University Press, 1988), 3.

[6] Kang Li, Research on the Rural Elites, unpublished. 1997.

[7] Huirong Fang, *No-event situation and the "reality" of the life world: Memory of the social life in Xicun Village during China's Land Reform*, Master's thesis, Peking University, 1997.

[8] Duara, *Culture, Power and the State*, 267.

[9] Shangli Lin, "Rural self-rule and rural political development", in Chong-Pin Lin, ed., *PRC Tomorrow: Development under the Ninth Five-year Plan* (Gaoxiong: National Sun Yat-Sen University ROC, 1996), 329–339.

[10] Duara, *Culture, Power and the State.*

jurisdiction. This passivity was a result not only of the fact that rural politics had now incorporated broader and more general concerns and considerations, but also of the fact that the objectives of rural politics were now being informed by goals and expectations that originated beyond its limited horizon. So is rural politics really a reflection of national politics? Have the interests of the rural population been now systematically factored into the political calculus of those organizations and administrative units set up by the state? Can we now make sense of or perhaps even find some basic answers to questions regarding rural conflicts and tensions by applying analytical approaches that have been used to study national politics?

Here, the question that Duara asked, phrased in different ways, is not only interesting, but still relevant today. Duara noted that in much of the rural areas in northern China in modern times, the relationship between the landlord and the tenant "did not constitute a major contradiction", and that "rent and interest reduction were not important revolutionary tasks, since they could neither activate the majority of peasants nor weaken the forces of feudalism in the countryside".[11] Duara seems to be trying to argue that it was not so much the relationship through rent (between peasants and landlords) that peasants wanted to see changed, but the relationship through taxation (between them and the state). If so, then local authority would not have been the peasants' target, and the feudal system (the relationship through rent) would have been collateral damage from peasants' political actions (targeted at taxes). Duara wants to show through this argument that it was resentment toward what the peasants saw as wanton exploitation by the state that was fueling rural political activities. Today, we can apply the same logic—determining the animating force behind rural political activities—in our efforts to answer the above questions. However, we may arrive at answers different from the conclusions Duara drew based on his own observations of modern China.

When we try to understand what people in the countryside are trying to achieve through their political actions, it helps to distinguish among different sets of issues. For example, we can focus on things such as basic ideas, objectives, interests, organizations, and motives or incentives. The questions would be whether local politics and the strategic objectives of national politics have "merged seamlessly", and whether local politics displays signs suggesting the "expansion of the political power of the state". Scholars who believe that modern rural politics are fundamentally different from traditional rural politics are agreed, almost unanimously, that shifts in the objectives and the role of local authority figures mean that local politics are no longer localized in their scope and concerns. The question we must try to answer is how and why it is that these individuals became not only the target of resentment among the rural population but also the subject of attack by the state? If indeed these are the people who helped extend the reach of the state into rural areas, then why is it that protests and resistance among the rural population often included efforts

[11] Duara, *Culture, Power and the State*, 266.

by the aggrieved individuals to secure support for their cause from the state? In some cases, they would ally with forces associated with the state to combat the local authority. How do we explain why these actions have failed to weaken the control and influence of the state in the countryside? What are the root causes of these rural conflicts? And how are the interests and demands of the parties involved organized into a coherent and worthy political voice?

Today, despite the large number of politically significant activities, given the challenges researchers face in obtaining documents and materials, written complaints and petitions constitute the main source of textual information we are able to obtain about rural politics. For this reason, I shall presume, for purpose of analysis, that these forms of correspondence are a commonly used method for communicating one's grievance to the government, while acknowledging that these are not the only ones. I discuss four cases in this chapter, which took place in different locations. I hope the analysis will shed light on some of the general features of rural politics, including the goals of the participants, their underlying ideas, and their organizational structure. The first case involves two complaints—an initial complaint and a counter-complaint—from two villages in Shaanxi province.[12] The story was the subject of a literary non-fiction by Yuegang Lu. The second case concerns complaints filed by farmers who lived in the flood zone for one power station in Sichuan province.[13] The interviews were done by Jin Jun and Ying Xing. The third case involves the complaints filed by a group of CPC members and some residents in one village in Hebei province about the incumbent village cadres. The documents related to the case came directly from those who filed the complaints.[14] The fourth case was the "anti-Qi campaign" (Qi being the village CPC committee secretary) that took place in a Shandong village. The investigation was done by Chunlin Xia. The first two cases never went beyond various administrative organs, the third one ended up in court, while the last one, which happened toward the end of the 1980s, has basically gone nowhere. Among the cases, some involved individual complainants, while others organizations, some complainants were members of the public, while others cadres. What the cases have in common is how long they went on. I have chosen these "protracted" cases specifically in order to minimize the influence contingent events may have had on them.

6.2 Four Cases and Analysis

Case One

This case happened in Fenghuocun village and Yuanjiacun village in Liquan county, Shaanxi province. Both were officially designated model villages by the provincial, municipal, and county governments. But the two villages were

[12] Yuegang Lu, *Great Country, Weak People* (Beijing: China Film Press, 1998).

[13] Jun Jin, *Divergent Logics: Elite versus Disaster Victims* (Master's Thesis, Sociology Department, Peking University, 1998).

[14] Petition letter from June 1998 pertaining to X village, Hebei province titled "Reporting Economic Corruption in My Village".

adversaries. Over the span of nearly two decades, they were locked in a bitter feud, in which both sides were prepared to use whatever tactics to take down the other, including blackmailing, divulging secrets, framing people, planting evidence, giving false testimony, and making false accusations. Things were so intense the two sides were at each other's throat, and one would be hard pressed to find anybody in Xianyang or even the entire province who did not know about it. The protracted case spanned the terms of several counties, prefectural and provincial CPC committee secretaries, and nobody succeeded in bringing it to a resolution.

The conflict unfolded between the two villages' cadre/model workers (Wang and Guo). Wang had been a model worker who had wholeheartedly embraced the leadership's call to action since the 1950s. This is how he was described in his evaluation by the commune cadres: "When we called on people to engage in mutual assistance and cooperation, he responded by setting up mutual assistance cooperatives; when we called on people to learn and become educated, he responded by setting up an evening school; when we called on people to adopt scientific farming methods, he responded by working on increasing corn yield, earning a name for himself for around the country".[15] Guo, a younger rising start, came of age in the 1980s, and distinguished himself with his achievements in technological transformation of agriculture, increasing crop yield, and running successful and profitable village enterprises that improved people's lives. Guo served in a number of leadership positions, including the Yuanjiacun village CPC committee secretary, standing member of the county CPC committee, and a member of the provincial CPC committee. Wang's leadership positions included Fenghuocun village CPC committee secretary, former county CPC committee secretary, deputy mayor (retired). When the successes of the younger Guo and Yuanjiacun village threatened to eclipse the records of Wang and Fenghuocun village, Wang decided he was not going to let Guo and Yuanjiacun village take the place of himself and Fenghuocun village. In his word: "Whoever who has anything negative to say about Fenghuocun village is against me being the model, and by extension, against the provincial authority's choice of exemplar". Wang was determined to put Guo and Yuanjiacun in their place. Guo, for his part, vowed to take down Wang, who he called a fake model, and went around telling people that Wang had monkeyed with the numbers and inflated his yields, used the vast amounts of money he had received from the government to enrich himself, did not pay back on loans he had taken out, and also owed taxes. This is somebody, Guo charged, "who lack the qualifications to be an exemplar, and as a village cadre he should not have been eligible to become either model worker or model CPC representative".

As the fierce mutual attacks raged on, the government was compelled to step in to even things out.

[15] Lu, *Great Country*, 380.

> We must exercise extreme caution while trying to handle the relationship between the two sides. When outside visitors come, they will be taken to both places, with absolutely impartiality. Especially when it comes to personnel arrangement, both villages have to be taken into consideration. If somebody from one of them is put on a committee, then somebody from the other village must be given a comparable position to achieve parity. The same is true of decisions made by the municipal leadership, the two villages must be considered in conjunction with each other (interview with county CPC committee member).[16]

If it is true that "one's performance as a cadre is a function of their contribution to the country", as Wang had himself said, then why is it that even though Fenghuocun village received more money from the government in loans, it inflated its yield numbers more than any other village, and did not disclose its records on land (so they can cheat on their grain contribution quota)? "This is how they do it. First they would collect half of the money for the grain [they sold to the government]. Secondly, instead of sending grain to the national granary, they store it locally at Fenghuocun, while claiming that what is stored there nonetheless belonged to the state. Yet the exact amount they are holding is fudged, and often the grain that should already have arrived in the granary in the first six months of the year is not delivered until the second half of the year. Thirdly, they always wait until all the other villages have reported their output to report theirs so they can make sure to put in a higher number, effectively guaranteeing that Fenghuocun village always comes out number one".[17] In this case it is unclear if by relying on these "pioneers" to guide the evolution of the rural society the state has secured either more control or more benefits. "Higher-ranking officials" cannot micromanage how things should be run in the village by sidestepping these two individuals. Indeed, since they have already been awarded the model worker title, "higher-ranking officials" cannot pretend as if they didn't know this and award the same title to others. And if this is done specifically for the purpose of invalidating an earlier award decision, that would be tantamount to denouncing the approach used to arrive at that decision and discrediting the predecessor who made it, thereby wiping out historical achievements and even condemning the political prospects of an individual or even an entire village.

The terminology used in describing the two cases is revelatory of larger differences between the two periods in which the two model workers came of age. But we can see that more than anything else the feud is about the rivalry over who gets the top spot. Instead of seeing this as a case in which their actions and behavior were influenced by the state, it would be more accurate to say that these individuals co-opted the national political discourse to gain an edge over their rival. Wang was designated a model worker in the 1950s, and his claim to fame was his achievement in boosting agricultural yield. Guo, on the other

[16] Lu, *Great Country*, 387.
[17] Lu, *Great Country*, 277.

hand, is a model for the new generation of farmers of the 1980s. Had they not become adversaries in the political sphere, there would still likely have been a showdown between the two in some other form. Both lived in an era when being a model worker gave one a ticket to moving up the political ladder, and every model worker had the stalwart support of the entire village, since the village leadership counted on the acclaim the model worker received to translate into benefits and even special treatment for the village, including generous loans, marketing initiatives, and preferential policies. "In the names of the model worker and the cadres, Fenghuocun village went around to the county bureau of water conservancy and management, bureau of electric power, bureau of resources and logistics, and the bureau of education asking for money and things. Sometimes Wang did the asking himself, other times the village cadres would do it in his name". And if the request was turned down, that would be seen as "taking out the [model worker's] red flag, and shaming them". Most government officials felt that not much could be done about such a situation: "Failure to hold on to the red flag in [one's] province would make everybody look bad".

Obviously, this is a war over the control of resources. The rivals are not interested in lining the rural population up with any particular side in national politics, or emulating any particular ideological value at stake in national politics. What they are really after are fame, status, and control over and access to resources. Driven by this rather self-evident connection the village figurehead and the rest of the village came together to demand things from the bureaucratic establishment of the state that they believe would be useful to them. And the emergence of their "political struggle" can be attributed to the desire to eliminate possible rivals. This rivalry can be partly explained by reference to the bureaucratic establishment that is lurking in the background, insofar as it makes both political and material resources available. Nor is there any doubt that such background influences rural cadres' behavior. In fact, this is why the feud between the two villages has the appearance of "state actions". Yet what this appearance reveals is that the rivals have managed to make use of cues and forms of expression that are approved by and familiar to the establishment. Nevertheless, the feud is driven by self-interest: securing assistance and aid from the government. Or as some provincial officials put it, it is to use the model worker title as a prop in their efforts to milk the government of money and things.

> According to the most conservative estimates, between 1958 and 1995, the government injected at least 2.5 million yuan (not adjusted for inflation) worth of cash and material into Fenghuocun village. As of July 1997, Fenghuocun village owed 1,121,578 yuan in loan repayment, and 7.26 million yuan, 11.60 million yuan and 2,448,000 yuan to the county finance bureau, the county construction bank, the county agricultural bank and the municipal credit union, respectively. Between 1980 and 1996, the total amount of taxes Fenghuocun village paid the

government was less than two million yuan. The "costs and the benefits are totally out of proportion" in this model worker village.[18]

The establishment, from the village figurehead's point of view, is a form of resource with not only economic but also political value. Marketing campaigns, loans and preferential policies create propitious development conditions in a model worker's village, which can then help village leaders enhance their reputation, boost their standing, and rule more effectively. Rather than trying to outdo one another in tax collection or other kinds of contribution, the leaders of different villages compete over loans, promotion to higher government positions for one of their own, and dominance. Over time, village cadres adopted a policy of expediency. When dealing with higher authorities, they learned to be cynical and shrewd and vied for status while withholding information. You want high yield, we will give you the numbers, you call on the farmers to take up cultural and athletic activities, we will organize a basketball game featuring players who are old women with bound feet. The upshot is that some things are done entirely only for show, and these are the things that are truly useful to oneself. In private conversations, the model worker Wang imparted the following advice, based on his own political experience, to the entire cohort of his fellow Fenghuocun village cadres:

1. It's imperative to take the initiative, it's imperative to grab hold of the initiative, never be the one in a passive position;

...

4. One must learn to manufacture public opinion;
5. Don't be afraid to use your power, unless you showed people you would not hesitate to use the power you have, others would not take you seriously, and if you are reluctant to use your power, you should not wonder why others would not submit to the power;
7. When you are a cadre, act as if you were Qin Shi Huang, and centralize power (cadre diary).[19]

Such "experience in politics" has as its starting point the interests of the village. These sorts of behavior can scarcely be said to be consistent with what [these individuals] openly profess to believe in their capacity as "model workers". Indeed, it is far worse than inconsistency, the two are often blatantly at odds with each other. For example, after the death penalty was carried out in the "Wu Fang Case", a case that happened in Fenghuocun village but garnered nationwide attention, village cadres used bullhorns to order the village residents to attend the funeral service for the executed, claiming that "because he is different from others". The call whipped the local population into a frenzy. They bought funerary products with great fanfare, then went to the city with great fanfare, and parked their vehicle on the street at the most conspicuous

[18] Lu, *Great Country*, 317–8.
[19] Lu, *Great Country*, 291.

spots, signifying to others how strongly they felt about the ruling by the county court. That they might be accused of contempt of the nation's laws did not seem to bother them. Such a grand funerary service, as some insiders would reveal, would help even out the relationship between two factions of the Wang clan, and allow the "Madao" faction, which had dominated the clan for the previous four decades, to maintain their status as the "protectorate". For this, nothing would have stopped these people from doing what they wanted, not one's "model worker" label, or one's position as an official, or placards that say either "gone with the old in comes the new" or "progressive civilization". None of these would have made any difference to how they thought and their basic interests. Despite the fact they had access to both the credibility and support afforded them by the establishment, which would have helped them boost their leadership standing in the village and gain more clout, they still governed their own way, even though their own way runs afoul of the state's rules. Local leaders' desire to boost their own reputation and standing by capitalizing on the establishment can also be seen in model worker Wang's attempt to help "pave the way" forward for his son when he was about to retire.

> Wang is old now, and is no longer a player. But as somebody who was always somebody his whole life, he wanted to make sure his son could take over, so he meticulously put together a plan tailor made for his son that was based on his own experience: starting with becoming "delegate", then onto "model worker", followed by gaining more power in the village by enlisting the support of the provincial CPC committee secretary, and arranging frequent media coverage. Just about everything he could do to prepare an easy journey towards a bright future for his son he did, then came this Yuanjiacun village that threatened to sabotage his plan, how could he not try to clear it out of the way?[20]

This was a political feud between the cadres of these two villages. Each side was opposed to the other. Yet the village residents were nowhere to be seen in all of this. And the reason is that even as the cadres fought tooth and nail to gain more power and control, what they did had little adverse effect on the collective economic interests of their respective villages. If anything, they succeeded in generating recognition for the village and raking in loans, from which different groups of people in the village population were able to benefit. However, should the opposite have been the case, that is, should their actions have advanced their own self-interest at the expense of the village's collective assets or its ability to access more resources, that is, should a village cadre's attempt to meet certain targets set by the government end up hurting the village's collective interest, and should their personal political gain have come at the cost of the village's economic gains, there can be little doubt that other influential characters with different agendas would have been drawn into this political battle. As for the village residents, while they are indifferent to how

[20] Lu, *Great Country*, 401.

deeply mired in politics the village cadres are, they do care a great deal about how much their own interests might be impacted. If the two are mutually beneficial, then all is good, but if it is a mutually destructive relationship (even if the embezzler did not end up benefiting personally), then trouble is brewing. This is even more pronounced in case four.

Case Two

It took exactly ten years for this case to be resolved. The complaint had been filed by people who were affected by the flooding of farmland as a result of the construction of the Dahe power station. Of all the cases I studied, this one lasted the longest, and was also more "organized" than all the other cases. The Dahe power station, located where Shanyan and Fengxian, both in Wanshan region, border each other, was the largest hydropower plant in the region. It was completed in 1978, and was under the jurisdiction of the regional administration. The Dahe power station supplies electricity directly to the power grid that served the two counties. After its completion, nine production brigades in the four townships that had been flooded or damaged lost their land. Village residents relentlessly complained to the authorities, seeking compensation for "disaster relief" paid out in either grain or cash. Until 1982, the complainants filed their complaints in the name of the production brigade, then the team and then the commune. Their argument was the farmers had lost their land on which their livelihood had always depended, and was plunged into material hardship, and they should be allocated earmarked funding with which to pay for "disaster relief" and "compensation". As a matter of course, the money would be allocated to the commune. But as the money and the grain began to run out, disagreements over the eligibility requirements for receiving them also grew, as did questions about where the money had gone. Complaints by farmer representatives intensified. Over the next several years, some of the village and production team cadres who had been involved in these petitions gradually ended their involvement. They then became a kind of activists, and organized a village delegation that was not part of any existing production team, village, or commune. The delegation took it upon itself to pass "resolution" on petition-related matters such as strategies, specific requirements, deployment, and post-petition work. Around this time, the number of issues covered by these complaints and petitions began to grow. In addition to continuing to demand to take over the ownership and the management of the calcium carbide plant (i.e., demanding that management of the calcium carbide plant near the electric power station be handed over to the villages, so that jobs can be created for the large number of surplus labor in surrounding areas), people also wanted to know what had happened to the earmarked funding, to see the accounting records, and corrupt cadres to be investigated and disciplined. Moreover, petitions and complaints around this time were also being sent to higher levels of government, had a broader scope and greater numbers of participants, and more drastic tactics were also used. For example, on more than a few occasions, flash mobs of farmers showed up at the electric power station's staff canteen to "loot food". In documents prepared by higher government bodies, descriptions of such incidents changed from "reasonable effort towards reporting problems and issues" to "disorderly conduct". Some of the delegates ended up being charged and punished.[21]

Materials collected by researchers indicate that this wave of complaints and petitions had two fairly straightforward objectives. The economic objective was securing larger cash payment and grain payout and giving the victims ownership of the calcium carbide plant (including controls over worker recruitment, profit distribution, and power of control). The political objective was to have "corrupt officials" who had embezzled the earmarked funds investigated and disciplined. The political objective was to find the stolen money and have it returned to the people (the demands laid out in the complaints did not explicitly include the removal of any particular cadre). So one might say that ultimately the purpose of the complaints was to secure more economic assistance through pressure. It was basically the people versus the electric power station and entities that are behind and in charge of the station, both trying to gain control over resources essential to survival. During these petition trips, the petitioners manufactured overt confrontation on multiple occasions. For example, one incident involved people submitting an "urgent joint petition" to the office of the State Council in which they alleged some cadres had "beaten people up". In another one, several dozen elderly people lied down cross-wise in the middle of the road in order to stop the car in which the CPC committee secretary was traveling and to ask for money and things from the secretary.

There was the case where cadres that had been stationed in rural communities were mobbed and assaulted by local residents. And in one case cadres were falsely accused and framed for illicit expenditure on meals. More notoriously still, one time the delegates altogether rejected not only the conclusions reached by the task force that had done the investigation, but also official documents that had been prepared by the county government.

> At the meeting of public representatives, where three hundred people were in attendance, the deputy county chief said that some former leader in Shanyang township had misappropriated disaster relief funds and diverted them for other purposes. For example, money that had been earmarked for the reconstruction of the riverbanks was instead used to build a calcium carbide plant. And then they couldn't find the right people to run the plant once it was built. The plant was incompetently run and suffered losses, and the disaster victims never received any benefit. Former commune leaders failed to take this problem seriously or try to address it, and ought to be held accountable. But an investigation found that no cadre had committed embezzlement. The task force's main objectives are to review the accounts, track down the misappropriated earmarked funds, help the local population boost economic production, address some of the everyday issues they were facing, and allocate disaster relief fund in the amount of 9,000 yuan

[21] Jin, *Divergent Logics*, 1998.

towards alleviating hardship. We must have trust in the government, and know that no problem can be solved by just a handful of people. The calcium carbide plant used to be operated by the township government, but now it is in the hands of your team of nine groups. It is now up to you to make of it what you can, and if you do it well it will be able to help you make ends meet.

These remarks were immediately met with opposition. Several representatives who had been handpicked proceeded to negotiate with the task force, putting forward four demands. First, four representatives of the public must be allowed to work with the task force on the review, while another eight must be allowed to monitor the task force's review; Secondly, all loans are forgiven; thirdly, all outstanding labor corvée is forgiven; and fourthly, the area of the flood zone would be set at 200 *mu* for purpose of calculating how the profit earned by the plant would be distributed. After deliberation, the task force did not agree to all of them, but did propose six compromise measures: (1) the accountant would be physically present at the review to present whatever evidence needed to address issues, concerns, and questions raised by the task force; (2) 80 percent of the recruitment quota for the calcium carbide plant would be evenly distributed among the nine teams; (3) money equivalent to the depreciation of machines and equipment at the calcium carbide plant would be deposited into the funds of the nine teams, to be used toward repairing the riverbanks (4) the results of the review would be made public, and whatever members of the public wanted to know more about would be subject to further investigation; (5) reclaiming of misappropriated funds must be pursued resolutely; (6) ownership transfer of the calcium carbide plant would also cover all the debts, and none of the loans or labor corvée obligations would be reduced or written off. But these were rejected by the representatives, who insisted that work would not resume unless and until all four of their demands were met, and those who go back to work would risk having their heads smashed to pieces. Then people forcibly removed the accounting records of the calcium carbide plant, sent the workers home, locked the vehicles and the main buildings, to prevent the resumption of production and the review.[22]

Under "collective" or state ownership of land, it is commonplace for higher level government bodies to requisition land from lower level ones whenever the need arises, and pay a nominal amount in compensation. Such requisitions are not transfer of ownership, so the only issue is how much compensation is paid, and whether one party agrees to have their land requisitioned is a "non-issue". Yet land tenure such as this also provided primary-level collectives reasons to try and justify their "ownership" of land, insofar as it allows them to use their control of the land as a bargaining chip, and haggle endlessly with higher authorities over the rate of the compensation. The collective ownership of enterprises and land puts the government on the other side of these transactions. The situation turns what would be straightforward conflicts over property rights under some other ownership system into clashes between an individual or entity on one side and the government on the other. It effectively

[22] "Report on Response to the Incident", cited in Xia, *Image Capital*, 1998, 34.

turns what might have been *economic* issues into a *political* one. In the case of the calcium carbide plant, there were no preexisting contracts between two legal persons that might have helped to avoid disputes, since the electric power station was built on land that had not been requisitioned or purchased following proper contractual procedure, including negotiations over the terms and the compensation rates. The station is often seen as government property and its construction state action. Under these circumstances, using land in flooded areas to build the station would have seemed entirely proper, and the only thing open to discussion is how much compensation would be acceptable to the concerned party. The role the government plays in all of this makes the setting of the standard tricky, since this cannot be handled the way other regular transactions and contracts are, nor would a contract be binding on economic matters the way contracts between straightforwardly legal persons would be (since it has repercussion for political stability). That means that how the rate is decided depends largely on the personal attitudes, experience, and the luck of the individuals involved: if the other party does not agitate, then maybe the rate will be set lower, or no compensation is given at all, but if the other party makes a big fuss and is persistent, then maybe they will get more in compensation. The point is that everything is uncertain, and depends on how the situation develops. This case is yet another illustration of how much disorder can be created in the absence of systems of property rights and of contracts: stakeholders can have unlimited rights, and economic principles are of little help in resolving disputes, and so long as hardships and grievances exist, people will always be making demands. This is in fact nothing new, and legal scholars have called this "the nonexistence of the statute of limitations".[23]

We can conclude, therefore, that an ostensible "political conflict" really turns out to be an economic dispute (over property right). The petitioners clearly were seeking economic benefits, ownership rights, and control over property. They wanted exclusive control over the calcium carbide plant and oversight over the review done by outsiders, and refused to give permission to the task force to check the accounting books once transfer of control is complete. Moreover, they demanded all loans to be forgiven, and that the transfer be conditioned upon not only loans but also labor corvée obligations being summarily forgiven. From their point of view, the loan that was used toward building the power station had in fact been disaster relief funds that had been allocated to them that was diverted by the commune, and so the transfer of control over the calcium carbide plant was essentially restoring stolen property to its rightful owner, and any talk of loans is simply beside the point. And it is precisely because the dispute is essentially over economic matters, the political demands of the petitioners, such as the call for investigation of and disciplinary

[23] Zhiping Liang, "Law and order in China's rural society", in Mingming Wang & Sifu Wang, eds, *Order, Justice and Authority in Rural Society* (Beijing: China University of Political Science and Law Press, 1997), 415. Yu Fan, Fan, Y. (1998). "The Value, Operational Mechanism and Social Effects of Litigation," *Peking University Law Review*, Vol 1, No.1 (1998): 158.

action against corrupt officials who misappropriated public funds, gradually fell by the wayside. In the end, the dispute was still primarily about economic issues.

> Minutes from the meeting of representatives of petitions, June 26, 1986
> Attendees: six people from team no. 4 from Liuping, four people from team no. 5 from Liuping, three people from team no. 14 from Baiyang, one person from team no. 13 from Baiyang, and two people from team no. 6 from Feilong.
>
> Agenda: Report by two petitioner representatives on petition delivered to regional authorities. Since the matter was not resolved, attendees deliberated on the following questions: whether to continue these petitioning efforts, what would petitions cover, who would represent them to deliver future petitions, and the budget.
>
> Resolutions: (1) unanimous agreement on continuing the petitions; (2) The issues covered included funding for the power station; funding for the 1982 flooding disaster relief; funding for family planning measures; funding for water conservancy projects; (3) Petitioner representative candidates and person(s) in charge (omitted); (4) petition budget; reimbursement for travel expenses, disbursement to representatives of allowance for missed work shifts; convening representative meeting, per diem allowance for representatives; compensation for all forms of losses caused by participation in petitioning (representative meeting minutes).[24]

Something that also emerged during this process is single-issue interest groups. These started as groups that included people who worked within the administrative establishment and who "reported on what they saw on the ground". As these groups evolved, however, they became separated from the administrative establishment, and more and more members that also served in leadership positions left, until they became basically hodgepodge groups of activists and petitioners and anybody else who shared certain objectives. The petition activists would be the leaders of these groups by default, and members included people from all nine teams (and later on fissure appeared between teams from upstream and those from downstream), even though representatives of the local population would still be representing specific teams. The meeting minutes above seem to indicate fairly sophisticated organizational structure of these groups. They have rules that require proposed solutions to problems to be deliberated and decided at the representative meeting, and the decision ultimately lies in the hands of the public, and nobody else can interfere, and no representative can announce where they stand on an issue at will. Binding rules also apply to the representatives of each team. For example, they must arrive at the meetings on time, and cannot be absent. As for the "mob looting of food" at the power station, organizers stipulated that "one person from each household must participate, and each participant would be paid two yuan for each day they went, and each person who failed to show up would be subject to a fine of five yuan per day (though it is unclear how this money

[24] Xia, *Image Capital*, 58.

would be collected), and nobody is allowed to bail out once they arrived on the scene. Organizers also asked participants to follow orders, and until other matters have been satisfactorily resolved, nobody is allowed to claim the grain subsidy that had been distributed by the task force, and whoever who did so would be considered a traitor". Documents show that members of the public had been non-committal. Some would side with the petitioners as soon as they saw signs that the government might be ready to make concessions, while others felt that they had been "compelled". The prospects of being labeled a traitor meant that they did not have the freedom to disengage from the petition.

The appeal this group had among the public had to do with what the local population was demanding in terms of the allocation of disaster relief funds and benefits. However, traditionally, in rural areas, people do not see the distribution of disaster relief funds and benefits as something to which clear and rigid eligibility requirements apply. Relief and aid were distributed according to the severity of the disaster and the self-reported needs of survivors. And it was not tied to corresponding obligations on the part of the survivors. This created uncertainty and instability in the demands, which had important implications for how much the local population wanted to support the petition efforts. As we can see, the support would wax and wane depending on shifts in the attitudes of the government and of the leaders of the petitions, but especially that of the former. When the government shows no signs of trying to meet the demands, support for the petitions would wane, but when some in the government look as though they might be sympathetic or willing to budge, support would go up. Sometimes support of the local population is strong, while other times it is lukewarm, and sometimes people simply take a wait-and-see attitude and are non-committal. As the organizational structure of the petition grew more sophisticated, more rules were introduced, but this also made it more challenging to keep people's interests aligned. Petitioners often had to resort to mandatory measures to organize effectively, including levying fines and meting punishments to "traitors". These "representative meetings" are another form these mandatory measures take. The resolutions that are passed for the most part reflect what the petition activists want, and this is why incentives such as allowances and subsidies and disincentives such as fines are even needed.

What is obviously, however, is that these demands have no connections whatsoever with national politics. The village populations are not driven to act by national politics, and the petition leaders have no political ambitions beyond gaining control over the calcium carbide plant and how the profits are distributed. And because their demands are so specific to the case, the petitions share no common cause with other groups in the society with which they might have pooled resources and worked together. In fact, the petitioners try to establish direct connections with and secure support from government officials above the local level. Whenever there is a confrontation or crisis, the petitioners would cite some "order from on high" or some "backdoor channel" to justify what they are doing. When we look at the relationship between the petitioners and outsiders, it is hard to see any well-defined and long-lasting objectives beyond the specific demands for economic "disaster relief". Even though a dispute over property right turned into a political conflict (that manifests itself as a conflict between the cadres and the local population), at least in this case, the interests of each side never developed into something around which a larger group of people can coalesce. The position taken by each side in this conflict was not a function of their social or political identity, but contingent on how much disaster relief they were able to secure for themselves. Who they chose to ally themselves with, and over which issues were all matters of uncertainty, and it had no discernible correlations with such factors as CPC membership, being on the village committee or a farmer representative, or a member of any other social class, or rung on the social ladder, or the position taken by any outside entities. Any individual petitioner and government official at whichever level of the bureaucratic hierarchy might have conceivably belonged to some different group. Indeed, what they openly professed to believe and what they actually believed may not even be the same. Our general observation is that while individual cadres, CPC members, and members of the public may come together for some specific cause or issue, such *ad hoc* alliances typically do not outlast the incident itself and would fall apart once what brought them together has been resolved. Moreover, their actions were never aimed specifically at any particular organization or entity. The forces petitioners were able to marshal also seemed to have great difficulty securing a seat at the table within the establishment in their negotiation, suggesting that they were not yet motivated by a strong and distinct desire to have a voice in the decision-making process. So instead of seeing these actions as targeting some specific body within the political establishment, it would be more accurate to describe them as a spontaneous reaction among certain groups within a confined area to economic disputes over the electric power station. Of course, the government's disaster relief policies, the expectations these policies created among their intended beneficiaries, and poor management and incompetence of the relief distribution agencies all contributed to how the petitioners were able to press their demands again and again with ever higher levels of government until they reached the state.

Case Three

This case took place in village X, Hebei province, and it involved people accusing the members of village leadership of engaging in "unlawful conduct", so was clearly targeted at a very specific village-level government body. Among the signatories of the petitions were more than 50 senior CPC members and several members of the public, and the figurehead of the group was the immediate predecessor of the current CPC committee secretary. Over the course of several years these individuals filed a number of petitions, in which they demanded four things: (1) impeachment of the incumbent village leadership in its entirety, and hold elections to select its replacement; (2) reversal of the decision to grant CPC membership to six individuals, which had not been preceded by proper deliberation at the CPC member meeting, or convene a CPC member meeting to discuss these individuals' qualifications and allow the CPC members to exercise their right to vote on such a matter; (3) investigation of village cadres for economic misconduct by superior government officials (petition dated February 1998); (4) investigation of township and county-level officials for covering up the misconduct by village cadres (petitions dated October to December 1997). The petition also noted that other individuals besides the four senior members of the village leadership (who were on bail awaiting trial) were also suspected of unlawful conduct.

> Other cadres have also engaged in activities that are economically and legally problematic. The village residents on the whole do not approve of the job the leadership is doing, and have many complaints and grievances. How can work be properly carried out if these individuals are allowed to stay in power? Why would the village residents have any trust and confidence in them? This is why we the petitioners, acting on behalf of all the village residents, bringing with us their grievances and their financial donations, will continue to press our case, and will never give up until these misconduct has been thoroughly investigated.[25]

This political "opposition" within one village was not between the CPC establishment and a non-CPC entity or two different organizations, instead, the two parties were both made up of CPC members: the signatories of the petitions were mostly senior CPC members in the village and the individuals named in the petitions were mostly senior members of the village leadership. Of the 100 CPC members in the village, 57 had signed the petitions (the petition dated May, 1997). And the main charge in the petitions was that the village CPC committee secretary had "deprived" them of the right to vote and to express their opinions.

> The CPC committee secretary never once convened a CPC member meeting throughout his eight-year tenure on the job. The current members of the CPC leadership were not selected through elections, six members of the CPC committee had been granted CPC membership without their qualifications having been reviewed at a CPC member meeting. Many CPC members do not know how these individuals were able to become CPC members. Of these six individuals, more than half did not have the qualifications needed for CPC membership. We hereby demand intervention by superior CPC leadership to redress these irregularities, and restore CPC members' right to vote, uphold the integrity of organizational rules and the CPC charter, and prohibit the approval of CPC membership without proper discussion at CPC committee member meetings. Only those individuals whose membership applications have been voted on by CPC members will be recognized as legitimate CPC members, and we do not recognize those who did not go through this process. Nor should their membership be recognized by CPC committees and any level (petitions date December 1997 and February 1998).

[25] Petition letter addressed to the Provincial Party Committee, January 1998.

The organizer of the petition was a former CPC committee secretary S. He authored most of the petitions and signed them, and enlisted other CPC members to sign the petitions. But he never denied that in launching this campaign to "discredit" the incumbent village leadership he had been motivated by his personal ambition to join and become part of the village leadership through elections. His reason for criticizing the current leadership is that "its members are people who got their jobs as a result of favoritism and nepotism on the part of certain former members of the leadership". S believes that the previous CPC committee secretary had managed to have himself replaced by a close ally after being arrested on charges of financial misconduct, allowed his other allies to become CPC members without due process, promoted them to leadership positions, all so that he could hold on to power. The person who is currently number one within the leadership is a customary (i.e., not consanguineous) relative of the person who preceded him, which means that the current leadership is built within the same mold of the previous one. This is ground, according to S, for stripping the customary relative's CPC membership (petition dated October 1997). But S also claimed that since due process had not been followed, it would be technically improper to sanction [the customary relative] according to Party rules, since he believes the process by which he was given CPC membership was itself in breach of relevant rules (petition dated February 1997). And like most other petitions, the ones authored by S also included charges related to various financial misconduct by the village leadership, including accounting irregularities, something that would seem to have required some cooperation of the accountant.

Exposing Financial Misconduct in Village X[26]

(1) In 1993 one farmer surnamed Tian contracted 37 *mu* of sand pit, ZH abused his power and did not hold an open bidding process, and set the price arbitrarily at 260,000 yuan, of which only 110,000 yuan had been paid, and the remaining 150,000 yuan could not be accounted for. When Tian resold the sand pit later on, the size of the sand pit was determined upon measurement to be 43 *mu*, which means the sale was for an area 6 *mu* larger than the one he had contracted, and there are no records about the additional 6 *mu*.

(2) In 1995 cadre M commandeered 48 *mu* of sand pit, and ZH set the price arbitrarily at 13,000 yuan per mu, for a total 624,000 yuan. But only 590,000 yuan was credited to the production brigade's account, with an outstanding balance of 34,000 yuan. Only cadres were allocated shared, and no member of the public was allocated any shares. In the next village over where open bidding is held for the sale of sand, the unit price (per *mu*) is 6800 yuan higher than what it is in our vil-

[26] Petition letter, June 1996.

lage. We reckoned that just selling sand at such low price alone amounted to a massive loss of public assets.

(3) In 1993, ZH failed to issue receipts for taxes he had collected in the amount of 40,000 yuan. Investigations show that the money was notrecorded by either the production brigade or the tax bureau, and cannot be accounted for.

(4) In 1992–1995, production brigade cadres racked up a total of 17,301 yuan in expenses for weddings and funerals that were improperly invoiced or declared.

(5) In 1992–1995, the total bonus for the entire leadership was 54,800 yuan, but without the knowledge of the rest of the leadership, the top four members, two full-appointment and two deputies, decided behind closed doors that the amount for "the person at the helm" would be 39,800 yuan. Oughtn't this be regarded as corruption?

(6) In 1994–1995, contracting fees totaling 24,000 yuan owed to the village was never entered into the ledger, and cannot be accounted for.

(7) In 1995, production brigade cadres traveled in automobiles, incurring expenses in the amount of 9,158.5 yuan (Table 6.1).

(8) In 1995, each village resident paid 90 yuan in cotton-related fines, and a total of 36,000 yuan should have been collected. Only 28,000 yuan was entered into the ledger, and the rest cannot be accounted for.

(9) In 1994–1995, the government allocated around 100,000 yuan to village X to support cotton cultivation. The fund was not distributed to all households (some suggest that only two households received any money at all), and was not entered into the ledger, and cannot be accounted for.

(10) In 1993 the government allocated 30,000 yuan toward disaster relief following a hail storm. The money was not entered into the ledger of the production brigade and cannot be accounted for.

(11) In 1992–1994, the village sold 200 *mu* of land designated for household cultivation and residential use was sold at high prices. Calculations based on the number of households who made payments show that around 900,000 yuan should have been received. Review of the ledger shows that only 440,000 yuan was recorded. The households we visited all told us that they had indeed made the payment to the production brigade. But the money cannot be accounted for.

(12) In the fall of 1995, another township made a compensation payment in the amount of over 74,000 yuan to village X, which was not entered into the ledger and cannot be accounted for.

(13) In 1997 contract fees totaling 50,000 yuan should have been collected, but only 12,000 yuan was received, and those who had failed to make payment were able to renew their contract for 1998.

(14) In 1995 somebody from another village hauled away 100,000 pieces of bricks, for which 10,000 yuan should have been collected. Not only did the ledger not show this money, it actually showed that 10,000

yuan was paid for the purchase of the bricks. Why should public fund be used to pay for bricks for private use?

(15) In 1992–1995, 154,000 yuan in expenditure on meals by village cadres was improperly invoiced or declared. In the period that spanned all of 1995 and the first two months of 1996, the amount reached 170,000 yuan. These expenses even took place on the first day of the Lunar New Year, at the clip of more than 400 yuan a day.

(16) In 1992–1996, cadres drew from public fund to make illicit cash payments to various individuals at weddings and funerals, racking up wasteful spending in the amount of 17,301 yuan.

It is worth noting that the petitions to which 57 CPC members had affixed their thumbprints had been meticulously prepared by just two people. Not only did the names of these two individuals appear on the majority of the petitions, judging by the handwriting, one of them was responsible for drafting the list of the names of CPC member references. This person apparently wrote down on the petition the names of the 57 CPC members before collecting

Table 6.1 Travel expenses for automobile trips taken by village cadres (Unit: yuan)

Date	*Purpose*	*Amount*	*Approved by*
Jan. 4, 1995	Use of automobile	900	Liu
Jan. 16, 1995	Gas	48	Liu
June 8, 1995	Use of automobile for official trip, for work done for the family planning commission	1100	Liu
Nov. 30, 1995	Use of automobile for work-related trip	500	Liu
October 8, 1995	Use of automobile for work-related trip	400	Liu
October 12, 1995	Use of automobile for work-related trip	250	Liu
January 19, 1996	Gas	54	Liu
March 2, 1996	Use of automobile for work-related trip	500	Liu
March 4, 1996	Use of automobile for work-related trip	500	Liu
March 3, 1996	Use of automobile for work-related trip	1500	Liu
January 6, 1996	Use of automobile for work-related trip	500	Fa, Zhi
November 29, 1995	Gas	57.6	Zhang
January 18, 1996	Gas	265	Tian
January 18, 1996	Gas	200	Zhang, Zhi
December 25, 1995	Gas	64	Zhang
October 12, 1995	Use of automobile by family planning commission	550	Li, KU
November 12, 1995	8 times of automobile use	560	Zhang
January 14, 1996	Use of automobile for work-related trip	1006	Zhi, Ku
January 3, 1995	Gas	104	Tian
November 15, 1995	Gas, use of automobile	105.9	Tian
Total		9158.5	

Note: Data on suspected economic irregularities are provided by the petitioners, and must be investigated by the cadres

their thumbprints. It must have taken quite a bit of work to get this done, including persuasion, visits, and meetings and organizations.

> The two of us, I and Tian, visited and met with 57 CPC members, all of who said they had no idea how [these newly minted CPC members] had managed to join the Party. All of these CPC members expressed concern with the situation, and affixed their fingerprints [on the petition]. Later, two county cadres brought along the fake CPC members W and M, and one member of the public, together they interrogated each one of the CPC members who had affixed their fingerprints [on the petition], demanding to know what the fingerprint was for, and who had asked them to do it, which seriously rattled these whistleblowers. Superior government officials who became involved in disclosing the identity of whistleblowers should have been held to account. Should any one of the 57 CPC members be targeted for retaliation, county authorities should take full responsibility (petition dated May 1997).

Interestingly, during the investigation by higher governments, many of the signatories on the petition declined to admit that they had done so in the presence of village cadres. Later on, somebody, organized by the petitioners, wrote something called "Certification", indicating that these people would rather not let their involvement become widely known, and wanted in particularly to make sure current village cadres did not know.

> County leadership:
> On March 8 two people from the commune and two cadres from my village came to see me, wanting to know more about the fingerprinting. All I said was I did affix my fingerprint to a document prohibiting the creation of new sand pits. As for the other two fingerprints (approval of CPC membership applications, senior CPC members having been kept in the dark, and reviewing accounting ledger of the village) the people didn't ask me about them, and I said nothing. Since a newly-minted cadre W was part of the group, and he is in fact one of the people whose CPC membership approval had not gone through proper review by the CPC member meetings, I didn't say anything.

So apparently while economic misconduct and issues related to CPC membership qualifications of certain individuals may have triggered the petition, there is ample evidence to suggest that this campaign to "discredit" the current village leadership is fundamentally motivated by the desire to join the leadership. The others who became involved and the two figures at the center of the petitions were all affiliated with the same organizations. But the two central figures' decision to do what they did had a lot to do with their experiences with losses they had suffered in past power struggles. We may very well consider this a typical and new round of contest over power. After the four former senior-most members of the village leadership were removed from office after their arrest for economic misconduct, they "set up" a new group, and also granted CPC membership to ZH, who had not been a CPC member until then, so that ZH could take on the top-most leadership position. As such, members of this new group became the center of the power struggle and also the target of the petitions. The petitioners filed a lawsuit with the county procuratorate, deploying the same tactic they had previously used on the former leaders: demanding an investigation of the new leadership for financial misconduct. To that end, the petitioners collected and organized evidence for the alleged financial misconduct by the new leaders, and submitted them along with the petition as support materials. But apparently township and county-level administrative departments and the judiciary could not agree on what to do, and offered scant support for the procuratorate, making it difficult for the procuratorate to proceed with the case. But when the procuratorate took no action, the petitioners began to accuse some county officials of "covering up for allegedly corrupt cadres".

> A number of county officials and the commune CPC committee secretary asked people to speak in their favor, a number of officials put labels on procuratorate staff assigned to the case, putting pressure on the procuratorate, resorting to both coercion and manipulation. The harassment made it impossible for the procuratorate to get any work done. The ledgers that were handed over to the procuratorate have yet to be reviewed, and so far nobody has bothered to take a look at the petition and support materials we submitted. The reason the procuratorate has been deterred in its investigation has more than a little to do with how certain individuals have reacted, and cover-ups by certain county leaders and the commune (petition dated August 1997).

When the petitioners press their demands again and again with ever higher levels of government, their goal is to make sure those who are engaged in cover-ups do not get away. And in so doing they are not treating village cadres of higher-level officials as being on a par with one another. Ultimately, the petitioners' end is to topple the incumbent village leadership, and uncovering financial misconduct by these village cadres is the means, and those who cover up these misconducts were, as far as the petitioners are concerned, obstacle that had to be cleared out of the way. Since within the existing institutional framework at the village level there is no space for this kind of political acts, these are "channeled" into the administrative system instead, and filing petitions with superior levels of government became for them a means to beating their political rivals in a power struggle. In a letter addressed to a freshly minted county CPC committee secretary, the petitioners wrote:

> I have worked in the countryside for three decades, and I know this all too well. Those cadres who have been installed by higher levels of government do not care about the people, and looking down on all the rest. But cadres who have been elected by CPC members and the general public do in fact serve the farmers, and try to make themselves readily available to the community. This makes it easier for them to get things done, and to stay in power longer. [But] the leadership of village X is corrupt, it does everything to advance their own interests and is willing to hurt the farmers. They would provide false testimony on behalf of their prede-

cessors, and should be punished for violating Party disciplines and the law. They have acted improperly in many areas, especially in economic matters. Materials are being collected on each one of them, and will be submitted to senior officials next time. What qualifications have they got for serving as cadres, can the public trust them? There are many outstanding problems that have existed for quite some time, and the freshly-minted leadership is deterred from tackling them, unwilling to tackle them, and could not solve them even if it tried (petition dated August, 1997).

Case Four

One surnamed Qi is the top-most official in Gucun Village, Shandong province. He came up through the ranks in the 1980s. Once0 his term began, he rallied to the government's call and launched a series of projects aimed at boosting the income of the local population, and supporting the development of the private sector. With the village's own financial assets and bank loans, he invested in a sleuth of projects, including a farmer-run cupboard box factory, electric transmission cable factory, Jixian Restaurant, plastic factory, chemical shipbuilding materials factory, electric power utility worker team, shoe factory, paper bag factory, ice rink, amusement park, cineplex, and so forth. Qi's achievements were recognized by the county authorities, who described him as somebody who "dared to dream and dared to act, and who built valuable experience in developing the tertiary industry and optimizing the economic structure, somebody who made major contribution to the development of tourism in the county".

The freshly-minted county chief attending the ribbon-cutting opening ceremony for the amusement park, and spoke in glowing terms of Qi's achievements, calling him somebody who actually got things done, somebody who took what Deng Xiaoping had called for in his "Southern speech" to heart and carried it out through concrete actions. The county chief's speech was broadcast on TV, which once again catapulted Qi to fame within the county. And there was not a meeting of county cadres where he was not mentioned as an exemplary reformer.[27]

Within the space of just a few years, thanks to Qi's reputation, the village of Gucun was awarded the title of model enterprise village, and Qi himself the title of an exemplary entrepreneur, became a county people's congress delegate, and a candidate for vice president of the county Party school, among others. He was the kind of person that every county and township leadership would want to have, somebody who was quick to grasp what the government wanted to achieve, quick to take actions to carry out the government's strategies and to rally the village population around the goal of doing their part to achieve the goals the government had set for this new era. And because of his swift response to the government's calls and quick actions, Qi was officially

[27] Xia, *Image Capital*, 29.

recognized across the board by the government, which supported him in what he did in every way possible, guaranteeing loans he was taking out. Apparently this was somebody who embodied national politics in this new historical period. But, as far as the rural population is concerned, the only thing that mattered was the results. If the results of Qi's actions ended up hurting the interests of the village, it mattered little how strongly the government supported his plans, his standing in front of the local community would be shaky. It was not long before it became clear that the above-mentioned projects were not turning a profit. Not only did the village residents see no increase whatever to their income, but now they also found themselves burdened with massive debts from unpaid bank loans. To turn things around, starting in 1995, the village resumed the practice of imposing mandatory contributions and collecting payments from the residents, which until then had been paid for by the village, which drew on its own collective assets. To alleviate the financial strain the village was under, Qi had to slash public expenditure by suspending a large number of welfare programs. For example, publicly funded medical services were halted, the electricity and water bills for the apple orchids were no longer paid by the government, and the residents were now being asked to pay for a range of things that until now had been effectively subsidized. The local population became resentful.

This widespread "discontent" provided an opportunity to a challenger, who filed a complaint with the township authority, and demanded backing from superior officials for his own candidacy as the village CPC committee secretary. The challenger knocked on many doors, plastered posters in many places, wrote articles, all in an effort to find an opening. He was able to garner support from some former members of the village leadership who had been removed from office because they were considered by township officials to have fallen behind the times. Together, they started a campaign to "oust Qi". Forty-seven farmers filed a joint petition demanding Qi's removal. At one point, disgruntled farmers cut off the telephone lines to Qi's residence, occupied it, took out the wheels from his car, and demanded to "dialogue" with him.

It is noteworthy that the subject of the petition was not an entire organization, but Qi as an individual. Not only did the petitioners not demand accountability from the top decision-makers for his mistakes, in fact, it was the no. 2 in the village leadership and a number of senior CPC members that led the petition. This would seem to suggest that, despite their objection, within the existing institutional parameters, there was no way for these people either to stop Qi from being elected or to make a real dent to Qi's prospects.

> The proposal for building an amusement park was presented to township officials, who gave their blessings. But when the matter was discussed at the village CPC member meeting, a majority opposed it... We are not going to say anything about this project this time. Why? Because it makes no difference what we say. In the countryside the CPC committee secretary is the emperor. He calls all the shots. In the past emperors at least had ministers who could help him weigh

things. But now the village CPC committee secretary has got nobody who could check his judgments, and he has the final say."[28]

Apparently, people turned against Qi because of his eagerness to be subservient to superiors. In fact, Qi never tried to deny his role as a foot soldier doing the bidding of those ranked higher: "Higher officials helped me rise to this position precisely because they wanted to see some fundamental changes, so neither not doing what they ask of me nor failing to deliver the results they expect is really an option for me. Nor could I use having been outgunned by others as an excuse. So whoever who can beat their rivals and come out on top gets to be the hero". Since there was nothing village residents could do to persuade Qi, committed as he was to the development goals set by his superiors, to give due consideration to the interests of the village, they resorted to demanding his replacement as a way to resist being "buffeted by the gusty winds" that came down on them from higher governments. In their petition letters long-time CPC members accused Qi of selling off land to orchestrate projects, from which the village residents did not benefit at all. All the enterprises that Qi had started ended up collapsing. The factory director's pocket got fattened, but the village as a whole suffered huge economic losses. It is clear that the "gusty winds blown in" from higher governments was at odds with the interest of the village residents, who objected to both the idea and the practice of pushing things through recklessly and hastily. And this was the crux of the conflict. One person who was involved recalled:

> I took part in the 1989 anti-Qi activities, as one of the three CPC members who did. Later I was asked to write a note of self-criticism, expressing my belief that all CPC members must fully support the national policy of reform and opening-up, and since Qi has been exemplary in this regard, we must all support him. Supporting him would be tantamount to supporting national policies, and to hewing to the official line. You see, he has wrought such havoc in Gucun Village, yet he ends up getting the label of model.[29]

Yet as far as higher officials are concerned, Qi had done nothing wrong.

> We cannot pin everything on him, since at the time that way of doing things was prevalent. County and township officials were all in favor of launching as many projects as possible, and he was acting under such historical conditions, so he must not be completely discredited. In the past, when the village was flush with money, residents were exempted from contributing toward village reserve or township endowment fund, which was entirely covered by the village's collective savings. People got used to that and took it for granted. Now we are cash-strapped, and people have been asked to pay, and such effort is met with resistance, so that is the problem. Before the projects were launched, the decision was

[28] Xia, *Image Capital*, 29.
[29] Xia, *Image Capital*, 24.

put up for a discussion among the CPC members. But regardless of whether they approved it, he went ahead with the project anyway… so he could be arbitrary and presumptuous, but when it comes to handling matters in the countryside, you have to make your own decisions no matter what others thought. All the projects that were launched had been part of the effort to rally to what county and township leadership had been calling for, so we cannot just blame him if things didn't work out as had been hoped, then nobody would ever want to do this kind of work (interview with township officials).[30]

Such sharp contrast between how the two sides thought of the matter is indicative not only of how misaligned higher governments and the primary-level were in their objectives, interests and thinking and how far apart they were in their interests, but also of how poor a job Qi had done in forging buy-in from the village residents and ensuring they accepted the goals of the "superior" and would participate in the various "movements". For the rural population, "national policies" and whether they were "in line" with superior governments was not a factor in their deliberations. What they cared about was the impact something would have on their personal interests, and they had no tolerance for village cadres who failed to think like them, even if there is no evidence that those individuals had themselves been corrupt or taken bribes. This case in Shandong involving petitions calling for Qi's replacement did not produce any evidence suggesting he had either broken the law or embezzled money. Yet people strongly demanded that county leadership removed him from his office, since despite the fact that he was relatively clean in financial matters, he was no longer somebody who could be trusted to speak on behalf of the village, and was even regarded as a threat to the village. The objectives of petitions like this go beyond simply getting rid of corrupt primary-level officials. They reflect the tension between two ways of thinking and two different standards: the rural communities strongly objected to and rejected people like Qi, who purported to be "agents of the state". Therefore, this is an example of the failure of a village cadre who embodied what superior governments wanted to achieve. He was rejected because he betrayed the interests of the primary-level community. And it did not matter if he had the backing of superior officials, since within the village, Qi could, despite the support he had, no longer control the situation, given the widespread efforts among the residents at sabotage and resistance. Even though Qi was nominally still holding on to his office, he had lost his mandate.

Conditions are dire in the village, with all the enterprises having gone under, and projects that had been launched still in the red. Local residents were critical of how the cadres had run things, and refused to contribute toward the village reserve. With little money in the coffer, the village could not pay cadre salaries, or collect enough money to meet the fundraising targets imposed by township authorities, and it would be too much pressure to take out a bank loan in the

[30] Xia, *Image Capital*, 32.

> amount of 2 to 3 million yuan, and people couldn't even make ends meet. Under such circumstances, village often resorted to making required payment toward the township by taking out loans, and the local residents would rather pay extra to water their orchards than paying the 10 yuan the village asked of them. The village authorities would not supply the water needed for the orchids unless the residents paid up first, while the residents insisted they would pay nothing unless they got water first for their orchards, and even threatened to pay nothing even after they received water. The two sides were at a stand-off for a long time. In the end, just so that the order from the superior government for them to help fight the drought could be carried out, the township cadres had to pay 500 yuan out of his own pocket, and a privately-owned enterprise contribute some money to pay for the water for the orchards, and that was how the tension was alleviated, albeit just barely (interview with township cadre).[31]

Several dozen village residents coming together to take down Qi may have been a chance occurrence in one village, but there are larger lessons to be learned from events like this. First, by committing themselves to the development goals set by county and township officials village cadres find what is in their own political interest to be at odds with what is economically beneficial to the village. Secondly, a group of adversaries emerge who are savvy at mobilizing, and who manage to gain support because they put forward a standard of interest that captures village residents' own development plans distinct from those imposed from above. And by doing what he did, Qi had in effect given these adversaries a reason to take action, since in the eyes of most village residents, the adversaries are on the right side, from a moral point of view. While Qi's action could apparently be explained by reference to his desire to carry out orders issued by the state, he was, however, unsuccessful in securing buy-in from the local residents. If anything, what he did had the opposite effect and led to tension between the primary-level community and the state. As for Qi himself, despite having squandered many village resources, he was in the end unable to make meaningful contributions to the realization of the higher government's development goals.

Can we say that by trying to "take down Qi" the village residents had in fact taken aim at the state, too? Not necessarily. As in case one, the fact that a particular cadre has earned approval and even praise from their superior need not constitute sufficient reason for village residents to want to get involved in political conflicts. What really matters is what impact cadres' attitudes toward orders from higher government have on the interests of the village residents. If the cadre's actions benefit the village, then he is held in higher regard in the village than even those cadres who may not have been recognized by superior officials (Wang and Guo in case one are examples). As far as the village residents are concerned, it is not necessarily a bad thing when some village cadre is promoted to higher offices, since the higher village cadres rise, the more likely it is the village itself will end up benefiting (preferential policies, loans, poverty alleviation support, and projects). And even when economic benefits are absent,

[31] Xia, *Image Capital*, 32.

there may still be benefits in terms of protection, i.e., reduced damage caused by one's own mistakes or rivalry from others. For those who rise slowly, even though their standing as authority figures in the village is not adversely affected, their ability to parlay their status into extra resources and preferential consideration would be compromised. However, if the political tailwinds for the rise of a cadre run counter to the interests of the village residents, who typically want welfare benefits and "relief from burden", that cadre's political capital could be jeopardized. Since the "structural alienation between the public and the cadres in terms of their interests" has a long history, village cadre cannot defy higher authority by acting as a collective entity. Instead, they would try to maintain their power by segregating insiders, on whom they rely, and outsiders, from whom they seek assistance when needed. But the same structural alienation from the interests of the village residents could also lead some village cadre astray. Blindsided by what they see as their own interests or the interests of the cadre cohort, some may end up making poor judgments deleterious to their own standing.

If we try to explain these trends in rural politics by reference to national politics, it would be fairly easy to find cues that point to obvious connections, such as slogans used, the organizations to which petitioners submitted their complaints, the kinds of argument that are made and the kinds of demands that are pressed, and especially the relationship between key figures at the primary level and higher-ranking officials. So it would not be entirely correct to conclude that rural and national politics are completely unrelated. However, even if this can help explain the experiences of some village cadres, who, say, may have tried to hang their own political career on orders from superior governments in the hopes of building the "image capital"[32] needed to climb the bureaucratic ladder, it does not necessarily offer a complete explanation for group participation in rural politics. A closer examination would reveal that, what ultimately motivates people to get involved in local politics in rural areas is when a large number of them press demand for some kind of benefits that they believe have been denied them. Demands like that are usually highly localized but also representative of what an entire group wants. It is natural for the rural population to believe that village leadership has a moral responsibility to stand up for the interest of the village, and this belief entails rejection of anybody who may have aligned themselves with other groups outside the village. In this way of thinking, the village constitutes a self-standing and unique entity that is separate and distinct from any other. It is not in and of itself problematic that village cadres serve as agents of the state at the primary level, what really matters is whether they are able to translate that role into tangible benefits for the village community. This is the only circumstance under which the local population can be successfully mobilized to get involved in the jostling for leadership positions and political power, and the only way for the contestants to attain influence and opportunities.

[32] Xia, *Image Capital.*

6.3 Discussion I: Features of Rural Politics

While these cases are different, they do have one thing in common: they seek to mount political challenges through accusations about financial misconduct. The petitioners all share a certain kind of value, which is reflected in their demands for village leadership to be chosen through elections, for disclosure of village finance, for punishment for embezzlement, wasteful spending and diversion of public funds, and for truthful financial reports. Yet such value thus reflected does not lie at the crux of the adversary between them and those they oppose. After all, the latter not only approve of the principle behind these practices but invariably claim that they have adhered to them when discharging their responsibilities. As far as they are concerned, the petitions are only targeted at those few individuals who have engaged in transgression, mistakes the rest of the cadre cohort would not hesitate to call out. Obviously then, the real point of the adversary between the two sides, regardless of what they purport to claim openly, is rivalry over turf, control, and power. The rivalry between Wang and Guo for the position of the provincial people's congress delegate is, at its core, over who gets to maximize their side's political interests, and also the clout of their respective village within the region. As for the case in Sichuan, in addition to the size of the compensation for the displaced population, the two sides also locked horns over control of the calcium carbide plant. In the Hebei case, where 57 CPC members "refused to recognize" the CPC membership of some newly minted members, the tension could clearly be traced back to leadership rivalry that had taken place a decade earlier. Lurking in the background to the "anti-Qi" campaign in Shandong was one deputy's scheme to take Qi's position. In all these cases, the petitioners/challengers accused an opponent of economic misconduct in order to destroy their political careers. Their goal is very clear, and it is to stake a claim in some kind of resource or certain leadership position.

We may, therefore, conclude, that there are two types of motives: (1) vying for political position and power; and (2) vying for (economic and welfare) interests and benefits. The *modus operandi* of rural politics is also unique to the system we have. People want more than external influence on, interference with or oversight over village affairs, they want instead to take over power, political or economic, from those they are trying to topple. People's objectives in competing over economic benefits tend to be open for all to see, but people do not typically advertise contests over political positions and power. In fact, the latter kind of contest is often masqueraded as conflicts over economic matters, and the usual tactic involves gathering as much evidence as possible of one's opponent's alleged "financial misconduct". This kind of political activity is highly localized, and concerns events that are confined to a specific locale. When and if people reach out to people outside the locale and in higher governments their goal is not to challenge a large body politic but simply to seek help.

In terms of organizational structure, these petitions do not pit one side against another neatly along familiar lines that divide the population, such as CPC members versus non-CPC members, cadres versus the public, higher governments versus primary-level government. In fact, they may feature different mixtures of participants, including both people who hold official positions and those who do not. Still, most of those who take part in these petitions have some kind of connections to either organizations or individuals within the primary-level political establishment. In rural politics, former "insiders" play a particularly important role in gathering evidence, mobilizing and transmitting information, especially in letting information flow from the leadership to the public. This usually requires the participation of somebody who has knowledge of critical information, and they are often people who once held leadership positions, or people, such as accountants or clerks, who have little power but know a great deal. Thanks either to the position they hold or their experiences, these individuals are familiar with how public assets operate and what the problems are, and they know who the important figures are in the process and their average income. So they can easily provide evidence to back up suspicions by the village residents. Without the participation of these individuals, without the "evidence" they provide, many allegations would have no way of being substantiated and gone nowhere. In other words, had it not been for the participation of people within in the primary-level political establishment rural political activities would not have reached the scale they in fact did. All the central figures in each of these four cases had at some point worked within the establishment. Even though the primary-level officials that were involved in the Dahe power station incident in the beginning pulled out later on, their subsequent silence was in effect their way of expressing where they stood on the matter. It would not have been a bad thing for their team to prevail in its struggle to attain control of the calcium carbide plant, and by not participating themselves these primary-level officials could not be held accountable as "organizers", something they must not be since they were prohibited from doing so in their official capacity.

In rural conflicts triggered by economic disputes, more often than not a group of cadres would mobilize some members of the public to work with them toward some common goal. When a group of people share a set of common goals, they usually share the benefits, while excluding and competing against those who are not part of the group. This principle of benefit sharing provides incentives to those who are part of a group to treat outsiders as rivals, yet the bond between participants is very weak, and fissure can easily occur in how they identify with one another. At these times, clearly demarcated groups of common interests constitute the units of (organized) action, while different groups rarely share the same set of goals and interests. This also goes to show the localized nature of rural political objectives: people take actions in response to some local event or development, and their demands are local in scope, are not readily generalizable, and do not easily cohere with those of others. Moreover, groups that form on the basis of shared economic interests tend to be highly volatile and short-lived, and disintegrate as soon as their demands are met.

As for competition over leadership positions and political power, the "organizational" model antagonists typically resort to involves the rivals forming their own group of supporters or faction. And the "organization" is usually carried out privately. For example, the residence of a central figure might be used as a meeting place, where meetings can be held overnight where strategies are thrashed out. Even though activities like this can mobilize some members of the local population, it is not their goal to overthrow the *status quo*. Instead, the strategy is to relay the pressure from the public to higher levels of government, and to demand them to take action to topple primary-level authority by providing them with information. This is why universal agreements are rare in rural politics. More often than not, each side has its own groups of supporters, and officials at different levels, whether it is townships, regions or cities, may support a wide range of different groups. Each group has a different set of backers, and it is common for people to co-opt the opinion of some particular official for purpose of stoking public sentiments, to attack one's opponents, and each side in a rivalry may resort to mobilizing a group of people from the local population to file a joint petition, just so that they can show that they have support of the public.

> You bring 50 people, I bring 100 people. You have your people go to the municipal CPC committee, I have mine go to the provincial CPC committee, or even the State Council, with both sides trying to outgun the other. The game of accusation and recrimination drags on, until the animus between the two sides becomes white-hot. During the three years in which the petition saga was going on, nobody in the village was selling grain to the government as required, nobody was in charge of implementing the family planning policy, and normal operations were suspended, and disorder and chaos reigned.[33]

It is worth noting that rarely do people involved in these rural primary-level activities offer detailed reform plans, so rarely do these events produce any constructive outcomes. So far as these years-long petition sagas are concerned, in addition to personnel changes and economic and material benefits, they did not help push forward any institutional reform or introduce an alternative set of governance principles. So a pattern emerged in which one leadership cohort that had been caught with misconduct was replaced by another one that performs their administrative and managerial duties under basically the same set of operational logic and within the same institutional framework, with the only difference between the two being how much self-discipline is exercised. So it is only a matter of time before the new cohort comes up against the same political

[33] Discipline Inspection Office of the Central Commission, *Transparency in Village Affairs and Democracy in Village Management* (China Fangzheng Publishing House, 1997), 131–2.

hurdles. This recurrence is ultimately attributable to the fact that in rural politics the goals are always local in scope: they concern specific individuals but not the system as such, yet personnel changes can do little more than mitigating tension in the short run. Therefore, so long as rural politics never set their sights on something beyond personnel changes nothing great will ever come of it.

The reason for the lack of progress has to do with the lack of a legal institutional framework and institutional configurations that can provide space for fair and open competition. That makes it impossible for personnel selection to take place through mobilization, organization, and campaigns. Consequently, political competition was shoehorned into the space in either the administrative or the economic domain, and passivity and trying to come up with dirt on a rival's financial record became the dominant tactics. This means not only do primary-level cadres feel compelled to get involved in various factions if for no other reason than to seek protection, but officials at higher levels of government also found themselves having to invest a great deal of time toward handling these conflicts.

Yet the most serious ramification of people's inability to resolve these incessant political conflicts and social tension over interests and benefits is the disruption it causes in administrative operations. In response, higher government often had to resort to personnel changes in order to keep everyday businesses running. This practice has in effect turned personnel change into the default approach to dealing with problems at the primary level. But the political rivalries triggered by personnel disputes do not thereby come under control in an orderly fashion. Since personnel changes require involvement of higher levels of government, higher officials tend to pick people who are compliant and subservient, and who are ready at their beck and call. This will inevitably lead some people to try to cover up the misconduct of others. This kind of behavior not only has deleterious effects on the public reputation of administrative operations but it can also intensify resentment toward higherups among the rivals. Sometimes the antagonism can escalate to the point where the opposing sides see each other as archenemies. In fact, this accounts for a large share of the antagonism between officials and the public (although such antagonism is aimed at "cover ups" and not higher governments themselves). Whether it is higher-level officials or petitioners, personnel change becomes the only solution to these political conflicts, yet these shifts hardly do anything to introduce new principles and new ways of choosing leadership, exercising control, imposing constraints or effecting changes. So while personnel changes can bring about temporary relief from the crisis, they have only led to new wine in old bottles. Instead of putting in place a new order, the old set of institutions have been patched up. In this sense, the significance of rural politics consists in its value as a balance used for restoring the status quo.[34]

[34] Francis L. K. Hsu, *Americans and Chinese: Passage to Differences*, translated by Kaiping Peng and Wenjing Liu. (Beijing: Huaxia Publishing House, 1989): 321.

Another observable aspect of rural politics is the level of organization to which interests and benefits are subjected. Even though rural conflicts take aim at the authority, and can generate public opinion critical of the authority, no organizational structure of interests and benefits that is independent of the authority has emerged from them. Members of the public were mobilized by different factions trying to enlist their support, and they were buffeted in different directions by different information, characters and relationships, and developed allegiance with different groups. An outstanding feature of this process is that people were mostly responding to very specific events and individuals. They were treated as mere means to an end by the different groups that enlisted their support, and once the dispute is resolved, they would once again be left with nothing more than their peripheral status as unaffiliated atomic individuals. The disorderliness and instability of how social interests become organizationally structured mean that the individuals who get involved in these political activities have no firm stance on any particular issue, and even hold different views in private and in public on the same matter. Their attitudes depend on who is calling upon them for help, and they often feel compelled to do whatever necessary to make sure these people who have turned to them do not "lose face", to comply with "restrictions" and to maintain "relationships". Therefore, if and when a central figure is no longer there, the *ad hoc* coalition among those who have been pulled into their orbit would immediately disintegrate. In the Dahe power station case in Sichuan, for example, some members of the public even said to the work team: "If you can get rid of teacher Xu (a key petitioner), we would go with your proposal". All of this goes to show that one of the most difficult issues in rural politics is the fluidity of people's allegiance.

Institutional and organizational deficiencies and underdevelopment contributed to the frequent occurrence of rural conflicts, in which higher governments were always forced to get involved. Such "invitation" to higher governments to help maintain order at the primary level does more than encouraging higher governments to intervene, it also means the loss of opportunities for developing the capacity for self-governance at the primary level. The reason political crises are not taken advantage of for purpose of forestalling future crises is that it was never the goal of rural politics, dominated as it was by competition for leadership positions, to demarcate the scope of power and to establish institutional constraints. Rural political conflicts do not lead to breakthroughs on the basis of the compartmentalization or organization of interest groups, nor do they facilitate the establishment of either a fair and amicable set of procedural rules governing competitions, or institutions that can enforce these rules. Given such institutional deficiency, while political disputes often seem to be triggered by damages to the interest of the public, they almost never achieve the kinds of changes needed to ensure such wrongs do not happen again. So in the absence of their own resources with which to settle these disputes and to prevent future ones, rural communities resorted to seeking support from higher administrative authorities.

These vertical connections, through which rural political disputes spill over to other areas and other government authorities, are different from the kind of horizontal connections that are common in political activities. Therefore, even though they occur frequently, and enjoy plenty of support from the public, they do not produce institutional improvements and a new order. All of the four cases we have examined involve efforts to get higher authorities to intervene, and in two of them (cases two and four), the unrest was put down despite fierce opposition from the higher authorities. It seems that the participants are not interested in the establishment of a new system, for fear that it might place constraints on what they themselves can do politically, how they can do it, and the ways in which they might justify their activities. So in addition to changes to the composition of the village leadership, these political activities do not bring about the formation of well-ordered social forces that can make up for the ineffectiveness of the administrative establishment by acting as a check and balance on the incumbent leadership.

The rural population, therefore, is condemned to watching the recurrence of efforts to take down one cohort of leaders after another. These regime-change campaigns disrupt the social order, are a waste of people's energy, counterproductive, and yet difficult to reign in. They are similar in not only what triggers them, but also in how they unfold, and their outcome: rivalry within the rank of the incumbent leadership is always the cause, and higher authorities are always drawn into the ruckus, and they always end with some personnel shuffle. Members of the public were enlisted to "hop on the petition bandwagon", and they went along not because they wanted to fight for some universal, general right of their own (to grant power to primary-level leaders and to monitor their behavior), but because they want something very limited, namely, leaders who would do a better job looking after their interests. Despite the public's massive involvement in rural politics, the politics they are drawn into are nothing more than turf wars and power struggle among primary-level "bureaucrats", in which the public plays a supporting role. The recurrence of these campaigns has not brought about fundamental institutional changes.

6.4 Discussion II: Rural Politics and National Politics

While these cases have to do with national politics, the connections are limited to the way in which rural and national politics tried to use the resources the other has at their disposal as a means to furthering one's own ends. But they are not otherwise connected to each other with respect to either how political disputes are triggered or what kinds of interests are at stake. For example, in the Shaanxi case, the rivalry between Wang and Guo began when the two tried to elevate both their own standing and that of their respective villages. Neither was trying to establish a presence on the national stage. Both Wang and Guo are peasants, and had won the title of model workers, and both were cadres, and CPC members. According to the logic of national politics, the two should have been allies and not rivals. Yet since they belonged to different collectives (villages), they were adversaries. In the Dahe power station case, the peasants' efforts to claim control over the calcium carbide plant were aimed at the power station and not the government, which is why some of the officials demanded that complaints be lodged against the government, instead of the power station. What the public wanted was for the government to make sure they get the money and in-kind benefits promised them and that township and commune cadres were held accountable. In the Hebei case, where 57 CPC members "refused to recognize" the CPC membership of some individuals, they were apparently trying to have the incumbent leadership replaced. But since they did not have the mandate to impeach an incumbent, and only the mandate to hold discussions about an individual's qualifications for CPC membership, they could claim that insofar as the proper consultative procedure was not followed before some individuals were granted CPC membership, they could not recognize these individuals as CPC members. This petition did not take aim at the procedural rules of the organization concerned. On the contrary, it cited these rules as the very basis of the petition. By contrast, it was the confluence of several things that led to the "anti-Qi" campaign in Shandong. One of Qi's uncles, also surnamed Qi, who was serving as the deputy CPC committee secretary at the time, had set his sights on the same leadership position that Qi was after. But the primary reason that the public was readily mobilized was their resentment toward Qi for having squandered the village's wealth on vanity projects that had been launched ostensibly to rally to calls from higher government to start up as many enterprises as possible. This CPC committee secretary pooled local resources, and secured buy-in from the local residents to invest in ill-fated "get rich movement". He earned praise from the higher government, but because he could not generate tangible benefits for the local population, a gap emerged between what he wanted and what the local population did. The attitude of the peasants suggested that they were committed to their own objectives, but it also meant that Qi had simply failed in his bid to rally the village community around the goal of meeting the development targets set by higher governments. By betraying the interests of the primary-level community he was supposed to represent, he breached what was an eternal logic that underpins how everything works at that level, thereby creating the condition for the "anti-Qi" movement, and giving his rivals an opportunity to strike.

These political conflicts and disputes had been triggered by something that had occurred locally, and were causally linked closely to the interests, status, and objectives of collective entities at the local level. They also co-opted the discourse typically associated with national politics, but only in order to lend credibility to what they were doing, and to be taken seriously. It does not mean that these people either are taking aim at or otherwise endorse the values and interests that animate national politics. These kinds of conflicts would not have been best explained by reference to such concepts as "tension between officials and the public", "social resistance", "the state and the society", "civil society", and "introducing consolidated primary-level forces into new political relationship".[35] These notions are inapplicable because in rural China, people's interests, values, and objectives are not organized within the parameters set by these ideas. Macroscopic politics has little explanatory value for understanding rural politics, which has very parochial focus, does not interrelate, and has very limited if any interest in broader issues. Even though it is true that many cases of rural conflicts do occur between the public and primary-level cadres, still, the objectives are confined to primary-level personnel matters. The subjects of the grievances are invariably seen personally, that is, as individuals, rather than as people representing some external monopoly power. Nevertheless, petitioners are particularly keen to find evidence that those they are trying to take down have violated national rules, and they do so by citing things such as the CPC's charter, official documents issued by higher governments, opinions of and speeches by high-ranking officials, and the constitution. In other words, they make a point of separating the people they are targeting from the body or organization they belong to, so as to demonstrate that they are fully in support of and are pursuing full compliance with the genuine social order such as laid out in the rules promulgated by the state. To make sure the state knows about and would be willing to intervene in their problems, rural petitioners demand investigations by higher government, and are prepared to accept leadership by different individuals from the same organization. In most if not all these political incidents, instead of avoiding it, intervention by state political entities is sought after.

This shows two things. First, the goal of these political activities is not to resist the presence of state political apparatus in the rural communities in the countryside. To the contrary, petitioners are eager to have the support of state intervention in their effort to resolve local issues. Second, unlike in other societies, where the state is asked to relinquish its governing power over rural areas, rural political activities at this historical stage show strong dependency on the state's ability to serve as an agent of arbitration and a cultural symbol. These activities do not touch on recalibrating the relationship between officials and the public, nor are they aimed at bringing certain social forces that have been mobilized into the fold of national political relationship. All they are concerned with are local groups and local disputes over political and economic interests and benefits, and the reallocation of control over local resources.

Moreover, we can conclude that rural politics do not take aim at any particular class, political party, or political or social force. Instead, their focus is the behavior of primary-level officials. Ample evidence suggests that petitioners do not make the connection between primary-level government with state organizations. In fact, they tend to believe that it is only in that space beyond the reach of state apparatus that one can do whatever one wants. So it is primary-level government that seeks to establish such connection, which they hope

[35] D. Kelliher, *Peasant Power in China: The Era of Rural Reform, 1979–1989* (New Haven: Yale University Press, 1992).

would not only help cement their own authority and standing but also afford them the kind of protection that nothing else can provide. In local politics, the state is drawn in to play the role of a third-party arbiter, and not an opponent, or the backer of any one side in the dispute. Almost all government bureaucrats would do whatever they can to escape the countryside. They would seize the first opportunity they get to move to the city, put an end to their status as rural residents, so they can forever leave the countryside and its problems behind. Cadres both within and outside rural communities share a tacit mutual understanding of the way control of local resource clearly distinguishes between insiders and outsiders. This is the very basis of the strong sense of clearly demarcated "jurisdictions", a sense that has long been in existence but that is also largely informal (i.e., not codified in law). This shared understanding ensures that officials of different jurisdictions not only respect each other's turf, but would also be willing to coordinate with each other when needed, such as when their involvement has been requested by the other.[36] Such influence is mutual, and utilitarian, which is to say that the primary level is not passive or reactionary.

But it is important to distinguish between influence and jurisdictional scope on one hand, and objective and interest on the other. Such influence does not entail that either side tries to establish authority over or solve problems within their own jurisdiction by adopting the other's principles of governance. Nor does it mean that either party in rural political disputes is bound up with the state through shared interests. Conflicts emerge in rural society as a result of local disputes over political and economic interests. Salient as their causes and objectives are, they do need to evolve with the changing macroscopic social backdrop, and package themselves using the latest discourse deployed by the state so they not only can always seem justified but are always adaptive and, just as important, capable of shielding themselves from harm.

[36] Weiya He, *Reading*, Aug (1998): 65.

CHAPTER 7

The Personal Versus the Public: The Mixed Permutation of Two Types of Relationship

At the end of our first visit to Xicun Village in northern China, the four of us—three of my students and myself—were getting ready to return to Beijing after completing fieldwork. If we wanted to take a mini-van to the county seat, it would be a 20-minute walk to the "station" (the courtyard to the van owner's residence). It had rained heavily the day before our departure, and the roads in the village were covered with mud, making it unfeasible to walk the distance while pulling our suitcases. So I thought I would ask the mini-van owner to come to where we were lodging to pick up the students' luggage, and pay him twice as much for it. To my mind, this was a win-win deal and there was no reason why it wouldn't be acceptable. But I was wrong. Despite my desperate plea, the owner would not budge. It was not because the roads were waterlogged or the rate unreasonable. What worried him was his relationship with the person who owned the place we were staying at. He explained that the two of them have been neighbors for many years, if he agreed to what I was proposing (and took our money), it would make him look bad in front of his fellow village residents. But if he gave us a ride for free it would mean forfeiting an income. So by not giving us a ride, he could avoid the dilemma, neither having to provide a service for free nor doing something disreputable.

In essence, this is a dilemma caused by the lack of clear distinction between rules governing public relationships (transportation service and customers) and those governing personal relationships (friends helping one another out). As far as the van owner is concerned, customers that he did not personally know

An earlier version of this chapter first appeared in *Journal of Huazhong Normal University (Humanities and Social Science Edition)*, No. 3 (1995). I would like to thank my graduate students Lipeng Zhang, Dongtao Qi, An Li, Fuhai Xu, Lei Zhang, and Min Zhang for their contribution to questionnaire design and information gathering and organization.

J. Zhang, *Primary-Level Government*,
https://doi.org/10.1007/978-981-96-6209-8_7

had an impersonal or "public" relationship with him, and he needed to follow rules that apply to the handling of public affairs. But one's fellow village residents are family (personal relationship), and he would become a subject of ridicule should he take money in exchange for a ride, because he would have applied the wrong set of rules (norms). Since we were lodging at a place that belonged to someone he considered family, and we were treated as family by these people, by extension the van owner could not treat us as outsiders, either. Gripped by this kind of logic, it was unthinkable to him that people who are acquainted might nonetheless have an impersonal or public relationship with one another. It follows, therefore, a perfectly ordinary deal and potentially a win-win for both parties—allowing him to make some money and giving us the convenience we wanted—could not happen because the personal relationships on which the deal is predicated cannot be converted into impersonal or public relationships.

7.1 Personal Relationships and Impersonal/Public Relationships

Personal relationships and impersonal/public relationships differ in terms of their functions and the norms that govern them. In impersonal/public relationships, the two parties are equals, and must be treated alike, otherwise it would be discrimination. In personal relationships, the two parties are different individuals and must be treated as individuals, and each personal relationship is different from any other. And the rules governing personal relationships are entirely different from those that govern impersonal/public relationships. Impersonal/public relationships are inclusionary, but personal relationships are unique and exclusionary. Parties in an impersonal/public relationship are held to account according to the rules applicable to these relationships, and are not subject to change according to personal preferences. By contrast, in personal relationships, the parties are responsible for one another, so how people act depends on the specific individual(s) they are related to. Impersonal/public relationships are essentially instrumental, i.e., focusing on how things operate; whereas personal relationships are primarily expressive, i.e., with a focus on how people feel. Entities in impersonal/public relationships are abstractions, and they possess individualities that have been forged of social expectations with respect to their rights, duties and responsibilities, and it matters little who they are as people. Whereas in personal relationships, the entities are specific persons, each with their own distinct personality.

Prototypically, public affairs presuppose the existence of impersonal/public relationships. This means treating the stakeholders as individuals in an impersonal/public relationship, who, at this point, has already shielded their individuality. Therefore, impersonality is a prerequisite for any role in an impersonal/public relationship. Impersonal/public relationships are important for public affairs because such relationships are what sustain and solidify the ideas underlying public affairs, ideas that define the parameters of public roles and the norms governing how these affairs are handled. Public affairs include, among other things, the distribution of wealth, the leasing of land, the creation of a budget, making spending decisions, recruiting cadres. If personal rules are used in the handling of these matters, many different kinds of criteria would have to apply. Impersonal/public relationship must be built on rules that are broadly accepted, rules that apply universally, impartially, and do not vary according to different interests and situations. Work performed in one's public role is supported by taxpayer money, i.e., the public's money, and the precise scope of the responsibility associated with that role is determined by the needs of, and subject to oversight by the public. The person who plays that role must, therefore, act within these parameters.

For many scholars, whether a set of institutions makes a clear distinction between the impersonal/public and the personal marks the distinction between the traditional social structure and the modern social structure. But just as importantly, such a distinction also points toward cultural differences. The distinction between what is personal and what is impersonal/public is instrumental for keeping the former from making inroads into the domain of the latter. The former is exemplified by market relationships, legal relationships, political relationships and labor relationships, while the latter is pervasive within families (and clans). Personal relationships form by building on family-based and clan-based relationships. It has been noted, for example, that in East Asia, it is common for businesses to establish close working relationships with local governments and for personal relationships to be used for purpose of guaranteeing business transactions. But in Europe and North America, such necessary guarantee is provided by law, whereas across Asia, something else is needed for business transactions to materialize, and that is one of the strongest elements of East Asian culture, namely, close personal ties that are built on clan connections and extensions.[1] Of Chinese culture in particular, some have observed that one of its distinctive features is the way in which networks of personal relationships are formed. Basically, family ties were extended to include members of a clan, and then those of the society. These networks bring together individuals who have shared interests and values. Once people form this kind of relationship with others, regardless of whether they are personally acquainted, they can expect others to share the same responsibilities as they themselves have.[2]

So far as these analyses are concerned, the above-mentioned duties are personal, so are the related responsibilities, and are essentially not impersonal or public. But in societies across Asia, the absence of such a distinction means impersonal/public relationships are lumped together with personal ones. Our preliminary hypothesis is that rules governing conduct associated with personal

[1] Dwight Perkins, "Law, Family Ties, and the East Asian Way of Business," in Lawrence E. Harrison and Samuel P. Huntington, eds., *Culture Matters: How Values Shape Human Progress*, eds. by Lawrence E. Harrison and Samuel P. Huntington, New York NY, Basic Books, 2000.

[2] Lucian W. Pye, "Asian Values": from Dynamos to Dominoes?", in Lawrence E. Harrison and Samuel P. Huntington, eds., *Culture Matters*, 2000.

relationships cannot evolve into impersonal/public relationships, or associated responsibilities and duties. But why not? Because personal interests could come into conflict with each other. These interests are different but have limited scope, which expands as personal relationships do. However, even though these relationships based on bloodlines, ancestral lineage, and geography are capable of expanding in reach, they are ultimately unable to evolve into public interest, public welfare, or the notion of fairness based on public rationality that transcends these limitations. But interests and fairness thus delimited would be unable to expand to cover the public sphere (outsiders), or to give rise to attitudes associated with universality or impartiality, or to grow into an affirmation of impersonal/public relationships. In short, personal relationships are different from, and are unable to transform into impersonal/public relationships.

It is natural, therefore, that when researchers deploy these notions in capturing the rural society, they tend to conclude that the rural population do not have any awareness of or appreciation for impersonal/public relationship, including its underlying ideas, and roles, areas and norms associated with them. Indeed, many researchers have offered examples that purport to show the absence of the notion of publicness among the rural population.

> In one village, the vegetable fields of six families are expected to be flooded by a dam that is being planned. They insisted that unless they are compensated for the Bok choy they would lose they would block the construction of the dam. Village cadres spent three days trying to change their minds, and were eventually able to arrive at an agreement with them. However, just as construction was about to commence, a woman from one of the families lied down in front of the bulldozer and demanded an increase to the compensation. In another village, well digging is being planned as part of the infrastructure construction. However, everybody wanted to have the well dug for them first and nobody would budge. In the end, nobody had a well dug for them. The village is planning to raise the elevation of the water-pumping rig, something that would benefit both irrigation teams. But team no. 1 thought that they got the short end of the stick, and that team no. 3 stood to benefit more, so team no. 1 announced that unless team no. 3 paid up they would not let the project go ahead… The village cadres have little trust in the residents. According to the cadres, if you are counting on money collected from the village residents to finance any infrastructure project, you'd never get anything accomplished.[3]

That things like this are common in rural areas is beyond dispute. But they raise a difficult question for all those trying to study issues related to the idea of publicness in the rural areas. That question has to with how we understand social relationship in the rural areas. Do impersonal/public relationships such

[3] Li Zhang, "'Manna' Puts Village Democracy to the Test," *Southern Weekend*, May 22, (1993): a7.

as how we typically understand them even exist in that setting? If not, how are impersonal matters handled? And how is public information transmitted and dispersed? And how are they organized to engage in collective actions?

7.2 Thinking and Doing: The Uniformity of Contradiction

Do the residents of Xicun village not have a sense of [the existence of] a public sphere? Yes they do. Let us use personnel changes, a fairly typical kind of public matter, as an example. Among the survey respondents, 62.5 percent reported paying attention to leadership recruitment and promotion. And among those, the most commonly cited reason (72.8 percent) for their interest was that they wanted to see that "people who are fair-minded and reasonable are selected to become cadres". That is what most people wanted, it's a public demand, because it is not directed at any specific individual or any particular personal interests. The following are residents' answers to questions about the differences between "public" and "personal". The patterns are quite self-explanatory (Tables 7.1, 7.2, 7.3, and 7.4).

These responses clearly indicate that residents of Xicun village do have the notion of a public sphere, since most of them did not approve of cadres who

Table 7.1 Answer to "Would you vote for somebody who is personally close to you in cadre election?"

Answers	*Number of responses*	*Percentage of the total*
Yes	17	8.5
No	117	58.5
It depends	66	33

Table 7.2 Answer to "If you are in charge of land leasing, who would you lease it to?"

Answers	*Number of responses*	*Percentage of the total*
Those who are closest to me	25	12.5
Those who pay the highest price	159	79.5
Those who would do something to benefit me personally	16	8

Table 7.3 Answer to "Your evaluation of morally scrupulous cadres"

Answers	*Number of responses*	*Percentage of the total*
Satisfied	173	86.5
Neutral	25	12.5
Dissatisfied	2	1

Table 7.4 Answer to "Your evaluation of cadres who show preferential treatment for those they have special relationship with"

Answers	*Number of responses*	*Percentage of the total*
Satisfied	18	9
Neutral	41	20.5
Dissatisfied	141	70.5

Table 7.5 Answer to "What would make you vote for somebody in cadre elections (choose as many answers as apply)"

Reason	*Number of responses*
Personally close to me, and can give me some preferential treatment when the need arises	17
Close to higher officials, and can secure tangible benefits for the entire village	41
Can offer protection to the village residents, so reduce the amount of fees and charges we have to pay	61
Is fair and impartial	142
Can help us increase our income	132
Is careful with the village's money	90

treated people they know differently and were easily compromised. When asked to imagine they were a cadre and could decide how to lease the land, most respondents did not say they would lease it to neighbors and friends, and most said they would not vote for somebody who was personally close to them in cadre elections. All of this goes to show that the respondents were able to distinguish between general principles and what is in some specific person's interests, and that most residents of the village were in favor of transcending the interests of specific individuals while handing matters of the public. Moreover, they realized that, insofar as they wanted to make sure their own interests were not hurt, that goal is more likely to be achieved when the cadres are impartial than when they are not.

However, despite residents having the idea of a public sphere, in point of practice, the principle (all are treated equally no matter how close the personal relationship) and private interests (helping the villages increase their earning, protecting the villages and reducing fees and charges) are on a par with each other (Table 7.5).

These answers are not consistent with the beliefs the respondents had reported earlier. Even though they do not like it when cadres treat those they personally know differently, they nonetheless expected the cadres to deliver maximum benefits for the village residents. This tendency to take specific benefits and interests into account grew as consideration of practical issues deepened. It would be easy to see that, in practice, cadres were primarily motivated in how they act by concerns for particular benefits and interests (Table 7.6).

Table 7.6 Answer to "Who ends up getting elected cadre?"

Answers	*Number of responses*	*Percentage of the total*
From a large clan	10	5
Has support from a clique	37	18.5
Has support from higher officials	88	44
Has money	6	8
Has superior capability	27	13.5
Follows the law in handling matters	17	8.5
Did not answer	5	2.5

Table 7.7 Reaction to the statement "I support what is just, even if it does not benefit me personally"

Answers	*Number of responses*	*Percentage of the total*
Agree	164	82
Indifferent	26	13
Disagree	10	5

Table 7.8 Opinion on the statement "I support what would benefit me personally"

Answers	*Number of responses*	*Percentage of the total*
Agree	70	35
Indifferent	59	29.5
Disagree	70	35
Did not answer	1	0.5

This indicates that even though people profess to want fair-minded people elected cadres, their actual choices when it comes to specific issues bely that proclamation, and show a preponderance of concern for their personal interests. What they say and what they do are misaligned with each other, and are, without much tension, held together. We intentionally designed our survey to include choices that are at odds with one another, and the results show that the "unity of contradiction" is a genuine phenomenon (Tables 7.7 and 7.8).

While a large proportion of the respondents supported "what it just", on the question about whether they supported what would benefit them personally, the same number of people said they would as that who said they would not, and a fairly large percentage of the respondents said they did not care. This seems to suggest that as far as the village residents are concerned, while principles of fairness are important, when it comes to specific issues in practice, the interests of individuals also matter greatly. Between these two considerations, neither prevails absolutely. Even though most of the residents did not believe that personal relationships should play a role in the handling of public affairs, and that cadres in particular should not, given their status as people who are supposed to serve the public's interest, let their decisions be swayed by personal relationships, they would not necessarily adhere to such principles in their decisions about who to vote for. Since casting the ballot is an act that, compared to that of filling out a survey, allows for greater anonymity and is more impactful on one's personal interest, we may infer that when it comes to choosing their leaders in Xicun village, people's notion of a public sphere, assuming that is represented by a belief in the principle of fairness, carries equal weight with a concern for their personal interests, and it may be difficult to tell the influence of each apart on people's decision about who they support.

7.3 Parlaying Personal Relationships in Managing Public Affairs

What happened in Xicun Village, as we have recounted above, suggests that in the absence of powerful norms that govern how people behave in the public sphere, they are likely to try to protect their private or collective interests by building various kinds of relationships. Yet these interests they seek to protect do sometimes have properties associated with the public sphere. Results of the survey we conducted revealed that most Xicun village residents believed that if one wished to benefit from public affairs, it was not enough to rely on their own devises, and it was very important to be able to secure assistance, making connections (from 79 percent of the respondents) and lobbying (from 67 percent of the respondents) from particular individuals, especially those who work in some kind of public capacity. Among the different kinds of personal relationship that might be worth cultivating, the most important was those with cadres. Most respondents (51 percent) replied that this was the most effective way to get something done, much more important than relationships with relatives and friends (35.5 percent). As far as meeting the needs of village residents is concerned, it was far more useful to have the right kind of relationship with somebody who worked in a public capacity than to have relatives and friends. This reminds us that it would be wrong to think of these relationships as being useful only to the handling of personal affairs, where people help either other out, and pass on information to others. We ought to pay special attention to the role these personal relationships play in public affairs, because we would otherwise not be able to understand why it is that most (more than half) survey respondents said that the most effective way to get something done is to establish some kind of relationship with cadres (people who handle public affairs).

In Xicun village, you can build these relationships in a number of ways, including giving gifts, ceremonial adoption of your target as a relative, and having messages passed onto them through a third party. However it is done, the goal is to build a relationship where none used to exist, or didn't exist quite in the form that makes it useful. Apparently these relationships serve to safeguard personal interests, but since they typically pertain to everybody, they become something of "generalized personal interests with some public features". For example, one Xicun resident who had been fined for violating the family planning restrictions wanted the fine reduced asked the husband of a cousin of his who worked in the county seat to call up a cadre to make a plea at his behest. Working in the county seat made one a member of the state officialdom, a position that comes with some influence. This county official then contacted village cadres to inquire about the case, and the fine was reduced by a considerable amount. In another example, one resident of Xicun village who earned his keep by working in the transportation industry wanted to have the amount of money he had to pay in taxes for his truck reduced. So every year he would bring gifts to the cadre before the Chinese New Year, claiming to wish them a happy holiday. In their own words, they needed to resort to such tactic to secure reduction to the taxes precisely because they did not otherwise have any kind of personal relationships with the cadres. These individuals were perfectly honest about what their objectives were in acting this way, which was to advance their own personal interests. What was different, however, was that it pertained to a matter that was essentially public, namely, taxes.

Things such as these, where people turned to personal relationships to address issues that were public in nature, whether it was to have one's taxes reduced or to ensure that one was treated fairly, were no means rare, and most Xicun residents who engaged in such activities did not do them stealthily either. On the contrary, such practice has become common and normal. It is an open secret that people would advertise and strongly recommend to others. To most village residents, there is nothing embarrassing about this because it is motivated by the desire to make sure one is not treated unfairly in public affairs, e.g., being asked to pay more in fines, taxes, and homestead fees than others. In order to avoid being taken advantage of in public affairs, village residents resorted to cultivating personal relationships with the right people to secure protection for themselves.

People adopted the same approach when pursuing their personal interests. Residents who happen to have close personal ties with certain village cadres are more likely to prevail in an open contract bidding. They simply have a better chance at landing a contract. In this one case, for example, "the 23 rows of land reserved for homestead behind the village are worth 4000–5200 yuan apiece, but two thirds of the people leasing them have never paid anything, since these are either friends or relatives, or people who have bribed or given gifts to the concerned cadres, and the few who did pay paid only a puny amount, and the money was not properly recorded in the ledger".[4] "There used to be a supply and distribution center in the village, but it was later taken over entirely by two village residents. The authority wanted to hold to two to account, but one cadre tipped them off, and the two bribed some cadres and the investigation never happened."[5]

Whether the goal was to secure benefits for oneself or to avoid being given short shrift in public affairs, village residents had to be proactive in building the

[4] Transcript of the June 2002 interview with local resident ZHXL.

[5] See the transcript of the June 2002 interview with local resident TXK.

necessary personal relationships. Personal matters and public affairs become inextricably intertwined, forming complex causal chains, and provided justification and also precedents for differential handling of public affairs in Xicun village. Residents would cite these precedents again and again, making it almost impossible to show that some different ways of doing things may be "just", or acceptable. Even if some people may have wanted things to be done differently, it would have been unfeasible to actually translate that wish into concrete action. For example, some former village cadre refused to pay the three mandatory fees to the village and the five mandatory fees to the county to the new village leadership, claiming that they had not been paid for six months. Some village residents who had contracted land refused to pay the contracting fees, citing as their reason the fact that they had yet to receive compensation from the government for losses associated with the growing of cotton. Some village cadres refused to pay taxes on the orchid to the township tax bureau, claiming that the orchid had already been leased to individuals, and these individuals did not want to pay the taxes, insisting that the 38,000 yuan they already paid the village council each year in contracting fees should have been sufficient to cover the taxes. All of these matters, whether they were personal or public in nature, were lumped together as a matter of course by the village residents, who simply did not see how they could have been dealt with separately.

There were times when things got so complicated that we were simply unable to tease out the various motives, because each seemed to have some kind of "justification". This was apparently how public affairs in Xicun village were handled, and the basis on which their future plans were made: in order to spare oneself the hassles of paying taxes, contractors frequently resorted to giving cadres gifts such as fish (fish pond), fruits (orchard), chicken (chicken farm) and flour (flour mill), all in an effort to secure some kind of benefits for themselves. Sometimes people did this entirely for personal reasons, e.g., so they could evade taxes, but other times it was driven by the desire to be treated in a certain way in public affairs, e.g., not being subject to arbitrary fees and charges. The fact of the matter is that personal connections were commonly used in the handling of public affairs.

This means it was normal to resort to personal relationships in handling and operations of public affairs. When it came to routine matters, such as bidding for contracts, applying for homestead, and paying taxes, the first thing people would do before taking any action is to weigh up where they stood in terms of their relationship with concerned cadres. For example, in contract biddings, half of the village residents (50 percent) showed no interests in participating. But this is not because these people did not want to enter, 17 percent of them were deterred because they could not afford the contract, while 51 percent did not enter because they "did not know the right people", and thought they would not succeed even if they entered the bidding process, so basically gave up. The common practice of resorting to personal relationships to settle public affairs left village residents (58 percent of them) with the impression that the most effective way to win contracts was through "building connections". The numbers of residents who cited different reasons they believed somebody won a contract were, in descending order: because they had power (114), because they had bribed a cadres (110), because they knew the right people (96), because they had influence on others (79), because they offered the highest price (68). The first four of these reasons pertained to personal relationships, while the fifth one had to do with somebody's financial wherewithal, but this was ranked the least important by the interviewees. This speaks to the fact that personal connections are by far the most important factor in how public affairs, such as competition for and distribution of economic benefits, are managed in Xicun village.

Other events that transpired in Xicun provide further corroboration of this.

> Appointment of Electrician
>
> A row broke out between the two key members of the village leadership in 2001. One was the deputy director, the other was a member of the village committee, who would later be in charge of electricians and the collection of utility fees. Xicun already had two staff electricians at the time, the older one of which had been appointed by the county electric power office, but then the deputy director appointed two more electricians. The village committee member in charge of the electricians objected to the two appointments, and wanted the two replaced. He pointed out that every time these two electricians submitted the electricity fees they had collected to him the amount did not add up, falling short of the amount of electricity that had in fact been used. This meant that the village owed money in electricity bills to the county electric power office, which then punished Xicun village by cutting off power, disrupting production activities such as water pumping and residential use. "The village residents thought this was due to mistakes I had made in my work as the person in charge of power supply, while in fact it was because of the incompetence of the two electricians the deputy director had hired, who had possibly pocketed some of the money they had collected from the residents in electricity fees".[6] This village committee member thought that he should be given the authority to appoint people to become the electrician since he was the person who had been put in charge of electric supply for the village. So he went ahead and removed the two electricians that had been hired by the deputy director and replaced them with two people he had hand-picked. But when the deputy director learned about this he objected, and claimed that such behavior is baseless, and amounts to slandering the electricians. But according to the village committee member, the reason the deputy director objected to the replacement was that the two electricians who had been replaced were his relatives. The position of the electrician is much sought after, the workload is light and the pay is steady, and anybody with some power wanted to put their relatives in this job.

What we see here is that even though electricians are civil servants, who gets to fill the position is a decision made on the basis of personal relationships, and dispute over this led to a row between members of the village leadership. More

[6] Transcript of the August 2001 interviews with some village-level committee members.

importantly, however, the row was not essentially about whether the decision should be based on public considerations or personal considerations, but rather about the two people involved, whose personal considerations would be decisive.

> SXZ Negotiations
>
> SXZ has been, more than anybody else blowing the whistle on irregularities within the Xicun village leadership even since the 1990s. Using their personal ties with the accountant, SXZ and his associates were able to collect a considerable body of evidence of financial misconduct by village leaders. And they were relentless in their effort to disperse this material by filing complaints, in the hope of getting government agencies to start an investigation. Within the space of a few years, SXZ personally drafted numerous complaints sent to higher officials, blowing the whistle on financial misconduct by the incumbent village leadership. These complaints were mailed to judicial organs and also county and county-level CPC and political leadership, and a few even to administrative organs above the provincial level. Once these complaints were received, the government dispatched task forces to the village to investigate. To put a stop to this behavior by the whistle-blower, and to avoid harm to concerned individuals, key members of village leadership passed a message on to SXZ through a third party, offering him three things in exchange for his agreeing to handing over all the materials he had collected and stopping filing complaints. The three things were: (1) a plot of homestead so the elderly in SXZ's family could have a place to live by themselves, apart from their adult children; (2) a "cadre" monthly supplemental allowance for the rest of SXZ's life and (3) exemption from the cotton fine.

The deal never happened because SXZ did not agree to it. However, there is much that we can learn from it. It is notable that the conditions were put forward by a village cadre. These people have both the resources and the power associated with public affairs, and when negotiating with individuals, the conditions they offer all pertain to public affairs, or public welfare more specifically. Obviously, the distribution of welfare benefits is normally subject to uniform criteria, and people should not be given differential treatment, that is, if SXZ is entitled to something, then he should receive it whether or not he has blown the whistle, and if he is not entitled to something, then it should not be given to him as a way of stopping him from filing these complaints. But what actually happened illustrates how easily these public policy and public criteria can be personalized in practice, and specifically for the purpose of getting some public figure who is in some kind of trouble out of it. Had it not been for the power a person in a position of authority has to distribute homestead, to make decisions about cadre allowances and the amount of a fine, and had not been because the person who is impacted is a key member of the village leadership, would SXZ have as a matter course been entitled to these benefits? If he is not otherwise entitled to these things, and was given them only as a condition for him agreeing to stop filing complaints, then clearly the line between public affairs and personal affairs is completely blurred. People are able easily to switch between using public resources and using personal resources.

And people with power are not the only ones who can benefit from these exchanges, so can ordinary village residents. After all, these exchanges do not take place only among those who are acting in their civil servant capacities, but also among village residents who are representing their own private interests. For example, there were cases where residents were able to obtain legal documents proving their claim to the land used by their flour mill. According to the rules, land designated for residential use cannot be legally repurposed for production use. So if everything was done according to the rule, this village resident should not have been able to receive a legal stamp of approval for his use of land to build his flour mill. But thanks to his personal connections to village cadres and a *quid pro quo*, he got the legal papers he wanted for the land. This shows that the lack of clear distinction between what is public and what is personal can benefit just about anybody, whether it is those who work in some public capacity or ordinary members of the community. Whether one has power associated with public office may affect how often they actually benefit, but it does not change the fact that in principle nobody is precluded from benefiting.

Further complicating things is the fact that often the objectives of such trading of benefits based on personal relationships have directly to do with affairs of the public. For example, when the new leadership of Xicun took office, the village was experiencing fiscal difficulties: the roads were in poor shape, tractors could not safely be driven on these roads, the village was behind on payment of irrigation fees and utilities bills, owed teachers back pay, schools had to suspend normal operations, some of the teachers were transferred elsewhere and the primary school classes were on the brink of being suspended. In response, some cadres proposed setting up a sand plant to make ends meet by selling sand. However, county authorities had already closed all the sand plants that the village once had citing their adverse impact on land availability for farm use and implications for soil erosion, and instituted a ban on all new sand plants. So the Xicun cadres got in touch with anybody with any influence at all, lobbying them, showering them with gifts, and promising that county and county officials in charge would get a cut of the profit. Finally, the efforts paid off, "they relented, and the sand plant is set to open any day now".[7]

What we can learn from these cases is that, in Xicun, there is no clear line separating personal relationships and impersonal or public ones, and there are no two different sets of rules applicable in two separate spheres. Any rule may apply on any occasion and for any individual, and the goal may be the advancement of either personal interests or public ones. This kind of fluidity is sometimes out in the open, and meets with no objection or resistance, but other times is only practiced in private. Given how common this practice is, it is safe to infer that it is widely accepted. Any individual has the discretion to apply any rule that they may see fit for any specific purpose at hand, whether it pertains

[7] Transcript of the August 2001 interviews with tax officials in Xicun Village.

to their own interests or the interests of the community. Of course, people who hold public office have more opportunities to exercise this discretion, and the beneficiaries could be specific individuals or the community.

7.4 Extending Personal Relationships into the Public Sphere

That rules governing the personal and the impersonal or public can be used interchangeably means that in Xicun the line separating the two is blurred. So far as public affairs are concerned, this has two consequences. First, personal connections help impersonal or public relationship grow; and second, how closely people work together on public affairs depends on how close the underlying personal connections are.

For example, reciprocity, a mark of personal relationships, is not only commonplace in impersonal connections, it has also become the main way in which these connections expand in both scope and depth. In Xicun, people commonly believe that one expands one's social circle in one of two ways: giving gifts, and adopting people as relatives. Sixty-one percent of the residents said that gift-giving has increased in recent years, which obviously cannot have been driven only by people's desire to advance their personal interests. Since personal relationships can be passed on, traded, and introduced to other in exchange for favors, they have wide application in both personal and public affairs. In this sense, they are also key to establishing impersonal and social connections. We found that in Xicun, recipients of gifts, were, in descending order, cadres (52 percent), people in charge (29.5 percent), it depends (11 percent), and finally friends and family (trailing at 3.5 percent). Because of the role personal relationships can play in public affairs, 68.5 percent of respondents said that giving gifts is especially useful (16.5 percent saying it was somewhat useful, 10 percent that it depends, and 5 percent that it was not useful). Meanwhile, 83 percent of respondents said the practice of adopting people as their relatives has increased in recent years, with 58 percent saying candidly that the goal of doing so is to "build connections", and 18 percent said that goal was to provide mutual aid, and 17 percent said it was to make sure the two sides get on well with each other. These numbers are fairly self-explanatory.

Another common practice was for individuals to present gifts to cadre to express their gratitude. Among the residents we interviewed, practically everybody had done that. And they did not mind acknowledging their reasons for doing it. These included: hoping to have their fine for violating family planning policies reduced, wanting to make sure their orchard contract would be renewed, wanting to be allotted homestead land, wanting to be granted a business license for a self-proprietor transportation business, and wanting to have one's taxes reduced. In the case of one resident who had contracted a fishpond, when people from the tax bureau came to his house for collection, the cadres accompanying them put in a few words on his behalf and that resulted in a reduction of his taxes by a few hundred yuan. The grateful villager gave a few live fish to the cadre. The mutual exchange of gifts in the context of public affairs is seen as being on a par with such exchange in the context of private affairs, and nothing illustrates this better than the fact that village cadres receive more visitors and gift cash at the weddings and funerals of family members. Obviously these interactions should not be seen as strictly personal, because whether you want them to be or not, these private matters (weddings and funerals of family members) provide opportunities for interacting with the cadres. There can be no other explanation for why these occasions draw in more people and money than anything else.

By contrast, in personal relationships, even large favors do not necessarily have to be repaid with gifts, for the simple reason that the two sides are personally close to each other.

> When I became pregnant with a second child, my distant uncle's nephew was a cadre in the county seat (who calls me his sister "aunt"). After my older sister told him about me, he made a call to somebody in the county leadership. Had it not been for this I would surely have been given a hard time, either a heftier fine or even prison time. But in the end everything was settled after I paid just 1,700 yuan. Afterwards one county official said to me they hadn't realized that somebody in my family holds office in the county seat.[8]

Upon hearing this story I made a point of asking whether they would prepare some gifts for this relative to thank him for his help, and was told that no gift was necessary since people from one's children's relative by marriage is also considered one's own family, and they are supposed to help. Here again we see how gift-giving is something primarily done in the context of public affairs, with the express purpose of establishing the right connections to the right people. And the closer people are to one another personally, the less necessary it is to give gifts. It would not be an exaggeration to say in Xicun gift-giving has become the means to maintaining impersonal or public relationships. The practice is commonly engaged in, widely condoned, and universally accepted.

It is precisely because of the impact personal relationships can have on the public sphere that the gift registry at the weddings and funerals of cadre' family members becomes particularly important as a kind of record, and is taken very seriously by the concerned cadre and their family. One of my graduate students followed the funerary process for the family member of one cadre from beginning to end in order to try to understand its underlying mechanisms. This particular cadre lived in Xicun, and the funeral was for his mother. For most of her life, however, she had lived in another village (where this cadre's brother lived), and did not know many people in Xicun. But her son set up a funerary table in front of his house in Xicun, on which people were expected to place gifts, and made arrangement for people to be picked up by cars and taken to

[8] See the transcript of interview No 1, conducted in August 2001, with a local resident.

the other village to attend the funeral ceremonies. Early in the morning, the cadre's family played music and made announcements over the PA system, and some service staff was put specifically in charge of keeping a log. Villagers would pass the information on to others, and many went to the house. My student also went, and put down five yuan, which was not recorded (could it be because he was an outsider? Or because the amount was too puny to be worth recording?) But the person who took the money did give him a pack of cigarette in return, and inquired whose family he was from. The reason record keeping and inquiring about family membership were important was this allowed the recipient to know to whom they owed the obligation of reciprocity. My student then boarded the car that took people to the funeral in the neighboring village. They were in and out of there very quickly, and the whole exercise was entirely for show. According to my student's observation, during the short trip people did not talk much, but the number of people who went was considerable. Another graduate student who worked with us was a native of this area. He told us that you can pretty much tell if the householder is a cadre by how many people show up at a wedding or funerals and the amount of gift delivered.

We were able to obtain the record for family weddings and funerals for one Xicun family, which listed the gifts, both in-kind and in cash.[9] We examined the record, and was quite astonished to see that the death of an ordinary elderly in the family reveals how extensive a social network this particular household has. Its reach extends to 15 surrounding villages and, and included more than one hundred of organizations (grade schools) and individuals (village residents). The host of these weddings and funeral is surnamed Song, but except for the people from this one village listed on the gift registry who are mostly also surnamed Song, everybody else had other surnames. This gift registry does not belong to a village cadre, nor are they a prominent family in the area. It just so happened that the son of the old woman who died had been quite close to some village cadres. Still, we never expected that the death of an old woman would have set in motion so much action on the part of so many people from so many places. If this had been entirely something within a family, such a vast social network would seem unnecessary, because of how costly it must have been to maintain it. Obviously, what is personal here has gone beyond what is needed to meet one's personal needs, and it is an extension of the public sphere. If and when the need arises, all of these people would be mobilized, and they can mobilize still others from counties farther away, all of whom being potentially ready to do what they are asked, whether it is lobbying or participating in something in other ways.

Thanks to these what are apparently personal relationships, some businesses of the public are handled more efficiently than otherwise. One example is the exposure of financial misconduct among former village leaders. It started when a friend who was working in the county procuratorate passed on some

[9] The list shall not be disclosed in compliance with publisher's policies.

information, and promptly received a response. But the same information that was sent to other government agencies in the county seat generated no response. When it comes to collecting evidence for alleged financial misconduct, the whistle-blowers also capitalized on their personal relationship with the accountant, who helped them track down a massive amount of spending records, all of which were later used as incriminating evidence. We might contrast this case with another one that happened in another village, in Hebei. There the people trying to investigate were not as lucky, since they did not know the accountant, who not only did not help them, but obstructed their efforts.

> When AYZ, a resident of Baochengcun Village, went to try to review the ledgers, the accountant said they could not be found. During the re-allocation of land things were recorded, and AYZ went to the accountant again with the same request, and was given the same answer. The accountant was doing everything they could to make sure AYZ didn't lay eyes on the ledgers, and that was the end of that. He said the ledgers couldn't be found, and nobody else knew if that is true, and what can you do to him?
>
> Q: Is it not the responsibility of the accountant to keep the ledgers and the accounts safe? If the accountant is unable to produce the accounting records, would they not be penalized for dereliction of duty?
>
> According to the accounting law, the accounting records are to be kept for a certain period of time. And some of the important contracts should be permanently kept. But in the countryside, if something goes missing then it goes missing, and there has never been any investigation.[10]

When we look at these two cases side-by-side, we can see that one's personal relationship with the accountant clearly makes a difference to how successful one is in trying to review the accounting record for a public cause. When these public affairs are perfectly legal and legitimate, the role of the accountant is to work in concert with the investigative team. Yet in the absence of personal relationships, such cooperation may or may not happen. The same logic applies to what happens within the administrative establishment. If Xicun cadres wanted to make sure their application for an agriculture loan is approved, it is not enough to have prepared all the necessary documents. One must also work one's connections. Obviously, personal relationships can hold the key to whether a public matter gets done.

> Trying to secure a loan for the village, something that every village does, so the cadres have to work their connections, prepare some goodie bags. This is beneficial to the village, but it is not legal.[11]

[10] Fuhai Xu's transcript of the March 2002 interview with ZHZQ of the Agricultural Economic Station in Qianxi County.

[11] Fuhai Xu's transcript of the March 2002 interview with ZHZQ of the Agricultural Economic Station in Qianxi County.

The police precinct does not help us every time we go into the village to mediate, according to director Yu, and what makes a difference is the fact that the director of the precinct happens to be a classmate, and it's a bit easier to get help from him, and to get things done. In other places, it is common for the precinct to withhold assistance to the mediators, who had to work with the village council in their capacity as representatives of the Women's Federation.[12]

When personal relationships become the basis of cooperation among people who are working on affairs of the public, opportunism and uncertainty grow as a result. But it also provides a channel through which village residents can register their support for public office holders in an organized way. People who have extensive personal social networks but who are not necessarily committed to fairness in handling affairs of the public are far more likely to become office holders than others, since the public approves of cadres like that. Ordinary village residents would also try to find out where others stand on particular issues, and if somebody is dissatisfied with something, then that person can capitalize on their personal relationships and engineer collective resistance to and obstruction of public actions even without having to resort to mobilization, knocking on doors or building alliances. The problem of course is that personal social networks are after all limited in scope, and since where people stand on officer holders depends importantly on their social network, those from different networks would often refuse cooperation with one another. Cadres would then have a hard time convincing people to carry out their orders, and they often needed to resort to personal relationships to do their jobs (Tables 7.9 and 7.10).

7.5 A Permutation of Public Relationship: A New Patron-Client Relationship

Conflating rules that apply in the private and the public sphere in ways just described are in effect to apply notions that apply in personal relationships, such as closeness and whether somebody is an insider or outsider, in building impersonal or public relationships. The behavioral norms thus constituted are

Table 7.9 Answers to "If the person elected is not your preferred candidate, would you help them do their job when needed?"

Answers	*Number of responses*	*Percentage of the total*
Would	32	16
Would not	69	34.5
It depends	97	48.5
Don't know	1	0.5
Did not answer	1	0.5

[12] Guoliang Cai, *What Makes Mediation Effective: A Mediation Case Study* (Master's thesis, Peking University, 2003), 12.

Table 7.10 Answers to "Do residents of the village help the cadres with their work when needed?"

Answers	*Number of responses*	*Percentage of the total*
Would	32	16
Would not	69	34.5
It depends	97	48.5
Don't know	1	0.5
Did not answer	1	0.5

not those that call for equality, independence, value commitment, and universality. Instead, they call for judging people and things according to the closeness of a relationship, dependence, interests, and particularism. This kind of relationship divides people up into groups according to how close or distanced they are from somebody, and different people are able to exert different kinds of influence on affairs of the public depending on how close they are to a particular central figure. This is what is often called cliches or factions that are formed around different elite figures. Our survey shows that 75.5 percent of the respondents in Xicun felt that cliches and faction were playing a greater role in public life than ever before, and the areas in which their influence was most pronounced where, in descending order: cadre recruitment and promotion (47 percent), land leasing (34 percent), homestead allocation (12.5 percent). Obviously, these are among the most important matters in public life in a place such as Xicun.

It is worth noting that this kind of relationship is not the same as the traditional patron-client relationship. Traditional patron-client relationship, which is distinct from impersonal or public relationship in the modern era, can be found in certain social groups, especially in clans and other informal groups, and sometimes even in some formal organizations (in modern societies). According to S. N. Eisenstadt, traditional patron-client relations have the following features:

(a) Patron-client relations are usually particularistic and diffuse.
(b) The interaction on which they are based is characterized by the simultaneous exchange of different types of resources, above all instrumental, economic, as well as political ones (support, loyalty, votes, protection) on the one hand and promises of solidarity and loyalty on the other.
(c) The exchange of these resources is usually effected by a 'package-deal,' i.e., neither resource can be exchanged separately but only in a combination that includes both types.
(d) Ideally, a strong element of unconditionality and of long-range credit and obligations is built into these relations.
(e) As a corollary, there is a strong element of solidarity in these relations—an element often couched in terms of interpersonal loyalty and attachment between patrons and clients—even though these relations may

often be ambivalent. The element of solidarity may be strong, as in the restricted primary relationship of the classical type of patronage, or, as in many of the more modern political machines, very weak, but to some degree it is to be found in all of them. Solidarity is often closely related to conceptions of personal identity, especially of personal honor and obligations, and it is also evident that some, even if ambivalent, personal 'spiritual' attachment may exist between patron and clients.

(f) At the same time, the relations established are not fully legal or contractual; they are often opposed to the official laws of the country and are based more on informal—although tightly binding—understandings.

(g) Despite their seemingly binding, long-range and, in their ideal portrayal almost life-long endurance, patron-client relations are entered into voluntarily, at least in principle, and can, officially at least, be abandoned voluntarily.

(h) These relations are undertaken between individuals or networks of individuals in a vertical fashion (the simplest kind is a strong dyadic one) rather than between organized corporate groups. They seem to undermine the horizontal group organization and solidarity of both clients and patrons, but especially of clients.

(i) Last and not least, patron-client relations are based on very strong elements of inequality and of differences in power. Even at this stage of our discussion it should be evident that the crucial element of this inequality is the monopolization by the patrons of certain positions that are of vital importance for the clients; especially, as we shall see in greater detail later, of the access to the means of production, major markets and centers of the society.[13]

Obviously, the traditional patron-client relationship is a relationship between groups that is forged through personal relationships. Key players, including the patron, the client, the middle man, the gatekeeper, key organizations and mediators function in ways that are interconnected, and on the basis of which collectives or local communities are constituted. The patron-client relationship is highly effective as a means to organize people because it forges identification with authority figures and can mobilize effectively. Even though these local communities can repel exploitative offenses launched by external forces, and retain their autonomy, they have little in common with public relationships in the modern sense in terms of their internal relationships (Table 7.11).

According to this analysis, then, the patron-client relationship is an expansion of kinship relations in traditional society. It is based on feelings of attachment, and tends to be quite stable. Clearly, public relationships in Xicun, which had been forged through the expansion of personal connections have similarities with the patron-client relationship. Both feature exceptionalism, are interest-oriented, dependent on personal networks, reciprocity and the moral duty to provide assistance.

[13] S. N. Eisenstadt, *Power, Trust and Meaning: Essays in Sociological Theory and Analysis* (Chicago: University of Chicago Press, 1995), 202–38.

Table 7.11 Comparison between patron-client relationship and modern public relationship

Traditional patron-client relationship	*Modern public relationship*
Personal	Non-personal
Instrumental	Value (ideological)-driven
Informal (not institutionalized)	Formal (institutionalized)
Exceptionalism	Universalism
In private	In the open
Highly cohesive	Loosely structured
Hierarchical	Division of labor and post
Moral obligation: Justified in both providing and receiving help	Moral obligation: Compliance with the law
Loyalty to individuals	Commitment to the law (rules)

A: Why is it that despite his financial misconduct, retired village cadre ZGZ was nonetheless able to stay in power for as long as he did?

Q: At the time he had the support of the village [leadership]. Cadres in key positions were allied with him, or otherwise his relatives or friends. And ordinary members of the village community did not oppose him. People who were associated with him either had some emotional attachment to him, or were friends with him, or had paid for that association. Back then the village was doing well financially, with its own orchards, and team of foresters, and he often took actions that benefited the village residents, such as drawing on the village's public funds to help villagers pay for mandatory contribution toward village reserve and township endowment, and reducing fines. But the people he was helping had to be reliable allies, people who would support him no matter what.[14]

Evidently, the situation in Xicun does not run counter to the basic model of the patron-client relationship. However, there are points of departure that are worth noting. These differences may indicate changes in certain factors.

First of all, the factions and alliances in Xicun transcend lineages. In Xicun, there are a number of "major dynasties", with large populations, and are connected to another. Of the village population, 23.5 percent belonged to large clans, and 63.5 percent belonged to medium-sized clans. These two groups together accounted for vast majority of the village population. However, we did not see any indication that when it came to matters of critical importance, where their interests are at stake, people necessarily allied with those from the same clan. For example, only 5 percent of respondents noted that they would back people from their clan or who were their relatives in personnel decisions. Nor was there evidence to suggest that village residents preponderantly favored people who shared the same last name for leadership positions. In fact, we

[14] Transcript of the No. 6 August 2001 interview with a local resident.

often found people who shared the same family in factions and alliances that were opposed to each other. Nor was whether people were close neighbors a strong predictor of whether they would be allies. Neighborly amicability apparently did not necessarily make people want to become allies with one another, or translate into shared interests or similar stance on matters. This means that the patron in these relationships is not necessarily the elderly members of a clan, but somebody else. The decline in the importance of lineage members and relatives suggests that belonging to the same clan was no longer a necessary condition for being allies, having shared interests and reciprocity.

Moreover, in contrast to the stability of patron-client relationships these alliances and factions in Xicun are highly volatile and unstable. Fragmentation, withdrawal, and betrayal were common. For example, somebody who succeeded in securing a position in the village leadership after blowing the whistle on a former member for allegedly breaching financial rules could soon become their former collaborators' adversaries vying for power. The collaborator-turned-rivals almost came to blows over the appointment of village electricians. One side is outgunned, and shifts their allegiance toward those who had previously faced accusations. These factions and alliances have porous boundaries and are compositionally fluid. They can disintegrate as soon as they form, depending on the specific needs of the situation. This seems to suggest that personal loyalty is weak in these relationships, and is entirely at the mercy of the ever changing situations. To the extent that the clients have greater room to choose, patrons are compelled to adapt, and to expand their social networks by providing assistance. In interviews, village residents admit that ZGZ, the central figure in one faction in Xicun, was always prepared to help whoever asked for it, regardless of which faction they belong to. ZGZ would help just about anybody who came to him asking for help, whether it was somebody from an opposing faction, and it mattered little if they were relatives. In fact, some of the people who belonged to opposing factions had once been adoptive relatives.[15] ZGZ not only treated people from his own village like this, he also treated those from outside the village in the same way.

> ZGZ calls my father uncle, and they were quite close. He was on good terms with just about anybody from the county leadership who had any power at all. A number of public security bureau chiefs, and tax bureau chiefs had been on good terms with ZGZ, and they frequently exchanged gifts. But he would not hobnob with people who had no power. The relative of some village resident became the deputy county chief, and as soon as ZGZ learned about this he reached out to them. Until then, they barely knew each other, and the two were not in the same faction during the Cultural Revolution. ZGZ is the kind of person who likes to help others out, regardless of who was asking for help. If people ask, he would help, driven by a sense of generosity and duty. Many people would come from the

[15] Transcript of the No. 4 August 2001 interview with a local resident.

county to him asking for help, with cars lining up in front of his house, and even higher officials would frequently present him with gifts. When the commune CPC committee secretary visited ZGZ's house, he spoke to ZGZ's daughter as if she was family.[16]

As far as the local residents are concerned, they do not necessarily have to turn to relatives or neighbors, these relationships, after all, are variable in terms of distance.

When something comes up and help is needed, it doesn't matter who it is, whether they are cadres or not, if they have experience, and seem dependable, then you can go to them, whether they are relatives or not. Some of the conflicts are legacies of the Cultural Revolution, even though they are not too serious. People who are friends now may not have been during the Cultural Revolution, things like this happens a lot.[17]

When compared with patron-client relationships, the kind of factions and alliances in Xicun tends to be more strongly utilitarian, where the basic principle is to attach little importance to other people's preexisting stance on issues and the groups to which belonged, and to take into consideration only what kinds of resources and benefits they are able to provide, and if they promise to support and who they would help. Clearly, this kind of patron-client relationship is more flexible and open, and this openness allows factions and alliances in Xicun to expand freely, and interest alignment changes, people show great agility and adaptiveness. Such relationships can reach far inside public relationships, try to achieve their ends by leveraging the administrative apparatus constitutive of public relationships, or mobilize supporters by taking advantage of the symbolic import of and norms inherent to public relationships. This is exactly what happened when one group of petitioners collected signatures from 60 CPC members. In fact, there are no more than a few people at the core of this faction, and its reach fell far short of all CPC members. However, the petitioners were able to secure the votes of most CPC members on the strength of the morally compelling case they were making with their whistleblowing. And this support was later key to the petitioners' success in prevailing in the election for representatives, which allowed them to form an alternative village leadership, one which is made up entirely of people who were sympathetic to the petitioners. Seizing the opportunity of the cotton fine, the petitioners were able to build trust and support among the local population, which rallied together to resist the fine. These all illustrate how preexisting public organizations and relationship can be turned into instruments for building new public relationships and expanding existing ones.

I would like now to discuss briefly a number of points at which the new patron-client relationship departs from the traditional one. On the traditional

[16] Transcript of the No. 3 August 2001 interview with a local resident.

[17] Transcript of the No. 2 August 2001 interview with a local resident.

model, the transmission of information is carried out by specific individuals. By contrast, on the new model, the relationship can involve a large number of people, be open-ended and take the form of mass mobilization. Yet this kind of relationship is often short-lived, loose-knit and fluid, subject to change depending on the needs associated with specific events and interests. The mobilization is often fueled by people's values. For example, CPC members signed the petition because they are opposed to economic corruption and to the practice of approving CPC membership application without a proper discussion of the qualifications of the applicant, and the local population rallied against the cotton fine in support of the petitioners because they believed the fine was unjustified. To this extent, this kind of relationship is similar to modern public relationship in some respects, where conflicts may be driven by differences in values or in interests. Information can be transmitted through individuals, or via public channels; the groups involved do not have clear boundaries and have porous borders, and are practically open to anybody. It is not necessarily a pyramid-shaped structure, but rather one that features a relatively small group at the core, poorly defined boundaries, parity of standing, and that does not impose mandatory rules about rights and obligations. Nor is it a unitary system of rule based on the authority of particular individuals, there is no prohibition against anybody pressing their claims and concern,[18] or anything clearly resembling an institutionalized and stable structure... All of this would seem to suggest that public relationships in Xicun were unlike both the traditional patron-client relationships and the typical modern public relationships, but were something of a mixed permutation of the two. Both personal matters and public affairs were handled within its parameters.[19]

7.6 Discussions: Potential Problems

Assuming that we accept the definition of the modern state according to which it is a public organization, it would logically follow then that the foundation of state-building should be the construction of public identities and associated relationships. People with these public identities would be compelled to comply with rules and norms that govern the public sphere, and act in these public capacities to manage affairs of the public. Evidently, what we were able to

[18] Andrew MacIntyre, "Business and Politics in Indonesia," Pacific Affairs 1990 ASAA Southeast Asia Publications Series, especially the discussion about "patrimonial cluster".

[19] As Francis Hsu correctly pointed out, relationships of control are a kind of social relationships above all other structural relationships. These other relationships not only become less important, and their properties change too. As a result, people who grow up in these institutions are fundamentally shaped by them, and their behavior is to a large degree determined by the properties of superior structural relationships. (See Francis L. K. Hsu, *Clan, Caste and Club*, New York: Van Nostrand Reinhold, 1963. Gang Xue, trans. Huaxia Publishing House, 1990. And *Americans and Chinese: Two Ways of Life*, New York: Henry Schuman, 1953. Kaiping Peng & Wenjing Liu, Trans. Huaxia Publishing House, 1989.)

observe in Xicun gave us no reason to believe that state-building understood in this way had been completed there. Some scholars are of the view that unless the public and the private spheres are clearly demarcated from each other, personal activities are wont to corrode public relationships, and even destroy them altogether. This would then allow the state to monopolize the public space, and function as the arbiter with the power of control.[20] Unless a clear distinc tion is first made between what is public and what is private, it would be meaningless to speak of the "relationship" between the two, and impossible for what is in the interest of the society to be clearly represented.

But in Xicun, since there is no clear distinction between what is public and what is personal, we were able to observe the corrosive effects personal relationships can have on public ones on one hand and the ways in which personal relationships can be utilized to extend and transform public ones on the other. It is two-sided, instead of one-sided. Because personal relationships are often instrumental in the handling and the expansion of public affairs, they can expand in an open-ended way, and reach considerable scale, and because how commonplace it is to tackle difficulties one encounters in public affairs by drawing on one's personal relationships, and how effectively they can function as a kind of medium in relation to public affairs, they are constitutive of a special kind of structure of the opportunity to act. Such structure is by no means the prerogative of the cadres only, as regular village residents can also generate benefits for themselves by being proactive and exerting influence on the allocation of public resources. When it is permissible to handle public affairs through interpersonal exchanges, anybody and everybody could presumably get the public authority to act on one's behalf by making the right deal, or come into contact with public figures by navigating complex and intricate social networks. This helps to explain why the number of people who adopt cadres as relatives, who give gifts to cadres, who visit cadres at home or otherwise show up at weddings and funerals in a cadre's family have all been on the rise. So long as it is possible to execute exchanges in private, these channels of contact are open to anybody, and they provide incentives to those who want to be proactive in securing benefits, whether it is for a collective or for themselves.

Obviously, this admixture of the personal and the public makes is easy for people with different objectives to establish their own structure of opportunities for action. For example, village cadres who are keen to see themselves promoted would try to cultivate relationships with higher-ranking officials, and use such village public resources they have some control over as the orchard, the mine, the chicken farm, and the brick factory as bargaining chips in their negotiations with people with power in either the township or the county. Those cadres who are interested in control and personal material wealth would do whatever they can to get done what village residents ask of them and are

[20] Lucian Pye, "The State and the Individual: An Overview Interpretation," ed, Brian Hook, *The Individual and the State in China* (Oxford University Press, 1996), 16.

willing to pay for, by making use of the power they wield. This unique model facilitates exchanges between these individuals of a variety of resources. Since these are essentially personal interactions, each is different, each is unique.[21] This may have created opportunities for ordinary village residents to take actions. For them, interpersonal exchange of wealth is both a costly and uncertain means to securing the public service one needs. For the cadres, getting things done for the village residents can augment their authority and boost their wealth, and is a traditional way to improve the effectiveness of their rule and governance, and to solidify their standing in the community, which in turn helps to cement the cadre-centered primary-level political apparatus.

This amounts to community members' "purchasing" public services through individual negotiations and exchanges. These are of course not one size fits all, and there is no one flat fee. Instead, each transaction is different, with a different price, and the applicable rules and principles are also variable. The admixture of what is public and what is personal gives people stronger reasons to try to secure public service for themselves through the exchange of wealth and personal relationships. This is both a last resort, and something people do of their own volition. Clearly, given its inherent complexity, rural social relationships do not easily fit into the model in which one side dominates the other. Indeed, they most definitely deviate from the very premise of the "state vs. society" model, namely, the sharp opposition between cadres and village residents in terms of their values and principles. What we observed in Xicun illustrates that more often than not the two groups share the same values, and adopt the same rules of conduct. These are simply the facts, whether or not we would like them to be.

Under such conditions, public organizations and social members are weakly separated from each other. Public affairs and decision-making are constantly being shaped by the actions of private individuals, and constantly changing to meet the needs of the public. As the sociologist Crozier noted, on one hand, personal relationships prevent social lockdown and closure, on the other hand, they allow the society to operate with flexibility.

But this is no reason why state-building, or the establishment of a uniform and modern public affairs system should not be pursued. Insofar as we agree that the kind of value and identity associated with public roles as Pye sees them, and public relationships defined by a unified administrative and bureaucratic system are not yet in place in Xicun, how could we conclude that centralized administration has already been established? So far as the uniquity of personalized exchanges between the public and the individual at the primary level is concerned, the myriad rules governing social relationships probably play a larger role in regulating cadres' conduct than do the norms intrinsic to the government's bureaucratic system.

[21] Lucian Pye, "The State and the Individual: An overview Interpretation," ed, By Brian Hook, *The Individual and the State in China* (Oxford University Press, 1996), 16.

Contrary to Crozier's view, the mainstream view about modernity would easily see Xicun as being in a pre-modern state, since superficially it has features representative of "feudal" relationships. According to Strayer, feudalism is distinguished from other types of social organizations in the following ways. First, the fragmentation of power, even though authority is absence in some places. Second, power is regarded as a kind of personal possession, something that can be allocated, gifted, loaned, and traded. Personal agreements and family background determine administrative and judicial authority, the public generally recognizes the public power of authority in the hands of the individual, something that is considered normal, nobody sees it as unacceptable. Third, real power can be exercised through the consent of individuals, where it is not because somebody is the citizen or the subject of a state that power and the ability to exercise power is granted them, but rather because they have pledged to do something in return. A mechanism like this can expand, and be manifested as individual, racial, rural community, or even government power.[22]

What we need to know is, how is it that there have been no structural forces to change them? Why, instead of establishing modern standards and expecting the society to adapt to (and comply with) them, are rules of public governance expected to bend in order to meet the needs of the society? Why do these problems noted above stubbornly remain despite state power reaching far into rural communities in the modern era, something that is quite widely acknowledged by many researchers? If we apply the logic of functional efficiency, we can easily see that the admixture of public and personal relationships helps to maintain the structural homogeneity of bureaucratic administration and the society and associated rules of conduct. Homogeneity means they are similar, not different. This considerably lowers the cost of public governance, i.e., the costs of building a system of public identity that is different from the prevailing behavioral norm in society, of training its members (cadres) to accept the new set of norms, of securing their loyalty so that the system would operate efficiently, or adjusting and consolidating social relationships so they can play their role within the new paradigm, and so forth. Cutting down on the number of tasks undertaken toward state-building does not necessarily undermine the stability and authority or governance.

This governance model is primarily focused on augmenting authority and keeping things generally under control, and not institutional evolution. It makes use of existing forms of social relationships to effect consolidation, and the traditional administrative institutions cope with changing conditions without trying to start afresh and build a new kind of public relationships or activities by public organizations that are based on those relationships. This would effectively ameliorate the tension between what norms call for and what is done

[22] J. R. Strayer, *Feudalism* (New York: D. Van Nostrand Company,1965), 12–13, cited in Xueliang Ding, "When Chinese Students Meet Western Social Science Concepts -- Three Roots of Misunderstanding," www.cc.org.cn, 2003.

in practice. This makes it possible for people to take on public identities and play the corresponding roles by doing what they are already familiar with, adhering to their current beliefs and values, mobilizing the relationships they have already built, and discharging their new responsibilities by agreeing to "conditions" of reciprocity with the people they already associate with. Meanwhile, this offers a cost-effective way to address the difficulty associated with accepting new values and new roles, and with maintaining loyalty among those who must do so. The admixture of what is public and what is personal provides insurance that their own objectives can be attained, and at such disincentives for these objectives to change. After all, if people are able to get things done in the public sphere by following familiar norms that govern personal relationships, then there would be little need for them to learn new rules and to abide by them. All they would have to do is to continue to build more of the old kind of relationships and to expand upon them, and rely on these to solve various problems. People will continue to maneuver and manipulate their existing networks to optimize return for all stakeholders in discharging their public responsibilities.

I concur with Pye that this structure faces the risk of exposing public relationships to persistent moral scrutiny, and it makes it too easy for people in public relationships to treat each other in a utilitarian mindset, instead of with mutual respect and beneficence. After all, public resources and personal resources can be exchanged for each other, or become the pawn for each other. For example, so far as social capital is concerned, it does not distinguish between reputable and dependable relationships and disreputable and corrupt ones, it can be used either in pursuit of ill-gotten gains or to help the vulnerable. Another risk this admixture of the public and the personal faces is over-politicization. Given the large number of factions in the public realm, social members have a strong incentive to strengthen and consolidate their own power, and to protect that power by building alliances. An alliance would act collectively to resist the political rival and to refuse to work with them, so that even when one has been removed from office, one's political rival would not be able to govern effectively. The need for alliance strongly motivates public figures to cultivate their network, and to ensure that their allies are placed in important positions.

At the same time, the proliferation of factions means that decision-makers are not isolated individuals, and that many matters call for collective decision-making, so that the many people in any faction can have their interests catered to. This increases the cost of organizing and coordinating. More often than not, things such as information exchange, trades and decision-making do not go through the normal organizational system, but are executed through internal channels within factions. It generates an information market among insiders in which decisions and information is dispersed. As for public policy decisions, people are not so much concerned with their actual content but are more focused on who made them and whether they themselves stand to benefit. So far as implementation is concerned, people are indifferent about the issue of efficiency, but are concerned about who is pushing it, and whether these people would be partial toward one's own faction. As for the attitude, people do not care about values and beliefs, and their primary objective is to make sure they stay on the same page with the rest of their faction. Because this competition mechanism is indifferent about what is right and wrong, and attaches a great deal of importance to the difference between outsiders and insiders. People do not make decisions about who to support on the basis of principles or beliefs, but on preexisting relationship. This is tantamount to the politicization of social life. In fact, this is exactly what is going on in Xicun.

CHAPTER 8

Compartmentalized Jurisdiction

According to one rather mainstream view, social development in China in the modern era has been deeply influenced by the process of state-building. This view has informed many analyses of rural communities, which purport to show that as the state apparatus continues to make inroads into the countryside, the governance structure that had long been in place in rural communities began to break down, so did the communication channels between those communities and the central government that once operated under rural self-governance, thereby replacing dual-track politics with single-track politics.[1] Since state-building was geared toward suppressing or overhauling the native tradition of order in rural society, its odds of success were slim to begin with.[2] The enlargement of state political apparatus changed the existing leadership configuration in the countryside, gave rise to a new kind of political leaders, who introduced new policies, and the disconnect between the government and the society in terms of their basic interests was largely a product of the enormous strain from exorbitant taxes.[3] These views are primarily concerned with the impact the transformation of state political apparatus has had on social life within rural communities. On these views, the relationship between the state and rural communities is presumed to be one in which the former imposes its will on the latter, which reacts to that coercion. This is to say, the state is a dictatorial independent variable, while rural communities are the passive and reactionary dependent variable.

[1] Xiaotong Fei, *From the Soil: The Foundations of Chinese Society* (Tianjin: Tianjin People's Publishing House, 1994).

[2] Torajirō Naitō, *Complete Works of Torajirō Naitō*, Vol. 5, Tokyo, 1972; Cited in Shiga Shuzo et al. *The Civil Trial and Civil Contract in the Ming and Qing Dynasties* (Beijing: Legal Press, 1998), 359.

[3] Prasenjit Duara, *Culture, Power, and the State: Rural North China, 1900 to 1942*, translated by Wang Fuming (Nanjing: Jiangsu People's Publishing House, 1995) 3, 219.

J. Zhang, *Primary-Level Government*,
https://doi.org/10.1007/978-981-96-6209-8_8

This view places emphasis on the external factors that contribute to social change, which does help us see the broader context within which these changes take place. However, as an explanatory account, it is problematic because it over-estimates how much control the state exercises in rural communities, and overlooks these communities' ability to advance their own objectives by taking advantage of external factors, especially the different ways in which they construct a space of self-governance and repel competition from outside for jurisdictional reach, often by adopting styles and discourse that would suit the external players. In fact, because of activities like these, many external changes have, as far as the primary level is concerned, amounted to little more than putting the status quo in a new packaging. Considering that many changes that have taken place in China in recent decades have in fact had their seeds sown at the primary level, and the state has typically had to accept these changes *ex post facto*, albeit reluctantly, it cannot be concluded that rural communities are entirely passive, i.e., merely being on the receiving end of external forces acting on it.

The essence of jurisdiction is the issue of the center of authority. More specifically, it concerns *whose* rules are adopted, i.e., which political body has the *de facto* power to interpret as well as to set the rules. If a person or a body with supreme authority has, in theory, the ultimate say, but lacks the ability to use this power to enforce its rules, or to ensure the uniformity of these rules and how they are interpreted, then doubt must be cast on the effectiveness of their rule is over their own jurisdiction. In modern China, even though "compartmentalized jurisdiction" is based neither on the constitution nor on rural communities' unequivocal demand for power (to the contrary, primary-level cadres unanimously consent to the symbolic significance, even if only in principle, of the authority of the state), if in practice agencies set up by the state at the primary level cannot genuinely function as the agents of the state despite their being nominally under its leadership, then there is insufficient reason to believe that the state actually is the controller, sets the rules, and exercises sanction. These powers may appear to be in the hands of the state, in fact they are not.

One fairly typical view holds that when state-building fails, it is due to serious administrative inefficiency, which does not otherwise affect state-building at its core. In other words, it is bureaucratic efficiency and other "technical" reasons that may have prevented the power of the state from reaching into rural communities: "The state's monopoly of ideological orthodoxy (by consensus of the elite), combined with an extremely low level of effective governmental penetration of the society, meant that for substantive urban autonomy to be achieved it was unnecessary, indeed undesirable, to provoke legalistic confrontations—by demanding municipal charters, for example".[4] Now if we apply this logic to the modern society, we would find ample evidence that suggests that "an extremely low level of effective governmental penetration of the society"

[4] William T. Rowe, *Hankow: Commerce and Society in a Chinese City, 1796–1889* (Redwood City: Stanford University Press, 1984), 344–345.

may in fact be symptomatic of the competition (openly or covertly) over compartmentalized jurisdiction. Such competition is revelatory of the extraordinary control primary-level cadres have over their own actions. By putting in place a complex mechanism for reacting, primary-level officials are able to impose a limit to how efficiently the state bureaucracy pursues the objectives of the state. If primary-level bureaucrats do not wish (instead of acting slowly), or do not know how to carry out the order of the state, perhaps because doing so would undermine their ability to maintain their own power, and if such resistance has to some degree been consented to by the state, which has given it *de facto* protection, it would mean that far from having things done to it, primary-level government has full agency capable of achieving its own ends by taking advantage of existing institutions. In this kind of tug of war between the state and local authorities with well-defined objectives, both parties try to increase their own power of control by making use of the other, and serious inefficiency is simply the outcome. And this in fact suggests that more often than not the expansion of the scope of state power is short on substance. Is it really the expansion of the principle of governance, of jurisdiction, or veto power, and the power of arbitration?

In this chapter I address these and other related issues. I differ from those who assume that the primary level is merely passive, and try to show instead how primary-level government defines the area over which it exercises power, what strategies it uses to prevent the state from making inroads into its own turf, and what impacts this has on who prevails in determining social norms in rural communities. In light of the earlier analysis of the issue of structural (in)stability, we shall in this chapter leave aside the relationship between primary-level government and the construction of social institutions, and focus instead on the rivalry between primary-level government as a body with its own objectives, interests and agency, and other forces in the country and the society. The discussion will revolve around one basic question: have the actions primary-level government engages in expanded the base of state power, or prevented state power from making inroads, while expanding its own power?

8.1 Regional Financial Responsibility System: The Tacit Consent to Collect Taxes

The economist Douglas North has once noted that for any level of government, what makes economic sense does not necessarily make political sense. Economists are always trying to tell the government that tariff is a bad idea, and how best to address political problems. They believe, naively, that politicians would accept and adopt these recommendations. But politicians have nothing but contempt for these recommendations.[5] This raises the questions:

[5] Douglass North, "Past, Present and Future of the State's Economic Role" in Joseph Stiglitz, *The Economic Role of the State* (Blackwell Publisher, 1989).

why is it so hard for these rules that clearly can stimulate the economy to be implemented, and sometimes just the contrary is true?

The reason is that many organizations, political organizations included, try everything they can to protect their vested interests through legislation. So far as efficiency is concerned, these protectionist measures can mean both competition (allowing efficiency to develop) and protection (preventing it from growing). However, in terms of their implications for power, they are entirely rivalrous. North recognizes that the principle of property right, which has profound consequences for allocative efficiency, is not the same as the principle of efficiency that it might impact. Even though property right and also the rules of politics built on its basis are a powerful guarantee for economic activities, they can also impede change and the emergence of new forms of economic organizations. The power of control, whether it is property rights in economics or the mandate to govern in politics, can only achieve the efficiency they are pursuing through its ability to maintain itself. This is why economic objectives do not always coincide with political ones. Looked at this way, notwithstanding his spectacular description of this kind of phenomenon,[6] Olson is not able to offer an explanation from the point of view of political activities why such perverse economic consequence should occur.[7] North recognizes that political rules and economic ones are different from one another. While the former is extremely important for the latter, it is often overlooked. Its importance lies in the fact that whether it is in economic or political rules, the *power of control* is usually the most effective way to protect one's interests. In this sense, the key to rivalry over economics (profit) consists in the rivalry over politics (power of control).

This kind of rivalry, in the minds of those operating at the primary level, is clearly of supreme importance. It manifests itself most prominently in rivalry over the power to control finances. At the primary level, whoever has control over money, land or material assets, or can influence the way resources are allocated by either granting or denying approvals is considered to have real power. The market's ability to coordinate and move material assets and currency can very effectively stimulate economic activities. However, this principle is applicable only with respect to those that are above or on the outside, and does not apply in relation to one's own group or jurisdiction. Because of the importance of "having control over the economy", obtaining opportunities through fair competition does not benefit those people who have the power to allocate opportunities. As V. Nee once noted, market competition tends to erode the power to redistribute, because the power to distribute typically must be attained through maintaining monopoly.

Apparently, the "power of control" must be based on considerable autonomy and agency. Yet while in theory primary-level apparatus is in charge of

[6] Mancur Olson, *The Rise and Decline of Nations: Economic Growth, Stagflation and Social Rigidities*, (New Haven: Yale University Press, 1984).

[7] North, "Past, Present and Future".

implementation, and does not "legitimately" have such autonomy or agency, this is not the case in fact. This is illustrated by how taxes are collected and spent. The basic feature of this system is the decentralized nature of tax collection, "the central government is heavily dependent on local governments for tax collection, as almost all of the taxes the central government collects is in practice collected by the local government".[8] On the surface, the central government is the source of local governments' fiscal revenue (e.g., the "Central government outlay" and "share of tax revenue" columns of Table 8.1). Yet in practice, neither of these two kinds of revenue constitutes the financial basis of primary-level government (see Table 8.2).

Evidently, the sub-total of outlay from higher-level government and their share of tax revenue was hardly enough to cover all the expenses. And more often than not primary-level officials had to rely on contribution from enterprises, extra-budgetary revenue, and discretionary fundraising as the main sources of fiscal income. Without money from these three sources, these governments would not be able to balance their budget. As for the expenditure, it mostly includes the salaries of township and local staff (at administrative public institutions, party organizations, radio and television, culture and education, agricultural management, public security, the procuratorates, the courts, health and medical care, and care for the disabled, family planning, and so forth) and administrative overhead. And less than 10 percent is allocated toward the provision of "public goods" (see Table 8.3).

In theory, "the central government sees local governments as its extension, where the latter collects taxes, hands over what it collects to the central government, which then allocates some of this money to local governments in the form of outlay".[9] Yet clearly higher governments have no control over what kinds of and how much taxes local governments collect. This means that even

Table 8.1 Fiscal revenue of TD Township, Zhejiang province, 1992–1996 (Unit: 100 yuan)

Year	*Central government outlay*	*Share of tax revenue*	*Contribution from enterprises*	*Extra-budgetary revenue*	*Discretionary fundraising*	*Total*
1992	2567	6520	6133	2458	486	18,164
1993	3030	12,652	8684	3675	1144	29,185
1994	7747	12,7890	11,568	4424	5411	41,939
1995	7968	13,243	25,499	8706	21,550	76,966
1996	8976	13,162	17,899	9065	12,332	61,398

Data source: TD Township financial breakdown, Aug. 1998

[8] Guoguang Wu & Yongnian Zheng, *Central-local Relations: A key Issue for Institutional Transition in China* (Hong Kong: Oxford University Press, 1995), 75–6.

[9] Guoguang Wu & Yongnian Zheng, *Central-Local Relations: A Key Issue for Institutional Transition in China*. (Hong Kong: Oxford University Press, 1995), 75.

Table 8.2 Fiscal spending in TD Township, Zhejiang province, 1992–1997 (Unit: 100 yuan)

Year	*Total*	*Wage*	*Subsidy*	*Benefit*	*Guarantee*	*Public Affair*	*Procurement*	*Repair*	*Business Administration*	*Others*
1992	17,775	2653	2414	1089	1449	282	60	667	1144	8017
1993	28,021	3129	3022	1081	1776	796	135	4544	300	13,238
1994	41,326	4551	4655	1764	4748	1456	590	6200	240	17,122
1995	77,879	5536	4696	4936	6213	867	–	4980	1476	49,175
1996	60,667	5123	5391	2940	3084	1380	–	3800	380	38,569

Data source: TD Township financial breakdown, Aug. 1998

Table 8.3 Total fiscal spending and total fiscal spending on agriculture at the township level (Unit: 100 yuan)

	1992	*1993*	*1994*	*1995*	*1996*
Total spending	17,775	28,021	41,326	77,879	60,667
Total spending on agriculture	1264	1259	51	486	2849

Data source: Itemized financial breakdown for this township, August 1997

though it is not codified in law, in practice primary-level authorities have considerable discretionary power (within their own jurisdiction) to decide what taxes to levy and to collect those taxes. Rural governments would never be able to make ends meet if they had only what they could collect in those taxes sanctioned by the central government. The proportion of their revenue that comes from other ways to raise money is far greater than what they get from the central government. This is also the reason primary-level governments can hire more people than can fill the regular permanent positions, since such expansion does not impose a particular budgetary strain on the primary-level authorities given their relative financial sovereignty. Evidently, without such broad latitude, and without the rural population's tacit consent, it would have been unimaginable for extra-budgetary revenue, enterprise contributions, and *ad hoc* fundraising to constitute the main sources of money needed to pay for primary-level administrative overhead. In other words, these ways of raising money are only considered justified if primary-level administration has sovereignty, for there would be no other way to make sense of why "[tax] burden relief" at any level should be as difficult as it is.

Evidently, this bureaucratic bloat at the primary level must be materially supported by fundraising capabilities. Yet even more fundamentally, this very ability to "amass resources" presupposes jurisdiction over a particular area. Such jurisdiction would allow any "public organ" at the primary level to engineer projects designed to "raise fund" for itself. A review of one document presenting "opinions regarding the management of village reserve and township endowment" reveals some common features of these engineered fundraising schemes, and these also tend to be what the rural population feels most strongly about.

- Requiring mandatory contribution toward old-age care security fund, issuing targets in relation to such fund, requiring all farmers to enroll regardless, and the contributions from enrollees are not even deposited into bank accounts, but are instead managed [by those who impose these requirements], and the money is often diverted for other uses;
- Imposing newspaper and magazine subscription requirements, announcing subscription targets and quota at distribution meetings, and including subscription numbers among the indicators used for performance evaluation for cadres, and individuals are not allowed to set up subscription at the post office according to their own interests and preferences;

- Charging marriage certificate applicants a host of miscellaneous fees such as family planning deposit, prenuptial physical exam, permit for having a child, national ID replacement, sales of books and magazines about marriage and childbirth, and the money thus collected is not handed over to the national coffer;
- Arbitrarily issuing documents announcing fees imposed onto primary and secondary school students, frequent education-related fundraising organized without formal review or official approval, peddling stationaries;
- Instead of drawing the money needed to improve hygiene and health from the collective endowment, it is raised by imposing mandatory contribution requirement onto rural households;
- Requiring households to purchase iodine-based rat poisoning, with specific sales targets, and specific cadres held accountable for meeting them, and not to be paid for with money from the collective endowment;
- Price gouging for electricity, not closing electricity rate, and tagging on miscellaneous fees to the electricity bill;
- Requiring those applying for household registration to pay for public security maintenance, without disclosing the specific types of fees being collected and the exact rates;
- There are no set criteria or rates for homestead, land requisition or household registration quota, and the money collected is not deposited into the designated land fund;
- Charging extra for miscellaneous items when selling agricultural products.[10]

In the analysis of Wu et al,[11] such behavior represents primary-level authority's attempt to milk the local population by exercising its prerogative to collect taxes on behalf of the central government. Yet in reality, it is widely known such behavior is explicitly prohibited by higher governments. Pertinent central government rules have been promulgated, and reiterated again and again: local governments' mandate is to collect taxes at rates set by the central government, they do not have the power to set their own tax rates. Knowingly and openly flouting rules is one thing, opportunistically tagging on extra charges is another. The former is based on a sense of control associated with jurisdiction over an area, whereas the latter must be done stealthily. Yet most of the different kinds of charges and fees we have seen have been openly approved and listed in official documents released by primary-level authorities, documents that are treated by clerks and runners as guidelines ("orders"). In the minds of primary-level cadres, such behavior is legitimate and justified so long as the money collected does not end up in their own pockets, and that it is done by the

[10] See government of SHZ County, Hebei province, "On Rectification, [Tax] Burden Relief, Management of Special Programs, and Regulation of the Management of Village Reserves and Township Endowment", 1997.

[11] Wu & Zheng, *Central-local Relations*, 1995.

"institution". Therefore, "documents" and "opinions" abound that are put out by the "institution" and in blatant violation of higher governments' rules, an act of contravention ("against the headwind" in government lingo) that has practically become the norm at the primary level. For example, even though higher governments set the rates—which are updated yearly—for individual contributions toward the infrastructure provident fund and the public welfare fund and also how the money should be used, these rules are rarely used as the basis for decision-making at the primary level, where few people take them seriously, and just as few would raise any concerns about this kind of overreach. The following notice contains rules regarding village reserve and township endowment, yet the rules that village cadres actually follow are rather different.

Excerpts from Opinions on the Implementation of Some Policies in Township BB[12]

1. In the previous year farmers in this township already saw significant reduction in the amount of money they had to pay toward fees and charges, and in order to provide further incentives to farmers to engage in production, all the villages much make sure to continue measures designed to help ease [economic] strain on the population;
2. The amount farmers must pay toward each of the three items in the village and team reserve will be calculated according to the size of the land they have under contract, and the per *mu* amount should not exceed around 5 yuan, of which 3 yuan will go toward the infrastructure provident fund, and 1–2 yuan toward each of the public welfare fund and management fee. And to demonstrate industry's role in supplementing agriculture, in villages where conditions permit contribution toward the public welfare fund and the management fee should be waived.
3. As for how money collected for the three items in the reserve is used, decisions in relation to the infrastructure provident fund should be made by the contract team, and priority should be given to water conservation, the installation and repair of machinery, equipment and appliance; decisions in relation to the public welfare fund and the management fee should be made by village cadres, and that money should be used toward public interest projects and other social causes.

And what does one particular village in this township do to implement these rules that have been officially adopted by the township government? Minutes from the village cadre meeting show that the actual rates at which they are collecting fees from the village residents are "7 yuan per *mu*, 2 yuan toward the infrastructure provident fund, 2 toward the public welfare fund and 3 toward the management fee,", changes that represent a 40 percent increase. Furthermore, the village's decision about how money in these three funds is to be allocated is also different from what was laid out in the "Opinions" released

[12] Document No. 92-53 of XT Village of BB Township.

by the township government. According to the village: "The 2 yuan collected for the public welfare fund will be handed over to the village, of the 3 yuan collected in management fee, 2 will be kept by the team, while 1 yuan will be handed over to the village".[13] In the following year, the same village drafted and adopted a "Opinion on Land Contracting". The document stipulated that, "adhering to the principles set out in documents released by the township CPC committee and government, and taking into consideration current conditions in the village", the village has adopted a "minimum standard" with no cap, and codified its decision in village-level [government] documents, according to which:

> The amount collected for the three items in the village reserve shall in principle be no less than 7 yuan per *mu*, of which no less than 3 yuan will go toward the infrastructure provident fund, and 1–2 yuan toward management fee, double for mulberry plantation, and 2 yuan will go to the public welfare fund, apportioned according to the number of laborers.[14]

In practice, when dealing with the same kinds of matter, the authority at each level can make whatever revisions to the rules as they see fit before applying them. These revisions are made not just when higher-level rules are too general and leave space for the primary level to formulate their own opinions "to optimize outcome for the local community" but also when higher-level rules are clear and unambiguous. This indicates that even at the village level, there is tacit understanding with regard to the existence of room for setting the tax rates. Except when some kind of special movement is taking place or widespread criticism has been generated (alarming higher officials), higher officials do not bother to scrutinize whether such power is being properly exercised. They understand that once this relationship based on tacit consent with regard to the distribution of power is perturbed, higher-level rules would be less efficiently implemented at the primary level. For example, in village YJZH in Zhejiang province, village cadres complained that the money collected for the three items in the village reserve (totaling 70,000–80,000 yuan excluding the part retained by the team) "is not even enough to cover the salaries of the cadres, in case the enterprises turn a reasonable profit, another 20,000–30,000 yuan may become available, but otherwise, there is practically nothing to be done about it".[15] Yet according to the rules, the majority of the money collected for the three items must be used on public interest projects, and only a small amount categorized under "management fee" (about one fourth, with infrastructure provident funding accounting for 50 percent, public welfare fund for 25 percent, and management fee for 25 percent) can be used toward cadres remuneration (Table 8.4). Apparently, if these rules are actually

[13] Minutes of the annual meeting of village cadre in XT Village of BB Townships.

[14] XT Village Committee, "Opinions on Stabilizing and Improving Land Contracting."

[15] Transcript of the August 1997 interviews with the village cadres in YJZH village, Zhejiang province.

Table 8.4 The amounts collected for the three items for this village in 1997

Item	*Amount (10,000 yuan)*	*Percentage (%)*
Infrastructure provident fund	6.9	54
Public welfare fund	3.04	23
Management fee	3.04	23
Total	12.98	100

implemented in the village, the remuneration would be so meager nobody would want to work as a cadre (from the same interview), then who would be carrying out higher governments' policies?

These blatant violations are not particularly surprising, since tacitly acknowledging the "right" of each level of authority to not follow the rules, and tolerating what they choose to do with their own interests within their own jurisdiction appear to have become the institutional norm. So long as such behavior involves public affairs, people who perpetrate these blatant violations typically face little risk of being penalized. In most cases, authorities get away with doing things according to rules they have themselves created. Other cadres would also apply pressure on those who are in charge of a particular matter, demanding that they put the interest of their own organization first. As for their playbook, rule No. 1 is to "whine", and argue that unless they are allowed to do things their own way they simply cannot carry on, and higher governments tend to be sympathetic to such pleas, and rule No. 2 is to impose a total ban on the upward flow of information, that is, to make sure higher governments do not know that they intend to act differently, thereby preventing them from interfering.

The reason these tactics work is that typically "reports" submitted by primary-level clerks are the sole source of information higher-level officials have about conditions in rural communities, and rarely do these officials try to verify the information by pursuing alternative channels of information, or receive information from the occasional whistle-blowers (while reports by whistle-blowers are not exactly rare, most do not end up reaching their intended recipients since they are blocked by somebody along the chain of command). In addition to the risk of information distortion, this heavy reliance on information supplied by lower-level administrators can also create opportunities for lower-level officials to falsify information or even fabricate it. As far as the primary level is concerned, this is an important strategy for protecting itself from external interference, since they have the opportunity to make sure higher governments receive the information that would be favorable to them, instead of what they really need to know. Doing this within one's own jurisdiction is minimally risky, and even if one gets caught in a stroke of bad luck in, say, the midst of a crackdown, one can simply cease and desist, and in most cases would not be subject to a thorough investigation by the establishment (unless one encountered a political opponent who is hellbent on getting to the bottom of it). For example, in the "Opinion" cited early regarding village reserve and township endowment, higher-level governments demanded that "money illegally collected for fees tagged onto the charge for application for marriage certificate is to be returned". However, there is no penalty for either the type of decision that led to such illegal collection of fees or the individuals involved in these decisions. In fact, the said "Opinion" even contained a clause stating that in case the money that had already been collected could not be returned, then it must be "handed over to the central government's coffer".[16]

At the primary level, decisions to add new fees to be collected are usually made without much fanfare, and rarely does it involve a rigorous process of review and approval, or even a careful calculation. Rarely is the legitimacy of such decisions questioned. Even though, as required by higher governments, each village must set up its own symbolic "village resident financial oversight team", the list of the individuals who make up the team is put together entirely as a matter of pure formality, to comply superficially with the rules. The village cadres hand-pick who sit on the team, and the team is answerable to these same village cadres, and have no autonomy or mandate independent of the power given them by the village cadres. Even worse, in many villages, the final decision on all major financial matters rests with a single individual, and other cadres only find out about these decisions at meetings, at which only those matters that have large impact and require the cooperation and coordination of all the cadres are brought up for discussion. Most members of the village leadership have a keen notion of independent finance (a private piggybank). Not only are they familiar with such practice as keeping two sets of books, they quite approve of it (because it tends to protect the interest of the organization to which they belong), and are committed to keeping their lips sealed about it with higher-ups. All such behavior makes it easier for just one or at most two people to oversee primary-level finances.

It is even less certain how money that is collected is to be used. The power to set tax rates at the primary level does not translated into the pressure to improve public services, as the two are unrelated to each other. Even when collection faces difficulty that leads to substantial and persistent tax shortfall, administrative overhead in the village is unaffected, and it is usually welfare programs that are on the chopping board. In many villages, we saw structures that had not been planned and were built willy-nilly, "streets" in villages that had been created simply by people treading on the ground repeatedly, and otherwise unpaved, and also electricity and water supply facilities that had yet to be built. Many paved roads had been financed by alternative sources of funding, and built for such reasons as boosting the locale's chance of winning excellence awards, or serving as vanity projects designed to impress visiting officials or reporters. Yet inadequate public services have not led to cuts to cadre salaries. Which is more important—cadre salaries or public services—and who gets

[16] See government of SHZ County, Hebei province, "On Rectification, [Tax] Burden Relief, Management of Special Programs, and Regulation of the Management of Village Reserves and Township Endowment", 1997.

to make that decision not only demonstrate the dominant role played by primary-level organizations but also manifest the relationship between taxes and public services.

> Ahead of this year's election, many cadres pledged to fix the dirt roads in the village, but it has been many years, and we have brought up the issue countless times, yet we haven't seen any real action, have we?[17]

> This year the township authority collected money from the residents of all the villages for the purchase of rat poisoning, but no rat poisoning was ever distributed, and for the few who did receive it, the thing didn't work, which means it is fake, and our money had gone down the drain. It's the same story for the swine vaccines. Everybody had to pay for it, whether they raised pigs or not, yet nobody came to give the shots.[18]

What is interesting, however, is that at the primary level, the right to make rules about taxes and the right to evade taxes are linked in the sense that neither is subject to binding requirements. Not only is the use of tax money not a legal issue for the cadres, it is quite normal among the village residents. Not only is tax evasion not subject to moral condemnation, on the contrary, it is looked upon favorably, and does not amount to "the crime of tax evasion". Many rural cadres complain about how hard it is to collect taxes, claiming that it is "just about the most headache-inducing work", so they do everything they can to avoid doing it, and try to do without collecting taxes if at all possible, and instead divert money from elsewhere to meet the collection target whenever they can. This has led to a phenomenon where, despite the large number arbitrarily imposed taxes, a large number of households owe taxes, including many cadres who have not paid what they should for many years. To get around the difficulty associated with collection, some villages have resorted to make up the shortfall by drawing on money enterprises that have paid the local government. Some well-to-do villages can go years without the residents having to pay a single penny in taxes toward the reserves and the endowment, because the enterprises and contracting firms in the village have picked up the tab. Other villages have fallen behind on tax collection for years, so they usually end up withholding from the residents money dispensed by the central government for relief or as other forms of aid. In some villages in which tax shortfall has been going on for many years, when the township authority decided to "take the matter seriously", and demand that residents started paying, such attempt is usually met with stiff resistance, and ends in failure.

> For many years contribution toward the endowment was never collected. Last year the township was in financial straits and started collecting military draft fee (from those who are eligible to enlist but do not, at the rate of 50 yuan per person per year) and also education surcharge (24 yuan per person per year). It was

[17] Transcript of the July 1998 interviews with residents of Lishu County, Jilin province.
[18] Transcript of the July 1998 interviews with residents of Lishu County, Jilin province.

> difficult, nobody wanted to pay, and collection was almost impossible, so this year they didn't even bother to collect. Ordinarily the team leader would visit each household to collect the money, and hand the matter over to the village leadership should this initial attempt fail. The village cadres would then repeat the effort, one group at a time, and if they fail again it would be recorded as unpaid taxes. The reason for such difficulty is for a number of years farmers were not required to pay anything. Collection resumed in 1988, but proceeded in fits and starts. During collection season all the cadres in charge of economic affairs would fan out across the village to visit residents in their homes, dividing them up into smaller groups, down to the production team, and setting up collection targets, aiming for no less than 80 percent of the total. Whenever the village enterprises were profitable, collection from residents would be suspended, and enterprise contribution would be used to make it up. When this was not possible, collection could not be gotten around. But it was difficult. The village cadres didn't want to be subject to the ire of the village residents, so would refrain from collecting money from them whenever there was any possibility to divert funds from elsewhere to cover the amount. Many village enterprises also had difficulty making contributions, resulting in delayed payment for cadre salaries again and again. The cadres in some villages experiencing economic hardship are still owed their salaries from last year.[19]

> Collecting taxes and getting public interest projects done are the hardest, as both involve money. Last year the village paid a total of 70,000 yuan in agricultural taxes, but the money was not collected from the residents, and had been drawn from funds intended for other purposes. Village-owned enterprises were not doing well, with little demand for their products. Still, we wouldn't agree to selling them to private individuals, as that would leave even fewer collective resources at our disposal.[20]

What all of this goes to show is the village authority has *de facto* power to offer tax exemption and grant extensions. At least in practice, should they decide to exempt somebody's taxes, or give somebody an extension on tax payment, or take no action on those who pay late, they would not be penalized. Such power is not stipulated in the law, but does exist *de facto*. This means that whatever power of control higher government has with respect to financial and tax matters is in reality pared away at each lower level of government.

8.2 Land Contracting: Tacit Control over Resources

Control of land is another important area in which competition over jurisdictional power plays out. In 1993–1997, the central government released a number of directives in quick succession which extended the term of land contracts. The new rules extended by 30 years the first round of land contracts that were

[19] Transcript of the July 1997 interviews with a township cadre of Zhejiang province who was in charge of the village affairs of a certain village.

[20] Transcript of the July 1997 interviews with the village cadres in YJZH village, Zhejiang province.

due to expire. The central objective was to make sure the status quo is continued, prevent frequent changes in land leases, and to keep the size of contracted area constant despite population changes. The larger goal of these policies is two-fold. On one hand, they are designed to delink land and people, and prevent land from being carved into ever smaller plots as a result of demographic development; on the other land, they are meant to remove a major source of uncertainty for farmers so they can focus on operating their land, and help maintain stability in economic relations and the associated institutions.

However, in townships and villages, where local needs determine how land is allocated, this policy to extend land contracts was not welcome. One reason is that, even though such policy is beneficial to farmers who had already attained land contracting rights, provides them with the right incentives, and boosts confidence in and support for the government's agricultural policies among farmers, it also poses an existential challenge to primary-level authorities insofar as it threatens to undermine its control over, i.e. ability to make allocation decisions about collectively own assets. In a document titled "Solving Current Problems by Meeting Local Needs and Responding to Reality on the Ground, Diligently Implementing the Central Government Policy to Renew Land Contract", diplomatic language is used to convey staunch resistance to the policy. The purpose of this county document is to explain to cadres in the villages and the townships the reasons for their decisions to make adjustments to land allocation the central government policy notwithstanding.

> There can be no doubt that the central government policy is absolutely correct. It is bound to have far-reaching and historic impact on efforts to stabilize conditions in the rural areas, deepen reform in the countryside and facilitate agricultural development. So far as this county is concerned, how to resolutely implement the central government policy to renew land contract and how to make sure land contracts are renewed properly are new issues we are currently facing. We have been deliberating about this question since 1995. We have found through our investigation, that since we adopted the household contract responsibility system in 1983, no change has been made to land allocation, and many problems and tensions in land management have been building up. The first is the tension between people and land. Over the last more than a decade, demographic changes, land requisition by higher governments and the local authority have resulted in severely uneven distribution of land among the households. Large households with little land have registered strong discontent. The second is the strain compensation by the collective has placed on the local authority. In recent years, a significant amount of land has been requisitioned by the government, allocated toward enterprises, public interest causes, homestead, high-tech agriculture and other uses. According to statistics, between 1987 and 1996, a total of 8,974 *mu* of land was allocated toward these purposes. As a result, villages had to set aside a significant amount of money to pay compensation to the farmers whose land was taken, ranging from tens to hundreds of thousands of yuan. And because the rates of compensation for government land requisition and land use by the local authority are fairly low, plus continuous rise in grain and cereal

> prices in recent years, the money that had been received for the land use had already been depleted, forcing the authority to tap into collective revenue and reserves to make the compensation payments. In some villages the majority of the yearly revenue had gone toward this, and in some cases the revenue fell short, placing enormous budget pressure on local governments.[21]

Even though such "financial strain" is the result of years of improper use of farmland by primary-level authority, to alleviate the problem, the county leadership decided to turn to a simple solution that can be used again and again, namely, reallocation of land. The goal was to remedy past mistakes in land use and institutional defects by adjusting how land is allocated. Evidently, from the point of view of county officials, land reallocation is a good way to strengthen control and maintain power over financial matters. To that end, county leadership called for things such as "strengthening of leadership, making sure the cadres are committed, and the plans are specific", "village and township leadership to personally lead the reallocation efforts, setting up dedicated bodies that would be tasked specifically with overseeing and coordinating the reallocation work", and "the establishment at the village level special task force on the matter, so that adequate time, staff and attention can be brought together to implement these measures down to the last detail".

In addition, the county CPC committee vigorously promoted land reallocation through publicity campaigns, pointing out that 78 villages in the county underwent land reallocation in 1996 and 1997, as a result of which "households that had had land taken from them were reallocated land, and subsidy by the collective was eliminated, effectively lifting a huge burden that had weighed the collective down for many years, allowing the collective economy to improve markedly. Ending the subsidy alone accounted for a saving of four million yuan".[22]

It is clear that for the primary-level authority, having control over land allocation constitutes a necessary condition for their ability to deal with financial uncertainties when the need arises. Under the current land ownership system, no individual is able to initiate changes to land allocation or to requisition land, which are things only the collective or individuals who are acting as representatives of collectively owned enterprises can do "legally". Holding on to the power to make land reallocation decisions is evidently beneficial to the primary-level authority. First, it entails power over financial matters. As land is carved up into smaller and smaller plots and allocated to more people, it saves money for the collective strengthening the collective's control over finances.

[21] Party Committee of ZHD County, Hebei Province, "Solving Current Problems by Meeting Local Needs and Responding to Reality on the Ground, Diligently Implementing the Central Government Policy to Renew Land Contract", November, 1997.

[22] Party Committee of ZHD County, Hebei Province, "Solving Current Problems by Meeting Local Needs and Responding to Reality on the Ground, Diligently Implementing the Central Government Policy to Renew Land Contract", November, 1997.

Second, reallocation of public resources offers one way to remedy development imbalances that have been caused by the power over land, to mitigate conflicts, cover up social tension, and indeed to lend legitimacy to these land grab by the collective in the past.

On multiple occasions we saw that land requisition had to go through the primary-level authority, and no deal was ever possible if those involved had nothing to gain. In some places farmers received no compensation at all for the land that had been requisitioned by the village or the township (which is what we found in our investigation in Village YJZH in Zhejiang province in 1997), so that whenever conflict arises the local authority would immediately resort to land reallocation as a way to adjudicate it. In other places the local authority would ask the enterprise that was taking over the land to make a one-time compensation payment to the affected farmers, thereby obviating the need for long-term obligations. Sometimes land under long-term contracts would simply have their ownership transferred to the contractor (a vast number of such agreements can be found in the countryside). There are still other villages in which 5 percent of the farmers did not want any land, and would rather have their land taken in exchange for cash. It is easy to see from these cases that the fundamental reason why primary-level authority would try to reallocate land by citing any pretext possible is that this would allow them to hold on to in the long term those key resources needed for both production and for everyday life in the countryside in the name of management.[23] The need to be able to do this is especially acute when the distribution of these resources is inextricably linked with the political and economic interests of primary-level politicians.

However, on the issue of the term of the land contracts, central government policy is incommensurate with what is in the interest of the primary-level authority. Implementing the policy would chip away at the amount of space primary-level authorities have in which to exercise control, make it increasingly difficult for them to commandeer land, and deprive them of the benefits they would otherwise be able to receive from land reallocation, contracting, and trade. Measures enacted by the central government aimed at optimizing stability in land usufruct have effectively if also quietly "deprived" primary-level authority of its control over land, hollowing out collective ownership of land—which primary-level control over land essentially amounts to, and replacing it with a combination of state ownership (ownership rights) and individual ownership by farmers (operating right). Obviously, this represents a serious threat to primary-level authorities' control over resources, something they have *de facto* enjoyed for a very long time. And this is why they would use any excuse they can think of to prevent state policies from taking effect at the local level and to defend their power of control. In this sense, the so-called tension between people and land is to a large extent caused by a default system that is

[23] Li Ding, "To make Adjustments to Land Contracts or not (Rural Survey No.4)." *Economic Highlights*, February 4, 1998.

problematic. Such a system exacerbates the chronic conflict between people and land, and rendered state policies impotent for the purpose of resolving such conflict.

Of course, not all results of efforts to defend the rights of the primary-level authority are negative, as these efforts may be an effective way to push back against policies the central government tries to impose on rural communities that are wrong, merely superficially sensible and deeply unpopular among the rural population. Since such policies hurt the interest of farmers, implementation is often a challenge, and "obstruction" and "superficial compliance" by primary-level authorities can help safeguard local social order. For example, when the government was pushing for dividing collectively owned land into two subcategories—land used to support personal consumption and land used to supply the market—in many places over-night mobilization sessions were held, and even with the cadres personally going to the front line advocating for the system the results were abysmal. This is because every village had their own ways of subverting the rules: lumping together the land of many different contractors under one name, which is marked as a "large contractor" on the paperwork submitted to higher authority, while otherwise changing absolutely nothing in the contractual relationships. Still, these positive effects do not cancel out the negative impacts, what is important is that whether to divide up collectively owned land based on two different uses does not depend on whether such a system meets the needs of farmers but on primary-level authority's control of land. Even after August 1997, when the central government released a directive announcing its abandonment of the land division system there were still places where the primary-level authority sought to find ways to institute it through land reallocation.

Some Opinions regarding Effective Execution of the Second Round of Land (Large Plots) Contracting System (Second Draft)[24]

> The second round of land contracts is guided by the idea that, following the guidance of Xiaoping Deng's theory of building socialism with Chinese characteristics, in compliance with the CPC Central Committee and the State Council's policies on stabilizing and improving the land contract accountability system, [we endeavor to] gauge the condition on the ground, and commit resources toward understanding situations and problems we encountered during the first round of land contracts, in compliance with the requirement to establish ownership, stabilize contracting rights, unleash the potential of operating rights (user rights), and strengthening managing right, and take further steps to stabilize and improve the two-tiered operating system centered on household contract accountability and that organically combines aggregation and separation, and establish a system for transferring land operating rights, facilitate the operation of land at a suitable scale, and strengthen the collective's capacity for uniform operations and services.

[24] See a document drafted in August, 1997 by a local government in Zhejiang province made available to those who wished to comment on it.

As such, while the central government unequivocally mandates continuity and constancy in operating (contracting) rights, primary-level authority is guided by the basic principle of "keeping the system unchanged and the land economically fecund", essentially a contradiction (between state policy and local policy).

> Keeping the system unchanged means making sure the two-tiered operating system centered on household contract accountability and that organically combines aggregation and separation remains over the long term. Keeping the land economically fecund entails facilitating land use (operating) rights, improving the quality and efficiency of resources, and building a land transfer system that is suitable for a socialist market economy.

Yet it is not up to the farmers to negotiate and sign any land transfer contracts, as that is the prerogative of the economic cooperative, effectively to "ramp up regulation and management of village-level contracts". In practice, in addition to renewing existing leasing contracts, a range of other models have been used, including making adjustments to existing allocation before renewing the contract, separating the two uses (producing for private consumption and for supply to the market) of land, share-holding cooperation, where the number of shares is divided into privately owned shares by the contracting farmer, collectively owned shares by the collective and shares based on the discount prices of farming instruments, and the duties and responsibilities of the households and the collective would be defined according to the number of shares they are allotted. Whichever model is applied, the collective ownership of land, the *status quo*, must remain. This Opinion has even given considerable discretion to the local authorities, noting that while in principle the central government's policy to renew current contracts by 30 years must be complied with, in practice local governments *can exercise discretion* by considering conditions on the ground, specifying only that "leases for land designated for supplying private consumption should have terms longer than those for land intended to be used to supply the market", which is essentially to say that land in the latter category should continue to be allowed to be "transferred", and these decisions rest in the hands of the primary-level authority.

In order to justify land transfers, the author of the Opinion took pains to distinguish between contracting rights and operating rights, so as to be able to show that it is possible to "maintain the stability" of the former while allowing the "transfer" of the latter.

> In order to speed up the establishment of a land transfer mechanism, local authorities must be sure to clearly distinguish between contracting rights and operating rights under the collective ownership of land, so as to create the right conditions for realizing the mutual enhancement of the two rights, and for allowing the transfer of operating rights. Land contracting right is the right to lease land that is enjoyed by members of the village cooperative and one that is codified in the laws and policies of the government and aimed at promoting the welfare of the

population, land operating right is the right of the producer to exercise their autonomy in operating and utilizing the land while keeping the agricultural use designation for the land. Provided that farmers' contracting rights remain intact, the owner's (the collective) permission has been obtained, and the contract has not expired, they may transfer the operating right to their land, in whole or in part, to other individuals (including member of the same village or of other villages) or organizations engaged in agricultural operation, or otherwise revert it to the owner, which may then either grant other individuals or agriculture operators the right to operate the land or the owner may decide to operate the land itself. Farmers who have gained access to land through transfer or the bidding process do not have the right to contract the land to others, they only have the right to operate it. Land operating rights are transferrable, but not as a means for profiteering.[25]

Had the purpose of such a system been entirely to ensure that farmers or primary-level authority retained control over land, the following rule would have been unnecessary:

The only body authorized the contract out land is the village cooperative. As for the production teams that own land but lack the ability to grant contract or to manage the land, it would be best to have them placed under village supervision, and to allow village economic cooperative to oversee all contracting. Meanwhile efforts must be made to ensure that the relationships between the village and the production teams, and also between production teams are properly handled. Make sure that all land contracts follow a template, and contracts that have already been signed remain valid. However, clauses in existing contracts that do not serve the interests of the parties to the contract in the way they define their respective rights and responsibilities must be emended.[26]

Here the local policy evidently deviates from central government policy. While the central government's intent is to give more teeth to rural households' contracting and operating rights with respect to land, the local government instead wants their own contracting and operating rights strengthened. So even though it is public knowledge that the rules call for 15 years as the term of the land contracts, in reality, since this touches on the interests of primary-level authority, most villages have continued to make reallocation with some regularity since the contract accountability system was first implemented. Indeed, reallocation has taken place quite frequently.

Among the villages that we investigated, 219 had carried out land reallocation, accounting for 80 percent of the total, and the frequency had been quite high.

[25] One local government, in Zhejiang province, draft document released to solicit comments, August 1997.

[26] One local government, in Zhejiang province, draft document released to solicit comments, August 1997.

> Among these 219 villages, the shares of villages that had had land reallocation once, twice, three times, four times and more than five times were 43.4 percent, 38.4 percent, 16 percent, 3.6 percent and 9.6 percent, respectively.[27]

Meanwhile, primary-level authorities also did what they could to fend off social entities competing for the power of control. By emphatically stressing the management of collectively owned assets, which was their weapon in this fight, they tried to prevent non-governmental economic organizations from being able to expand their power of control. One example is "advancing reform of the rural collective ownership regime". According to one cadre from the rural economic committee in charge of the matter, the purpose of establishing township collective asset organization—Township Collective Asset Operation Cooperation—is to "manage assets collectively owned by the farmers on their behalf". He stressed that "there used to be economic associations and people's communes, which have been abolished, and the township government represents the government, then who would represent the farmers and manage their assets on their behalf?" Why should there be somebody else managing the farmers' assets on their behalf, instead of the farmers representing themselves? This is an interesting question in its own right, and nobody else except primary-level cadres would even ask it, revelatory of what they want: in reality, the variety of corporations operating collective assets are, unfortunately, organizations deliberately set up by primary-level cadres that control public resources for purpose of exercising further control over township finances. Such corporations are pitted against rural households whose control over resources has grown significantly.

> There used to be the Agricultural, Industrial and Commercial Corporation (AICC), but the problem was that amounted to trying to achieve political ends using economic means, and a great deal of tension existed between economic organizations and the government, with the latter being unable to reign in the former. For example, when it came to setting up enterprises, the township government did not have the authority to make the call, whenever the government needed money it turned to the AICC, and if the request was turned down, there was nothing the government could do. The AICC was an organization on a par with the township government in terms of administrative rank, so the government did not have control over it. [By contrast], the newly established Collective Asset Operating Corporation received no administrative ranking, and was under the leadership of the township CPC committee and the government. This was the proper relationship among the CPC committee, collective economic organizations and enterprises.[28]

[27] Policy Research Office of the CPC Central Committee & Ministry of Agriculture Office of Fixed Rural Fieldwork Sites, *Improving Two-tier Operating System* (CPC Central Party School Press, 1992), 15.

[28] Transcript of the August 1978 interviews with members of county-level agricultural economic committee.

For the primary-level authority, the go-to approach to keeping the power of control within its own grip was to recalibrate the administrative standing (ranks) of different bodies, so as to reassert who is dominant and who is subordinate.

> In the past the AICC and the township government were on a par with each other in terms of administrative standing, but now the former has been downgraded by one notch. In the past, among those in the three core branches of leaders – the CPC, the people's congress and the government, the manager of the AICC was on a par with the township chief. But now there are only two core branches of leadership, with the deputy secretary of the township CPC committee also serving as the AICC manager, and the deputy manager is also the assistant to the township chief, and the township chief financial officer also serves as a deputy manager.[29]

Through calibrating the ranking order, primary-level authority was able to become the official manager of corporate finances, effectively ending enterprises' status as independent legal persons. In addition, primary-level authority also took out bank loans using the government as a guarantor, then gave out loans to economic organizations and charged a management fee. It stipulated that those legal persons who became shareholders would be eligible for loan, which would not be available to those outside the region. This effectively allows primary-level authority to curtail enterprises' ability to enter into horizontal trading relationships, thereby rendering these enterprises more dependent than they otherwise would be on the management department of the local government.

An even more important consequence of the establishment of this kind of organization is that the number of economic entities officially entered into the tally for accounting purposes was drastically reduced. Take land as an example. While nominally it is collectively owned, in fact only those entities that are eligible to be tallied for economic accounting purposes can exercise genuine control over it, which is why that control is mostly in the hands of the village or even the production team. In the past, in relation to land transactions, for accounting purposes the production team (natural village) would set the price and the village by administrative designation would oversee the actual paperwork, and grassroots authority could only retain a 5 percent that goes toward management fee. Now we have the collective asset management corporations, and rules are in place according to which 20–40 percent must go toward higher governments as management fee. For the local government, reclaiming the right to manage land is an achievement in their ability to control economic benefit. Overtly, it signifies control over land transaction. But in fact, with each transaction, primary-level authority would also rake in a certain amount of money. Therefore, there was no need for local government at any level to

[29] Transcript of the August 1997 interviews with staff of the township agricultural economic committee.

impose serious restrictions on land transaction, all they needed to make sure was that they got to pocket a certain portion of the economic return.

In addition to charging money for land transactions, this economic management body also has the authority to collect fees from enterprises: land use fee, which must be paid once a year, management fee, which must be paid once every three to six months, and contribution toward the agriculture development fund, which must be paid once a year. On top of these, money may be collected for a host of other things, such as public welfare funds and provident funds. Evidently, in order to augment their control over resources, the primary-level apparatus established a series of organizations whose raison d'etre is to boost its standing, and to enhance its control over finances and resources.

> Boosting the standing of primary-level organizations requires strengthening the collective economy, and securing the public funds needed to get things done. It is very difficult to obtain this money through collection, so administrative measures must be resorted to. A large proportion of the extra-budgetary funds is held by the various departments, not by the primary-level government, and the primary-level government is not allowed any cut in whatever taxes collected by the departments, all of which must be turned over to superior governments. So obviously they have to come up with some other way.[30]

These attempts augmented the financial resources township government can command, and the power of control became increasingly concentrated in it. So while the number of village cadres declined, the number of township cadres grew year after year: "There are fewer village cadres and more township cadres now than before". We also heard that "with a lack of talents down at the primary level, and no fund at their disposal, how does one expect them to promote local development?" As for the townships, despite having received the money collected, the collective assets management corporations nonetheless failed to fulfill their responsibility of providing services to the enterprises. For example, when an enterprise being managed by this corporation tries to transfer its assets, the corporation would deny the request, because should it approve the transfer, it would then be subject to debt liability, but if it denies the request, and instead lets the enterprise make its own decision, then the enterprise would have to take full responsibility for that action.[31]

Even with such expansion of their power, the township cadres were not fully satisfied and wanted more latitude. According to one person in a position of responsibility at the primary level who spoke about this, the staff expansion at the primary level is really not of their own doing. It was the various government departments above that were pulling the strings, and people at the primary level were simply doing their bidding. Cadre appointment took place even without the primary-level organizations having been notified, all for

[30] Transcript of the August 1997 interviews with primary-level cadres.
[31] Transcript of the August 1997 interviews with primary-level cadres.

purpose of enlarging the power and interests of one's own department. At the township, the policy-making body was the CPC-government joint conference. But when it comes to such important matters as social development or investment, decisions were mostly made by specific administrative and economic departments. For matters such as wage increases, performance evaluation of cadres on probation, and promotion of outstanding cadres, if rules set by superior governments are followed to the letter, it would erode the overall power of the primary-level government, and weaken their central role. Therefore, primary-level cadres made three proposals: "The township government would be given preference in placement of the best and the brightest recruits, it would be given priority in the government's task list, and it would enjoy favorable treatment in the distribution of gains and benefits".[32]

8.3 The Function of Collective Ownership

Members of primary-level leadership are able to maintain a certain standard of living and social standing, which require certain material basis. However, it takes more than their salaries to sustain these material conditions. Not only is their salary not nearly enough for that purpose, in fact, there is nothing enviable about being dependent on one's salary as a way of life, and it certainly is not how the superiority of such a position manifests itself. In fact, one feature of the "prestige" of being a primary-level cadre is that it allows that person to meet their private needs, such as those related to production, daily life, transportation, social intercourse, and even personal needs for laborer by ("legally" and free of charge) taking advantage of a variety of public channels. When they need help with farm work or for a personal matter, some cadres would simply casually draft somebody to do the work for free. In return, they would dole out some favor to those who have done the work by exercising the power they have in administering public affairs, without having to pay anything out of their own pocket. Under the collective ownership system, it is commonplace for the personal expenditure of clerks and runners who do the grunt work on the ground to be "justifiably" covered by public funds (administrative overhead), and it is largely up to the cadres themselves to determine how much is spent based on their needs. This makes them staunch supporters of the collective ownership system, so far as how their interests are impacted by it.

From the point of view of both public and private affairs, given its inherent lack of constraints, the collective ownership system has effectively become a primary-level cadre group ownership system. Given their ability as a group to reap benefits from the operation of this system, they have every reason to ensure that it is maintained, that its associated power of control is maintained. These prospects for gain mean that this group of people is rivalrous with both the state and private individuals in terms of control, and this is something very important to understand about how officials at the primary level behave.

[32] Transcript of the August 1997 interviews with the organizational staff.

Responses to a questionnaire designed specifically for the village cadres make their attitude toward such matters unmistakable: As far as they are concerned, what is important is not whether central management of the economy is necessary, but which aspects of the economy should be managed centrally, which need not be, and more importantly still, who actually does the managing.

- Of all the cadres in the village, 72.6 percent believe that it is necessary to establish collective economy organizations and associated management bodies, and to build a stronger collective economy; 24.5 percent believe that these are not necessary, but among these, 86.6 percent believe that the village council should take up this management responsibility. In mountainous areas, this percentage is as high as 100 percent.
- Among those village cadres in favor of establishing a central management body, 58.8 percent believe the village council should be put in charge, 22.1 percent favor having integrated management of the Party, the government and the economy; 17.6 percent think a separate body should be established specifically for that purpose.
- Of all the village cadres, 82.9 percent think the collective economy organization should be set up within villages of administrative designation.
- Some comrades think that the level of mechanization has declined since farming on separate plots of land began, and that there has been a general deterioration in production methods. More should be done to ensure mechanization is applied across the board in collective production.
- Of all the village cadres, 84.5 percent believe that the most serious difficulty facing the collective in its effort to provide services is the anemic condition of the collective economy, leaving it materially inadequate for purpose of providing services. Obviously, boosting the collective economy has become the most urgent task for most villages trying to improve their capacity for providing services. In other words, if the collective is to take on the responsibility of providing uniform services to rural residents, it is imperative for the collective economy to grow stronger.[33]

Given that production is primarily organized at the household level, collective service provision plays a secondary role, and cooperative and personal services take up a small percentage (55.3 percent, 32.8 percent, and 11.9 percent, respectively), it is no coincidence that the majority of the cadres are in favor of having village organizations oversee the collective economy. Some surveys have shown that as a group village cadres are actually the largest beneficiaries of the collective operation of the economy: among rural households, whether one is a member of the cadre makes a difference to how they operate their land, with

[33] "Analysis of the Attitude among Village Cadres towards Improving the Two-tiered Operational System: Survey Results from 274 Villages," in *Improving the Two-Tiered Operational System*, ed. Policy Research Office of the Central Committee & Ministry of Agriculture Office of Fixed Rural Fieldwork Sites (Beijing: Central Party School Press, 1992), 70–71.

cadres households enjoying a notably higher level of service provided by the collective than do non-cadre households. In 1990, of all households where each aspect of their production was carried out through services provided by the collective, on average cadre households accounted for 47.4 percent and non-cadre households 31.2 percent, a difference of 16.2 percentage points. Of all households that carried out production using their own resources, on average cadre households accounted for 43.4 percent and non-cadre households 56.6 percent, a difference of 13.5 percentage points. Of all households where production was carried out through cooperation among households and personal services, on average cadre households accounted for 9.5 percent and non-cadre households 12.2 percent, a difference of 2.7 percentage points (see Table 8.5).

The differences reflected in Table 8.5 cannot be explained by reference to economic principles, what can explain is how control over resources is distributed. Obviously such control is not gained primarily through economic activities, whether it is competition or trade, but through political means (power of control). The difference between the two is that political control is not so much a means for profiteering as it is a form of parasitic existence.

Being a cadre gives one access to a range of benefits associated with individual and collective modes of operation. Collective control must be able to maintain cadre households' freedom to operate independently. We can, therefore, understand why it is that even though primary-level cadres tend in general to favor strongly the principle of collective management, they nonetheless disagree widely over many specific details, such as whether to raise the percentage of the contracting fees to be retained by primary-level administration, whether to lease certain selected plots of land at elevated rates for growing cash crops, and whether fruit, mulberry and tea plantations should be controlled and operated directly by the collective.[34] The reason for this, obviously, is that since their position as cadre already allows them to lease these resources as individuals and to enjoy the collective services associated with them, they have no incentive to see changes to such a system. I noted earlier that in one village in Hebei province the heads of the four major enterprises were all, without exception, either former or incumbent village CPC committee secretaries. Cadres "taking turns" to serve at the helm of local enterprises illustrates the ease with which people with official titles become business operators. How can it be shown that they are the most suitable candidates for these positions? It cannot, all that can be shown is that they are the most readily available candidates. Their position in the primary-level government makes it easier for them than for anybody else to control information and resources, and as contractors, they as a matter of course stand to reap profits. There is no better way to exercise control, and this brings the complex relationship between the collective interest of the cadres and collective operation and independent operation into sharp relief.

[34] "Analysis of the Attitude among Village Cadres," 71.

Table 8.5 Breakdown of different operating models for rural households in different regions[a] (Unit: %)

	Independent 1984	*Collective 1984*	*Others 1984*	*Independent 1990*	*Collective 1990*	*Others 1990*	*Change in Independent*	*Change in Collective*	*Change in Others*
Surveyed households	57.6	31.9	10.5	55.3	32.8	11.9	−2.3	0.9	1.4
Eastern region	50.9	39.3	9.8	50.8	37.8	11.4	−0.1	−1.5	1.6
Central region	60.0	28.6	11.4	56.9	30.2	12.9	−3.1	1.6	1.5
Western region	66.2	23.6	10.2	61.0	28.0	11.0	−5.2	4.4	0.8
Cadre	45.2	46.4	8.4	43.1	47.4	9.5	−2.1	1.0	1.1
Non-cadre	58.9	30.4	10.7	56.6	31.2	12.2	−2.2	0.8	1.5

[a]"Analysis of the Attitude among Village Cadres", 54–55

This means that how "collective" control is distributed is actually rather complicated. It is neither purely collective nor purely private, and this mode of property rights is best understood by looking at which group ends up benefiting by gaining or retaining control (over funds and resources) and profits. For example, in the Hebei case mentioned earlier, the township government's attempt to terminate a village enterprise chief's contract and sign a new one with somebody else failed because the village enterprise chief resisted. In this case, the township government, which was the legal person representing a collective enterprise, did not have the mandate to make decisions unilaterally. Yet obviously, the contractor in the original contract had only limited mandate to make decisions. This suggests that even though in reality the mode of property rights is closely linked to "the collective", because of staunch resistance from the primary-level cadre, in practice what happens in the end is a result of horse trading. I call this collective ownership in name only.

The feature of this collective ownership in name only is that control rests in the hands of individuals with official titles or groups, and outside this group, resources have no way of having their value effectively realized independently. Even though returns yielded by the operation of rural resources are designated public assets, because of reasons having to do with distribution, these returns are not in fact widely shared among all members of the rural community. We find further evidence of the existence of collective ownership in name only in Professor Shu-min Huang's anthropological oral biography. In one village in Fujian province that Huang visited, the disintegration process of the collective regime (in May 1984) showed signs of such a phenomenon. At the time, the egalitarian distribution of public land and agricultural instrument auctions was under way, and the hardest thing was deciding what to do with enterprises that had been set up and operated by the production brigades, and they became the coveted prize that anybody with some capital fought "tooth and nail" for. Under such circumstance, the secretary decided that he had to take action to make sure people outside their rank did not get hold of the power to control these assets and rule the village.[35] So he brought together several people and did all they could to prevent the worst eventuality from materializing, capitalized on his august standing in the community to destroy rivals, and bagged all the enterprises himself. He then divided them into 13 shares, and gave one share each to the former head of the production brigade and the incumbent cadre.[36] One month later, the secretary, who had secured the enterprise contracting right, decided to set up a brick factory in the village, and told Professor Huang that his plan was to raise eight shares, each worth 10,000 yuan, and just about every production brigade cadre would be invited to join. He noted that at the time, the government had not yet released rules governing the proper size of privately operated enterprises, so if he was able to

[35] Shu-min Huang, *The Spiral Road: Change in a Chinese Village through the Eyes of a Communist Party Leader* (Westview Press, 1993), 269.

[36] Huang, *The Spiral Road*, 271.

get the majority of village cadres on board for the investment, then he could get away with classifying the resultant enterprise as a collective one, thereby evading government restrictions.[37]

The reason this cadre cited for doing what he did was quite telling. He basically wanted to make sure that former and incumbent cadres were given some preferential treatment so they would not be reduced to members of the public as a result of the disintegration of the collective system. Lo and behold, when township cadres realized that the secretary had not tried to keep all the gains from such a move to himself but was sharing them with the rest of the cadres, they deemed the arrangement the right thing to do. However, what such a change meant was that collective accumulation, which is used toward enhancing the welfare of all the village residents, was being generated through the collection of rents, instead of profits, making corporate profits out of reach for the village residents, who were not shareholders. Can this kind of transfer of property rights be said to be more in line with the collective system than the one that existed before, allowing all village residents to have a share in the benefits? What we see is that while this kind of "cooperation" being arranged in this one village in Fujian does have some aspects to it that are motivated by economic considerations, such as when large brick factories in urban areas were allotted shares based on their technological contributions, other aspects are motivated by political considerations. This is evident in how assets were divvied up among powerful figures in the village in ways that would maintain the power relations status quo.

> Being a cadre makes a large difference in the redistribution of collective assets, and also in the redistribution of the profits yielded by the assets. Even though "by the end of 1984, in the vast majority of rural areas collectively-owned land had been leased to rural households, and collectively-owned animals and agricultural instruments had been sold at discounted prices or distributed to households, and the fixed assets of enterprises owned by the commune and the production brigade had mostly been contracted to collectively-operated enterprises to factory managers, with some having been converted to shares at a discounted value and resold to the production team or the farmers", still "some of the assets that did not lend themselves to being equally distributed – such as brick kilns, mills and orchards – would end up being leased out by village cadres in the name of the collective to technicians or farmers who had some kind of close relationship with the cadres". It is worth noting that what the farmers ended up getting in the distribution were only assets that belonged to the two organizational units ranked below the production brigade, and collective assets that once belonged to the communes were, as a result of the replacement of the communes by newly-established townships essentially turned over to either township government or departments under governments above the township level. These would have mostly included the fixed assets of commune-operated enterprises in the five small industries, and the buildings and other fixed assets that belonged to distribution departments, agricultural

[37] Huang, *The Spiral Road*, 303–4.

> instruments department, financial department and agricultural technology department. This constituted the source of most of the seed capital for both township enterprises that began to flourish in the mid-1980s and the agricultural social service system that was given serious attention later on. Even though the original value of these assets continued to grow, so far as the distribution of its profit yields is concerned, the portion that is invested toward "subsidizing and building agriculture using proceeds from industrial development" continued to contract.[38]

It is precisely a consequence of the collective ownership system in name only that despite profit increases there was no increase in investment toward collective welfare. As far as primary-level cadres are concerned, the advantages they are able to enjoy thanks to their positions have allowed their power of control to expand considerably. Whether it is information, funds, or resources (land, buildings, electric power, hydraulic facilities), they have easier access than anybody else. This is how it came to be that the operation, planning, management, and direction of rural economies are essentially in the hands of the cadres. Relative to rivals with other kinds of identities, primary-level cadres' control over resources is both exclusionary and monopolistic. Farmers are mostly workers for hire, and do not get to compete with the cadres on a level playing field.

8.4 Discussion: The Structure of Compartmentalization and the Role of the State

Earlier we discussed how, in modern history, as a result of the development of the manner in which the central government "endowed" local authorities "with power", the relationship between rural communities and local authorities with respect to their interests and goals had undergone vast transformation. One change is that, while local authorities used to serve (as it should) the community, now it serves those to whom they owe the power they had (usually higher governments). One corollary of this change is that it brought village authority and township authority closer to each other, effectively deepening mutual dependency among officials of different ranks within the bureaucratic hierarchy. In theory, this should have augmented the power of the bodies that endowed local authorities with power, thereby strengthening superior governments, i.e., the state's power of control. Yet this is not what happened. The reason has to do with the fact that jurisdiction at the primary level is divided up regionally, contributing to a governance structure defined by compartmentalization. From the point of view of the rural population, some authorities were merely symbolic, while others substantive.

[38] Tiejun Wen & Shouyin Zhu, "An Experimental Research on the Basic Operations in Rural China". *Chinese Rural Economy*, 1999.

With regard to symbolic significance, admittedly the state does in fact have the right to interfere, in the sense that it is possible for the state to take any action at any time that would have an impact on the lives of rural residents. However, to go from "could" interfere to "does in fact" interfere, and from interfering under extraordinary circumstances to interfering on a daily basis would require not only seamless coordination among officials up and down the bureaucratic hierarchy all of whom trying to carry out policies of the state but also the existence of uniform rules across different jurisdictions. Yet these conditions do not in fact obtain.

The facts we have been examining so far suggest that, in practice a "fragmented structure of authority"[39] is what defines the *de facto* relationship between the primary level and the state. Under such a fragmented system, the role of the state is not so much to govern but to coordinate. On one hand, government bodies on different levels partake in basically the same plan, yet none of them is capable of executing it on its own, and would require very effective coordination, and consensus building, so that disagreements and dissent can be prevented. But since disagreements and dissent will never disappear completely because conflicts of interest and rivalry over power will always exist, this "coordination" will be indefinitely necessary, and extremely costly. On the other hand, since the different departments do make decisions, and promulgate them, it means not only do they have decision-making power, such powers often come into conflict among different departments, leaving those who have to carry out the decisions having to make choices and find the right balance. In essence, these conflicts reflect the desire among the different bodies, of varying types and ranks, to compete for and expand their power. In fact, such a structure helps to lend legitimacy to the discretion primary-level officials' exercise when discharging their responsibilities. As a result, a multi-centered, multi-tiered authority structure forms. Superior governments and officials have no choice but to tolerate it, otherwise it would be even more of a challenge for their orders to be carried out.

This is a system with multiple centers of authority. It gives the primary level the space in which to continually consolidate and reconfigure its own interests, with the aim of maintaining its scope of influence in the face of constant competitive pressure, while at the same time deepening interdependency and mutual protection among local administrative bodies. The effect of this is that higher-level governments can only govern the population indirectly, i.e., via lower-level administrative bodies, on which they must depend for managing things on the ground, instead of directly. Faced with this reality, superior governments have no choice but to allow such a multi-centered, multi-tiered, and perhaps even motivationally "diverse" system to exist. Of course, this motivational "diversity" is only confined to the ranks of the cadres, and does not apply

[39] Kenneth Lieberthal & Michael Oksenberg, *Policy Making in China: Leaders, Structures and Processes* (Princeton: Princeton University Press, 1988). Their discussion is focused more on the power fragmentation within the bureaucratic system.

to the society at large. Therefore, in practice, any substantive attempt to centralize jurisdictional power would be bound to touch the fixed structure of local authorities, typically suggestive of changes to the location of the center of authority or alternative configuration, and would therefore be met with strong resistance.

More important still, should superior governments try to change this multi-centered system, and increase their ability to exercise uniform and direct control [of the rural population], this would, given the current interdependency among the different centers on different levels, threaten the stability of the administrative substratum on which these superior governments depend. For this reason, superior governments are always reluctant to challenge the power of lower governments. Indeed, this is why throughout much of history, new centers of authority—whether they occupy a high position or middling position on the bureaucratic hierarchy—have been very cautious when it comes to any action that constitutes treading on the turf of primary-level authorities. They understand that the wise thing to do, and what would be in their own best interest, is to support and protect primary-level authorities, rather than challenging or trying to supplant them. Doing this would maximize the "smooth" transmission of political commands, ensure the security of everybody's authority and standing, and basically keep in place a system under which everybody gets what they want. Therefore, except in cases where their authority and legitimacy are under threat, ordinarily, superior governments are far more likely to protect lower-level political organizations than they are to monitor or challenge them.

For their part, primary-level officials tend to be highly sensitive to actions that erode their authority. Their default response to threat is to call it quits altogether, complaining that "it's an impossible job". This tried-and-true tactic is often enough to raise concerns among higher officials about the continual functioning of the messaging mechanism, who usually just let primary-level officials manage things using their own methods, as long as this does not lead to consequences beyond control. Meanwhile, vigilance against interference from above, superficial compliance and resistance against outside influence are widespread among primary-level officials. "Resistance" often takes the form of passing for "accountability" by performing the absolute minimum.[40] This means that while the state is able to delegate some power to the primary level, this is a process of selection and permutation, and the power that the primary-level officials do end up with is only what they absolutely must have, power that would benefit these officials. This is what I called "structural resistance", i.e., efforts to prevent the state from making inroads into the country.[41]

[40] Kung-Chuan Hsiao, *Rural China: Imperial Control in the Nineteenth Century* (University of Washington Press, 1972).

[41] Jing Zhang, "Several Issues in China's Primary-level Governance," *China Book Review*, 1996 (10).

A system like this is different from both a centralized power structure where localities have only minimum power and a decentralized power structure where local authorities effectively shield themselves from state over-reach. In my view, this system is characterized by a combination of mutual vigilance and mutual support. Local officials cautiously try to make sure their own power is not chipped away on one hand while seizing every opportunity to increase their power by taking advantage of superior governments. They are particularly adept at milking their relationship with the state for opportunities to boost their own power. Because this relationship is different for different localities, regional differences exist in local power. Local cadres have the discretion to implement the rules as they see fit, without any rigid guidelines. Because their interests and needs are different, so are their preferred means to increasing their gains. But what they all have in common is the goal of protecting their turf, and preventing information, resources, and power from flowing toward the state. Building primary-level political apparatus is less about establishing an effective mechanism for the transmitting orders from superior government and implementing them but more about maintaining and strengthening local authority's own power. This strengthening did not correspondingly increase the state's power of control. To the contrary, where local authority gains, the state loses. Meanwhile, the rural population has barely benefited from this strengthening of the local authority, because to the cadres, any increase in the power of the individual and the prospect of threat to what they can gain from the collective economy would simply be unacceptable to them.

Consequently, we see a sharp contrast between rural and urban areas. For the most part, urban expansion either solidified state ownership or helped the state expand its authority.[42] In the countryside, however, state control of the assets, resources, information, and power in rural communities was more indirect and relatively weak. As the foundation of the system, the collective ownership of land was particularly conducive to efforts by primary-level cadres to reconfigure the power relationships among village, township, and other local officials. By capitalizing on their *de facto* control of resources and their political standing, they were able to build up gradually their control and power of distribution over local benefits, resources and assets, and grow their social network. As a result, control in economic affairs shifted downward, mostly toward cadres and their groups, not because they have outstanding capabilities or business acumen but because they occupy a certain privileged position in the administrative pecking order. Ample evidence shows that businesses set up and run by these individuals are far more likely to fail than to succeed.

Far from being pushed and pulled by blind impulses, primary-level cadres act with deliberation. They are adept at finding opportunities for growing their own power within the parameters of the relationship they have with superior

[42] Scott Wilson, "Competing Claims to Village Property and the Gradual Clarification of Property Rights", Prepared for "Property Rights in Transitional Economies: Insights from Research on China" (Hong Kong, 13–15, June 1996) p. 26.

officials. They make alterations to the core message of documents released by higher governments to suit their own purposes; they withhold information or choose whichever course of action that is most expedient, and they adroitly choose only those policies to comply with that fit within their calculus of cost and benefit, and then only in ways that optimize their own objectives. While they are in charge of the economy, most of them have but limited competence in business management, leaving them having to eke out an existence by subsisting parasitically on the cadre cohort to which they belong and trying to make sure that group's existential security. They do not aim at investing for profits or expanding the market, as they are not prepared to take on the risks and responsibility those would entail. Instead, they are simply trying to survive and to reap as much easily available gain as possible. Whenever primary-level cadres interfered with corporate management, it is not so much with the aim of helping enterprises become more profitable, but more with the aim of exercising their power of control and the right to extract fees out of them. They are always cautiously trying to protect their power of control over various things from being taken away, by, say, making sure that the person(s) in charge of managing land resources are not those most suitable but rather those individuals or organizations with the most power. The principle underlying all these actions has had deleterious effects on the reputation of primary-level officials, since the practice of reaping gains from one's position of control not only is inconsistent with market principles but also runs counter to the principle according to which public organizations should sustain themselves on tax revenue and provide public services. This has done significant damage to their credibility and image within the rural community.

Under such a system, the state is always in a position of unwilling passivity. It finds itself having to react to actions taken by primary-level officials: approve, grant tacit consent, or obstruct. Yet clearly, whatever the state can do to primary-level officials is highly inefficient, especially in comparison with what the latter can do themselves. For example, primary-level officials can successfully block the state from carrying out income distribution on its own, yet the state cannot quite do the same to primary-level officials over the same matter. Primary-level officials can successfully sabotage attempts by the state to reconfigure their relationship with the rural community, but the state can only afford to resort to such heavy-handed approach in extraordinary circumstances. Despite what may have been expected of them, state law meant to protect the rights of individuals in contractual relationships can offer only very limited help to the rural population, since primary-level officials have the discretion to decide which rules are appropriate within the local context, and the state hardly has the final say on these matters.

Even principles applicable to a market economy have no place at the primary level. For example, when primary-level organizations contract out land, they are acutely aware of the importance of that very power, and once the land has appreciated in value thanks to labor input from the contractor, the contractor stands to gain significantly from the contract, especially long-term ones. But this is when, in order to reap short-term gain, the village authority often unilaterally declares the contract void, using their position as stewards public goods, and effectively takes the land back from the farmers. Economic principles presuppose equality in standing between the parties to a contract, yet no such equality in fact obtains between primary-level officials and members of the rural population, so these contracts cannot produce the desired results. Primary-level authority's control over the livelihood resources of the rural population cannot be altered by the existence of the contract law, and the rights of the rural population cannot be protected by such a law. And there is no feasible way to establish a relationship between the rural population on one hand and the state, i.e., the legislature, on the other on the basis of the contract law. Obstruction by the local authority means the state's strategy to implement a market economy cannot get off to a fair start, and for the same reason, state measures designed to protect the operating rights of individuals proprietors cannot product the intended results. Instead, any project that would help the primary-level authority hold on to their power enjoys enthusiastic support.

We might conclude, it seems, that the relationship between the state and the primary-level authority is neither one between "oppression and reaction", as Duara has argued, nor one between the party that issues orders and the one that carries them out, as Tongzu Qu has argued. This has given some scholars reasons to believe that "state-building" is more a matter of form than of substance. Therefore, the state is not to be held solely responsible for the anemic control it has (altogether it shares considerable responsibility for it), but the enormous influence of the local authority on state apparatus must also be blamed. Such powerful influence prevents state apparatus from improving efficiency, and leaves it with no other choice but to maintain the *status quo*. The local authority is inevitably the winner in this, which not only retains the power it has, but is also given the space to increase its clout. The relative autonomy enjoyed by rural communities means that it would be inappropriate to see them as subordinate administrative units in the ordinary sense of the term. After all, local authorities have control over their own land, the structures on that land, and economic opportunities and resources, the power it has over its jurisdiction enjoys tacit consent from the state, which acts deferentially toward them and lets them improve their own policies based on local conditions. All of these have the effect of cementing the apparent legitimacy of local authorities. As for the state, since it is primarily interested in targets and results, it does not so much as try to articulate a set of alternative governance principle to the ones in effect at the local level, and it has basically adopted a laissez-faire approach to rural governance. Thanks to this, even as primary-level authority manages to earn credibility to the things it does by manipulating its relationship with the state, it does not share with the latter a common set of principles of governance.

CHAPTER 9

Rural Residents and the State

9.1 The Issue

According to one mainstream analytical paradigm in studies on social change in modern China, social corrosion within rural communities is explained by reference to the growing reach of state power inside the countryside. As an explanation for the changes in primary-level society in modern China, this has been an influential view. It is the direction in which the research by many scholars has taken place. According to them, the evolution of primary-level social order is attributable to the growing presence of state power in the countryside and the tendency toward structural centralization.[1] The scope of the influence of this line of thinking is not confined to research on historical China, it is also evident in writings on modern China.

It is worth noting that, on the issue of the state, the main point of contention among scholars is whether it is the power of the state or the power of the society that should be strengthened. There are two main opposing views. According to one, prosperity and strength of the nation has primacy, and it is imperative to strengthen the power and capacity of the state in order to achieve objectives such as correcting market failure, promoting equality, protecting the vulnerable, collecting taxes and mobilizing resources, objectives which can only be realized through a powerful state. However, when intellectuals articulate their ideal with regard to a powerful nation, they are mostly either speaking about a powerful state, or treating a powerful state, a powerful society, a powerful citizenry, a powerful nation and other powerful entities as if they were equivalent, while paying almost no attention to the powerful and institutionalized relationship among them. And should anybody cast doubt on this, they risk earning the ire of the public by touching off a sensitive nationalist nerve.

[1] Jing Zhang, "State Building and Self-governing Units in Rural China: Problems and Review," *Open Times*, 10, 2001.

J. Zhang, *Primary-Level Government*,
https://doi.org/10.1007/978-981-96-6209-8_9

According to the other view, interference of the state must be deterred, because, on this view, the expansion of the power of the state is responsible for perturbing the order of the market, obstructing the growth of the civil society and damaging the structure of primary-level power. Therefore, restrictions must be placed on such expansion, and the power of the state ought to return to where it belongs, namely the size prescribed for it under libertarianism that calls for small government, big society.

All these discussions are premised on the idea that a powerful state and a powerful society are on a par with each other or can otherwise be treated as being opposed to each other. And these discussions revolve around the question of whether to strengthen or to weaken the state. My question, however, is this: is that even *the right question* to ask?

I would like to use a case study of one village to illustrate what the power of the state means for legal order in terms of its capacity, significance, and consequences. By showing what the power (capacity) of the state means for one ordinary civil case, especially the relationship between such capacity and the creation of citizen rights, my goal is to help the reader recognize the differences among these different types of state capacity.

9.2 Rights Based on Membership Versus Rights Based on Citizenship

Gaoyu Village, Yinzhuang Township, Qianxi County, Hebei province, is located within the waste dump for the local iron mine that belongs to the Shougang Group. Many years ago, because the Shougang waste dump was being expanded, the authority requisitioned 3300 *mu* of land from the Gaoyu Village, of which 252 mu was occupied by homestead. For compensation, the county, township and village officials, and also Shougang Mining Inc. reached an agreement whereby the entire village of Gaoyu would be relocated to a nearby location, where it would be allotted 320 mu of land for building construction. All the residents of Gaoyu would have their household registration status converted from rural to non-rural, but would remain under the jurisdiction of the village. Those residents of the right age who meet the physical requirements would be placed in jobs at Shougang.[2]

Traditionally, when a woman marries her name would be added to her husband's family's household registration. So when a woman originally from Gaoyu village marries somebody outside the village, all of the things she was once entitled to as a Gaoyu village resident (homestead, contracted land, land

[2] See "Shougang Mining Co., Ltd. on the Agreement to Requisition the Hexi Mine Waste Dump and Resettlement for Gaoyu Village Residents," (February 2, 1993), 1. Data collected by Wen Wang, Xiaolei Gao, Rongman Chen, Qianxi Fu from the Peking University Legal Aid Society, and others. Master's thesis by my graduate student Wen Wang, in which some of the data on this case were used, has been published in the volume I edited: *Research on Identity* (Shanghai: Shanghai People's Press, 2005).

for growing food for personal consumption, dividend from land yield, year-end bonus, pension, and others) would be stripped from her as she loses her local household registration status. She would then become, in terms of her entitlements, the responsibility of the village council of the village where she now lives, and her husband and his family, and also her husband's employer. At the present time there are 54 Gaoyu village households in which there are women who have married into families outside the village, and the total number of women (and their children) who fall into this category is 77. Their husbands are workers at the nearby Shougang mine. Gaoyu village did not allocate them new homestead, but since they had retained their household registration as local residents, they were still living in their old houses where the village used to be.

By 2004, the Shougang waste dump had grown so large it was beginning to occupy some of the land near (50 meters from) some of the houses nearby, these women with husbands from outside the village began to press their demands. They asked that "through administrative channels the village council should see to the reinstatement of their rights to vote in village elections, to stand in village elections, to participate in democratic activities, to be allotted homestead to meet their urgent housing need, to be allotted grains and cereal according to pertinent standards that would sustain them, all so that they would be afforded the same level of care and support from the collective as all other village residents".[3] According to notes taken by researchers, in addition to these questions, there were other "hidden" entitlements that are also denied these women. For example, these women with non-native husband are not considered for temporary jobs for which village residents and their relations are often recruited; they are excluded from a cut of the compensation payment for land requisition, when they try to apply for certificate as proof they have only one child, they are denied the official stamp from the village authority, and they are also denied the in-kind benefits such as cooking oils and rice received by others at the time of the Chinese New Year.[4] The reason for this is that "the village has never recognized [this woman] as one of its own".[5] All these issues have generated deep resentment among these women who have married men from other villages, and they continue to file grievances with higher authorities, at times escalating the tension. Yet despite all of this, the village council stood its ground, firmly.

Q: So where does the village authority come down on this?

Chief: Even though they are registered residents here, they are not considered village residents. Their household registration status has already

[3] Letter dated May 9, 2004 by women in Gaoyu Village pleading for help. (Data collector: Wen Wang).

[4] Transcript of the November 20, 2004 interview with Fenglan Wang, whose husband is not from Gaoyu Village. (Interviewer: Ye and others).

[5] Transcript of the January 19, 2005 interview by Xiaolei Yang and others with the Politics and Law Committee Secretary surnamed Zhou.

changed from rural to non-rural, so even if they should go to any other village, they would not allocate land to them… In the village benefits are distribution according to the headcount, these women who have married men from other villages don't have land, we don't consider them one of our own.

Q: Why are there so many of women in this situation?

Chief: Their household registration status changed from rural to non-rural, should they go to other villages they would not allocate land to them either, so they have no choice but to stay put… All the land in the village has been requisitioned, the amount reserved for homestead is extremely limited, and there is not even enough housing for all the male residents of the village, we are still in talks with Shougang, and providing what these women who are married to men from other villages need would certainly be more of a challenge. Most of the compensation previously received for land requisitioned by Shougang and for the buildings on that land has already been spent by previous village cadres, and the enterprises they set up has made no money. The money owed to village residents for buildings requisitioned from them, totaling more than 3.6 million yuan, has yet to be disbursed. Now the village has neither land nor money, so there is nothing to be done.[6]

In the report sent to the township government, the village council noted that "at present there is no spare land in this village that can be allocated toward either homestead or farming, all of the land the title to which was transferred from Shougang to this village has been allocated".[7] As far as the village council is concerned, the household registration for these individuals (women who married men from other villages) should have been transferred to other places, but for one reason or another these women didn't want the change, and they want to continue to claim opportunities and benefits the village makes available. Because of this, "there is a lot of complaint among the public, and allocation of both land and funds in the village cannot proceed as usual".[8] "These women did not change their household registration and register as residents of other villages after marrying non-local men, and demanded from the village council to be allocated homestead and economic benefits, as a result of which the entire village leadership had to be replaced, jeopardizing normal administrative operation…" Moreover, "In July 1997, villager congress and Party congress were convened whose sole agenda was to consider issues related to women who had married non-local men. After deliberation, it was decided

[6] Transcript of the January 19, 2005 interview by Rongman Chen and others with Haibin Gao, the village committee director.

[7] Report "Current Condition of Gaoyu Village."

[8] "Investigation Report Prepared by the Village Committee for Yinzhuang Township Government" (August 2003).

that women who had been residents of Gaoyu village, married non-local men and declined to change their household registration even when they could do so would not be eligible for entitlements for Gaoyu village residents. Those who had genuine difficulty in changing their household registration had to have documents issued by the county public security bureau certifying their local household registration status if they are to be eligible for entitlements for Gaoyu village residents. According to survey conducted at the time, with the exception of one woman who had married a man registered as a Beijing resident, for the other 41 women who had married non-local men, the police precinct in the places where their husbands were registered residents were indeed able to add their names to their husbands' household registration". Therefore, should these women be allowed to continue to enjoy entitlements reserved for Gaoyu village residents "we would be unable to justify this to the public, and it would not pass".[9]

This decision by the village council had basis in the law. According to provisions in *The Organic Law of the Village Council*, important matters in the village must be discussed at the village congress and voted on for approval, the village delegates did not approve, women who married non-local men therefore were not entitled to benefits reserved for village residents. However, the case pressed by these women also had basis in the law. According to the *Marriage Law* and *the Law on the Protection of Women's Rights and Interests*, people had the right to choose where they reside after marriage, so these women could choose to keep their household registration in Gaoyu village, and enjoy the benefits to which village residents are entitled. Departments in the county CPC committee identified the legal documents pertinent to the case, and wrote a letter to the authority in charge urging them to treat these women who had married non-local men the same way they would any other village resident.

> The *Marriage Law*, the *Organic Law of the Village Council* and the *Law on the Protection of Women's Rights and Interests* were all laws promulgated by the National People's Congress, and there is not conflict among them. Even though *Organic Law of the Village Council* gave the village congress the authority to discuss important matters in the village and vote on them, the substance of the debate must be consistent with provisions in pertinent laws. The resolution that was arrived at the (Gaoyu) villager congress and Party congress was in contravention of the *Marriage Law*. Provision No. 9 of the *Marriage Law* clearly stipulates that: after the marriage certificate has been issued, the wife may become a member of the husband's family, and the husband may become a member of the wife's family. This means that the wife is officially registered as a member of her parents' family, and may choose of her own volition as to whether to join her husband's family instead for purpose of household registration. It is lawful to opt out of changing her household registration status, and she ought to be entitled to the

[9] Yinzhuang Township Government, "Report on the Implementation of Policies on Women Native to Gaoyu Village who Married non-local Men," (June 2, 2004), 1–2, unpublished.

> same treatment afforded all village residents. There are also provisions in the *Law on the Protection of Women's Rights and Interests* with stipulations to the same effects, and *Document No. 9* issued by the General Office of the Chinese Communist Party (2001) also contained similar provisions pertinent to the matter. Therefore, Yinzhuang Township government ought to order the Gaoyu village council to accord the same treatment to these women who married non-local men that is reserved for all village residents.[10]

Clearly, the body (village council) that determines the membership criteria for a village and the bodies (The National People's Congress and the General Office of the Chinese Communist Party) that determine the criteria for citizenship disagree on the status, standing and even the rights of these female villagers. However, since the economic interests of villagers are directly linked with their membership status, it is the village council that grants actual "recognition" of somebody's rights and takes charge of the allocation of benefits. Therefore, when the village council refuses to act or to grant the recognition, there is no mechanism, action, arrangement, or motivation that superior governments can use, take, make, or draw on to compel it to comply with existing laws and central government documents. The most they can do is "urge" the township government "to order" the village council to implement higher-level legal documents. In other words, higher government authority is reduced to the role of "urging" and issuing "requirements", but has otherwise no control over if the other party actually complies.

From the point of view of the village council, this has been standard practice in the village for many years, and the same is true in other villages, superior governments' "recognition" of the rights of these women who married non-local men is merely nominal and has little substantive meaning. So, several months after the letter from superior government, the village council has still not budged. And apparently, the so-called would not pass with the public is just a pretext. What really matters is whether it wanted to get it done, whether it tried, and whether it had the resources. In the words of the village chief when he spoke to the interviewer: "The key issue is there is no money, the economy is not doing well, should we have the land and the money, such a problem would have been solved long ago".[11]

We saw that in this case involving these wives of non-local men, there were two bodies in charge of determining what rights they had and if they could actually exercise these rights: the national legislature and the village council. The former set down the criteria for their status as citizens, while the latter the criteria for their status as village residents. Yet when it comes to the allocation

[10] County Women's Federation, "On How to Handle the Request by 12 Native Gaoyu Women Who Had Married Non-local Men to be Given Equal Treatment with All Other Village Residents," a letter addressed to county magistrate surnamed Li, August 18, 2004. (Data collected by Wen Wang and others).

[11] Transcript of the January 19, 2005 interview by Rongman Chen and others with the village committee director Haibin Gao.

of benefits, which in my view is really what matters, the only thing that matters is one's status as a village resident. On paper, it seems indisputable and the two bodies involved in determining the status of these individuals are not on a same rank on the bureaucratic hierarchy, and that the subordinate body ought to yield to the superior body, and it is up to the superior body to interpret the scope of the mandate given to the lower body. In practice, however, the two bodies have significantly disparate influence on the villagers' ability to exercise their rights.

What is particularly pronounced in this case is that the rights of a village resident and the rights of a citizen do not come to the same thing, and that different bodies have different kinds of impact on how these rights are exercised. According to *Document No. 9* issued by the General Office of the Chinese Communist Party, the *Marriage Law* and the *Law on the Protection of Women's Rights and Interests*, the demands of these wives of non-local men are valid rights, and ought to be protected. However, since the village council is in charge of allocating economic resources, and it has decided on the basis of customary practice to exclude these wives of non-local men from entitlements to benefits, a decision that was officially affirmed at the villager congress and the Party congress because it was in the interest of the entire village population. This is an interesting structure within the establishment that recognizes dual status at the same time: On one hand, there is the affirmation of a citizen's right to decide for themselves where they would like to live after getting married, while on the other hand there is the affirmation of a [community] member's right to terminate their local household registration. The former is largely economically inconsequential since it is not tied to economic benefits, yet it is just the opposite for the latter, and the connection has a long history and the [tacit] consent of the village population. For these wives of non-local men and other rural individuals in similar predicament, not only do their rights as members of the village and their rights as citizens not reinforce each other, the two are at odds with each other.

These problems are in part attributable to the uniquely Chinese system in which citizens are divided into registered rural residents and registered urban residents. Rural residency status and urban residency status correspond with different sets of rights, resources, and authorities with control over these resources. Customarily, these bodies are not required to follow the same principles and rules. This then gives rise to the issue we are presently concerned with, namely, the state's awareness of these conflicts and capacity for adjudicating and mitigating them. Of course, correcting discordance and tensions among laws is one important indicator of the state's governance capability, and such capacity has implications for how well the state is able to protect the legal rights of ordinary citizens and their need for and dependency on state organizations.

According to the constitution, "Land in rural and suburban areas is owned by collectives except for that which belongs to the state as required by law; housing sites and cropland and hillsides allotted for private use are also owned by collectives".[12] In addition, according to the Land Administration Law, "Land owned by peasant collectives that belongs lawfully to peasant collectives of a village shall be operated and managed by collective economic organizations of the village or by villagers' committees".[13] These rules governing the land suggest that what we are facing is the right to make allocation decisions about collectively owned land in villages of administrative designation, and the rights to operate, manage, and allocate collectively owned resources have been given to the village council. This means that once the measure has been approved by the villager congress, the village council has the mandate to act on behalf of the collective in stripping the wives of non-local men of the right to land in Gaoyu village.

As we saw, there are inconsistencies among the *Marriage Law*, the *Law on the Protection of Women's Rights and Interests*, *Document No. 9* issued by the General Office of the Chinese Communist Party, the *Constitution* and the *Land Administration Law* on the issue of rights. The first three laws give these wives of non-local men the freedom to change their place of residence for purpose of household registration and to choose where to live, yet the latter two give the village council the right to manage collectively owned land and benefits it yields. Obviously, such an arrangement offers no solution to the problem confronting those seeking help, namely, how to exercise their right, yet faced with such tension, there is nothing the state can do. In this case, despite the fact that county authority is clearly ranked higher than the village council on the administrative hierarchy, a letter from them urging the latter to take certain actions is of no help, it can neither effectively affirm or protect the rights of wives of non-local men nor influence the allocation of benefits within the village. As a result, these wives of non-local men effectively found themselves in a position where, even though according to the law they have the right of a citizen to choose their place of residence, such right is only symbolic and nominal, because it does not translate into real benefits.

Rights that cannot be exercised are no different from rights that do not exist, so does this indicate weak capacity of the state? Yes and no. Because in the experience of most people, the state's power of control is usually not weak, but very strong. This then gives rise to a more important question: how is it that the modern state should and must have capacity and power, which are in practice so limited?

9.3 Modern Transformation of the Role of the State

Capacity and power are related, but are not the same thing. Capacity points toward the outcome and effectiveness of the exercise of power, and different kinds of power strengthen different kinds of capacity. If we are to strengthen

[12] *The Constitution of the People's Republic of China* (April 1988 revised edition), Clause No. 2, Article No. 10.

[13] *Land Administration Law of the People's Republic of China*, (1989), Article No. 10.

the state's modern capacity, then, so far as we can tell from this case, the key lies not in whether to strengthen or weaken the power of the state, but in distinguishing between those powers that need to be enhanced and those that need to be curtailed and even between capacities of different nature and types. Given its organizational functions, the modern political establishment that purports to serve the public ought specifically to strengthen its capacity in such areas as defining the rights of citizens, ensuring that these rights are equally distributed in the population and can be exercised, which are its basic tasks.

Why do we say that? Once again, we need to look at something discussed earlier, namely, the historical process of state-building, and just what capacity has been "built" as a result of this transformation.

In the European experience, "state-building" describes a particular phenomenon in early modern history, where a scattered, multi-centered, and fragmented power structure was gradually replaced by a centralized one (with the modern state at the center). One of the haul marks of this structure is the establishment of new political entity: the nation-state, which now became the new center of authority, supplanting the fragmented authority structure that had been in place previously. Under the waves of industrialization and modernization, small and compact political units were dismantled, gradually incorporated into the new state. As for the collective identity of members of a society, such a transformation created a new kind of cultural landscape: as education and literacy became increasingly accessible, people's ability to connect with one another grew, and over time they became members in a larger political unit. This is the formation of nation-states in Europe, something that was made inevitable by industrialization.[14] As power became increasingly concentrated in the hand of the new political entity—the state—people's relationship with the political body to which they once belonged also underwent changes, changes that enlarged people's social networks, something that facilitated industrialization.

Tilly's articulation of the goals of state-building was even more specific: the ruler hopes to augment and deepen one's rule over the society, to control the social structure of places that have enjoyed considerable self-rule, to have greater control over local resources, and to establish new institutions with the support of the state. Tilly finds that the emergence of these goals is attributable to the development of class conflict, a decentralized authority structure, war, and the concentration of capital.[15] The concentration of power means the disintegration of a decentralized power structure. Characteristically, according to Tilly, states are "coercion-wielding organizations that are distinct from

[14] E. Gellner, *Thought and Change* (London: Weidenfeld and Nicolson, 1964); E. Gellner, *Nations and Nationalism* (Oxford: Blackwell, 1983); Cited in Tom Bottomore, *Political Sociology* (London: Pluto Press, 1979), 78–79.

[15] Charles Tilly, "Introduction," in *The Formation of National States in Western Europe* (Princeton: Princeton University Press, 1975); Charles Tilly, ed., *Coercion, Capital, and European States: AD 990-1990* (Cambridge University Press, 1990).

households and kinship groups and exercise clear priority in some respects over all other organizations within substantial territories".[16]

Clearly, this represents unprecedented growth in "state power". However, we must note that it is a different kind of power than what existed before, since the political structure of the modern nation-state is a reflection of a new kind of authority and social relationship: as rulers consolidated power through coercive means, they gradually shifted away from forming power alliances, and toward connecting with the general population, and acting as the body that defines and protects the latter's basic rights. This effectively destroyed the support base on which the traditional, fragmented authority structure depended, and it was impossible for this older structure to prevent members of the society from turning to higher and larger organizational bodies to recalibrate their source of collective identity.

> [K]ings rallying popular support by offering guarantees against cruel and arbitrary local magnates or by challenging their claims to goods, money or services, but not hesitating to crush rebellion when the people were divided or a sufficient military force was at hand; magnates parading as defenders of local liberties against royal oppression, but not hesitating bargain with the crown when it appeared advantageous. Ultimately, the people paid.[17]

Changes in the center of power inevitably led to intense conflicts. However, why was it that despite strong resistance among local authorities, this process nonetheless did not end in failure? The reason is that as a result of this process, a new kind of social identity emerged, namely, the citizen, an identity that was endowed with legitimate and protected rights. These rights had until then never been granted recognition by any other political body. What the affirmation of these rights in fact did was to create a new set of rules to generate solidarity among the populace. These rules reduced people's dependency on and sense of allegiance toward the local authority, which were replaced by ***dependency*** on protection from the state. Through this transition from indirect rule (through local proxy) to direct rule (by the state), the state was able to secure the support of the people for the expansion of its power.

What is important is the change in the nature of that power. Direct rule by the state would not have been able to achieve the success that it did had its basic philosophy been the same as that which underlined local rule. Its success is attributable to the fact that it won support of the people by creating citizenship as a form of identity and expanding the rights of citizens, including the rights to own property, to vote, to welfare and to public goods, and establishing institutions that would ensure the equal distribution of rights, safety and

[16] Charles Tilly, *The Formation of National States in Western Europe, Introduction* (Princeton: Princeton University Press, 1975); Charles Tilly, ed., *Coercion, Capital, and European States: AD 990-1990* (Cambridge University Press, 1990), 1.

[17] Charles Tilly, *The Formation of National States in Western Europe* (Princeton: Princeton University Press, 1975), 24.

security, and the delivery of legal justice. The fragmented political structure in the past was of course made up of political entities of substantial size, and power was highly institutionalized. Yet those entities represented a special kind of power, individuals of authority, or the interests of dynasties. This is not public authority, but the center of special privileges, which are an undifferentiated mixture that takes absolute precedence over the society. The power structure resembles a loose-knit feudal circle of unity, consisting of social alliances containing individuals in positions of power and their followers. The boundaries of these groups are fluid and uncertain, and the groups lack internal cohesion, sustainability or clear objectives, and no coercive means exists to bring people together into close associations. Yet the modern state makes it possible for the orderliness of social life to be built on a kind of rational connection.[18]

People's identity as citizens, which is protected by the modern state, has liberated the rights of the individual, which suggests that state-building was accompanied by changes in the role and the nature of authority and its relationship with those who are governed. Therefore, behind the structural "centralization" there lies something more concrete, namely, the formation of the modern government, a new public organization, and the establishment of a kind of relationship between authority and the public that is centered around the modern government and one in which the latter is not submissive to the former, as had been the case before. The mandate of public organizations comes from its defense of the rights of the citizens, and ordinary people, now with a new type of identity, namely, as members of a state, also have rights they never did before, and may be able, under the protection of the new forms of political bodies, overcome the oppression to which the local nobility and people with power had subjected them. To sum this up, in the European experience, state-building was not a competition for power in which the state alone emerged as the beneficiary. Rather, it was also a process that resulted in the emergence and growth of the civil society and the public sphere.[19] Without the establishment of citizenship as a type of identity or powerful protection it receives, the centralization of political power in the hands of the state would not have enjoyed the support of the people, nor would it have been successful at repelling resistance from those with power under the older system.

In this sense, state-building is not simply about the expansion of power, it necessarily involves changes to the very nature of power, including changes in the role of the state, that is, the role of a government that purports to serve the public, changes to institutions such as the law, tax collection, the granting of mandate and the model of governance, and also changes to the relationship between the authority and the people. This suggests that the key reason why

[18] Gianfranco Poggi, "The Nature of the Modern State," in Gianfranco Poggi, *The State: Its Nature, Development and* Prospects (Stanford: Stanford University Press, 1990), 19–33.

[19] Prasenjit Duara, "State, Civil Society and the History of Chinese Modernity," in Xi Wang & Frederic Wakeman, Jr. eds. *China's Quest for Modernization: A Historical Perspective* (Shanghai: Fudan University Press, 1994), 363.

state-building was eventually successful, and the state was able to supplant other forms of political body or collective entity, and become the object on which citizens hung their identity was the emergence of new principles of governance, new types of social identity, new ways of understanding what rights members of the state had and how they relate to one another, and the fact that public organizations became the political body that would safeguard and disseminate these basic principles, rights, and relationships. These particular aspects of state-building have enormous normative significance. State-building requires government organizations to be built on a new set of governance principles, and what these organizations do for the people must be supported and regulated by a set of institutions.

According to the neo-liberal economic conception of the state, the political restructuring in late medieval period is the foundation to the economic restructuring triggered by social change. The state is a kind of modern organization birthed from this kind of political restructuring, and its basic task is the "production" of public goods for the society, of which the most important would be social security and social justice. It does this by using power that it alone possesses—the power to determine and to protect the rights and duties of the people in relation to the obtainment, use and transfer of resources. This is how the state maintains monopoly over law enforcement and the use of violence and coercion. This monopoly over the determination and the protection of those relationship based on rights on which the society is existentially dependent is a sine qua non for the maintenance of order. The system of legal governance constitutes the basic institutions for ensuring that citizens' rights and social order are protected, and the taxation system serves to guarantee that these activities are adequately funded. Therefore, the establishment of a modern taxation system and legal governance system is an integral part of supporting state organizations at the institutional level. These two systems effectively institutionalize the relationship between the state and the citizens over public affairs.

If a state is unable to establish some kind of uniform tax system within its jurisdiction, it cannot really be said to exist at all. For example, within a kingdom, if the nobility at the primary level is fully capable of collecting taxes, the kingdom cannot be considered a "state"; conversely, if a duke, while seeming too small to matter, is able to effectively stand up to the king, and defend its financial independence, then for all intents and purposes it is a "state", albeit a small one. Therefore, the formation of the state involves not just the redistribution of political power, but also recalibration of the contract between the ruler and the ruled.[20] The same is true of legal governance, where a uniform system of legal governance will not have been built if the laws of the state cannot effective adjudicate the conflicts of interests among different local bodies, because that would mean that these local authorities continue to operate "autonomously" with respect to legislation and the judiciary. Judged from these perspectives, state-building increased, not decreased, the power and capacity of the state.

[20] Henri Lepage, *Tomorrow, Capitalism: Economics of Economic Freedom* (Common Wealth Publishing Co., Ltd., 1988), 82.

More specifically, as an integral part of state-building, the establishment of a modern taxation system and legal governance amounts to advancing a new set of norms for governance through the state, the "newness" of which consists in its having a broader scope for its publicness, beneficiaries, and representation. With respect to the tax system, essentially the contractual relationship between the government and citizens over financial matters, it not only guarantees financial wherewithal of the public authority, more importantly still, it mandates that tax receipts must be treated as "public property". This requires that the collection, management, and use of taxes must be in accordance with principles that the public has agreed to, and serve the interests of the public, and reflect governance on behalf of the public. The new taxation system makes a fundamental distinction between "public property" and "private property", and makes clear that public property is essentially different from royal property, and the two must be managed differently in terms of the body in charge, principles, and procedures. With respect to legal governance, [we saw] the establishment of professional organizations that are neutral with respect to group interests, organizations that cannot make use of the law in their attempt to outgun their rivals but are committed to upholding the principle that all are equal before the law. Law is no long used specifically as a political weapon, but the standard by which a diverse group achieves the balance needed to maintain order. Clearly, these beliefs associated with the public goods cannot be used by the state as an instrument to wrench financial and judicial powers out of the hands of local authorities. Instead, they are used to promote a new way of understanding of the relationship between public organizations and the rights and duties of citizens.

As the society and the economy continue to evolve, the relative costs and effects of social behavior change, changes that engender new forms of benefit and opportunities. This is when it becomes necessary to create new rights in order to encourage behaviors that are lower in costs and higher in efficiency. The "state" is thus "built", it takes it upon itself to protect economic freedom and to provide incentives, so that the needs of the society can be met. Otherwise, it would be either very costly or altogether impossible for either individuals or the society to make use of these economic opportunities. This requires the new political entity (namely, the state) to become a force promoting progress in law, and to safeguard the implementation of new laws on the strength of the authority of the state. But what is more important is the contents of these new laws, which aim to protect economic freedom and ensure efficient and lawful transactions by recalibrating the distribution of rights, and to build a sense of belonging to and identification with the state among members of the society. Unlike local rules such as rural covenants and village ordinances, common law and other norms applicable within a limited area, national laws reduce the cost of social transaction by redistributing rights and by enforcing these legal principles within the entire society.[21]

[21] Zhang, "State Capacity Building", *Open Times*, May 2001.

9.4 Concluding Remarks

Clearly, the modern transformation of the role of the state means the weakening of the state's traditional roles and the strengthening of its modern roles. The latter consist essentially in the creation of mechanisms for the equal distribution of the rights of citizens, for protecting these rights, and for ensuring their ability to be exercised. There are no modern public goods more important than these. The sustainability of the state's authority depends not only on support from the society, but also on the power and capabilities of both citizens and the state. Moreover, it is by virtue of the modern roles of the state that these factors shape one another, and maintain social stability through their strong mutual dependency. Therefore, the question is not how much capacity the state has and whether it should have any. The right question is which capacities should be augmented. Human experience tells us that some of the adverse capacities the state has sometimes had can have deleterious effects on the construction of legal order, reinforce indirect (fragmented) ruling structure, and erode the state's fundamental ability to provide its citizens with justice and safety and to protect their rights. And these would precisely be the reasons why some states lack the mandate to govern, stability or support.

Therefore, there is a question logically prior to that of state-building that is even more important, namely, how to distinguish among capacities of different kinds, so that the positive ones will be strengthened, while the society and even the state itself can be protected from the harm that might be caused by the negative ones.

CHAPTER 10

Issues in Rural Governance

As for the "conclusion" of this book, to put it simply, I have tried to demonstrate that the root cause of conflicts in rural society lies in the defects in a range of existing institutions and rules. There are tensions with respect to values, objectives, and interests inherent to these institutions, which shape the role of primary-level political authority, their rights and duties, and their social relationship with the rural population. The challenges facing rural politics can be attributed to these tensions.

10.1 Some Features

Unlike in the West, where what is public and what is private are kept separate, in rural China, the basic structure of social relationship is the intermixture of public and private relationships. Characteristically, it is as possible to increase one's personal gain by taking advantage of public relationship as it is to pursue publicly shared objectives using one's personal relationships. There is no clear separation or distinction between the two. Under such a system, some of the functions of the traditional patron-client relationship have been retained, albeit not without some change. While under the traditional patron-client relationship information was transmitted from individual to individual, the new form of patron-client relationship may feature universality, openness, and mass mobilization. However, such a relationship may be fleeting, loose, and fluid, and change as circumstances do. Conflicts that may arise in the relationship are about both values and benefits. Information is transmitted through either private or public channels, groups lack clearly defined boundaries, and do not exclude any individual from entering. It is not pyramid-like symmetrical in structure, but of a loose-knit structure with a small group at the core, and no rigidly defined rights or obligations. Nor is it a unitary system in which authority rests with a single individual. Instead, anybody may press for what is in their

J. Zhang, *Primary-Level Government*,
https://doi.org/10.1007/978-981-96-6209-8_10

interests, and there does not exist a stable set of institutions. These characteristics indicate that social relationships in rural China are the same as neither the typical patron-client relationships nor the typical public relationship associated with modernity, but some kind of mutated hybrid of the two, and one that is capable of handling both personal and public affairs.

With respect to institution-building, primary-level government has considerable control, which they use to solidify their influence and defend their turf. As the body primarily responsible for determining what rights village residents have and for making sure these rights can be exercised, primary-level government also has the authority to legislate, enforce the law, and exercise rule over a jurisdiction. Collective ownership of land and the role of the representatives of primary-level authority in managing the land by making decisions about contracts, trade and reallocation, help to ensure that it has control over important economic resources. The system of "nomination" by incumbents and other insiders as a mechanism for filling leadership positions facilitates the alignment of interests within the establishment, from which a local political network through which political operatives support one another is built. Such a network serves as an effective shield against oversight from both the central government and the public, making it easier for primary-level cadres to hold on to political, economic, and legal powers. This is the very existential foundation of what Shue calls "petty local despotism".[1] Primary-level governance may not comply with all the laws of the country, but only with those that would serve their interests, and it would do whatever it can to boost their own authority by taking advantage of the political discourse, which is constantly changing in response to evolving national ideology. Primary-level authority has manufactured a certain kind of "buffer zone" that separates the state from rural life, thereby preventing, in terms of both jurisdictional structure and governance principle, the power of the state from extending its reach downward.

These features can help us identify the properties of primary-level government. Despite what its official label might suggest, it is not an organ set up at the primary level by the state. Were that to be the case, presumably it would only be obligated to *carry out* the rules of the state, and not have the right to *determine or change* these rules. The documents we have reviewed suggest that primary-level government tends to punch far above its weight. Instead of managing production resources in rural areas on behalf of the state and in accordance with the rules created by the state, primary-level government has developed its own set of rules. Nor is it anything like a typical bureaucratic organ. It is at once a nominally official organization (insofar as it serves to advance the objectives of the state), and one that has its own political and economic interests, and an organizationally mature network. Overall, it does not share its interests with either the state or the rural population but is instead at

[1] Vivienne Shue, *The Reach of the State: Sketches of the Chinese Body Politic: a Comparative-historical Approach to the Modernization of Local Government in China* (Stanford: Stanford University Press, 1988).

odds with them. Over time, it developed into a special interest group that stands apart from both the state and the rural population. The overall effect it has on the rural community is generating conflicts and threatening primary-level order and stability.

But because of its role as an official body, primary-level government tends to turn these local conflicts into conflicts between the society and the state, and between the rural population and officials. In the modern era, the primary-level government embodies a synthesis of traditional rural authority and bureaucratic officials, and derives its legitimacy from this synthesis. On one hand, unlike what had been true of primary-level government in the past, it does not need to earn its mandate by contributing to the public affairs, since it receives its mandate to rule from the central government and such mandate is secure. On the other hand, nor is it like a typical bureaucratic organization that runs entirely on whatever power it has been endowed with by the central government and whatever incentive that can be provided by the remuneration. Instead, it has developed a political support network capable of sustaining and safeguarding its own interests, and the right to collect fees that serves as the financial basis to its very existence. By exercising control over (collective) financial assets, implementing its own special set of rules, and building its own mutual support network, primary-level government solidifies and strengthens order at the primary level that has itself at the center. Meanwhile, by formalizing state ownership and suppressing participation by the rural population, it is able to preserve a space in which to exercise relative autonomy, and keep to a minimum the amount of influence either the state or the rural population can have on it. The confluence of a host of factors—including the coalescing of interests among town and township cadres, blockage on information, the state's dependency on primary-level officials for everyday governance, and apathy among the rural population—helps to ensure primary-level government's security in its rule within its jurisdiction. Under such a system of divided authority, the ability of the state to institute direct governance by expanding the rights of citizens has also been curtailed, reducing the authority of the state to something with only symbolic, ideological, and advisory significance to the primary level, and leaving it with no substantive administrative mandate.

10.2 Politico-Sociological Significance

This is in fact a continuation of the system of decentralized administration that has a long history in China. What has changed, however, is that while before it was the gentry that served as primary-level authority, today that function is being performed by the nominal agents of the state, namely, primary-level officials. The reach of the authority of the state is largely confined to urban areas and small cities, and it mostly fell to primary-level officials to rule the countryside. As far as the rural population is concerned, the state's rules and authority, and the responsibilities it has toward them rarely have any direct and substantive impact on their everyday lives. These ordinary village folks hardly ever benefit from activities of the state. Yet, those state policies that effectively increase the power of primary-level government are fully "carried out". There have long been efforts to expand the local bureaucratic structure, power, and interests by appropriating the political discourse of the state. Even though village cadres are but marginal characters, they often become swept up in these activities. They unilaterally make "laws", such as those governing the terms of contracts, fees and methods, all in order to maximize the amount of control they have over resources. These village cadres raise funds for corporation from the rural population in their capacity as officials (public figures), and see to it that profits go to their own (private) groups. These are not activities aimed at expanding the public interests, instead, they alienate the public authority from the rural population, create widespread distrust, damage the moral standing of primary-level government itself, thereby making it a major source of conflicts and tension in the countryside.

State politics and local politics each has its own turf. Local politics, which revolve around competition for status and power, largely play out between local cadres and their network of patrons. Rather than seeing it as being influenced by state politics (or ideology), it would be more accurate to say that it parlayed the discourse of state politics into an instrument with which to beat rivals, largely an objective that is local in scope. While local politics of this kind are quite active, those who are involved hardly ever attempt to turn these local forces into reform of the state's political framework, and are always able to derive satisfaction from the maintenance of local control.

Even though this kind of structural separation has deleterious effects on public political power and even the authority of the state, it does not amount to a fundamental challenge to the system itself. There are two reasons for this. One is institutional, namely the interdependence between the two on issues of interest to each. On the one hand, primary-level government needs the state to provide it with the standing of a body serving the public, with administrative power, the opportunity to collect fiscal revenue, and ideological justification. On the other hand, the state needs primary-level government to collect taxes and maintain order at the primary level. The second reason has to do with ideology and culture, where both primary-level government and the state have something in common, and enjoy the same ideological justification. All of this means that while primary-level government generates institutional conflicts and creates difficulties for integration, it is nonetheless not a force antithetical to the establishment. While it may not be reliably committed to the state's institutions and ideology, it must do what is necessary to sustain the state's institutions if only to safeguard its own power and standing.

In its relationship with the state, primary-level government is not entirely passive. The very fact that village and township cadres work closely together and support one another means that they already constitute a body that exercises political power on its own terms. The state, as far as they are concerned, is but a force of deterrence that can be deployed when and where the need arises. More specifically, this means primary-level officials can solicit help from superior officials by seeking their intervention, albeit mostly when that suits their need. Or, they may mediate between officials at different ranks, or offer to provide guarantee for the handling of some internal matters, and when what is in their interest and what is in the interest of the state do not line up with one another, they may resist demands from above by citing all kinds of excuses. In all these areas, primary-level government has considerable room in which to make its own decisions as it sees fit. Therefore, perhaps we should not overstate either the amount of influence actions of the state have on local politicians, or, at the very least, the passivity of primary-level government (their complaints, which are passive, are mostly the outcome of strategies used in rivalry over power). In my tentative opinion, to the extent the state has a powerful impact on primary-level government, that impact is manifested not so much in either the organizational embodiment of the connections between the two based on their respective interests, or the hierarchical bureaucratic system or their respective rights and responsibilities, but more in the way both share the same culture, ideology, and governance principle. Because of these commonalities, primary level and polity and the state appear to merge into one single organization.

This kind of relationship is an indication of the way in which the different roles primary-level government plays are interwoven, and the multiple types of social relationships built into primary-level society as a result. This is amply illustrated in the fees and taxes primary-level government collects, including rent, state taxes, locally determined taxes, and money raised through fundraising. As far as the farmers are concerned, "rent" (the myriad rental fees and fees associated with contracting and subletting) signifies the relationship between the land owner and the tenant, while state taxes (such as agricultural taxes) signify the relationship between bodies that provide public services and taxpayers (citizens), "locally determined taxes" (including village reserve and township endowment, mandatory quota, education surcharge, construction of roads and water conservancy projects) signify the relationship between primary-level political authority and the farmers, while "fundraising" (for the economic cooperative fund, stock and financial activities, and corporate fundraising) signifies the roles of primary-level authority as investors and as operators. Among these social relationships, some, such as those between labor and the capital, and between landlords and tenants, are inherently antagonistic, and the absence of clear distinction between agent of the state and independent organizations makes it ever more difficult for people to tell which administrative body on which level of the hierarchical structure is responsible for imposing which particular fee of dubious justification.

As noted earlier, this admixture makes it very easy for one kind of conflict to turn into a different kind of conflict. For example, conflicts between landlords and tenants and between labor and capital (which would have been class conflict or conflict between different social strata in an earlier era) turned into conflicts over taxes (conflict between the public and the government). The refusal to pay rent represents antagonism among the classes, and it is aimed at the class with competing interests, and caused by the imbalance in economic gains between the capitalists and the proletariats. By contrast, the refusal to pay taxes represents the antagonism between what is public and what is private, and it is directed toward the illegitimate imposition and collection of taxes by public organizations, and caused by the lack of public acceptance of the right of these public organizations and some individuals to profit from what is collected, and the absence of the distinction between the rights of public organizations and the rights of individuals. Clearly, the two kinds of conflicts take place between individuals playing different social roles, have different objectives, and involve the state in different ways. Yet, because of the mixed roles of primary-level government, the distinction between these different kinds of conflicts becomes blurry or even disappears. As a result, all conflicts are reduced to that between "the government and the people". This is one consequence of the "mixed role" [of primary-level government]. Yet, for researchers, perhaps the more significant finding is that these common types of conflicts at the primary level are in some way a reflection of the main features of the local social structure. What we found was that most of the exchanges of the important economic resources and political power do not take place either among the people or even between the government and the people. Rather, they take place among the different cliques of primary-level cadres. This structure is unstable and is a breeding ground for political problems.

10.3 Several Related Issues

The above analysis can easily create the impression that primary-level government is "out of control", an impression that has led some to suggest the need to "build up" control again, including "building up" an effective and authoritative primary-level government altogether, and making it do what the state asks of it. Yet history has shown that this kind of control is usually not very successful.

And the reason for such failure is the mutual dependency between the state and primary-level government, especially the state's dependency on primary-level government for maintaining primary-level social order. While the bureaucrats are indeed subject to a range of "performance evaluation", these evaluations take place among individuals who have some interests in common. When both the evaluator and the evaluated are cadres, who have strong ties with each other as superiors and subordinates, the performance evaluation can only be themselves a mere performance. Obviously, any system where oversight is done among groups that stand in relation to one another as superiors and subordinates must contain inherent structural impediment, and other forces in society need to be called upon to contribute toward the oversight. Moreover, the participation of other social forces must not be confined to information disclosure or transparency in financial matters. What also need to be considered are ways to allow power to be more widely shared, to ameliorate the level of concentration of political, economic and legal powers, and to ensure that the rural population's power to perform oversight is more or less comparable to the primary-level authority's power to rule. This is what is meant by self-governance through representation, otherwise, "building" would only result in the recreation of self-governance through authority. Yet because self-governance through authority is impervious to pressure from both the state and the society, not only is it scarcely motivated to transform itself into political power that works for the public, it is in fact the basic source of conflicts at the primary level insofar as it amounts to "localized and local authoritarianism". In this sense, the establishment of self-governance through representation is not just for purpose of realizing information openness, but more importantly, for constitutional reform of the distribution of power in rural areas. This is key to building primary-level order that is stable, dynamic, and capable of self-repair.

On one optimistic view, when primary-level politicians are wrenched free of control by superior governments, they would be able to focus on building the local economy, "local state corporatism" is good for economic development.[2] This view assumes the perspective of the relationship between the central government and the local government. It is true that greater freedom gives primary-level government tremendous incentive to engage in economic activities, such that making a profit becomes an important goal for local politicians. Industrial and commercial development fueled by this profit motive has boosted local employment and the standards of living. However, we ought to be mindful of the differences between this and market activities: the economic activities of primary-level politicians do not engender any new principles of operation aimed at protecting the economic opportunities and the trading rights of *the individual*, these activities are based on such non-market principles as power monopoly and the nexus of personal connections. Primary-level politicians are taking advantage of those resources they have control over, such as their office, information and preferential policies, in order to create benefits, resources, and market opportunities that are not enjoyed by regular competitors. The system does not eliminate the different forms of monopoly rights, but encourages dependency and rent-seeking, instead of independent growth among *homo economicus*.

It is true that as the role of the state declines primary-level authorities have been able to enjoy more freedom. Yet this has not made them or their relationship with the rural population more modern. Everything they do is geared toward strengthening their own control over "collective" assets, and their power to allocate resources. As for the rural population's strong demand for resources and opportunities, they typically choose to be unresponsive, except

[2] Jean C. Oi, "The Role of the Local State in China's Transitional Economy," *China Quarterly* 144 (1995): 1132–1149.

when any change might end up benefiting them. This helps to perpetuate their own authority, while suppressing the economic freedom of others and the distribution of property rights and trading rights, and the principle of individual competition. In Weber's view, closed organizations exclude those who might compete with them, so that these outsiders do not share the social and economic opportunities offered by these organizations.[3]

In this way, the openness and liberty associated with "local state corporatism" exists not among economic actors that have the same standing as one another but rather among bodies on different levels and among different organizations within the polity. Yet the interlocking relationship between the political (control) and the economic (profit-making) roles of political entities has done enormous damage to the working principles governing those who work for the public interest and to their moral caliber. Therefore, I beg to differ from proponents of local state corporatism, and believe instead that much more evidence and careful analysis of it are needed in order to answer such questions as whether primary-level government is capable of playing a key role in the transformation of economic order, whether such transformation is really fueled by actions by primary-level politicians or by the rapid development of the market itself, and whether primary-level politicians play a positive or negative role in the expansion of the market principles.

Another related question is this. Some scholars skeptical of the idea of "planned changes" have criticized the historicist idea of modernization from the point of view of "the recreation of traditional resources", and argued that traditional orders and rules already contain within them considerable number of elements intrinsic to modernity, elements that are in fact far more effective than such imported notions as "the establishment of a system of laws" and "extending the reach of the laws into the countryside". The original intent behind such criticism is to overthrow the cognitive paradigm defined by the opposition between tradition and modernity. Yet the criticism brings to bear different perspectives in its analysis of these two kinds of rules, and conflates the *effectiveness* of orderliness at the primary level and its ***nature***. Such a discussion is based on the presumption that only primary-level orderliness is natural and historical while rules that are implemented by the state through administrative means are exogenous and artificially planned. But don't these "new" rules have historical ties with institutional history? Can we assume that all the (political and economic) forms of orderliness that have long been in place and effective at the rural primary level have served the needs and interests of the majority of the rural population? The materials we have been able to obtain do not support such a hypothesis. In fact, many common ingredients of primary-level order share similarities with some aspects of the principles of the state governance both throughout history and at the present time. These include

[3] Max Weber, *Economy, Social Sectors and their Rights*, Translated by Qiang Li (Shanghai: SDX Joint Publishing Company, 1998).

exceptionalism (instead of universalism), conditional reciprocity in relation to duties and powers (instead of natural rights), the doctrine of absolute authority (instead of contractarianism), flexibility and discretion (instead of legalism), among others. This means that the distinction between "statist" and "non-governmental" does not track the dichotomy between two different kinds of rules.

The pertinent question here would be just how we should make sense of "state-building" as a commonly applied analytical perspective. In the experiences of European societies, it refers to the process of cultural and institutional integration and consolidation that is centered on the nation-state. Superficially, state-building essentially involves the establishment and extension of governmental apparatus on different levels. This usually entails the power of the state reaching into a range of organizations in the society, over which the state now claims jurisdiction where it did not have any before. Yet even more substantively, state-building involves changes to *the role and the nature* of the state, and also to the *relationship* between the state and important entities and individuals in the society. We might, in this sense, call it a modern social "revolution". As it begins to unfold, whatever local control the nobility and the urban elite had commanded was supplanted, and the masses were delivered from the sense of identification with political entities of the past. A series of new principles emerged according to which they identified themselves with a nation-state, in a new kind of relationship, namely, that between the citizens and the modern state. This new kind of relationship is able to take root thanks to new tax systems and laws. Imperial power, once possessed by a dynasty, has now evolved into the collective organs that comprise a modern state, and serve to manage *public assets*, are bound by the law, subject to its mandates, in the interests of the public. Clearly, state-building is about more than the consolidation of the power structure, but also gives rise to new principles undergirding norms and orders. And the reason why these principles have been able to prevail despite fierce resistance among local authorities is that they represent the choice of the people, for whom these principles offer recognition and protection of their interests. This was a marked departure from the *status quo* before, under which the principles of governance served only to advance the interests of the authorities.

Therefore, we must not apply the label "state-building" to every and any set of actions that involve the expansion of state power. In many cases, while the institutional infrastructure is "being built", these key changes to social relations have not taken place on a significant scale, nor have the corresponding institutional transformations provided the kind of steady support needed for the emerging social relations to be sustained, or popular institutions reflect the new political, economic, and rights distribution principles. It is necessary, therefore, to step outside the perspective of institutional-building to observe "state-building". More importantly still, care must be taken to avoid mistaking any "tax statistics" or tax collecting activities for "state-building". We must remain critically alert to the existence of what is nominally considered "state-building" but that is either inappropriate or disingenuous. Unless something genuinely reflects a totally different set of principles of rights, it may not quite deserve the label of "modern".

I wish to end by noting that I have hardly addressed all the problems with and in primary-level government exhaustively. In China in particular, one must not overlook the issue of regional diversity. This is why I have not referred to the observations recorded in this book as "model", but have called them "issues" or "problems" instead. Still, I believe that these discussions will shed important light on some of the features of primary-level political authority.